monitoring the future

questionnaire responses from the nation's high school seniors

1975

Lloyd D. Johnston and Jerald G. Bachman

Survey Research Center • Institute for Social Research
The University of Michigan
Ann Arbor, Michigan

ISR Code Number 4155
ISSN 0190-9185
ISBN 0-87944-235-2

Published in 1980 by:
Institute for Social Research,
The University of Michigan, Ann Arbor, Michigan

Printed in the United States of America

Table of Contents

Appendices

References   177

Tables

Figures

Preface

This volume is the first in a series which presents descriptive statistical results from a national survey of young people entitled Monitoring the Future: A Continuing Study of the Lifestyles and Values of Youth. Each year the study surveys a large sample of high school seniors, located in approximately 125 schools nationwide, and drawn to be representative of all seniors in the coterminous United States. In 1975, the year covered by the present volume, 15,792 seniors in 111 public and 14 private high schools participated in the research.

The first four volumes in this series, dealing with the high school classes of 1975, 1976, 1977, and 1978, are being published simultaneously. Additional volumes are expected to appear on an annual basis. The most important contribution of this series is likely to be the opportunity it provides for the exploration of trends, a process that obviously involves the use of several different volumes. With that in mind, we have kept the format highly consistent from one volume to another, and we have developed an index (described below) which should facilitate the process of matching data across years. It should be noted that the volume presenting 1975 data is different from the others in several respects.*

Although we designed the volumes to fit together as a series, we also saw distinct advantages in having each volume able to stand alone — to be usable without reference to any of the others. For that reason, the introductory material on research design and questionnaire content, the instructions for accessing the data tables, and the appendices on

sampling errors are all included in each volume. Thus, the small price we pay for making each volume self-contained is that much of the text portion is repeated each year.

Purposes of this Series of Publications

Monitoring the Future, which is conducted by the University of Michigan's Institute for Social Research and receives its core funding from the National Institute on Drug Abuse, is an unusually comprehensive research project in several respects: surveys are conducted annually on an ongoing basis; the samples are large and nationally representative; and the subject matter is very broad, encompassing some 1,300 variables per year. Many people — scholars, policy makers, educators, and so on — will have an interest in the results.

The principal investigators are already writing for a number of these audiences and will continue to do so. Because of the limitations in our own time, interests, and expertise, however, there is an enormous amount of valuable information which may never be utilized if the initiative to digest and disseminate all of it must come from us alone. Further, since the project is in part a social indicators series, its value rests to a considerable degree on *timely* dissemination of the results. For these reasons, we wish to share the study's results with others in a number of fields on a rapid and regular basis. We have chosen to provide two major and complemen-

---

* The 1975 volume does not include comparison data for black and white subgroups, nor does it include data for the subgroups who did and did not plan to complete four years of college. Also, somewhat fewer questionnaire items appear than in the other volumes. These restrictions are the result primarily of missing data problems that occurred only in the 1975 survey when the questionnaires were longer than in subsequent years.

tary vehicles for doing this: (a) these annual reference volumes of descriptive results, and (b) machine-readable data archives for direct analysis by others.

We believe that many potential users who would not mount the effort required to conduct computer analyses of archived data will be able to get most of what they want from these volumes of descriptive results. The user of any one of these volumes can estimate — usually with considerable accuracy — a wide variety of characteristics of the high school class described in that volume. To take just one example, the user of the present volume can ascertain that 40.0 percent of seniors in the high school class of 1975 reported using marijuana at least once during the preceding year. Further, by utilizing two or more of these volumes the reader can describe recent trends in any such characteristic. To continue with the same example, the volume describing the high school class of 1978 indicates that 50.2 percent of those seniors reported marijuana use during the preceding year; and when that is combined with the data from the present volume the reader is able to discern a shift of 10.2 percent over the three years between the classes of 1975 and 1978. And if all of the first four volumes in the series are used, one can observe a steady increase in the proportion of high school seniors who report having used marijuana at least once during the twelve months preceding the survey:

> 40.0 percent of seniors in 1975
> 44.5 percent of seniors in 1976
> 47.6 percent of seniors in 1977
> 50.2 percent of seniors in 1978

A similar examination of trends can be carried out for over 1,300 different variables dealing with a wide variety of subject areas (listed in Table 2 of the Introduction). A simple indexing system (described below) has been developed which makes it quite straightforward for the reader wishing to do trend analyses to locate the results for a given question for any year of the study. The index in the present volume lists the location of all items included in the surveys for 1976 through 1978 and most items included in 1975.

Analyses such as those illustrated above need not be limited to the total sample. The data provided in these volumes also permit examination of a variety of subgroups (e.g., males, females, those from different regions, those with different levels of drug use experience). The principal investigators have already conducted and reported some analyses in the area of drug use and related attitudes (Johnston, Bachman, and O'Malley, 1977, 1979), but many other areas have not yet been explored extensively.

We recognize that providing ready access to essentially undigested data carries certain risks, particularly the risk of mistaken interpretations based on inadequate controls, lack of awareness of sample limitations, etc. More than offsetting the risks, in our view, are the advantages of prompt and widespread dissemination of these nationally representative survey indicator data. Although we are unable to eliminate the risks, we hope to reduce them by providing the reader with an extensive list of caveats presented at the end of the Introduction section. We ask all who use the data to read these caveats carefully and take them seriously.

A Guide for the Reader

This volume is divided into three main parts: (1) the introductory section, (2) the section giving the descriptive results from the current year's survey, and (3) the cross-time item reference index.

Introductory Section. The introduction contains a description of the study — its purposes, major content areas, design, field procedures, response rates, and methods of publication and data dissemination. Since most of this material remains unchanged from year to year, anyone having read another of the volumes may wish to skim this section. We do, however, suggest reviewing the caveats, located at the end of the introductory section, which deal with interpreting and extrapolating from these data.

Descriptive Results Section. In this section most questions contained in this year's survey are presented along with percentagized frequency distributions of answers for the entire sample and for selected subgroups. The questions in this section are organized according to the sequence of items used in 1976 and (with very few changes) in all subsequent years. The data are presented separately for each of the five questionnaire forms, with one important exception: the section which is common to questionnaire Forms 2 through 5 (Section B on drug use, background characteristics, and some other subjects) is presented only once, at the beginning of the Descriptive Results section, using the data from respondents on all four forms.

The first portion of the Descriptive Results section contains detailed definitions of all subgroups for whom data are presented. It also describes the statistical conventions used in generating the tables.

Cross-Time Index of Questionnaire Items. This index is intended to serve two purposes.

First it should be useful in locating items dealing with a subject area of interest. The subject area key at the beginning of the cross-time item index shows the alphabetical code assigned to various subject areas (e.g., "politics" or "work and leisure"). Having selected a subject area of interest, one can then scan the Subject Area column in the item index to locate all questions in any of the surveys (through 1978) which deal with that subject. To locate the results for any given question in the Descriptive Results section of this volume, simply look in column two of the item index for its page location.

The cross-time index can also be used to determine in which other years an item was used and where to locate it. If, in reviewing the Descriptive Results section, one locates an interesting item and would like to know in which of the other annual surveys of seniors it has appeared, it may be found in the cross-time index by its unique "item reference number." The index will indicate all years in which that same item appeared and show the questionnaire form, section, and item number for each year. This information thus can be used to decide which other volumes in this series might be of relevance; and the same item may be readily located by its reference number in the index of any other volume.

Sampling Appendices. Appendix A is provided for those wishing to determine the confidence limits around a percentage estimate, or to test the statistical significance of an observed difference between two groups, or to test the significance of a change from one year to another. It gives the necessary procedures and tables for such tests and provides the appropriate factors by which to correct for the fact that the study makes use of a multi-stage probability sample clustered in a limited number of schools (usually about 125). Appendix B provides further detail on sample design effects and the procedures which were used to derive the sampling error estimates.

Availability of Archived Data

As was mentioned earlier, this series of volumes will be complemented by an archiving of the raw data sets for direct analysis by others not associated with the project. The present volumes should be a considerable help to those wishing to access the archived data since they provide a verbatim statement of items and answer categories, and also because they include basic univariate and bivariate frequency distributions for all items, as well as the missing data rates. The cross-time index of items contained in each of these volumes also provides an efficient way to identify the relevant variables in various content areas, as well as to determine when they were measured and their questionnaire locations. In fact, we hope that the availability of this series will not only facilitate the use of the archived data but actually stimulate interest in their use.

Two major social science archives will hold the individual level data which are summarized in this volume:

> The Interuniversity Consortium for Political and Social Research (ICPSR)
> Institute for Social Research
> P.O. Box 1248
> Ann Arbor, Michigan 48106

> The Drug Abuse Epidemiology Data Center (DAEDAC)
> Institute for Behavioral Research
> Texas Christian University
> Fort Worth, Texas 76129

The ICPSR archive will make individual-level data available on tape to interested investigators for analysis at their own facility. However, it is presently planned that these data sets will not contain the drug use or delinquency measures. Because of the sensitivity of the latter measures — that is, those describing the respondent's own use of illicit drugs and other delinquent behaviors — only the data set in the DAEDAC archive will contain those measures. The Monitoring the Future file at DAEDAC will be treated as a "restricted data set," meaning that all analyses must be carried out by the archive staff (under the instructions of the outside investigator). Individual level data will not be released by DAEDAC, thereby ensuring that the answers of an individual respondent cannot be located through pattern recognition (i.e., using various descriptor variables in combination to make a unique identification). While the probability of such identification may seem remote, we feel that the potential seriousness of the consequences is sufficient to justify this high level of caution.

Other Publications from the Study

A number of different forms of publications based on Monitoring the Future data have been developed or are being planned. One series of annual volumes, dealing with trends in drug use and drug-related attitudes and beliefs, is being published by the National Institute on Drug Abuse. The first volume in that series, *Drug Use Among American High School Students 1975-1977* (Johnston, Bachman, and O'Malley), was published in late 1977; and the second, *Drugs and the Class of '78* (Johnston, Bachman, and O'Malley), in 1979.*

---

*Either the full volumes, or abbreviated highlights versions of each, may be ordered without cost from the National Clearinghouse for Drug Abuse Information, National Institute on Drug Abuse, 5600 Fishers Lane, Rockville, Maryland 20857.

An Occasional Papers series has been launched by the project. It includes papers on design and methodological issues as well as special substantive analyses and early, and sometimes more detailed, drafts of articles planned for journal publication. The first occasional paper, "The Monitoring the Future Project Design and Procedures" (Bachman and Johnston, 1978), provides a detailed description of the study and its underlying rationale.

The present series of reference volumes is being published by the Institute for Social Research. A new volume will be added to this series each year.

Articles for academic journals, as well as for journals serving various professionals working with youths, are also being written. In addition, several integrative books based on the Monitoring the Future project are in the planning stages.

To request particular papers, reprints, or periodic notification of publications available from the study, write to Monitoring the Future, Room 2030, Institute for Social Research, The University of Michigan, Box 1248, Ann Arbor, Michigan 48106.

Acknowledgements

A great many people have contributed to the launching and development of this research effort. We are indebted to a number of officials of the National Institute on Drug Abuse and the Special Action Office for Drug Abuse Prevention for their encouragement and advice at the outset — in particular, Richard Bucher, Robert DuPont, William Pollin, and Louise Richards. To the members of our Advisory Panel we also express our thanks for their review and suggestions regarding instrumentation and design. In addition to Drs. Bucher and Richards, the committee members are John Ball, Donald Campbell, Ira Cisin, Wilbur Cohen, O. Dudley Duncan, Dorothy Gilford, Eric Josephson, Robert Kahn, Donald Michael, and Lee Robins.

Our colleagues at the Institute for Social Research and elsewhere who shared their insights, and often their most cherished instrumentation, are too numerous to mention; but their contributions are greatly appreciated. To the director of the Survey Research Center's Sampling Section, Irene Hess, we owe a particular debt for the creativity of her sampling design for the study. The contributions of the SRC Field Section also have been very valuable.

Major contributions to the production of this particular volume were made by staff members Dawn Bare, Deborah Poinier, Maria Sanchez, and Ann Taylor. We would also like to thank the staff of the Publishing Division of the Institute for Social Research for their work in arranging publication.

The present and former members of the project staff (listed below) have, of course, contributed greatly to the building of this large and complex research series.

Finally, we would like to acknowledge the tens of thousands of high school seniors, their teachers, and their principals, whose cooperation and generous contribution of time make the Monitoring the Future project possible.

LLOYD D. JOHNSTON
JERALD G. BACHMAN

Present and Former Members of the Project Staff

Donna Ando	Walter Gruhn	Patrick O'Malley
Margaret Bailey	James Hersey	Dorothy Paulette
Dawn Bare	A. Regula Herzog	Sharon Pietila
Ellen Berger	Mark Krell	Joseph Pleck
Mary Lou Bewley	Sally Lawson	Deborah Poinier
Katherine Blatt	Ludmilla Litus	Judith Redmond
Mary Lea Bonucchi	A. Kathryn Loker	Barbara Renaud
Marcy Breslow	Regina Lumbard	Maria Sanchez
Mary Lou Davis	Oksana Malanchuk	Ann Taylor
Mary Dempsy	Wayne McCulloch	Richard Taylor
William Diedrich	Joan McGraw	Lynda Tolen
Karen Donahue	John Miller	Sandra Wronski
Leslie Eveland	Marion Morse	Thelma Wurzelbacher
Halford Fairchild	Jim Neveaux	

Introduction

The Monitoring the Future project is designed to explore changes in many important values, behaviors, and lifestyle orientations of contemporary American youth. Two general types of tasks may be distinguished. The first is to provide a systematic and accurate *description* of the youth population of interest in a given year, and to quantify the direction and rate of the changes taking place among them over time. The second task, more analytic than descriptive, involves the *explanation* of the relationships and trends observed to exist.

The task of description may be subdivided into three parts: (1) the description of static conditions (which may be accomplished through a single cross-sectional study); (2) the description of cross-cohort or, in longer time-spans, generational changes (usually accomplished using repeated cross sections of the same age groups); and (3) the description of changes with aging (usually accomplished by means of longitudinal studies). The Monitoring the Future project has the capacity to provide each of these three types of description, since it incorporates all three types of research design into a single study. (This complex design, in which multiple cohorts are followed longitudinally, has been referred to as a cohort-sequential design.)

The content of this volume exemplifies the first of these types of description in that it contains cross-sectional data on a single high school class. When the data in this volume are used in combination with data from other such volumes in the series, the nature, direction, and rates of change from one cohort of seniors to another also may be described — the type of reporting which is often labeled as the social indicator approach. The third class of description — dealing with the maturational changes which occur during the years after high school — will not be dealt with in this series of volumes but will be reported in other publications from the study.*

The accurate characterization of American young people and the description of important changes occurring among them is but one class of objectives for the study. The second class of objectives involves the development of a greater understanding of what causes these young people to be as they are, and why the changes being documented are occurring. Explanation will be sought through both the analysis of change at the aggregate level and at the individual level. The results of these explorations will be disseminated via the various publications discussed in the Preface.

The merging of the social indicator approach and the analysis of relationships (particularly longitudinal relationships) into a single cohort-sequential design is, in our view, synergistic: the effectiveness of the two approaches combined is greater than if the two were undertaken separately. Because the present series of volumes deals with senior year data only, our remarks here focus primarily on the project's social indicator contributions — the accurate description of high school seniors and the documentation of trends over time. It is worth not-

---

*Panels of students from each graduating class are being randomly selected and followed longitudinally for six years. Thus it soon will be possible to characterize the changes which seem to take place consistently with aging during the early adult years. Not only will longitudinal development in the years after high school be studied, but once enough of these longitudinal panels have accumulated, it will also be possible to characterize cross-sectionally most American young people aged 18 to 24, (at least the major segment of the population who completed high school — roughly 80-85 percent), and to describe the changing characteristics of that age group each year.

ing, however, that even the limited amount of bivariate data included in the present volumes will suggest promising directions for relational analyses, many of which can be carried out using the archived data tapes from the project.

The Need for Social Indicators

The fundamental argument for developing social indicators is that there are considerable scientific and practical benefits derived from having accurate information about current social realities and the way those realities have been changing. For the scientific community such indicators provide a rich set of information against which existing theory may be tested and from which new theory may be suggested. For the community at large, social indicators permit the "reality testing" of common perceptions and beliefs about the nation and its people. Past experience has demonstrated that widely held conceptions, which themselves may serve to create or exacerbate problems, can be most inaccurate. One example is the exaggerated popular conception of the size and nature of the "gap" between generations (see Adelson, 1970, 1979); another is the mistaken assumption that most young people condone the use of a variety of illegal drugs (Johnston, 1973; Johnston, Bachman, and O'Malley, 1977; 1979).

While deflating exaggerated perceptions, a continual monitoring of indicators on youth also can reveal the beginning of new problems and thus give rise to corrective efforts at a relatively early stage. For instance, most would view with concern the emergence of new types of drug use. Monitoring the Future has already documented and reported a sharp increase in regular marijuana use among high school seniors, and as a result more attention has been paid to the issue by policy makers, the media, and the general public. The discovery of such trends may trigger more intense efforts to discover the causes, consequences, and (when appropriate) preventatives of such behaviors.

Although social indicators seldom translate directly into specific policy decisions, the availability of descriptive information can substantially enhance the decision-making capabilities of policy makers. These data provide considerable insight into the size and nature of problems, the rate of change occurring nationally and in subgroups, and in some instances information about related factors and even the likely impacts of major social interventions (such as changed drug laws, or new incentives for recruitment into the military, to name but two). They also provide the possibility of feedback on the consequences of some social interventions as well as major historical events.

The particular topics included in our monitoring system are summarized later in this introduction and, of course, they are presented fully in the complete set of data tables. For present purposes, it is enough to indicate that the range of topics is very broad. This breadth is partly due to the wide interests of the principal investigators; but it also reflects our conviction that the concurrent examination of trends in a variety of areas is not only much more cost efficient but also more scientifically productive.

Research Design and Procedures*

The basic research design involves annual data collections from high school seniors during the spring of each year, beginning with the class of 1975. Each data collection takes place in approximately 125 public and private high schools selected to provide an accurate cross section of high school seniors throughout the coterminous United States. The design also provides for the longitudinal study of a subsample from each class of participating seniors; but since the focus of this series of volumes is exclusively on the data collected annually from seniors, the follow-up procedures will not be discussed here.

Reasons for Focusing on High School Seniors. There are several reasons for choosing the senior year of high school as an optimal point for monitoring the behaviors and attitudes of youth. One is that the completion of high school represents the end of an important developmental stage in this society, since it demarcates both the end of universal public education and, for many, the end of living in the parental home. Therefore, it is a logical point at which to take stock of the accumulated influences of these two environments on American youth.

Further, the completion of high school represents the jumping-off point from which young people diverge into widely differing social environments, including college, business firms, military service, and homemaking. But these environmental transitions are not the only important changes which coincide with the end of high school. Most young men and women now reach the formal age of adulthood shortly before or after graduation; more significantly, they begin to assume adult roles, including financial self-support, marriage, and parenthood.

Finally, there are some important practical

---

*A more extensive description of the research design and procedures may be found in Bachman and Johnston (1978).

advantages to building a system of data collections around samples of high school seniors. The last year of high school constitutes the final point at which a reasonably good national sample of an age-specific cohort can be drawn and studied economically. The need for systematically repeated, large-scale samples from which to make reliable estimates of change requires that considerable stress be laid on efficiency and feasibility; the present design meets those requirements.

One limitation in the design is that it does not include in the target population those young men and women who drop out of high school before graduation (or before the last few months of the senior year, to be more precise). This excludes a relatively small proportion of each age cohort — between 15 and 20 percent (Golladay, 1976, 1977) — though not an unimportant segment, since we know that certain behaviors such as illicit drug use (Johnston, 1973) and delinquency (Bachman, O'Malley, and Johnston, 1978) tend to be higher than average in this group. However, the addition of a representative sample of dropouts would increase the cost of the present research enormously, because of their dispersion and generally higher level of resistance to being located and interviewed.

For the purposes of estimating characteristics of the entire age group, the omission of high school dropouts does introduce certain biases; however, their small proportion sets outer limits on the bias (Johnston, O'Malley, and Eveland, 1975, Appendix B). For the purposes of estimating *changes* from one cohort of high school seniors to another, the omission of dropouts represents a problem only if different cohorts have considerably different proportions who drop out. We have no reason to expect dramatic changes in those rates for the foreseeable future, and recently published government statistics indicate a great deal of stability in dropout rates since 1967 (Golladay, 1976, p. 62; 1977, p. 81).

Some may use our high school data to draw conclusions about changes for the entire age group. While we do not encourage such extrapolation, we suspect that the conclusions reached often would be valid, since over 80 percent of the age group is in the surveyed segment of the population *and* since we expect that change among those not in school are very likely to parallel the changes among those who are. Nevertheless, for purposes of characterizing the entire age group we would urge the user to check the results emanating from the present monitoring system against those emerging from other data collection systems using different methods, such as household interviews. (It is encouraging to note that when we have compared drug use data for this age group from the present study with those

from interview studies, the findings have shown a high degree of similarity.)

Sampling Procedures. The procedure for securing a nationwide sample of high school seniors is a multi-stage one. Stage 1 is the selection of particular geographic areas, Stage 2 is the selection of one or more high schools in each area, and Stage 3 is the selection of seniors within each high school.

Stage 1: Geographic Areas. The geographic areas used in this study are the primary sampling units (PSUs) developed by the Sampling Section of the Survey Research Center for use in the Center's nationwide interview studies. These consist of 74 primary areas throughout the coterminous United States — including the 12 largest metropolitan areas, which contain about 30 percent of the nation's population. Of the 62 other primary areas, 10 are in the Northeast, 18 in the North Central area, 24 in the South, and 10 in the West. Because these same PSUs are used for personal interview studies by the Survey Research Center (SRC), local field representatives can be assigned to administer the data collections in practically all schools.

Stage 2: Schools. In the major metropolitan areas more than one high school is often included in the sampling design; in most other sampling areas a single high school is sampled. In all cases, the selections of high schools are made such that the probability of drawing a school is proportionate to the size of its senior class. The larger the senior class (according to recent records), the higher the selection probability assigned to the high school. When a sampled school is unwilling to participate, a replacement school as similar to it as possible is selected from the same geographic area.

Stage 3: Students. Within each selected school, up to about 400 seniors may be included in the data collection. In schools with fewer than 400 seniors, the usual procedure is to include all of them in the data collection. In larger schools, a subset of seniors is selected either by randomly sampling classrooms or by some other random method that is convenient for the school and judged to be unbiased. Sample weights are assigned to each respondent so as to take account of variations in the sizes of samples from one school to another, as well as the (smaller) variations in selection probabilities occurring at the earlier stages of sampling.

The three-stage sampling procedure described above yielded the number of participating schools and students indicated in Table 1.

One other important feature of the base-year sampling procedure should be noted here. All schools (except for half of the initial 1975 sample) are asked to participate in two data collections, thereby permitting replacement of half of the total sample of schools each year. One motivation for

Table 1

Sample Sizes and Student Response Rates

	1975	1976	1977	1978
Number of Public Schools	111	108	108	111
Number of Private Schools	14	15	16	20
Total Number of Schools	125	123	124	131
Actual Number of Participating Students	15792	16678	18436	18924
Number of Weighted Cases (Total)*	15104	15299	15839	18924
Student Response Rate**	78%	77%	79%	83%

* Sample weights are assigned to each respondent to correct for unequal probablities of selection which arise in the multi-stage sampling procedure.

** The student response rate is derived by dividing the attained sample by the target sample (both based on weighted numbers of cases). The target sample is based upon listings provided by schools. Since such listings may fail to take account of recent student attrition, the actual response rate may be slightly underestimated.

requesting that schools participate for two years is administrative efficiency; it is a costly and time-consuming procedure to secure the cooperation of schools, and a two-year period of participation cuts down that effort substantially. Another important advantage is that whenever an appreciable shift in scores from one graduating class to the next is observed, it is possible to check whether the shift might be attributable to some differences in the newly sampled schools. This is done simply by repeating the analysis using only the 60 or so schools which participated both years. Thus far, the half-sample approach has worked quite well; an examination of drug prevalence data from the classes of 1975 and 1976 showed that the half sample of repeat schools yielded drug prevalence trends which were virtually identical to trends based on all schools.

School Recruiting Procedures. Early during the fall semester an initial contact is made with each sampled school. First a letter is sent to the principal describing the study and requesting permission to survey seniors. The letter is followed by a telephone call from a project staff member, who attempts to deal with any questions or problems and (when necessary) makes arrangements to contact and seek permission from other school district officials. Basically the same procedures are followed for schools asked to participate for the second year.

Once the school's agreement to participate is obtained, arrangements are made by phone for administering the questionnaires. A specific date for the survey is mutually agreed upon and a local SRC representative is assigned to carry out the administration.

Advance Contact with Teachers and Students. The local SRC representative is instructed to visit the school two weeks ahead of the actual date of administration. This visit serves as an occasion to meet the teachers whose classes will be affected and to provide them with a brochure describing the study, a brief set of guidelines about the questionnaire administration, and a supply of flyers to be distributed to the students a week to 10 days in advance of the questionnaire administration. The guidelines to the teachers include a suggested announcement to students at the time the flyers are distributed.

From the students' standpoint, the first information about the study usually consists of the teacher's announcement and the short descriptive flyer. In announcing the study, the teachers are asked to stress that the questionnaires used in the survey are not tests, and that there are no right or wrong answers. The flyer tells students that they will be invited to participate in the study, points out that their participation is strictly voluntary, and stresses confidentiality (including a reference to the fact that the Monitoring the Future project has a special government grant of confidentiality which allows their answers to be protected). The flyer also serves as an informative document which the students can show to their parents.

Questionnaire Administrations. The questionnaire administration in each school is carried out by the local SRC representatives and their assistants, following standardized procedures detailed in a project instruction manual. The questionnaires are administered in classrooms during normal class periods whenever possible, although circumstances in some schools require the use of larger group administrations. Teachers are not asked to do anything more than introduce the SRC staff members and (in most cases) remain in the classroom to help guarantee an orderly atmosphere for the survey. Teachers are urged to avoid walking around the room, so that students may feel free to write their answers without fear of being observed.

The actual process of completing the questionnaires is quite straightforward. Respondents are given sharpened pencils and asked to use them because the questionnaires are designed for automatic scanning. Most respondents can finish within a 45-minute class period; for those who cannot, an effort is made to provide a few minutes of additional time.

Procedures for Protecting Confidentiality. In any study that relies on voluntary reporting of drug use or other illegal acts, it is essential to develop procedures which guarantee the confidentiality of such reports. It is also desirable that these procedures be described adequately to respondents so that they are comfortable about providing honest answers.

We noted that the first information given to students about the survey consists of a descriptive flyer stressing confidentiality and voluntary participation. This theme is repeated at the start of the questionnaire administration. Each participating student is instructed to read the message on the cover of the questionnaire, which stresses the importance and value of the study, notes that

answers will be kept strictly confidential, states that the study is completely voluntary, and tells the student "If there is any question you or your parents would find objectionable for any reason, just leave it blank." The instructions then point out that in a few months a summary of nationwide results will be mailed to all participants and also that a follow-up questionnaire will be sent to some students after a year. The cover message explains that these are the reasons for asking that name and address be written on a special form which will be removed from the questionnaire and handed in separately. The message also points out that the two different code numbers (one on the questionnaire and one on the tear-out form) cannot be matched except by a special computer tape at The University of Michigan. (The content of the inside and outside of the standard questionnaire cover, including the tear-out form, may be found in Appendix C.)

Content Areas and Questionnaire Design

Drug use and related attitudes are the topics which receive the most extensive coverage in the Monitoring the Future project; but the questionnaires also deal with a wide range of other subject areas, including attitudes about government, social institutions, race relations, changing roles for women, educational aspirations, occupational aims, and marital and family plans, as well as a variety of background and demographic factors. (Table 2 provides an outline of the 19 general subject areas into which all items are categorized in the Question Index toward the end of this volume.) Given this breadth of content, the study is not presented to respondents as a "drug use study," nor do they tend to view it as such.

Table 2

Measurement Content Areas

A. **Drugs.** Drug use and related attitudes and beliefs, drug availability and exposure, surrounding conditions and social meaning of drug use. Views of significant others regarding drugs.

B. **Education.** Educational lifestyle, values, experiences, and environments. Media usage.

C. **Work and Leisure.** Vocational values, meaning of work and leisure, work and leisure activities, preferences regarding occupational characteristics and type of work setting.

Table 2 (continued)

D. **Sex Roles and Family.** Values, attitudes, and expectations about marriage, family structure, sex roles, and sex discrimination.

E. **Family Plans and Population Concerns.** Values, attitudes, and expectations about personal family plans. Views on sexual mores and concerns about overpopulation.

F. **Conservation, Materialism, Equity, etc.** Values, attitudes, and expectations related to conservation, pollution, materialism, equity, and the sharing of resources. Preferences regarding type of dwelling and urbanicity.

G. **Religion.** Religious affiliation, practices, and views.

H. **Politics.** Political affiliation, activities, and views.

I. **Social Change.** Values, attitudes, and expectations about social change.

J. **Social Problems.** Concern with various social problems facing the nation and the world.

K. **Major Social Institutions.** Confidence in and commitment to various major social institutions (business, unions, branches of government, press, organized religion, military, etc.).

L. **Military.** Views about the armed services and the use of military force. Personal plans for military service.

M. **Interpersonal Relationships.** Qualitative and quantitative characteristics of cross-age and peer relationships. Interpersonal conflict.

N. **Race Relations.** Attitudes toward and experiences with other racial groups.

O. **Concern for Others.** Radius of concern for others; voluntary and charitable activities.

P. **Happiness.** Happiness and life satisfaction, overall and in specific life domains.

Q. **Other Personality Variables.** Attitudes about self (including self-esteem), locus of control, loneliness, optimism, trust in others, somatic symptoms, importance placed on various life goals, counter-culture orientation.

R. **Background and School.** Demographic and family background characteristics, curriculum and grades in high school, victimization in school.

S. **Deviant Behavior and Victimization.** Delinquent behaviors, driving violations and accidents, violations and accidents under the influence of drugs, victimization experiences.

Because many questions are needed to cover all of these topic areas, much of the questionnaire content is divided into five different questionnaire forms which are distributed to participants in an ordered sequence that produces five virtually identical subsamples. About one-third of each questionnaire form consists of key or "core" variables which are common to all forms. All demographic variables and some measures of drug use are included in this "core" set of measures. This use of the full sample for drug and demographic measures provides a more accurate estimation on these dimensions and also makes it possible to link them statistically to all of the other measures which are included in a single form only.*

Representativeness and Validity

The samples for this study are intended to be representative of high school seniors throughout the 48 coterminous states. We have already discussed the fact that this definition of the sample excludes one important portion of the age cohort: those who have dropped out of high school before nearing the end of the senior year. But given the aim of representing high school seniors, it will now be useful to consider the extent to which the obtained samples of schools and students are likely to be representative of all seniors and the degree to which the data obtained are likely to be valid.

We can distinguish at least four ways in which survey data of this sort might fall short of being fully accurate. First, some sampled schools refuse to participate, which could introduce some bias. Second, the failure to obtain questionnaire data from 100 percent of the students sampled in participating schools could also introduce bias. Third, the answers provided by participating students are open to both conscious and unconscious distortions which could reduce validity. Finally, limitations in sample size and/or design could place limits on the accuracy of estimates. Each of these issues is treated extensively elsewhere (Johnston, Bachman, and O'Malley, 1979, especially Appendices A and B), so in this section we will present only the highlights of each of those discussions.

School Participation. As noted in the description of the sampling design, schools are invited to participate in the study for a two-year period. With very few exceptions, each school which has participated for one data collection has agreed to participate for a second. Thus far, from 66 percent to 80 percent of the schools initially invited to participate have agreed to do so each year; for each

school refusal, a similar school (in terms of size, geographic area, urbanicity, etc.) was recruited as a replacement. The selection of replacement schools almost entirely removes problems of bias in region, urbanicity, and the like that might result from certain schools refusing to participate. Other potential biases are more subtle, however. For example, if it turned out that most schools with "drug problems" refused to participate, that could seriously bias the drug estimates derived from the sample. And if any other single factor were dominant in most refusals, that also might suggest a source of serious bias. In fact, however, the reasons for schools' refusals to participate are varied and largely a function of happenstance events of the particular year. Thus, we feel fairly confident that school refusals have not seriously biased the surveys.

Student Participation. Completed questionnaires are obtained from three-fourths to four-fifths of all students sampled. The single most important reason that students are missed is that they are absent from class at the time of data collection, and in most cases it is not workable to schedule a special follow-up data collection for them. Students with fairly high rates of absenteeism also report above-average rates of drug use; therefore, there is some degree of bias introduced by missing the absentees. That bias could be largely corrected through the use of special weighting; however, this course was not chosen because the bias in estimates (for drug use, where the potential effect was hypothesized to be largest) was determined to be quite small and because the necessary weighting procedures would have introduced undesirable complications (see Johnston et al., 1977).

In addition to absenteeism, student nonparticipation occurs because of schedule conflicts with school trips and other activities which tend to be more frequent than usual during the final months of the senior year. Of course, some students refuse to complete or turn in a questionnaire. However, the SRC representatives in the field estimate this proportion to be only about one percent.

Validity of Self-Report Data. Survey measures of delinquency and of drug use depend upon respondents reporting what are, in many cases, illegal acts. Thus, a critical question is whether such self-reports are likely to be valid. Like most studies dealing with these areas, we have no direct, objective validation of the present measures; however, the considerable amount of inferential evidence which exists strongly suggests that the self-report questions produce largely valid data. A number of

---

*These core variables are the first ones on which data are presented in the Descriptive Results Section.

factors have given us reasonable confidence about the validity of the responses to what are presumably among the most sensitive questions in the study: a low nonresponse on the drug questions; a large proportion admitting to some illicit drug use; the consistency of findings across several years of the present study; strong evidence of construct validity (based on relationships observed between variables); a close match between our data and the findings from other studies using other methods; and the findings from several methodological studies which have used objective validation methods.*

As for others of the measures, a few have a long and venerable history — as scholars of the relevant literatures will recognize — though some of these measures have been modified to fit the present questionnaire format. Many (probably most) questions, however, have been developed specifically for this project through a careful process of question writing, pilot testing, pretesting, and question revision or elimination. Some already have been included in other publications from the study, but many have not; therefore, there currently exists little *empirical* evidence of their validity and reliability. On the other hand, the fact that virtually all results presented in this volume are based on individual items, rather than indexes or abstract concepts, should make it easy for the reader to judge the degree to which each item has "face validity" and also the degree to which there is some evidence of construct validity in the bivariate results.

Accuracy of the Sample. A sample survey never can provide the same level of accuracy as would be obtained if the entire target population were to participate in the survey — in the case of the present study, about three million seniors per year. But perfect accuracy of this sort would be extremely expensive and certainly not worthwhile considering the fact that a high level of accuracy can be provided by a carefully designed probability sample. The accuracy of the sample in this study is affected both by the size of the student sample and by the number of schools in which they are clustered. Appendix B presents a discussion of the ways in which this clustering and other aspects of the sampling design are taken into account in computing the precision or accuracy of the samples. For the purposes of this introduction, it is sufficient to note that virtually all estimates based on the total sample have confidence intervals of ±1.5 percentage points or smaller — sometimes considerably smaller. This means that, had we been able to invite all schools and all seniors in the 48 coterminous states to participate, the results from such a

massive survey would be within an estimated 1.5 percentage points of our present sample findings at least 95 times out of 100. We consider this to be a quite high level of accuracy, and one that permits the detection of fairly small trends from one year to the next.

Consistency and the Measurement of Trends. One other point is worth noting in a discussion of the validity of our findings. The Monitoring the Future project is, by intention, a study designed to be sensitive to changes from one time to another. Accordingly, the measures and procedures have been standardized and applied consistently across each data collection. To the extent that any biases remain because of limits in school and/or student participation, and to the extent that there are distortions (lack of validity) in the responses of some students, it seems very likely that such problems will exist in much the same way from one year to the next. In other words, biases in the survey estimates should tend to be consistent from one year to another, which means that the measurement of *trends* should be affected very little by any such biases.

Caveats to Users of the Data

In attempting to understand and interpret the statistical results contained in this volume, the reader should keep in mind the several considerations discussed below.

Estimation of Sampling Errors. Appendix A provides figures which allow the reader to determine the 95 percent confidence interval around any observed percentage for both the total sample and the several subgroups for which statistics are given. Appendix A also provides tables and guidelines for testing the statistical significance of observed differences between subgroups (e.g., males vs. females) and the significance of year-to-year changes for the entire sample and for the various subgroups on any given variable. Estimates based on subgroups containing relatively few cases (e.g., those who have used heroin) will have substantially larger margins of error than those subgroups with large numbers of cases.

Subgroup Definitions. At the beginning of the Descriptive Results section there is a careful definition of each of the subgroups analyzed in this series of volumes. It is important for the reader to read these definitions so as not to be misled by the

---

*A more detailed discussion of the evidence for validity of the measures of illicit drug use may be found in Johnston et al. (1977), Appendix A.

necessarily abbreviated descriptions given in the column headings of the data tables. For example, several column headings in the lifetime illicit drug use index use the term "pills"; however, these categories contain people who indicate that they used any of a number of drugs — including some which usually are not taken in pill form (e.g., cocaine, and narcotics other than heroin).

Missing Data Notes. Each column of percentages for a given variable adds to 100 percent (with slight variations due to rounding), whether based on the entire sample or any one of the subgroups being described. Missing data were not included in computing these percentages, so it is up to the reader to determine whether an exceptional level of missing data exists on any given question. This can be done by comparing the weighted number of cases on which those percentages were based (given in italics under each percentage distribution) with the total number of weighted cases who took the questionnaire (given at the top of the same column). As would be expected, the missing data rate tends to rise modestly toward the end of each questionnaire. Occasionally there is an exceptional level of nonresponse for some other reason, the most common being that the respondent has been branched around a question or set of questions which are inappropriate for him or her. In this case the percentages are based only on those for whom the question was appropriate *and* who answered. A footnote has been entered to help call attention to the fact that completing a particular question is contingent upon the answer on a prior question. Most such cases are contained in Form 1 of the questionnaire, which has several sets of detailed questions about drug use which are answered only by those respondents who have used a particular class of drug during the past year.

Characterizing Heroin Users. Because this project places a special emphasis on the study of drug use, one set of columns distinguishes respondents according to the extent to which they have been involved with illicit drugs. The five drug use categories are based on an index of seriousness of involvement. The index has Guttman-like properties — that is, anyone classified at a given level is also very likely to have exhibited any drug-using behaviors which are associated with the lower levels in the index.

The most extreme category in the index is defined in terms of the respondent's ever having used heroin during his or her lifetime. However, any interpretations made about heroin users from these data must be tempered with extreme caution, not only because the small number of cases makes

estimation in a given year relatively unreliable, but also because heroin users are probably the most selectively represented of all of the subgroups presented here. Heroin users — especially continuing users — are among those most likely to drop out of high school (Johnston, 1973). Therefore, we feel that heroin users are particularly underrepresented in a sample of high school seniors. Furthermore, most of those included in the study report only very occasional heroin use. Frequent users — addicts, if you will — are not well represented in these data.

Given these problems with the representation of heroin users, the reader may wonder why it was decided to present them as a separate category of drug users. There are two reasons for doing so. First, because even occasional heroin use represents such an extreme point on the continuum of drug involvement, it seems preferable that the heroin users not be mixed in with the next highest category of use (the "more pills" category). It remains quite possible, of course, for anyone to *combine* any two or more categories in the drug use continuum (by computing means of percentages weighted by the number of cases in each category); therefore, those wishing to incorporate heroin users with the next category can do so whenever they wish. The second reason for keeping them separate is that we suspect the data based on high school seniors provide some indication of the characteristics which might be found among heavier heroin users who dropped out of school. Some variables in the study are strongly correlated with the drug use continuum, and the present heroin user category provides both an end point for that continuum and an indication of the direction (further out on the continuum) in which heavier heroin users are likely to lie.

In sum, the reporting of separate percentages for heroin users among high school seniors permits greater clarity in analyzing other levels of drug use and provides data which may be suggestive about the larger population of young heroin users. But the particular data are clearly limited and should be interpreted with these cautions in mind.

Interpreting Racial Differences in Later Volumes. All subsequent volumes in this series contain data for the two largest ethnic subgroups in the population — those who identify themselves as white or Caucasian and those who identify themselves as black or Afro-American. Data are not given for the other ethnic categories (American Indians, Asian Americans, Mexican Americans, Peurto Ricans, or other Latin Americans (since each of these groups comprises less than three percent of the sample in any given year, which means that the small Ns (in combination with their clustered groupings in a limited number of schools) would yield estimates which would be too unreliable, In fact, even blacks — who constitute approximately 12 percent of each year's sample — are represented by only 350 to 425 respondents per year on any single questionnaire form. Further, because our sample is a stratified clustered sample, it yielsd less accuracy than would be yielded by a pure random sample of equal size (see Appendix B for details). Therefore, because of the limited number of cases,. the margin of sampling error around any statistic describing blacks is larger than for most other subgroups descrived in the series.

There exists, however, a quick way to determine the replicability of any finding involving racial comparisons. Since most questions are repeated from year to year, one can readily establish the degree to which a finding is replicated by looking at the results for the same question in prior or subsequent years. Given the relatively small Ns for blacks, the reader is urged to seek such replication before putting much faith in the reliability of any particular racial comparison.

There are factors in addition to unreliability, however, which could be misleading in the interpretation of racial differences. Given the social importance which has been placed on various racial differences reported in the social science literature, we would like to caution the reader to consider the various factors which could account for differences. These factors fall into three categories: differential representation in the sample, differential response tendencies, and the confounding of race with a number of other background and demographic characteristics.

Differential Representation. Census data characterizing American young people in the approximate age range of those in our sample show that somewhat lower proportions of blacks than whites remain in school through the end of twelfth grade (Golladay, 1977, p. 197). Therefore, a slightly different segment of the black population than of the white population resides in our target population of high school seniors. Further, our samples appear to underrepresent slightly those black males who, according to census figures, are in high school at the twelfth grade level. Identified black males comprise about 6 percent of our sample, whereas census data suggest that they should comprise around 7 percent (U.S. Bureau of the Census, 1978). Therefore, it appears that we are losing more black males from our target population than white males or females of either race. This may be due to generally poorer attendance rates on the part of some black males and/or an unwillingness on the part of some to participate in data collections of this sort.

In sum, a smaller segment of the black population than of the white population of high school age is represented by the data contained here. Insofar as any characteristic is associated with being a school dropout or absentee, it is likely to be somewhat disproportionately underrepresented among blacks in our sample.

Differential Response Tendencies. In examining our full range of variables, we have noted certain racial differences in response tendencies. First, the tendency to state agreement in response to agree-disagree questions is generally somewhat greater among blacks than among whites. For example, blacks tend to agree more with the positively worded items in our index of self-esteem, but they also tend to agree more with the negatively worded items. As it happens, that particular index has an equal number of positively and negatively worded items, so that any overall "agreement bias" should be self-cancelling when the index score is computed. Since all data in this volume are based on single items, however, group differences in agreement bias are likely to affect results on questions employing the agree-disagree format. Fortunately, most of our questions are not of that type.

We have also observed a somewhat greater than average tendency for black respondents to select extreme answer categories on attitudinal scales. For example, even if the same proportion of blacks as whites felt positively (or negatively) about some subject, fewer of the whites are likely to say they feel *very* positively (or *very* negatively). We do not have any ready explanations for these differences in response styles, but what seems important for our present purposes is that, in the process of interpreting racial differences, the reader should be aware that differences in responses to particular questions may be related to these more general tendencies.

A somewhat separate issue in response tendency is a respondent's willingness to answer particular questions. The missing data rate, which can be determined by dividing the number responding to a question by the number taking the questionnaire (given at the top of each page), may reflect willingness to answer particular questions. If a particular question or set of questions has a missing data rate higher than is true for the prior or subsequent questions, then presumably more respondents than usual were unwilling (or perhaps unable) to answer it. We have observed such an exaggerated missing data rate for black males on the set of questions dealing with the respondent's own use of illicit drugs. Clearly a respondent's willingness to be candid on such questions depends on his or her trust of the research process and of the researchers themselves. We interpret the exaggerated missing data rates for black males in these sections as possibly reflecting, at least in part, less trust. The reader is advised to check for exceptional levels of missing data when making comparisons on any variable in which candor is likely to be reduced by lower system trust.

Covariance with Other Factors. Some characteristics such as race are highly confounded (correlated) with other variables — variables which may in fact explain some observed racial differences. Put another way, at the aggregate level we might observe a considerable racial difference on some characteristic, but once we control for some background characteristics such as socioeconomic level or region of the country — that is, once we compare the black respondents with whites who come from similar backgrounds — there may be no racial difference at all.

Race happens to be correlated with important background and demographic variables much more than some of the other variables dealt with here (like the respondent's sex). When we compare males and females in this sample we know that observed differences between them are not likely to be explained by differences in their family background (such as the socioeconomic level of their families, the region of the country, or the size of the cities in which they grew up) because males and females on the average come from extremely similar backgrounds. A perusal of Section C of Questionnaire Forms 1 through 5, however, will illustrate that on the average the black subgroup in this sample is quite different from the white subgroup in a number of such respects. A higher proportion of blacks live in the South and a higher proportion grew up in large cities. Blacks are more likely to report low levels of parental education (an indication of a lower socioeconomic background more generally). A greater than average proportion of blacks grew up in families with the father and/or mother absent, and more had mothers who worked while they were growing up. A substantially higher proportion of blacks are Baptists, and blacks tend to attribute more importance to religion in their lives than do whites. Fewer are enrolled in a college-preparatory curriculum (though a higher proportion say they plan to attend some type of college). A slightly higher proportion of black respondents are married and have children, and on the average they are slightly older than the white sample. As was mentioned earlier, black males are more underrepresented in our sample than black females, with the result that any attempt to understand *why* a racial difference exists, one would want to be able to examine the role of these covarying characteristics. It is not possible, given the amount of data contained in this each year roughly 58 percent of our black sample is female versus roughly 51 percent of the white sample.

We note these differences in demographic, background, and ascriptive characteristics because, in volume, to "factor out" the contribution of most of these covarying characteristics when interpreting racial differences. Therefore, while the data here may provide a relatively accurate *description* of racial differences (keeping in mind our earlier cautions about representativeness and response style), they do not by themselves yield a great deal by way of explanation. However, since the full data sets now reside in two archives, described in the Preface, it is possible for the reader to conduct a more in depth exploration of observed differences — or nondifferences, for that matter. We particularly encourage readers interested in racial comparisons to make further explorations in the data in order to determine the possible role of the other variables discussed here. Users of the data are also encouraged to contact the principal investigators for information on the most recent analyses of racial differences, some of which are already underway.

Given the long list of caveats about interpreting racial differences, one might ask why we chose to publish the statistics for racial subgroups at all. After considerable deliberation among ourselves as well as with colleagues more knowledgeable in the field of race relations, we concluded that the expected benefits of making these data available (along with this cautionary discussion) outweigh the potential costs of having them misused. Unfortunately, because blacks constitute a relatively small proportion of the American population, they constitute too small a number in most surveys to be characterized separately. Because the sample sizes in the present survey are large in comparison to most, we have at least sufficient numbers of cases to consider publishing data on blacks separately. Further, given the iterative nature of the series, we are also able to provide checks for replication of findings on different samples each year. While there may be some risk that findings will be taken out of context or used carelessly in ways that might tend to increase racial misunderstandings, there is substantially greater risk that valuable information concerning the races (and relevant to their well-being) will be lost if it were not included here.

Unique Aspects of the Data Tables for 1975. The first data collection for the Monitoring the Future study took place in 1975. It was a considerable success in nearly all respects; however, one important problem was the fact that the questionnaire forms proved too long for many respondents to complete within the time available. Accordingly, the questionnaires were shortened substantially in 1976, and the 1976 format (which seemed to be an optimal questionnaire length) was continued with only minor changes in subsequent years.

For a number of reasons it seemed useful to organize the 1975 data in the same sequence as that used in 1976 (and, with only relatively few variations, in later years as well). This means that the format for the present volume departs from that used in the other volumes in several respects:

1. The order of the items does not always correspond to the order in which they appeared in the 1975 questionnaires. The questionnaire numbers are shown in the data tables, so the reader can usually reconstruct the original sequence if that is desired.

2. Items which appeared in the 1975 questionnaires but were omitted in the 1976 questionnaires have not been included in this volume.

3. The final segments of each questionnaire form in the 1975 data collection had sufficiently large proportions of missing data that we decided those segments should not be published.

4. A further restriction in the present volume is that a considerable proportion of respondents in 1975 failed to reach the specific items near the end of each form which asked for racial identification and also college plans. Accordingly, the present volume does not include separate data on four subgroups which are included in all subsequent volumes: whites, blacks, those planning to complete four years of college, those not planning to complete four years of college.

One other characteristic of the 1975 data should be noted. Although the most severe instances of missing data have been avoided (point 3 above), there remain some fairly high rates of missing data in the latter portion of Part B in questionnaire Forms 2 through 5. Thus the reader should be alert for missing data in Part B items, and should use caution in interpreting percentages based on such items.

Changed Item Order May Lead to Spurious "Trends." As noted above, the questionnaires were shortened considerably after 1975, and that means that the arrangement of items was different in all subsequent years. Early analyses of some of these data indicate that response distributions are sometimes shifted appreciably when questionnaire items appear in different contexts. Thus, for example, the question "How good do you think you would be as a worker on a job?" is answered differently by some respondents depending upon whether the preceding questions have dealt with job matters. Undoubtedly there are many instances in which changes in item sequence have not systematically influenced responses; in other instances the effects may extend to only one or two items; in still other instances the effects may be more far reaching. Unfortunately, we cannot begin to specify such distinctions in advance, although we can sometimes make after-the-fact estimates of whether changes in context are responsible for apparent "trends."

What should the user of this volume do about the possibility that changes in item context may be producing spurious "trends" when data from 1975 are compared with later years? We can offer two specific suggestions:

1. When comparing 1975 data with data from later years, examine the sequence of items preceding the item of interest. If the ten or twenty preceding items are identical, there is probably little basis for worry about effects of different contexts (although we cannot be sure how far back one ought to go). If, on the other hand, there are differences in immediately preceding items, then some judgment must be made about whether such differences are likely to have differential impacts on the item of interest.

2. Do not compare 1975 data with only one other year. If several years of data are used (e.g., 1975, 1976, 1977, and 1978), it may be clear that a fairly regular and steady trend is involved, with the 1975 data falling into the "proper" place. On the other hand, if the 1975 data seem to "stand apart" from the other years, there is reason to suspect that a different item context in 1975 contributed to the difference in responses.

Given the above list of caveats that are unique to this volume, one might ask why we chose to publish percentages for the class of 1975. We considered that question carefully, and concluded that the advantages of publishing the 1975 data more than outweighed the limitations noted above. Most of the questionnaire items which appear in later volumes are also included in the present one, and making them available adds a full year to the longitudinal span covered by this series of volumes.

Descriptive Results: 1975

Introduction to the Table Format and Conventions

Univariate and selected bivariate percentagized distributions are given in this section for most questions asked of the 1975 senior class. The definitions of column headings and the source of the standard contents for each table are given below under the numbers indicated in Figure 1. It should be noted that the *sequence* in which the questions are presented in this section has been arranged to match as closely as possible the sequence used in the other volumes. As a result, some of questions appear "out of order," i.e., they appear in the order used in 1976 (and subsequent years) rather than the original order used in the 1975 questionnaires.

Definitions of Column Headings

① **Questionnaire Form.** The form from which all data on the page were derived is given here. When the designation "Forms 1-5" is used, it indicates that responses from students completing all five questionnaires have been combined; accordingly, the numbers of respondents in each column are five times as large for questions contained in a single form only.

② **Total Sample.** Univariate percentagized distributions based on the total sample of respondents are given in this column.

③ **Sex.** Percentagized distributions are given separately for males (M) and females (F). Respondents with missing data on the variable asking the respondent's sex (or who could not be characterized accurately as male or female based on their first name) are omitted from both groupings.

④ **Region.** Percentagized distributions are given separately for respondents living in each of four mutually exclusive regions of the country. The regional classifications are based on Census categories and are defined as follows:

Northeast (NE): Census classifications of New England and Middle Atlantic. Includes Maine, New Hampshire, Vermont, Massachusetts, Rhode Island, Connecticut, New York, New Jersey, and Pennsylvania.

North Central (NC): Census classifications of East North Central and West North Central. Includes Ohio, Indiana, Illinois, Michigan, Wisconsin, Minnesota, Iowa, Missouri, North Dakota, South Dakota, Nebraska, and Kansas.

South (S): Census classifications of South Atlantic, East South Central, and West South Central. Includes Delaware, Maryland, District of Columbia, Virginia, West Virginia, North Carolina, South Carolina, Georgia, Florida, Kentucky, Tennessee, Alabama, Mississippi, Arkansas, Louisiana, Oklahoma, and Texas.

West (W): Census classifications of Mountain and Pacific. Includes Montana, Idaho, Wyoming, Colorado, New Mexico, Arizona, Utah, Nevada, Washington, Oregon, and California.

⑤ **Illicit Drug Use: Lifetime.** Percentagized distributions are given separately for five mutually exclusive subgroups differentiated by their degree of involvement with illicit drugs. Eligibility for each category is defined below.

None. This column contains data from those respondents who indicated that they had not used marijuana at any time, and also did not report use of any of the following illicit drugs in their lifetime: LSD, other psychedelics, cocaine, amphetamines, tranquilizers, methaqualone, barbiturates, heroin, or other narcotics.

Marijuana Only: This column contains data from those respondents who indicated that they had ever used marijuana (or hashish) but who also indicated that they had never used any of the other illicit drugs just listed.

Few Pills. This column contains data from those respondents who indicated having used one or more of the above listed drugs (other than marijuana) but who had not used any one class of them on more than three occasions *and* who had not used heroin at all.

More Pills. This column contains data from respondents who had used any of the above listed drugs (other than marijuana) on more than three occasions, but who had never used heroin.

Any Heroin. This column contains data from those respondents who indicated having used heroin on one or more occasions in their lifetime.

⑥ **Weighted Number of Cases.** This row contains the number of students who turned in questionnaires in each of the categories indicated by the column headings. The number of cases is stated in terms of the weighted number of respondents rather than the actual number, since all percentages in the tables have been calculated using weighted cases. The actual number of respondents generally is slightly higher than the weighted number for data collected in 1975, 1976, and 1977. (For a comparison of weighted and unweighted numbers, see Table B-2 in Appendix B). For data collected in 1978 or later, the actual number of respondents is roughly equal to the weighted number.

⑦ **Percentage of Weighted Total.** The percent of the total number of respondents who fall into the category indicated by each column heading (e.g., Female) is contained in this row. Unlike all other percentages on the page, which can be summed vertically, these percentages sum horizontally. To the extent that the subcategories in a column (e.g., Males and Females) fail to sum to 100 percent, cases have been eliminated because of missing data

on the variable in question (e.g., Sex).

Table Contents

⑧ **Questions and Answers.** Each question along with its accompanying answer alternatives is presented verbatim. The alphanumeric prefix to the question indicates the section of the questionnaire in which the question was contained and the sequential question number by which it was identified in that section of the questionnaire. So, for example, a prefix of B12c indicates that the item was question 12c in the the B Section of the questionnaire.

⑨ **Item Reference Number.** This is a unique identification number permanently assigned to each question. Any question may be located in the cross-time item index of this volume (or any other volume in this series) simply by using this reference number.

⑩ **Percentagized Distribution.** Each column of numbers beside a question gives the percentage of each group (defined by the column heading) who chose each answer alternative. Percentages are rounded to the nearest tenth of a percent and add vertically to 100 percent (with some rounding error). Nonrespondents to the question are excluded from percentage calculations.

⑪ **Number of Weighted Cases Answering (N Wtd.).** The number of students in the relevant group (defined by the column heading) who answered the question is given just below the percentage distribution. The number of nonrespondents may be determined by subtracting this weighted number answering from the weighted number of cases taking the questionnaire, shown at the top of the same column. Nonresponse may be due to the subject not answering the question, even though it pertains to him or her, or to the subject skipping inappropriate questions as instructed on a prior item.

Figure 1
Guide to Table Format

Circled reference numbers: ① ② ③ ④ ⑤ (top); ⑥ ⑦ ⑧ ⑨ ⑩ ⑪ (left side)

QUESTIONNAIRE FORM 2-5 1975	TOTAL	SEX			REGION					ILLICIT DRUG USE: LIFETIME				
		M	F		NE	NC	S	W		None	Mari-juana Only	Few Pills	More Pills	Any Her-oin
Weighted No. of Cases:	12108	5571	6100		2695	3832	3857	1724		4400	1894	1113	1989	216
% of Weighted Total:	100.0	46.0	50.4		22.3	31.6	31.9	14.2		36.3	15.6	9.2	16.4	1.8

The following questions are about cigarette smoking.

B01: Have you ever smoked cigarettes?

	TOTAL	M	F		NE	NC	S	W		None	Mar	Few	More	Her
1. Never	26.3	24.2	28.3		25.3	24.5	27.1	30.3		44.5	11.8	16.2	9.4	3.4
2. Once or twice	26.8	28.5	25.5		23.8	26.4	27.4	31.0		32.0	30.3	27.3	14.6	10.2
3. Occasionally but not regularly	16.4	16.6	16.1		13.7	18.4	17.0	14.9		13.8	21.9	18.9	15.7	10.2
4. Regularly in the past	8.6	8.5	8.5		10.4	7.7	7.4	10.0		4.3	9.5	12.4	13.5	16.1
5. Regularly now	22.0	22.2	21.5		26.8	23.1	21.1	13.7		5.4	26.5	25.3	46.9	60.0
Item 760 N(Wtd)	10081	4554	5416		2336	3104	3213	1427		4338	1878	1097	1961	205

B02: How frequently have you smoked cigarettes during the past 30 days?

	TOTAL	M	F		NE	NC	S	W		None	Mar	Few	More	Her
1. Not at all - incl. (1) in b01	63.2	62.6	64.1		59.8	60.4	63.8	73.7		84.0	54.1	55.3	36.3	23.8
2. Less than one cigarette per day	9.8	10.2	9.5		8.7	10.9	10.0	9.0		7.2	13.6	12.9	9.7	10.2
3. One to five cigarettes per day	9.0	7.3	10.2		9.3	9.7	9.3	6.0		4.8	12.8	11.9	12.4	12.1
4. About one-half pack per day	8.3	8.1	8.3		9.4	8.5	8.1	6.4		2.5	10.1	10.4	17.2	15.5
5. About one pack per day	7.3	9.0	5.7		9.5	7.8	6.8	3.8		1.2	7.7	7.9	18.1	23.8
6. About one and one-half packs per day	1.9	2.1	1.7		2.6	2.0	1.7	.9		.3	1.2	1.4	5.2	10.2
7. Two packs or more per day	.5	.6	.4		.7	.7	.3	.2		.1	.4	.4	1.0	4.9
Item 780 N(Wtd)	10010	4517	5383		2326	3084	3173	1427		4324	1873	1095	1954	206

B03: Next we want to ask you about drinking alcoholic beverages, including beer, wine, and liquor.

Have you ever had any beer, wine, or liquor to drink...

	TOTAL	M	F		NE	NC	S	W		None	Mar	Few	More	Her
1. No	9.2	7.8	10.5		4.8	7.7	11.5	14.7		18.1	.8	4.5	1.6	1.5
2. Yes	90.8	92.2	89.5		95.2	92.3	88.5	85.3		81.9	99.2	95.5	98.4	98.5
Item 790 N(Wtd)	9787	4404	5281		2279	3009	3098	1401		4270	1852	1089	1919	196

B04A: ...in your lifetime?

	TOTAL	M	F		NE	NC	S	W		None	Mar	Few	More	Her
1. 0 occasions - incl. (1) in b03	9.5	8.0	10.8		4.9	8.0	12.0	15.0		18.6	.8	4.7	1.6	1.5
2. 1-2	7.5	5.0	9.7		4.5	6.5	10.3	8.6		13.2	2.6	5.2	1.7	1.0
3. 3-5	8.8	6.7	10.6		6.8	8.7	10.9	7.7		14.3	4.8	6.8	3.0	1.5
4. 6-9	8.3	6.7	9.7		7.2	8.6	8.9	7.7		11.7	7.0	8.1	2.5	2.0
5. 10-19	12.6	9.7	15.1		12.5	13.1	12.6	11.6		15.1	12.6	14.8	7.2	4.0
6. 20-39	13.5	12.4	14.4		15.9	14.3	11.1	13.5		10.8	18.0	16.9	13.6	11.5
7. 40 or more	39.7	51.5	29.6		48.3	40.8	34.1	35.7		16.2	54.1	43.6	70.2	77.5
Item 810 N(Wtd)	9486	4277	5108		2208	2929	2976	1374		4163	1818	1040	1891	200

B04B: ...during the last 12 months?

	TOTAL	M	F		NE	NC	S	W		None	Mar	Few	More	Her
1. 0 occasions - incl. (1) in b03	15.1	11.8	17.9		8.1	12.4	20.0	21.8		27.6	3.7	8.8	3.7	4.1
2. 1-2	12.8	9.8	15.5		10.4	12.7	14.7	12.8		20.1	7.6	10.6	4.5	2.0
3. 3-5	12.5	9.8	15.0		12.0	12.7	12.5	12.8		16.4	10.8	15.1	5.7	2.5
4. 6-9			12.2		12.6	11.2	11.1	10.7		12.1	12.8	12.8	8.6	4.1
5. 10-19					18.1	16.8	13.7	13.5		11.7	20.6	20.3	17.4	12.7
6. 20-					15.3	14.0	10.6	12.2		6.6	19.6	14.2	19.9	16
					23.4	20.2	17.4	16.2		5.6	24.8	18.1	40.3	
						2944	1364			4111	1807			

QUESTIONNAIRE FORM 2-5 1975	TOTAL	SEX			REGION					ILLICIT DRUG USE: LIFETIME				
		M	F		NE	NC	S	W		None	Marijuana Only	Few Pills	More Pills	Any Heroin
Weighted No. of Cases:	12108	5571	6100		2695	3832	3857	1724		4400	1894	1113	1989	216
% of Weighted Total:	100.0	46.0	50.4		22.3	31.6	31.9	14.2		36.3	15.6	9.2	16.4	1.8

The following questions are about cigarette smoking.

B01: Have you ever smoked cigarettes?

	TOTAL	M	F		NE	NC	S	W		None	Mari	Few	More	Any
1. Never	26.3	24.2	28.3		25.3	24.5	27.1	30.3		44.5	11.8	16.2	9.4	3.4
2. Once or twice	26.8	28.5	25.5		23.8	26.4	27.4	31.0		32.0	30.3	27.3	14.6	10.2
3. Occasionally but not regularly	16.4	16.6	16.1		13.7	18.4	17.0	14.9		13.8	21.9	18.9	15.7	10.2
4. Regularly in the past	8.6	8.5	8.5		10.4	7.7	7.4	10.0		4.3	9.5	12.4	13.5	16.1
5. Regularly now	22.0	22.2	21.5		26.8	23.1	21.1	13.7		5.4	26.5	25.3	46.9	60.0
Item 760 N(Wtd)	10081	4554	5416		2336	3104	3213	1427		4338	1878	1097	1961	205

B02: How frequently have you smoked cigarettes during the past 30 days?

	TOTAL	M	F		NE	NC	S	W		None	Mari	Few	More	Any
1. Not at all - incl. (1) in b01	63.2	62.6	64.1		59.8	60.4	63.8	73.7		84.0	54.1	55.3	36.3	23.8
2. Less than one cigarette per day	9.8	10.2	9.5		8.7	10.9	10.0	9.0		7.2	13.6	12.9	9.7	10.2
3. One to five cigarettes per day	9.0	7.3	10.2		9.3	9.7	9.3	6.0		4.8	12.8	11.9	12.4	12.1
4. About one-half pack per day	8.3	8.1	8.3		9.4	8.5	8.1	6.4		2.5	10.1	10.4	17.2	15.5
5. About one pack per day	7.3	9.0	5.7		9.5	7.8	6.8	3.8		1.2	7.7	7.9	18.1	23.8
6. About one and one-half packs per day	1.9	2.1	1.7		2.6	2.0	1.7	.9		.3	1.2	1.4	5.2	10.2
7. Two packs or more per day	.5	.6	.4		.7	.7	.3	.2		.1	.4	.4	1.0	4.9
Item 780 N(Wtd)	10010	4517	5383		2326	3084	3173	1427		4324	1873	1095	1954	206

B03: Next we want to ask you about drinking alcoholic beverages, including beer, wine, and liquor.

Have you ever had any beer, wine, or liquor to drink...

	TOTAL	M	F		NE	NC	S	W		None	Mari	Few	More	Any
1. No	9.2	7.8	10.5		4.8	7.7	11.5	14.7		18.1	.8	4.5	1.6	1.5
2. Yes	90.8	92.2	89.5		95.2	92.3	88.5	85.3		81.9	99.2	95.5	98.4	98.5
Item 790 N(Wtd)	9787	4404	5281		2279	3009	3098	1401		4270	1852	1089	1919	196

B04A: ...in your lifetime?

	TOTAL	M	F		NE	NC	S	W		None	Mari	Few	More	Any
1. 0 occasions - incl. (1) in b03	9.5	8.0	10.8		4.9	8.0	12.0	15.0		18.6	.8	4.7	1.6	1.5
2. 1-2	7.5	5.0	9.7		4.5	6.5	10.3	8.6		13.2	2.6	5.2	1.7	1.0
3. 3-5	8.8	6.7	10.6		6.8	8.7	10.9	7.7		14.3	4.8	6.8	3.0	1.5
4. 6-9	8.3	6.7	9.7		7.2	8.6	8.9	7.7		11.7	7.0	8.1	2.5	2.0
5. 10-19	12.6	9.7	15.1		12.5	13.1	12.6	11.6		15.1	12.6	14.8	7.2	4.0
6. 20-39	13.5	12.4	14.4		15.9	14.3	11.1	13.5		10.8	18.0	16.9	13.6	11.5
7. 40 or more	39.7	51.5	29.6		48.3	40.8	34.1	35.7		16.2	54.1	43.6	70.2	77.5
Item 810 N(Wtd)	9486	4277	5108		2208	2929	2976	1374		4163	1818	1040	1891	200

B04B: ...during the last 12 months?

	TOTAL	M	F		NE	NC	S	W		None	Mari	Few	More	Any
1. 0 occasions - incl. (1) in b03	15.1	11.8	17.9		8.1	12.4	20.0	21.8		27.6	3.7	8.8	3.7	4.1
2. 1-2	12.8	9.8	15.5		10.4	12.7	14.7	12.8		20.1	7.6	10.6	4.5	2.0
3. 3-5	12.5	9.8	15.0		12.0	12.7	12.5	12.8		16.4	10.8	15.1	5.7	2.5
4. 6-9	11.4	10.6	12.2		12.6	11.2	11.1	10.7		12.1	12.8	12.8	8.6	4.1
5. 10-19	15.7	15.3	16.0		18.1	16.8	13.7	13.5		11.7	20.6	20.3	17.4	12.7
6. 20-39	13.0	14.2	11.9		15.3	14.0	10.6	12.2		6.6	19.6	14.2	19.9	16.8
7. 40 or more	19.5	28.6	11.5		23.4	20.2	17.4	16.2		5.6	24.8	18.1	40.3	57.9
Item 820 N(Wtd)	9430	4265	5063		2201	2921	2944	1364		4111	1807	1045	1889	197

B04C: ...during the last 30 days?

	TOTAL	M	F		NE	NC	S	W		None	Mari	Few	More	Any
1. 0 occasions - incl. (1) in b03	31.7	24.9	37.7		23.0	28.8	37.2	40.0		51.5	16.1	23.6	11.7	5.6
2. 1-2	22.0	19.1	24.6		22.0	21.8	22.1	22.5		24.6	23.8	25.3	14.7	8.6
3. 3-5	17.5	19.4	15.9		20.7	18.0	15.7	15.1		12.8	23.8	22.4	19.4	11.6
4. 6-9	12.8	14.6	11.2		15.5	13.5	11.4	10.0		6.2	16.9	16.5	19.3	21.2
5. 10-19	10.1	13.0	7.5		12.4	11.0	8.5	7.8		3.4	12.7	8.1	21.8	24.2
6. 20-39	3.5	4.9	2.1		3.7	4.3	3.1	2.3		.6	4.5	2.6	7.7	15.7
7. 40 or more	2.4	4.1	.9		2.7	2.6	2.1	2.3		.9	2.2	1.5	5.4	13.1
Item 830 N(Wtd)	9423	4276	5044		2192	2913	2952	1366		4103	1813	1040	1892	198

CAUTION: Items were rearranged after 1975; changes in context may produce spurious "trends" (see page 12).

QUESTIONNAIRE FORM 2-5 1975	TOTAL	SEX			REGION					ILLICIT DRUG USE: LIFETIME				
		M	F		NE	NC	S	W		None	Mari- juana Only	Few Pills	More Pills	Any Her- oin
Weighted No. of Cases:	12108	5571	6100		2695	3832	3857	1724		4400	1894	1113	1989	216
% of Weighted Total:	100.0	46.0	50.4		22.3	31.6	31.9	14.2		36.3	15.6	9.2	16.4	1.8

B05: On the occasions that you drink alcoholic beverages, how often do you drink enough to feel pretty high?

	TOTAL	M	F		NE	NC	S	W		None	Mar. Only	Few Pills	More Pills	Any Heroin
1. On none of the occasions	26.4	20.0	32.3		21.5	24.8	32.6	24.8		49.4	11.1	17.8	7.5	2.0
2. On few of the occasions	32.5	30.3	34.5		33.5	31.3	33.5	31.4		32.5	38.3	35.1	27.1	18.0
3. On about half of the occasions	16.9	19.6	14.6		18.6	18.6	14.2	16.2		8.8	22.5	19.5	23.7	24.9
4. On most of the occasions	16.5	19.6	13.6		18.8	18.1	12.5	18.0		6.1	21.1	19.8	28.1	25.4
5. On nearly all of the occasions	7.7	10.5	5.1		7.7	7.3	7.2	9.6		3.2	7.2	7.8	13.6	29.8
Item 840 N(Wtd) ★	8799	4038	4672		2163	2764	2696	1176		3489	1853	1044	1914	205

B06: Think back over the last two weeks. How many times have you had five or more drinks in a row? (A "drink" is a glass of wine, a bottle of beer, a shot glass of liquor, or a mixed drink.)

	TOTAL	M	F		NE	NC	S	W		None	Mar. Only	Few Pills	More Pills	Any Heroin
1. None - incl. (1) in b03	63.0	50.7	73.6		56.8	59.2	67.8	71.0		83.1	51.7	57.1	38.3	22.6
2. Once	11.4	13.0	10.1		13.4	12.4	9.9	8.9		7.4	15.5	17.5	13.0	7.7
3. Twice	9.5	12.2	7.2		10.8	11.1	8.0	7.5		4.8	13.2	10.6	15.0	16.9
4. Three to five times	9.9	14.1	6.3		11.8	10.4	9.0	7.5		3.3	13.2	10.4	19.2	21.0
5. Six to nine times	3.6	5.6	2.0		4.3	4.0	3.0	3.1		.9	3.8	3.2	9.0	12.8
6. Ten or more times	2.5	4.2	.9		2.8	2.8	2.2	2.2		.5	2.7	1.2	5.4	19.0
Item 850 N(Wtd)	9405	4208	5101		2209	2887	2969	1340		4176	1800	1043	1891	195

The next major section of the questionnaire deals with various other drugs. There is a lot of talk these days about this subject, but very little accurate information. Therefore, we still have a lot to learn about the actual experiences and attitudes of people your age.

We hope that you can answer all questions; but if you find one which you cannot answer honestly, we would prefer that you leave it blank.

Remember that your answers will be kept strictly confidential: they are never connected with your name or your class.

B07: On how many occasions (if any) have you used marijuana (grass, pot) or hashish (hash, hash oil)...

B07A: ...in your lifetime?

	TOTAL	M	F		NE	NC	S	W		None	Mar. Only	Few Pills	More Pills	Any Heroin
1. 0 occasions	52.5	47.1	57.3		43.6	52.9	61.1	47.4		100.0	-	33.8	12.8	1.0
2. 1-2	8.8	8.9	8.7		8.7	9.0	8.5	9.1		-	32.6	13.2	3.8	2.0
3. 3-5	5.1	6.0	4.4		6.7	5.0	4.1	5.1		-	18.0	7.3	3.4	2.0
4. 6-9	4.0	4.1	3.8		4.9	3.8	3.6	3.5		-	12.3	6.1	3.3	5.4
5. 10-19	5.4	5.8	5.2		7.5	5.0	3.9	6.3		-	13.9	10.4	6.5	2.9
6. 20-39	5.1	5.1	5.1		6.3	5.3	3.6	6.3		-	9.8	9.8	9.4	5.9
7. 40 or more	19.1	23.0	15.5		22.4	19.0	15.3	22.2		-	13.5	19.6	60.8	81.4
Item 860 N(Wtd)	9557	4287	5182		2235	2937	3021	1364		4400	1894	1086	1928	204

B07B: ...during the last 12 months?

	TOTAL	M	F		NE	NC	S	W		None	Mar. Only	Few Pills	More Pills	Any Heroin
1. 0 occasions	59.9	54.0	65.1		52.3	59.7	67.5	55.8		100.0	23.4	46.1	17.8	5.0
2. 1-2	8.7	9.6	8.0		9.9	8.6	8.1	8.5		-	28.6	14.4	6.6	3.5
3. 3-5	5.2	5.9	4.7		5.9	5.3	4.4	5.6		-	14.7	8.8	5.8	6.0
4. 6-9	4.3	4.3	4.2		6.0	3.6	3.5	4.8		-	10.9	7.0	6.4	2.5
5. 10-19	5.5	5.8	5.2		6.9	5.3	3.9	7.3		-	11.2	8.1	11.1	3.0
6. 20-39	4.5	4.6	4.3		5.3	5.3	2.6	5.5		-	5.8	7.2	11.0	12.1
7. 40 or more	11.9	15.8	8.4		13.7	12.2	10.0	12.5		-	5.4	8.6	41.2	68.3
Item 870 N(Wtd)	9513	4264	5162		2222	2932	3001	1358		4398	1865	1085	1915	199

★=excludes respondents for whom question was inappropriate.
CAUTION: Items were rearranged after 1975; changes in context may produce spurious "trends" (see page 12).

QUESTIONNAIRE FORM 2-5 1975	TOTAL	SEX			REGION				ILLICIT DRUG USE: LIFETIME				
		M	F		NE	NC	S	W	None	Mari-juana Only	Few Pills	More Pills	Any Her-oin
Weighted No. of Cases:	12108	5571	6100		2695	3832	3857	1724	4400	1894	1113	1989	216
% of Weighted Total:	100.0	46.0	50.4		22.3	31.6	31.9	14.2	36.3	15.6	9.2	16.4	1.8
B07C: ...during the last 30 days?													
1. 0 occasions	72.7	67.4	77.5		67.6	72.2	78.7	69.2	100.0	60.1	67.4	32.6	10.7
2. 1-2	7.7	8.9	6.7		8.6	7.7	6.6	8.7	-	20.8	13.2	9.4	7.6
3. 3-5	4.8	5.6	4.2		6.5	4.2	3.4	6.8	-	9.3	7.5	10.0	5.6
4. 6-9	4.0	4.1	3.9		5.6	4.1	2.6	4.0	-	5.4	4.5	11.1	7.1
5. 10-19	4.6	5.5	3.6		4.8	5.3	3.6	4.8	-	3.3	4.0	14.5	24.4
6. 20-39	3.1	4.0	2.4		3.6	3.2	2.6	3.3	-	.7	2.1	11.7	18.8
7. 40 or more	3.0	4.6	1.7		3.4	3.3	2.5	3.2	-	.5	1.3	10.7	26.9
Item 880 N(Wtd)	9514	4263	5162		2220	2931	3003	1359	4400	1863	1087	1915	197
B08: On how many occasions (if any) have you used LSD ("acid")...													
B08A: ...in your lifetime?													
1. 0 occasions	88.4	86.4	90.3		86.9	87.3	91.5	86.5	100.0	100.0	91.1	56.5	19.3
2. 1-2	4.7	4.9	4.5		5.8	4.7	3.3	6.2	-	-	9.0	16.7	14.5
3. 3-5	2.2	2.5	1.8		2.3	2.3	2.0	2.3	-	-	-	9.8	10.6
4. 6-9	1.3	1.4	1.2		1.3	1.5	1.0	1.4	-	-	-	5.6	7.2
5. 10-19	1.4	1.7	1.1		1.2	1.7	1.0	1.8	-	-	-	5.0	15.9
6. 20-39	.9	1.3	.6		1.1	1.1	.6	.9	-	-	-	3.4	10.1
7. 40 or more	1.1	1.7	.5		1.4	1.4	.6	1.0	-	-	-	3.0	22.2
Item 890 N(Wtd)	9643	4354	5201		2256	2958	3067	1361	4387	1886	1101	1955	207
B08B: ...during the last 12 months?													
1. 0 occasions	92.5	90.4	94.4		91.5	91.3	94.6	92.4	100.0	100.0	96.9	71.5	37.0
2. 1-2	3.9	4.6	3.3		4.6	3.9	3.2	4.4	-	-	3.1	15.1	23.0
3. 3-5	1.6	2.2	1.1		1.6	2.0	1.1	1.9	-	-	-	6.5	13.5
4. 6-9	.9	1.0	.8		1.2	1.0	.6	.7	-	-	-	3.3	10.0
5. 10-19	.6	1.0	.2		.5	1.0	.3	.4	-	-	-	2.2	6.0
6. 20-39	.2	.3	.2		.3	.3	.2	.1	-	-	-	.9	3.0
7. 40 or more	.3	.5	*		.3	.5	.1	.1	-	-	-	.6	7.0
Item 900 N(Wtd)	9634	4345	5201		2255	2954	3066	1360	4387	1886	1101	1952	200
B08C: ...during the last 30 days?													
1. 0 occasions	97.5	96.5	98.5		97.3	96.7	98.5	97.6	100.0	100.0	99.2	91.4	69.5
2. 1-2	1.7	2.4	1.2		2.3	2.0	1.0	2.0	-	-	.8	6.4	16.5
3. 3-5	.4	.5	.3		.2	.6	.3	.3	-	-	-	1.3	4.5
4. 6-9	.1	.2	.1		.1	.2	.1	.1	-	-	-	.5	2.5
5. 10-19	*	*	*		-	.1	-	.1	-	-	-	.1	1.0
6. 20-39	*	*	-		*	.1	-	-	-	-	-	.2	-
7. 40 or more	.2	.4	*		.1	.4	.1	.1	-	-	-	.3	6.0
Item 910 N(Wtd)	9629	4340	5199		2255	2952	3063	1358	4387	1886	1101	1947	200
B09: On how many occasions (if any) have you used psychedelics other than LSD (like mescaline, peyote, psilocybin, THC)...‡													
B09A: ...in your lifetime?													
1. 0 occasions	85.7	83.7	87.6		83.0	84.0	89.1	86.5	100.0	100.0	83.7	47.6	17.7
2. 1-2	5.3	5.3	5.2		6.1	5.9	3.8	5.7	-	-	16.4	15.7	9.1
3. 3-5	2.6	2.9	2.3		2.8	2.5	2.4	2.9	-	-	-	12.0	8.6
4. 6-9	1.9	2.3	1.6		2.5	1.6	1.7	1.9	-	-	-	8.3	9.6
5. 10-19	1.9	2.3	1.6		2.5	2.5	1.2	1.3	-	-	-	8.0	13.9
6. 20-39	1.2	1.4	1.0		1.7	1.4	.8	.9	-	-	-	4.2	15.8
7. 40 or more	1.4	2.2	.7		1.4	2.1	1.0	1.0	-	-	-	4.2	25.4
Item 920 N(Wtd)	9604	4341	5177		2252	2943	3051	1358	4369	1878	1100	1946	209

* = less than .05 per cent.   ‡ = Wording changed in subsequent years.

CAUTION: Items were rearranged after 1975; changes in context may produce spurious "trends" (see page 12).

QUESTIONNAIRE FORM 2-5 1975	TOTAL	SEX			REGION					ILLICIT DRUG USE: LIFETIME				
		M	F		NE	NC	S	W		None	Mari- juana Only	Few Pills	More Pills	Any Her- oin
Weighted No. of Cases:	12108	5571	6100		2695	3832	3857	1724		4400	1894	1113	1989	216
% of Weighted Total:	100.0	46.0	50.4		22.3	31.6	31.9	14.2		36.3	15.6	9.2	16.4	1.8

B09B: ...during the last 12 months?

	TOTAL	M	F		NE	NC	S	W		None	Mari. Only	Few Pills	More Pills	Any Heroin
1. 0 occasions	90.4	87.9	92.5		88.0	88.7	92.9	92.3		100.0	100.0	93.0	63.7	30.7
2. 1-2	4.4	5.0	3.8		5.2	5.0	3.4	3.9		-	-	7.0	15.9	16.6
3. 3-5	2.1	2.8	1.6		2.8	2.2	1.7	1.8		-	-	-	8.9	14.6
4. 6-9	1.3	1.6	1.0		1.6	1.5	.9	1.2		-	-	-	5.1	11.7
5. 10-19	1.0	1.2	.8		1.4	1.3	.6	.5		-	-	-	3.8	9.8
6. 20-39	.4	.7	.2		.4	.7	.3	.1		-	-	-	1.3	6.8
7. 40 or more	.4	.8	.1		.4	.7	.3	.2		-	-	-	1.2	9.3
Item 930 N(Wtd)	9602	4333	5184		2251	2942	3050	1359		4375	1879	1100	1939	205

B09C: ...during the last 30 days?

	TOTAL	M	F		NE	NC	S	W		None	Mari. Only	Few Pills	More Pills	Any Heroin
1. 0 occasions	96.1	95.1	97.1		95.0	95.4	97.2	97.4		100.0	100.0	98.9	85.7	60.9
2. 1-2	2.4	2.7	2.2		3.4	2.5	1.8	2.1		-	-	1.1	9.6	15.3
3. 3-5	.6	.8	.5		.7	.6	.8	.3		-	-	-	2.3	7.9
4. 6-9	.3	.5	.2		.4	.6	*	.2		-	-	-	1.2	4.0
5. 10-19	.2	.3	.1		.2	.3	.1	-		-	-	-	.3	4.5
6. 20-39	*	*	-		-	*	-	-		-	-	-	.1	.5
7. 40 or more	.3	.6	.1		.3	.5	.1	-		-	-	-	.7	6.9
Item 940 N(Wtd)	9600	4333	5181		2250	2943	3049	1358		4375	1879	1101	1939	202

B10: On how many occasions (if any) have you used cocaine (sometimes called "coke")...

B10A: ...in your lifetime?

	TOTAL	M	F		NE	NC	S	W		None	Mari. Only	Few Pills	More Pills	Any Heroin
1. 0 occasions	90.8	88.4	93.1		90.9	91.0	91.6	88.4		100.0	100.0	92.2	68.1	15.9
2. 1-2	4.3	4.8	3.8		4.4	4.1	4.4	4.7		-	-	7.8	14.9	19.2
3. 3-5	2.0	2.6	1.5		1.9	2.0	1.9	2.7		-	-	-	8.0	19.7
4. 6-9	.9	1.2	.6		1.0	1.0	.6	1.0		-	-	-	3.2	10.6
5. 10-19	.8	1.1	.6		.9	.7	.6	1.3		-	-	-	3.0	11.1
6. 20-39	.5	.8	.2		.4	.4	.5	.9		-	-	-	1.7	8.2
7. 40 or more	.6	1.0	.2		.4	.7	.4	1.0		-	-	-	1.3	15.4
Item 950 N(Wtd)	9603	4333	5185		2256	2938	3052	1357		4361	1876	1104	1949	208

B10B: ...during the last 12 months?

	TOTAL	M	F		NE	NC	S	W		None	Mari. Only	Few Pills	More Pills	Any Heroin
1. 0 occasions	94.2	92.1	96.1		94.5	94.5	94.5	92.2		100.0	100.0	97.4	79.5	35.5
2. 1-2	3.3	4.0	2.7		3.1	3.1	3.5	3.9		-	-	2.6	12.3	26.1
3. 3-5	1.0	1.5	.5		1.1	.8	.8	1.3		-	-	-	3.4	13.3
4. 6-9	.6	.8	.4		.5	.6	.5	.9		-	-	-	2.1	7.9
5. 10-19	.4	.7	.2		.5	.4	.3	.7		-	-	-	1.5	6.9
6. 20-39	.2	.3	.1		.2	.1	.2	.4		-	-	-	.6	2.5
7. 40 or more	.3	.6	.1		.1	.5	.2	.6		-	-	-	.6	8.9
Item 960 N(Wtd)	9592	4324	5184		2253	2935	3048	1355		4363	1876	1104	1938	203

B10C: ...during the last 30 days?

	TOTAL	M	F		NE	NC	S	W		None	Mari. Only	Few Pills	More Pills	Any Heroin
1. 0 occasions	97.9	97.0	98.8		98.0	98.0	98.3	96.9		100.0	100.0	99.2	93.4	69.3
2. 1-2	1.3	1.6	.9		1.2	1.3	1.1	1.7		-	-	.8	4.5	12.4
3. 3-5	.4	.6	.2		.5	.2	.4	.6		-	-	-	1.2	6.9
4. 6-9	.1	.2	.1		.2	.1	-	.4		-	-	-	.4	3.0
5. 10-19	*	.1	*		-	*	*	.2		-	-	-	.2	.5
6. 20-39	*	*	*		-	*	-	.1		-	-	-	.1	1.0
7. 40 or more	.2	.4	*		.1	.4	.1	.1		-	-	-	.3	6.4
Item 970 N(Wtd)	9587	4320	5182		2253	2931	3047	1356		4363	1876	1103	1936	202

B11: Amphetamines are sometimes prescribed by doctors to help people lose weight or to give people more energy. They are sometimes called uppers, ups, speed, bennies, dexies, pep pills, and diet pills. On how many occasions (if any) have you taken amphetamines on your own--that is, without a doctor telling you to take them...

* = less than .05 per cent.

CAUTION: Items were rearranged after 1975; changes in context may produce spurious "trends" (see page 12).

QUESTIONNAIRE FORM 2-5 1975	TOTAL	SEX			REGION				ILLICIT DRUG USE: LIFETIME				
		M	F		NE	NC	S	W	None	Mari-juana Only	Few Pills	More Pills	Any Her-oin
Weighted No. of Cases:	12108	5571	6100		2695	3832	3857	1724	4400	1894	1113	1989	216
% of Weighted Total:	100.0	46.0	50.4		22.3	31.6	31.9	14.2	36.3	15.6	9.2	16.4	1.8
B11A: ...in your lifetime?													
1. 0 occasions	77.5	79.2	76.3		76.9	75.5	81.6	73.8	100.0	100.0	60.3	21.6	14.4
2. 1-2	6.7	5.4	7.7		6.8	6.6	6.8	6.4	-	-	39.7	9.4	7.9
3. 3-5	3.4	2.9	3.7		3.6	3.5	2.8	4.0	-	-	-	15.8	7.9
4. 6-9	2.4	2.5	2.3		2.4	2.5	2.0	3.2	-	-	-	11.4	5.1
5. 10-19	3.3	3.2	3.3		3.1	3.3	2.7	4.7	-	-	-	14.6	13.0
6. 20-39	2.3	2.4	2.2		2.8	3.2	1.3	1.9	-	-	-	10.3	8.8
7. 40 or more	4.4	4.3	4.5		4.4	5.3	2.9	5.9	-	-	-	16.9	43.1
Item 980 N(Wtd)	9419	4237	5121		2228	2875	2980	1336	4270	1813	1092	1910	216
B11B: ...during the last 12 months?													
1. 0 occasions	83.6	83.9	83.4		83.3	81.0	87.3	81.5	100.0	100.0	83.6	36.5	27.4
2. 1-2	5.5	4.6	6.2		5.6	5.8	4.9	5.8	-	-	16.4	16.7	8.4
3. 3-5	2.8	3.0	2.6		2.4	3.0	2.6	3.7	-	-	-	12.8	10.7
4. 6-9	2.4	2.7	2.1		2.1	2.6	2.3	2.7	-	-	-	10.4	12.1
5. 10-19	2.4	2.3	2.4		3.2	2.7	1.5	2.3	-	-	-	10.6	10.2
6. 20-39	1.6	1.6	1.7		1.8	2.6	.4	2.1	-	-	-	7.1	9.3
7. 40 or more	1.7	1.9	1.5		1.6	2.2	1.0	2.0	-	-	-	5.8	21.4
Item 990 N(Wtd)	9399	4233	5105		2221	2873	2973	1332	4270	1813	1084	1897	215
B11C: ...during the last 30 days?													
1. 0 occasions	91.3	91.3	91.4		90.9	88.9	93.8	91.8	100.0	100.0	95.0	65.6	49.3
2. 1-2	4.1	3.9	4.1		4.2	5.1	3.1	4.1	-	-	5.0	15.9	15.2
3. 3-5	1.7	1.8	1.6		1.3	2.4	1.4	1.5	-	-	-	7.5	8.1
4. 6-9	1.1	1.1	1.1		1.5	1.3	.6	1.3	-	-	-	5.0	4.7
5. 10-19	1.1	1.0	1.1		1.3	1.3	.7	1.0	-	-	-	4.1	11.4
6. 20-39	.4	.2	.5		.4	.6	.2	.2	-	-	-	1.4	2.4
7. 40 or more	.3	.5	.2		.4	.5	.2	.3	-	-	-	.6	9.0
Item 1000 N(Wtd)	9387	4225	5101		2218	2868	2971	1329	4270	1813	1083	1890	211
B12: On how many occasions (if any) have you used quaaludes (quads, soapers, methaqualone) on your own--that is, without a doctor telling you to take them...													
B12A: ...in your lifetime?													
1. 0 occasions	91.7	90.5	92.7		91.2	91.3	91.0	94.6	100.0	100.0	94.5	69.2	33.7
2. 1-2	3.1	3.1	3.1		3.5	2.8	3.4	2.2	-	-	5.5	11.3	7.2
3. 3-5	1.4	1.6	1.3		1.5	1.5	1.4	.8	-	-	-	5.7	10.6
4. 6-9	1.0	1.4	.8		1.0	1.0	1.2	.7	-	-	-	4.4	6.7
5. 10-19	1.0	1.3	.7		.7	1.0	1.1	1.2	-	-	-	4.0	8.2
6. 20-39	.8	.7	.8		.8	1.1	.7	.2	-	-	-	2.4	13.5
7. 40 or more	1.0	1.4	.7		1.2	1.3	1.1	.2	-	-	-	3.0	19.7
Item 1010 N(Wtd)	9350	4192	5101		2223	2841	2971	1315	4251	1809	1082	1882	208
B12B: ...during the last 12 months?													
1. 0 occasions	94.7	93.3	96.0		94.5	94.2	94.2	97.2	100.0	100.0	98.3	80.2	47.8
2. 1-2	2.3	3.0	1.8		2.6	2.3	2.6	1.4	-	-	1.7	9.2	13.0
3. 3-5	.9	1.0	.8		1.0	1.1	.8	.5	-	-	-	3.6	7.2
4. 6-9	.9	1.2	.6		.9	.8	1.0	.5	-	-	-	3.5	7.7
5. 10-19	.6	.7	.4		.4	.9	.5	.3	-	-	-	1.8	9.7
6. 20-39	.3	.3	.3		.2	.3	.4	.1	-	-	-	.7	5.3
7. 40 or more	.4	.6	.2		.4	.5	.4	.1	-	-	-	.9	9.2
Item 1020 N(Wtd)	9346	4190	5097		2221	2843	2969	1313	4252	1809	1083	1875	207
B12C: ...during the last 30 days?													
1. 0 occasions	97.7	97.0	98.4		98.1	97.4	97.3	98.6	100.0	100.0	99.7	92.2	68.6
2. 1-2	1.2	1.5	.9		1.0	1.3	1.2	.9	-	-	.3	4.3	11.1
3. 3-5	.5	.6	.4		.4	.6	.7	.2	-	-	-	2.0	5.8
4. 6-9	.2	.3	.2		.2	.2	.3	.2	-	-	-	.9	3.4
5. 10-19	.1	.2	.1		.1	.2	.2	-	-	-	-	.3	3.9
6. 20-39	.1	.1	.1		*	.2	.1	.1	-	-	-	.3	1.4
7. 40 or more	.1	.3	-		.2	.2	.1	-	-	-	-	-	6.3
Item 1030 N(Wtd)	9340	4189	5095		2220	2839	2967	1314	4252	1809	1080	1875	207

* = less than .05 per cent.

CAUTION: Items were rearranged after 1975; changes in context may produce spurious "trends" (see page 12).

QUESTIONNAIRE FORM 2-5 1975	TOTAL	SEX			REGION					ILLICIT DRUG USE: LIFETIME				
		M	F		NE	NC	S	W		None	Mari-juana Only	Few Pills	More Pills	Any Her-oin
Weighted No. of Cases:	12108	5571	6100		2695	3832	3857	1724		4400	1894	1113	1989	216
% of Weighted Total:	100.0	46.0	50.4		22.3	31.6	31.9	14.2		36.3	15.6	9.2	16.4	1.8

B13: Barbiturates are sometimes prescribed by doctors to help people relax or get to sleep. They are sometimes called downs, downers, goofballs, yellows, reds, blues, rainbows. On how many occasions (if any) have you taken barbiturates on your own-- that is, without a doctor telling you to take them...

B13A: ...in your lifetime?

	TOTAL	M	F		NE	NC	S	W		None	Mari-juana Only	Few Pills	More Pills	Any Her-oin
1. 0 occasions	82.9	82.7	83.0		82.4	81.8	84.2	83.0		100.0	100.0	74.6	39.2	17.8
2. 1-2	6.1	5.5	6.7		6.3	6.2	5.7	6.9		-	-	25.4	15.2	6.5
3. 3-5	3.4	3.3	3.5		3.3	3.8	3.2	3.3		-	-	-	15.6	11.2
4. 6-9	1.9	2.0	1.9		2.1	2.1	1.7	1.9		-	-	-	9.1	4.7
5. 10-19	2.0	2.4	1.7		2.0	2.1	2.0	2.0		-	-	-	8.5	14.0
6. 20-39	1.3	1.4	1.2		1.0	1.8	1.1	1.4		-	-	-	5.1	13.1
7. 40 or more	2.3	2.6	1.9		2.8	2.3	2.1	1.7		-	-	-	7.5	32.2
Item 1040 N(Wtd)	9319	4185	5080		2216	2838	2945	1320		4230	1803	1077	1879	214

B13B: ...during the last 12 months?

	TOTAL	M	F		NE	NC	S	W		None	Mari-juana Only	Few Pills	More Pills	Any Her-oin
1. 0 occasions	89.0	87.7	90.1		89.5	87.2	90.1	90.0		100.0	100.0	92.1	57.8	31.6
2. 1-2	4.5	4.7	4.3		4.4	5.3	3.5	4.9		-	-	7.9	16.6	9.4
3. 3-5	2.4	2.8	2.1		1.9	2.4	3.0	2.1		-	-	-	10.6	13.2
4. 6-9	1.5	1.6	1.3		1.7	1.8	1.1	1.2		-	-	-	5.6	14.6
5. 10-19	1.4	1.4	1.3		1.3	1.8	1.0	1.3		-	-	-	6.0	7.1
6. 20-39	.5	.7	.4		.6	.6	.5	.2		-	-	-	1.7	9.4
7. 40 or more	.7	1.1	.4		.7	.8	.8	.2		-	-	-	1.8	14.6
Item 1050 N(Wtd)	9304	4179	5072		2215	2832	2941	1315		4233	1803	1074	1864	212

B13C: ...during the last 30 days?

	TOTAL	M	F		NE	NC	S	W		None	Mari-juana Only	Few Pills	More Pills	Any Her-oin
1. 0 occasions	95.1	94.7	95.4		95.5	94.1	95.2	95.9		100.0	100.0	98.2	81.4	56.5
2. 1-2	2.6	2.7	2.6		2.2	3.3	2.3	2.5		-	-	1.8	10.4	14.5
3. 3-5	1.0	.9	1.0		.9	1.2	.9	.9		-	-	-	4.2	6.1
4. 6-9	.6	.6	.6		.5	.6	.7	.5		-	-	-	2.3	5.1
5. 10-19	.4	.5	.3		.4	.3	.6	.1		-	-	-	1.0	8.9
6. 20-39	.1	.2	.1		.1	.2	.1	.1		-	-	-	.4	2.3
7. 40 or more	.2	.4	*		.3	.3	.1	.1		-	-	-	.2	6.5
Item 1060 N(Wtd)	9308	4180	5075		2214	2833	2942	1318		4233	1803	1074	1868	214

B14: Tranquilizers are sometimes prescribed by doctors to calm people down, quiet their nerves, or relax their muscles. Librium, Valium, and Miltown are all tranquilizers. On how many occasions (if any) have you taken tranquilizers on your own-- that is, without a doctor telling you to take them...

B14A: ...in your lifetime?

	TOTAL	M	F		NE	NC	S	W		None	Mari-juana Only	Few Pills	More Pills	Any Her-oin
1. 0 occasions	82.8	83.9	81.9		85.0	82.4	82.6	80.5		100.0	100.0	61.5	45.5	26.2
2. 1-2	7.7	6.7	8.6		7.2	8.1	7.2	9.2		-	-	38.5	14.7	13.1
3. 3-5	3.1	2.7	3.5		2.1	2.9	3.8	3.8		-	-	-	14.6	7.5
4. 6-9	2.1	2.2	2.0		2.0	2.0	2.2	2.2		-	-	-	9.2	10.3
5. 10-19	1.6	1.7	1.6		1.5	1.8	1.4	2.1		-	-	-	7.1	9.3
6. 20-39	1.0	.8	1.1		.7	1.3	1.1	.9		-	-	-	4.1	7.9
7. 40 or more	1.6	1.9	1.2		1.4	1.6	1.8	1.4		-	-	-	4.8	25.7
Item 1070 N(Wtd)	9250	4161	5040		2203	2819	2913	1315		4196	1789	1072	1869	214

B14B: ...during the last 12 months?

	TOTAL	M	F		NE	NC	S	W		None	Mari-juana Only	Few Pills	More Pills	Any Her-oin
1. 0 occasions	89.2	89.6	88.9		90.6	89.1	88.5	88.4		100.0	100.0	86.3	61.0	41.0
2. 1-2	5.4	4.8	6.0		4.8	5.2	5.6	6.7		-	-	13.7	17.1	15.1
3. 3-5	2.2	2.3	2.1		2.0	2.2	2.5	1.9		-	-	-	9.9	8.5
4. 6-9	1.2	1.2	1.2		1.2	1.3	.9	1.7		-	-	-	5.2	6.6
5. 10-19	.9	1.0	.8		.9	.9	1.0	.7		-	-	-	3.4	9.4
6. 20-39	.6	.5	.6		.2	.6	.9	.3		-	-	-	1.7	9.4
7. 40 or more	.6	.8	.4		.4	.8	.6	.4		-	-	-	1.6	9.9
Item 1080 N(Wtd)	9246	4161	5034		2203	2811	2916	1315		4204	1794	1062	1852	212

* = less than .05 per cent.

CAUTION: Items were rearranged after 1975; changes in context may produce spurious "trends" (see page 12).

QUESTIONNAIRE FORM 2-5 1975	TOTAL	SEX			REGION					ILLICIT DRUG USE: LIFETIME				
		M	F		NE	NC	S	W		None	Mari-juana Only	Few Pills	More Pills	Any Her-oin
Weighted No. of Cases:	12108	5571	6100		2695	3832	3857	1724		4400	1894	1113	1989	216
% of Weighted Total:	100.0	46.0	50.4		22.3	31.6	31.9	14.2		36.3	15.6	9.2	16.4	1.8
B14C: ...during the last 30 days?														
1. 0 occasions	95.7	95.7	95.7		96.5	95.4	95.2	96.0		100.0	100.0	96.2	84.5	67.5
2. 1-2	2.4	2.3	2.5		1.8	2.7	2.5	2.7		-	-	3.8	9.0	6.6
3. 3-5	.9	.7	1.0		.7	.7	1.2	.8		-	-	-	3.8	4.7
4. 6-9	.5	.5	.5		.5	.6	.5	.4		-	-	-	1.8	6.1
5. 10-19	.3	.4	.3		.4	.1	.4	.2		-	-	-	.8	6.1
6. 20-39	.1	.1	*		-	.1	.1	-		-	-	-	.1	2.4
7. 40 or more	.2	.3	*		.2	.3	.1	.1		-	-	-	.1	6.6
Item 1090 N(Wtd)	9232	4155	5028		2200	2808	2911	1312		4206	1794	1061	1845	212
B15: On how many occasions (if any) have you used heroin (smack, horse, skag)...														
B15A: ...in your lifetime?														
1. 0 occasions	97.7	96.9	98.3		97.9	97.0	97.8	98.2		100.0	100.0	100.0	100.0	-
2. 1-2	1.5	1.8	1.1		1.2	1.7	1.5	1.2		-	-	-	-	62.0
3. 3-5	.2	.2	.2		.2	.3	.1	.3		-	-	-	-	9.3
4. 6-9	.2	.2	.1		.1	.2	.1	-		-	-	-	-	6.5
5. 10-19	.2	.2	.1		.2	.2	.1	-		-	-	-	-	6.9
6. 20-39	*	.1	*		*	.1	-	-		-	-	-	-	1.9
7. 40 or more	.3	.6	.1		.4	.4	.3	.2		-	-	-	-	14.4
Item 1100 N(Wtd)	9229	4141	5037		2198	2809	2904	1319		4191	1774	1075	1857	216
B15B: ...during the last 12 months?														
1. 0 occasions	98.8	98.4	99.2		98.7	98.4	99.0	99.2		100.0	100.0	100.0	100.0	47.4
2. 1-2	.6	.8	.5		.7	.8	.6	.4		-	-	-	-	27.9
3. 3-5	.1	.1	.2		*	.2	.1	.1		-	-	-	-	5.1
4. 6-9	.1	.1	.1		.2	-	.1	-		-	-	-	-	3.7
5. 10-19	.1	.1	.1		.1	.1	*	.1		-	-	-	-	3.7
6. 20-39	*	*	*		*	.1	-	-		-	-	-	-	1.4
7. 40 or more	.2	.5	*		.2	.4	.2	.2		-	-	-	-	10.2
Item 1110 N(Wtd)	9256	4152	5052		2201	2819	2917	1320		4201	1782	1076	1866	215
B15C: ...during the last 30 days?														
1. 0 occasions	99.4	99.2	99.7		99.5	99.0	99.6	99.7		100.0	100.0	100.0	100.0	74.9
2. 1-2	.2	.2	.2		.1	.3	.2	.2		-	-	-	-	8.4
3. 3-5	.1	*	.1		.1	-	.1	.1		-	-	-	-	3.3
4. 6-9	*	*	*		-	.1	*	-		-	-	-	-	1.4
5. 10-19	*	.1	*		-	.1	*	-		-	-	-	-	1.9
6. 20-39	*	.1	-		-	.1	-	-		-	-	-	-	1.4
7. 40 or more	.2	.4	*		.2	.4	.1	.2		-	-	-	-	9.3
Item 1120 N(Wtd)	9261	4157	5052		2202	2820	2919	1320		4202	1785	1076	1865	215
B16: There are a number of narcotics other than heroin, such as methadone, opium, morphine, codeine, demerol, paregoric, talwin, and laudanum. These are sometimes prescribed by doctors. On how many occasions (if any) have you taken narcotics other than heroin on your own--that is, without a doctor telling you to take them...														
B16A: ...in your lifetime?														
1. 0 occasions	90.8	89.7	91.7		89.7	90.4	92.1	90.3		100.0	100.0	91.0	67.9	21.4
2. 1-2	3.7	3.8	3.6		4.9	3.2	3.0	4.6		-	-	9.1	12.2	10.7
3. 3-5	1.7	1.8	1.7		1.6	2.2	1.6	1.5		-	-	-	6.7	17.0
4. 6-9	.9	1.1	.7		1.0	1.0	.7	1.0		-	-	-	3.6	7.3
5. 10-19	1.2	1.4	1.1		1.0	1.2	1.4	1.1		-	-	-	4.4	15.0
6. 20-39	.5	.4	.5		.5	.5	.4	.5		-	-	-	1.6	6.3
7. 40 or more	1.2	1.8	.7		1.4	1.5	.8	1.1		-	-	-	3.5	22.3
Item 1130 N(Wtd)	9145	4093	5009		2185	2773	2885	1303		4165	1773	1056	1832	206

* = less than .05 per cent.

CAUTION: Items were rearranged after 1975; changes in context may produce spurious "trends" (see page 12).

QUESTIONNAIRE FORM 2-5 1975	TOTAL	SEX			REGION					ILLICIT DRUG USE: LIFETIME				
		M	F		NE	NC	S	W		None	Mari-juana Only	Few Pills	More Pills	Any Her-oin
Weighted No. of Cases:	*12108*	*5571*	*6100*		*2695*	*3832*	*3857*	*1724*		*4400*	*1894*	*1113*	*1989*	*216*
% of Weighted Total:	*100.0*	*46.0*	*50.4*		*22.3*	*31.6*	*31.9*	*14.2*		*36.3*	*15.6*	*9.2*	*16.4*	*1.8*
B16B: ...during the last 12 months?														
1. 0 occasions	94.1	93.0	95.2		93.6	93.5	94.9	94.6		100.0	100.0	97.5	79.1	38.7
2. 1-2	2.6	3.0	2.4		3.3	2.5	2.1	2.9		-	-	2.6	9.7	17.2
3. 3-5	1.1	1.3	.9		.9	1.3	1.2	.7		-	-	-	4.3	10.8
4. 6-9	.8	1.1	.6		.6	1.0	.8	.8		-	-	-	3.1	9.3
5. 10-19	.6	.7	.5		.6	.8	.5	.6		-	-	-	2.3	6.9
6. 20-39	.2	.2	.2		.3	.3	.1	.3		-	-	-	.7	3.4
7. 40 or more	.5	.8	.2		.6	.7	.3	.1		-	-	-	.9	13.7
Item 1140 N(Wtd)	*9148*	*4095*	*5009*		*2183*	*2774*	*2886*	*1306*		*4171*	*1775*	*1052*	*1829*	*204*
B16C: ...during the last 30 days?														
1. 0 occasions	97.7	97.0	98.2		97.3	97.4	98.0	98.1		100.0	100.0	99.5	92.2	67.2
2. 1-2	1.0	1.1	.9		1.2	1.0	1.0	.8		-	-	.5	3.8	10.3
3. 3-5	.6	.7	.5		.7	.6	.4	.6		-	-	-	2.1	5.9
4. 6-9	.3	.3	.2		.2	.3	.3	.2		-	-	-	1.0	2.5
5. 10-19	.2	.3	.1		.3	.3	.2	.2		-	-	-	.5	5.9
6. 20-39	*	.1	-		*	-	.1	-		-	-	-	.2	.5
7. 40 or more	.2	.4	*		.2	.4	.1	-		-	-	-	.2	7.8
Item 1150 N(Wtd)	*9143*	*4093*	*5006*		*2180*	*2773*	*2885*	*1306*		*4170*	*1775*	*1052*	*1828*	*204*

* = less than .05 per cent.

CAUTION: Items were rearranged after 1975; changes in context may produce spurious "trends" (see page 12).

QUESTIONNAIRE FORM 1 1975	TOTAL	SEX			REGION					ILLICIT DRUG USE: LIFETIME				
		M	F		NE	NC	S	W		None	Mari-juana Only	Few Pills	More Pills	Any Her-oin
Weighted No. of Cases:	3038	1437	1568		688	943	979	428		1374	528	225	523	39
% of Weighted Total:	100.0	47.3	51.6		22.7	31.0	32.2	14.1		45.2	17.4	7.4	17.2	1.3

A004: How much do you agree or disagree with each of the following statements?

A004A: The nation needs much more long-range planning and coordination to be prepared for the future

	TOTAL	M	F		NE	NC	S	W		None	Mari-juana Only	Few Pills	More Pills	Any Her-oin
1. Disagree	2.3	2.3	2.3		2.3	2.2	2.3	2.3		2.9	1.1	1.0	2.3	4.6
2. Mostly disagree	3.8	4.8	2.7		4.3	4.0	2.8	4.7		3.4	4.0	4.7	3.8	2.2
3. Neither	7.3	7.9	6.4		5.2	7.6	7.1	10.2		7.8	6.0	5.8	7.5	9.0
4. Mostly agree	41.4	37.8	45.0		42.0	45.1	37.8	40.6		41.6	41.7	45.2	43.0	28.7
5. Agree	45.2	47.2	43.6		46.3	41.0	49.9	42.3		44.4	47.1	43.3	43.4	55.4
Item 1200 N(Wtd)	3010	1430	1549		681	932	971	427		1364	527	222	520	38

A004B: I enjoy the fast pace and changes of today's world

	TOTAL	M	F		NE	NC	S	W		None	Mari-juana Only	Few Pills	More Pills	Any Her-oin
1. Disagree	21.2	23.0	19.7		24.2	20.4	20.3	20.2		23.3	19.0	20.3	18.0	15.4
2. Mostly disagree	20.7	19.9	21.4		19.1	18.8	23.0	22.3		20.1	20.1	19.4	23.3	14.0
3. Neither	17.4	17.0	17.6		16.5	18.4	14.4	23.4		16.9	18.3	19.5	17.2	13.9
4. Mostly agree	26.5	24.9	28.0		25.5	27.7	27.4	23.2		26.0	29.3	22.8	27.1	36.8
5. Agree	14.3	15.1	13.4		14.8	14.6	15.0	10.8		13.6	13.2	18.0	14.5	19.9
Item 1210 N(Wtd)	3019	1432	1556		680	937	974	428		1368	525	224	522	38

A004C: If we just leave things to God, they will turn out for the best

	TOTAL	M	F		NE	NC	S	W		None	Mari-juana Only	Few Pills	More Pills	Any Her-oin
1. Disagree	24.3	28.6	20.3		33.6	23.0	17.6	27.4		19.9	29.7	26.0	33.0	28.6
2. Mostly disagree	14.3	13.6	14.9		15.8	15.8	10.3	18.0		11.8	17.9	15.1	17.4	8.1
3. Neither	19.1	19.6	18.7		20.3	21.4	15.7	19.7		18.1	18.8	23.0	21.5	26.1
4. Mostly agree	19.1	16.2	21.8		15.8	18.5	23.8	14.9		21.9	18.0	13.2	14.7	22.5
5. Agree	23.2	22.0	24.2		14.5	21.3	32.6	20.0		28.3	15.5	22.7	13.4	14.6
Item 1650 N(Wtd)	2994	1412	1551		677	935	964	419		1357	522	224	517	37

A004D: Things change too quickly in today's world

	TOTAL	M	F		NE	NC	S	W		None	Mari-juana Only	Few Pills	More Pills	Any Her-oin
1. Disagree	10.4	11.4	9.2		11.7	9.0	11.9	8.4		9.8	8.9	13.1	12.0	19.2
2. Mostly disagree	17.6	17.7	17.4		15.6	18.1	17.1	20.6		16.1	20.8	15.8	18.8	26.5
3. Neither	15.6	15.3	15.9		14.9	17.4	13.6	17.6		14.4	20.4	10.9	17.7	17.2
4. Mostly agree	27.5	24.9	30.2		24.8	28.7	28.1	28.1		29.6	24.0	26.2	26.8	21.8
5. Agree	28.8	30.7	27.2		33.0	26.8	29.4	25.4		30.1	25.8	34.0	24.8	15.4
Item 1220 N(Wtd)	3015	1427	1557		680	935	975	425		1364	523	225	521	39

A004G: I think the times ahead for me will be tougher and less fun than things are now

	TOTAL	M	F		NE	NC	S	W		None	Mari-juana Only	Few Pills	More Pills	Any Her-oin
1. Disagree	20.1	18.7	21.6		21.1	18.5	20.4	21.5		18.7	20.1	21.2	22.6	40.4
2. Mostly disagree	22.8	20.1	25.4		24.0	23.0	21.0	24.5		24.0	21.6	18.8	24.3	11.8
3. Neither	12.6	12.2	12.9		14.1	13.0	11.6	11.5		12.4	15.0	13.7	11.6	12.1
4. Mostly agree	22.3	22.0	22.3		21.2	23.6	20.4	25.4		21.3	21.4	21.0	25.5	7.5
5. Agree	22.2	26.9	17.8		19.7	21.8	26.5	17.0		23.6	21.9	25.5	15.9	28.2
Item 1230 N(Wtd)	3023	1433	1560		684	938	976	425		1371	527	223	519	39

A006: Of all the time you spend with other people, about how much is spent with people over 30?

	TOTAL	M	F		NE	NC	S	W		None	Mari-juana Only	Few Pills	More Pills	Any Her-oin
1. Very little	21.4	24.2	18.7		23.2	18.9	21.3	24.1		18.4	23.1	24.1	26.5	13.8
2. Some	41.9	44.7	39.3		43.7	43.0	40.8	39.2		41.8	44.2	43.4	40.7	46.3
3. About half	29.9	26.1	33.5		28.1	31.6	29.6	29.6		30.9	28.1	28.3	27.0	35.2
4. Most	5.1	3.8	6.4		3.7	5.4	5.5	6.0		6.6	3.4	3.5	5.1	2.3
5. Nearly all	1.7	1.2	2.1		1.3	1.1	2.8	1.2		2.3	1.3	.7	.8	2.4
Item 1240 N(Wtd)	3029	1432	1565		687	937	977	427		1373	527	225	521	38

CAUTION: Items were rearranged after 1975; changes in context may produce spurious "trends" (see page 12).

QUESTIONNAIRE FORM 1 1975	TOTAL	SEX			REGION					ILLICIT DRUG USE: LIFETIME				
		M	F		NE	NC	S	W		None	Mari-juana Only	Few Pills	More Pills	Any Her-oin
Weighted No. of Cases:	3038	1437	1568		688	943	979	428		1374	528	225	523	39
% of Weighted Total:	100.0	47.3	51.6		22.7	31.0	32.2	14.1		45.2	17.4	7.4	17.2	1.3

A007: Would you like to spend more time, or less time, with people over 30 if you could?

	TOTAL	M	F		NE	NC	S	W		None	Mari-juana Only	Few Pills	More Pills	Any Her-oin
1. Much less time	3.1	3.4	2.8		3.7	2.8	2.6	3.6		3.2	1.8	1.8	4.2	1.8
2. Somewhat less time	7.7	7.7	7.8		6.6	8.4	7.9	7.7		5.9	7.7	8.4	10.8	18.0
3. About the same as now	67.6	70.0	65.1		70.7	66.1	67.0	67.0		65.9	71.0	71.7	66.1	61.6
4. Somewhat more time	18.7	16.6	20.6		17.0	20.0	18.6	18.5		20.7	17.9	17.3	17.1	13.2
5. Much more time	2.9	2.2	3.6		1.9	2.7	3.8	3.1		4.2	1.7	.9	1.7	5.3
Item 1250 N(Wtd)	3015	1422	1563		681	933	975	426		1366	526	224	517	38

A008: Would you like to spend more time, or less time, working with or helping younger children?

	TOTAL	M	F		NE	NC	S	W		None	Mari-juana Only	Few Pills	More Pills	Any Her-oin
1. Much less time	3.4	4.8	2.1		4.1	2.8	3.0	4.1		2.9	2.5	4.3	3.7	3.3
2. Somewhat less time	4.5	6.6	2.4		4.3	5.7	3.0	5.5		4.3	4.6	3.6	5.4	2.9
3. About the same as now	32.3	42.4	23.1		33.2	31.8	31.2	34.6		30.2	33.0	35.5	37.6	39.7
4. Somewhat more time	36.9	33.8	39.7		37.0	37.6	36.5	35.8		37.8	37.2	33.9	34.6	48.9
5. Much more time	23.0	12.4	32.7		21.3	22.1	26.3	19.9		24.8	22.7	22.7	18.7	5.2
Item 1260 N(Wtd)	3003	1416	1560		681	929	969	425		1363	526	223	516	38

A009: The next questions ask how satisfied or dissatisfied you are with several aspects of your life. For each question, mark the circle that shows best how you feel. If you are neutral about something, or are just as satisfied as you are dissatisfied, mark the middle answer.

How satisfied are you with...

A009A: Your job? (If you have no job, leave blank)

	TOTAL	M	F		NE	NC	S	W		None	Mari-juana Only	Few Pills	More Pills	Any Her-oin
7. Completely satisfied	21.5	21.0	22.0		18.7	22.0	24.3	19.4		25.7	20.1	17.2	16.5	25.8
6.	20.9	20.8	21.0		19.9	23.6	20.0	18.2		21.6	21.9	22.6	19.4	11.5
5.	13.0	13.4	12.6		15.0	13.8	9.1	15.2		11.0	14.0	11.9	18.1	19.8
4. Neutral	25.5	26.1	24.7		25.3	22.3	29.1	26.3		26.3	20.9	27.9	23.7	21.4
3.	8.3	8.2	8.4		8.0	8.5	7.8	9.2		6.7	11.4	5.1	10.6	3.8
2.	5.5	5.7	5.2		6.2	5.6	4.3	6.6		4.6	6.9	8.9	4.2	4.0
1. Completely dissatisfied	5.3	4.7	6.2		6.9	4.1	5.4	5.2		4.1	4.8	6.3	7.4	13.6
Item 1270 N(Wtd)	1767	927	822		427	578	503	258		771	347	135	311	20

A009B: The neighborhood where you live?

	TOTAL	M	F		NE	NC	S	W		None	Mari-juana Only	Few Pills	More Pills	Any Her-oin
7. Completely satisfied	31.1	31.2	31.3		28.8	31.1	34.6	27.3		36.2	25.6	31.2	23.0	31.9
6.	17.8	19.9	16.0		18.4	17.9	16.2	20.7		16.6	21.8	18.9	20.0	8.5
5.	10.5	11.4	9.6		11.0	12.9	7.5	11.0		8.8	12.1	9.5	12.7	15.6
4. Neutral	22.7	20.0	24.7		23.8	19.9	24.4	23.4		22.4	23.0	16.3	23.3	20.5
3.	7.0	7.3	6.7		7.0	7.7	6.2	7.0		6.4	7.5	11.5	6.5	7.3
2.	4.5	4.3	4.7		4.2	4.7	3.9	5.9		3.9	4.1	6.0	5.6	5.3
1. Completely dissatisfied	6.4	5.9	6.9		6.8	5.9	7.2	4.7		5.7	5.9	6.7	8.8	10.8
Item 1280 N(Wtd)	3021	1428	1564		682	935	975	428		1369	526	224	522	39

A009C: Your personal safety in your neighborhood, on your job, and in your school--safety from being attacked and injured in some way?

	TOTAL	M	F		NE	NC	S	W		None	Mari-juana Only	Few Pills	More Pills	Any Her-oin
7. Completely satisfied	39.5	42.5	37.2		39.5	42.5	38.3	36.0		40.6	39.6	42.4	38.6	27.4
6.	19.8	20.2	19.4		18.2	21.0	18.4	22.5		18.2	20.4	24.9	23.5	15.1
5.	10.3	9.6	11.0		11.4	10.2	9.3	10.9		9.7	12.1	9.5	9.8	14.8
4. Neutral	19.4	18.0	20.1		19.8	17.7	22.0	16.6		20.4	16.0	14.8	17.6	29.2
3.	4.3	4.0	4.5		3.9	3.7	3.9	6.8		5.1	4.2	2.1	4.5	2.6
2.	2.9	2.6	3.3		3.0	2.0	3.6	3.5		2.2	4.6	3.8	2.7	4.9
1. Completely dissatisfied	3.8	3.1	4.5		4.2	2.9	4.5	3.8		3.8	3.0	2.4	3.2	6.0
Item 1290 N(Wtd)	3017	1427	1560		684	937	969	427		1364	527	224	523	39

CAUTION: Items were rearranged after 1975; changes in context may produce spurious "trends" (see page 12).

QUESTIONNAIRE FORM 1 1975	TOTAL	SEX			REGION					ILLICIT DRUG USE: LIFETIME				
		M	F		NE	NC	S	W		None	Mari-juana Only	Few Pills	More Pills	Any Her-oin
Weighted No. of Cases:	3038	1437	1568		688	943	979	428		1374	528	225	523	39
% of Weighted Total:	100.0	47.3	51.6		22.7	31.0	32.2	14.1		45.2	17.4	7.4	17.2	1.3

A009D: The safety of things you own from being stolen or destroyed in your neighborhood, on your job, and in your school?

	TOTAL	M	F		NE	NC	S	W		None	Mari-juana Only	Few Pills	More Pills	Any Her-oin
7. Completely satisfied	18.3	18.0	18.8		22.0	19.4	16.0	15.0		19.0	16.0	20.2	17.1	12.1
6.	17.2	15.1	19.4		16.6	19.5	14.2	20.3		16.5	19.2	22.2	17.7	11.8
5.	13.0	12.9	13.0		13.6	16.0	9.2	14.1		12.3	14.2	14.0	12.9	11.6
4. Neutral	19.3	18.5	19.8		19.5	15.6	24.0	16.7		20.1	19.5	20.3	16.2	16.7
3.	12.2	14.2	10.5		10.9	11.7	11.8	16.3		11.2	11.8	9.6	16.2	11.9
2.	8.1	8.7	7.5		6.2	7.1	10.1	8.5		8.0	9.4	5.4	7.9	23.2
1. Completely dissatisfied	11.8	12.7	11.0		11.1	10.7	14.6	9.1		13.0	9.8	8.3	12.1	12.8
Item 1300 N(Wtd)	3012	1424	1559		681	932	974	425		1364	528	222	521	39

A009E: Your educational experiences?

	TOTAL	M	F		NE	NC	S	W		None	Mari-juana Only	Few Pills	More Pills	Any Her-oin
7. Completely satisfied	18.2	16.7	19.7		16.4	17.2	22.1	14.3		22.0	13.2	15.2	12.8	6.3
6.	20.7	20.7	21.1		20.8	22.3	18.6	22.1		24.1	22.5	19.3	15.4	8.6
5.	17.5	19.5	15.4		19.0	19.4	15.0	16.4		15.8	19.8	16.7	20.4	16.5
4. Neutral	23.3	23.1	23.2		24.5	22.8	23.5	21.8		22.6	21.2	24.3	25.3	12.6
3.	9.0	9.3	8.6		7.4	8.9	9.4	10.8		7.8	11.9	9.2	10.3	23.1
2.	6.0	4.9	7.0		6.1	4.6	5.4	9.8		4.4	5.7	10.0	8.5	16.6
1. Completely dissatisfied	5.4	5.8	5.0		5.8	4.7	5.9	4.8		3.4	5.7	5.2	7.3	16.2
Item 1310 N(Wtd)	3007	1422	1556		681	932	969	425		1363	527	222	521	39

A009F: Your friends and other people you spend time with?

	TOTAL	M	F		NE	NC	S	W		None	Mari-juana Only	Few Pills	More Pills	Any Her-oin
7. Completely satisfied	45.1	41.1	49.1		44.8	40.9	50.6	42.2		47.9	41.9	41.8	42.8	30.0
6.	27.6	28.7	26.7		25.7	31.4	24.2	29.9		25.7	29.5	30.9	30.0	37.1
5.	10.1	11.6	8.8		12.4	9.3	9.5	9.9		9.6	11.8	11.5	10.3	8.0
4. Neutral	10.8	12.1	9.1		10.3	11.6	10.2	11.3		10.4	10.2	7.5	10.8	20.3
3.	3.6	3.7	3.6		4.5	4.1	2.6	3.7		3.7	4.5	5.2	2.8	2.8
2.	1.3	1.4	1.2		1.3	1.3	1.1	1.3		1.1	1.2	1.0	1.9	-
1. Completely dissatisfied	1.4	1.4	1.4		1.0	1.4	1.6	1.6		1.4	.9	2.0	1.3	1.8
Item 1320 N(Wtd)	3018	1427	1561		681	936	974	428		1368	526	224	522	39

A009G: The way you get along with your parents?

	TOTAL	M	F		NE	NC	S	W		None	Mari-juana Only	Few Pills	More Pills	Any Her-oin
7. Completely satisfied	33.1	33.0	33.4		34.1	30.5	37.9	26.6		39.0	28.8	32.5	22.7	19.0
6.	20.9	21.3	20.7		19.8	21.6	19.5	24.4		21.5	23.4	15.4	20.3	25.9
5.	12.2	13.9	10.5		12.1	14.5	9.8	12.5		11.2	15.0	11.6	12.5	7.5
4. Neutral	17.5	16.3	18.4		18.0	16.9	18.0	17.2		17.0	16.4	15.5	19.4	18.9
3.	5.7	6.0	5.4		5.7	6.2	4.2	7.8		4.1	6.3	6.6	8.3	3.1
2.	4.9	5.1	4.6		4.6	5.9	3.7	5.6		3.4	5.6	7.9	6.9	10.8
1. Completely dissatisfied	5.7	4.3	7.0		5.7	4.4	6.9	5.9		3.7	4.5	10.5	9.9	15.0
Item 1330 N(Wtd)	3022	1428	1564		683	937	974	428		1369	528	224	523	39

A009H: Yourself?

	TOTAL	M	F		NE	NC	S	W		None	Mari-juana Only	Few Pills	More Pills	Any Her-oin
7. Completely satisfied	27.1	29.6	24.8		26.9	23.2	33.6	21.4		30.0	23.2	29.4	19.9	20.3
6.	25.2	24.1	26.2		23.5	26.2	23.3	29.8		26.6	29.0	20.6	25.2	23.7
5.	15.1	15.2	14.9		15.3	17.7	11.4	17.4		13.8	17.6	18.9	15.8	22.7
4. Neutral	21.9	19.5	23.9		23.8	21.9	21.2	20.5		19.8	21.2	17.2	26.4	13.1
3.	5.3	5.1	5.5		4.7	5.6	4.8	6.9		4.9	4.9	7.1	6.9	12.1
2.	2.4	2.8	2.0		2.5	3.1	2.0	1.4		2.3	2.0	3.6	2.6	1.5
1. Completely dissatisfied	3.1	3.6	2.7		3.3	2.4	3.7	2.7		2.6	2.2	3.3	3.2	6.6
Item 1340 N(Wtd)	3008	1423	1556		679	930	973	427		1363	523	222	520	39

A009I: Your standard of living--the things you have like housing, car, furniture, recreation, and the like?

	TOTAL	M	F		NE	NC	S	W		None	Mari-juana Only	Few Pills	More Pills	Any Her-oin
7. Completely satisfied	36.5	33.6	39.3		34.7	34.7	40.0	35.5		40.1	30.0	36.5	33.7	35.3
6.	25.5	27.0	24.3		26.1	27.2	22.5	27.4		25.2	28.3	26.7	24.4	13.3
5.	12.4	13.9	11.2		14.2	15.0	8.5	12.8		10.8	16.5	11.8	14.0	19.4
4. Neutral	14.7	13.7	15.5		16.5	12.7	17.1	10.9		14.7	14.3	12.7	14.3	16.3
3.	4.5	5.3	3.6		3.5	5.3	4.0	5.8		3.6	5.4	5.0	6.6	4.1
2.	2.8	2.9	2.8		2.9	2.2	2.4	4.9		1.9	2.8	3.3	4.3	6.9
1. Completely dissatisfied	3.5	3.7	3.3		2.0	2.8	5.5	2.8		3.6	2.7	4.0	2.8	4.8
Item 1350 N(Wtd)	3018	1427	1561		683	937	970	428		1367	527	224	521	39

CAUTION: Items were rearranged after 1975; changes in context may produce spurious "trends" (see page 12).

QUESTIONNAIRE FORM 1 1975	TOTAL	SEX			REGION					ILLICIT DRUG USE: LIFETIME				
		M	F		NE	NC	S	W		None	Marijuana Only	Few Pills	More Pills	Any Heroin
Weighted No. of Cases:	*3038*	*1437*	*1568*		*688*	*943*	*979*	*428*		*1374*	*528*	*225*	*523*	*39*
% of Weighted Total:	*100.0*	*47.3*	*51.6*		*22.7*	*31.0*	*32.2*	*14.1*		*45.2*	*17.4*	*7.4*	*17.2*	*1.3*
A009J: The amount of time you have for doing things you want to do?														
7. Completely satisfied	18.4	18.2	18.7		17.0	15.8	21.8	18.6		19.3	17.0	19.9	17.3	13.5
6.	16.7	17.0	16.5		15.7	17.8	15.8	17.9		17.3	18.3	18.5	13.9	11.6
5.	14.3	14.4	14.2		16.4	15.5	12.5	12.3		15.1	14.3	11.9	15.3	20.8
4. Neutral	16.4	15.3	17.3		18.3	15.4	17.0	14.4		17.5	16.1	13.5	12.5	14.2
3.	14.5	15.3	13.7		14.0	15.0	13.2	17.2		14.2	14.3	13.0	16.6	18.9
2.	7.9	8.0	7.9		6.9	10.7	5.7	8.7		6.4	9.0	12.2	8.5	13.0
1. Completely dissatisfied	11.8	11.8	11.6		11.8	9.7	14.1	10.9		10.2	11.0	11.0	15.8	7.9
Item 1360 N(Wtd)	*3018*	*1426*	*1563*		*683*	*935*	*973*	*428*		*1367*	*528*	*224*	*520*	*39*
A009K: The way you spend your leisure time--recreation, relaxation, and so on?														
7. Completely satisfied	28.0	28.5	27.3		27.5	25.7	32.3	24.3		28.6	26.2	33.8	27.0	20.2
6.	22.2	22.7	21.8		23.4	23.8	18.9	24.2		21.6	23.7	23.5	23.5	23.7
5.	15.9	16.8	15.1		15.4	18.5	12.9	17.5		16.4	15.9	10.0	17.4	18.8
4. Neutral	16.3	15.2	17.1		17.4	14.2	18.0	15.0		17.2	15.7	12.7	15.0	13.3
3.	8.5	8.4	8.6		7.8	8.4	8.7	9.1		7.6	10.7	7.3	8.0	12.9
2.	4.4	4.4	4.5		3.4	5.6	3.2	6.3		4.5	3.8	6.7	5.0	6.2
1. Completely dissatisfied	4.7	4.0	5.5		5.1	3.7	5.9	3.7		4.1	3.9	5.9	4.1	4.9
Item 1370 N(Wtd)	*3023*	*1429*	*1564*		*684*	*936*	*974*	*428*		*1371*	*527*	*224*	*521*	*39*
A009L: Your life as a whole these days?														
7. Completely satisfied	18.1	17.3	18.8		16.8	16.1	21.9	15.9		22.8	14.6	14.4	14.5	10.3
6.	27.3	26.9	27.8		25.6	27.8	26.9	30.2		27.6	29.8	27.7	26.2	26.4
5.	17.4	18.5	16.5		17.5	20.5	13.4	19.2		14.8	19.5	19.2	20.3	19.6
4. Neutral	23.7	23.6	23.5		23.8	22.6	26.6	19.3		23.1	22.9	26.1	22.6	17.0
3.	7.1	7.5	6.6		8.4	6.0	5.9	9.9		6.8	6.9	6.4	7.6	9.0
2.	2.6	2.7	2.6		3.4	3.4	1.4	2.4		2.1	2.9	2.2	3.5	6.3
1. Completely dissatisfied	3.8	3.5	4.1		4.5	3.6	3.9	3.1		2.7	3.2	4.0	5.2	11.3
Item 1380 N(Wtd)	*3016*	*1426*	*1563*		*681*	*934*	*974*	*428*		*1369*	*527*	*223*	*518*	*39*
A010: Generally speaking, would you say that most people can be trusted or that you can't be too careful in dealing with people?														
3. Most people can be trusted	34.5	34.4	35.1		33.7	37.7	31.1	36.8		37.6	35.5	34.9	32.7	25.3
2. Don't know, undecided	25.7	25.1	26.1		27.4	26.1	22.0	30.3		25.0	25.8	24.1	26.6	19.8
1. Can't be too careful	39.8	40.4	38.8		38.9	36.2	46.9	32.9		37.3	38.7	41.0	40.7	54.9
Item 1550 N(Wtd)	*3013*	*1423*	*1560*		*679*	*934*	*972*	*428*		*1366*	*526*	*224*	*521*	*37*
A011: Would you say that most of the time people try to be helpful or that they are mostly just looking out for themselves?														
3. Try to be helpful	32.5	28.5	36.2		34.6	33.4	31.2	30.2		33.1	33.1	30.6	30.2	20.9
2. Don't know, undecided	30.0	30.5	29.5		29.2	30.0	27.8	36.3		29.0	30.6	31.7	29.8	24.9
1. Just looking out for themselves	37.5	41.0	34.3		36.2	36.7	40.9	33.5		37.9	36.3	37.6	40.0	54.3
Item 1560 N(Wtd)	*3008*	*1422*	*1559*		*677*	*932*	*971*	*427*		*1365*	*526*	*224*	*517*	*37*
A012: Do you think most people would try to take advantage of you if they got a chance or would they try to be fair?														
3. Would try to be fair	28.2	25.9	30.6		28.7	28.5	26.0	31.8		29.2	28.9	26.8	29.5	17.9
2. Don't know, undecided	32.7	33.8	31.4		31.9	32.3	32.7	35.1		32.8	32.2	33.4	32.6	29.5
1. Would try to take advantage of you	39.1	40.3	38.0		39.4	39.3	41.3	33.1		38.0	38.9	39.8	37.9	52.6
Item 1570 N(Wtd)	*3011*	*1422*	*1559*		*677*	*934*	*973*	*427*		*1367*	*525*	*223*	*520*	*37*

CAUTION: Items were rearranged after 1975; changes in context may produce spurious "trends" (see page 12).

QUESTIONNAIRE FORM 1 1975	TOTAL	SEX			REGION					ILLICIT DRUG USE: LIFETIME				
		M	F		NE	NC	S	W		None	Marijuana Only	Few Pills	More Pills	Any Heroin
Weighted No. of Cases:	3038	1437	1568		688	943	979	428		1374	528	225	523	39
% of Weighted Total:	100.0	47.3	51.6		22.7	31.0	32.2	14.1		45.2	17.4	7.4	17.2	1.3

A13: How much do you agree or disagree with each of the following statements?

A013B: I feel a good citizen tries to change the government policies he disagrees with

	TOTAL	M	F		NE	NC	S	W		None	Marijuana Only	Few Pills	More Pills	Any Heroin
1. Disagree	5.7	5.6	5.8		8.9	4.7	4.5	5.8		5.9	4.5	5.8	4.5	4.1
2. Mostly disagree	9.7	8.7	10.3		10.0	9.5	9.4	9.9		9.0	10.2	9.5	12.2	-
3. Neither	21.1	19.4	22.5		20.3	22.7	20.6	20.1		21.1	23.2	22.0	18.8	14.0
4. Mostly agree	35.3	35.5	35.2		34.4	39.7	31.8	34.9		35.3	36.9	28.3	39.2	29.3
5. Agree	28.2	30.8	26.1		26.3	23.4	33.7	29.3		28.7	25.1	34.4	25.3	52.6
Item 1600 N(Wtd)	3000	1419	1552		677	929	969	425		1361	525	221	521	36

A013C: Despite its many faults, our system of doing things is still the best in the world

	TOTAL	M	F		NE	NC	S	W		None	Marijuana Only	Few Pills	More Pills	Any Heroin
1. Disagree	9.3	7.9	10.5		10.8	8.2	9.2	9.3		8.6	9.7	11.8	10.5	9.8
2. Mostly disagree	12.6	12.7	12.5		14.5	14.2	10.3	11.5		10.4	14.1	13.9	16.5	30.4
3. Neither	22.4	20.0	24.6		25.6	23.9	17.7	24.8		20.5	23.5	20.7	27.3	16.7
4. Mostly agree	28.5	27.8	29.2		25.6	28.9	29.2	30.6		30.4	28.4	25.8	24.1	23.0
5. Agree	27.2	31.6	23.2		23.4	24.7	33.6	23.8		30.1	24.2	27.9	21.5	20.1
Item 1630 N(Wtd)	2998	1420	1550		672	935	966	425		1359	525	223	521	36

A013E: America needs growth to survive, and that is going to require some increase in pollution

	TOTAL	M	F		NE	NC	S	W		None	Marijuana Only	Few Pills	More Pills	Any Heroin
1. Disagree	33.9	33.8	33.9		34.2	31.0	36.2	34.6		34.5	32.0	33.0	36.4	28.4
2. Mostly disagree	25.5	25.2	26.0		25.4	27.7	22.4	28.0		25.4	24.5	29.2	26.1	23.3
3. Neither	15.3	14.6	15.8		15.2	16.8	15.5	11.4		16.0	17.9	12.4	12.5	20.5
4. Mostly agree	14.4	15.0	13.9		14.3	15.9	13.4	13.4		13.5	16.2	11.9	15.2	13.1
5. Agree	10.9	11.4	10.4		10.9	8.5	12.5	12.5		10.6	9.4	13.6	9.9	14.7
Item 1640 N(Wtd)	2992	1415	1548		669	931	965	427		1357	522	219	521	37

A013H: Doing well in school is important for getting a good job

	TOTAL	M	F		NE	NC	S	W		None	Marijuana Only	Few Pills	More Pills	Any Heroin
1. Disagree	3.8	5.0	2.7		5.8	3.3	1.9	5.9		3.1	3.5	5.1	4.9	6.0
2. Mostly disagree	6.4	7.2	5.6		7.2	7.8	3.8	8.3		4.3	7.7	10.6	9.4	8.6
3. Neither	8.4	9.5	7.4		8.4	10.2	6.9	7.9		5.9	10.9	8.1	14.7	14.3
4. Mostly agree	29.5	30.1	28.9		33.6	27.6	26.3	34.4		27.2	32.7	32.8	29.5	32.7
5. Agree	51.9	48.3	55.5		45.1	51.2	61.1	43.5		59.5	45.3	43.4	41.4	38.4
Item 1670 N(Wtd)	3011	1426	1557		681	933	970	428		1364	526	224	521	37

A013I: Going to school has been an enjoyable experience for me

	TOTAL	M	F		NE	NC	S	W		None	Marijuana Only	Few Pills	More Pills	Any Heroin
1. Disagree	7.4	8.5	6.5		8.1	8.7	5.6	7.9		5.7	7.5	8.5	11.7	20.7
2. Mostly disagree	8.3	8.2	8.0		9.9	8.8	7.1	7.2		5.4	7.5	10.7	15.2	21.3
3. Neither	13.8	14.6	12.9		15.1	16.5	9.6	15.1		12.0	15.4	15.5	17.8	11.7
4. Mostly agree	36.5	38.3	35.1		38.8	36.6	34.8	36.7		37.5	37.8	31.7	35.2	26.2
5. Agree	34.0	30.5	37.5		28.1	29.4	42.9	33.1		39.5	31.8	33.6	20.0	20.1
Item 1660 N(Wtd)	3013	1425	1560		680	935	970	428		1367	526	224	521	37

The following questions are about CIGARETTE SMOKING.

A018: Have you ever smoked cigarettes?

	TOTAL	M	F		NE	NC	S	W		None	Marijuana Only	Few Pills	More Pills	Any Heroin
1. Never--GO TO Q.A023	26.0	23.2	28.9		23.7	23.5	27.9	30.9		42.9	9.9	12.1	7.0	11.0
2. Once or twice	27.8	30.0	26.0		21.8	28.4	30.0	30.9		33.6	27.3	23.3	11.1	15.9
3. Occasionally but not regularly	17.2	18.9	15.8		16.0	18.9	17.0	15.9		12.8	27.2	18.0	15.6	12.5
4. Regularly in the past	7.2	7.0	7.3		8.6	7.6	6.1	7.0		3.5	10.6	10.1	15.4	7.1
5. Regularly now	21.8	20.8	21.9		29.9	21.6	19.0	15.3		7.2	25.1	36.6	50.9	53.5
Item 760 N(Wtd)	2984	1414	1542		677	921	964	422		1349	525	220	520	37

CAUTION: Items were rearranged after 1975; changes in context may produce spurious "trends" (see page 12).

QUESTIONNAIRE FORM 1 1975	TOTAL	SEX			REGION					ILLICIT DRUG USE: LIFETIME				
		M	F		NE	NC	S	W		None	Marijuana Only	Few Pills	More Pills	Any Heroin
Weighted No. of Cases:	3038	1437	1568		688	943	979	428		1374	528	225	523	39
% of Weighted Total:	100.0	47.3	51.6		22.7	31.0	32.2	14.1		45.2	17.4	7.4	17.2	1.3
A019: When did you first smoke cigarettes on a regular daily basis?														
8. Never	58.3	59.1	58.3		50.6	58.2	60.6	65.5		77.0	49.8	42.3	24.3	27.7
1. Grade 6 or below	3.3	5.4	1.3		4.2	3.4	2.3	3.7		2.0	4.9	3.1	4.9	7.2
2. Grade 7 or 8	9.1	9.4	8.1		11.4	8.5	7.3	10.9		3.8	8.1	8.7	20.9	37.6
3. Grade 9 (Freshman)	8.2	7.7	8.7		9.9	8.4	7.9	5.8		3.5	10.1	14.8	16.3	16.3
4. Grade 10 (Sophomore)	9.4	9.0	9.9		11.6	9.0	9.9	5.7		5.0	10.9	14.2	18.6	6.2
5. Grade 11 (Junior)	7.8	6.1	9.4		8.2	8.6	8.3	4.4		5.9	10.9	13.2	9.4	1.6
6. Grade 12 (Senior)	3.9	3.3	4.4		4.1	3.9	3.7	3.9		2.8	5.2	3.8	5.7	3.4
Item 5570 N(Wtd)	2965	1406	1531		672	916	957	420		1340	520	222	515	38
A020: How frequently have you smoked cigarettes during the past 30 days?														
1. Not at all	49.3	50.8	48.4		39.2	49.7	53.4	56.6		68.2	47.1	36.3	25.7	20.0
2. Less than one cigarette per day	12.5	12.2	12.9		13.6	13.6	9.1	15.6		11.9	15.6	10.2	11.7	13.4
3. One to five cigarettes per day	13.3	12.6	13.9		14.4	12.8	14.0	10.9		9.6	13.8	17.9	14.9	7.6
4. About one-half pack per day	11.9	10.1	13.5		15.2	11.7	11.3	8.2		5.7	12.1	14.8	22.9	14.9
5. About one pack per day	10.5	11.6	9.1		14.3	9.9	10.0	6.2		3.5	9.1	17.4	20.0	29.8
6. About one and one-half packs per day	2.1	2.3	1.8		2.4	2.1	2.2	1.6		.6	1.7	3.0	4.3	14.3
7. Two packs or more per day	.4	.5	.4		.9	.3	-	.9		.4	.6	.4	.5	-
Item 780 N(Wtd) ★	2195	1078	1091		516	700	689	289		761	471	196	483	34
A021: Have you ever tried to stop smoking and found that you could not?														
1. Yes	18.1	17.9	18.3		22.0	17.9	16.3	16.3		9.3	17.9	22.6	28.6	48.1
2. No	81.9	82.1	81.7		78.0	82.1	83.7	83.7		90.7	82.1	77.4	71.4	51.9
Item 1690 N(Wtd) ★	2054	996	1033		486	660	648	260		697	439	185	469	33
A022: Do you want to stop smoking now?														
1. Yes	19.4	19.8	18.8		23.3	20.5	17.2	14.9		11.1	19.7	25.3	28.0	31.8
2. No	24.4	22.0	26.5		31.6	22.7	22.7	20.1		15.3	23.5	32.2	39.7	39.0
8. Don't smoke now	56.2	58.2	54.7		45.1	56.7	60.1	65.0		73.6	56.7	42.5	32.4	29.2
Item 1700 N(Wtd) ★	2119	1041	1057		493	682	670	273		733	457	192	467	32
A023: Do you think you will be smoking cigarettes five years from now?														
1. I definitely will	1.0	1.3	.7		1.2	.8	1.4	-		.8	.2	.5	1.3	6.8
2. I probably will	27.4	24.8	29.7		37.5	26.8	23.0	21.7		16.5	26.9	35.6	44.5	49.0
3. I probably will not	31.0	31.5	30.5		26.9	32.1	32.9	30.8		32.9	32.0	26.4	28.1	25.0
4. I definitely will not	40.6	42.4	39.1		34.4	40.3	42.7	47.5		49.8	40.9	37.4	26.1	19.2
Item 1710 N(Wtd)	2192	1076	1095		512	704	691	285		775	468	196	471	35

The next major section of this questionnaire deals with alcohol and various other drugs. There is a lot of talk these days about these subjects, but very little accurate information. Therefore, we still have a lot to learn about the actual experiences and attitudes of people your age.

We hope that you can answer all questions; but if you find one which you feel you cannot answer honestly, we would prefer that you leave it blank.

Remember that your answers will be strictly confidential. We never connect them with your name or your class.

★ = excludes respondents for whom question was inappropriate.

CAUTION: Items were rearranged after 1975; changes in context may produce spurious "trends" (see page 12).

QUESTIONNAIRE FORM 1 1975	TOTAL	SEX			REGION					ILLICIT DRUG USE: LIFETIME				
		M	F		NE	NC	S	W		None	Mari- juana Only	Few Pills	More Pills	Any Her- oin
Weighted No. of Cases:	3038	1437	1568		688	943	979	428		1374	528	225	523	39
% of Weighted Total:	100.0	47.3	51.6		22.7	31.0	32.2	14.1		45.2	17.4	7.4	17.2	1.3

The next questions are about ALCOHOLIC BEVERAGES, including beer, wine, and liquor.

A027: When did you first try an alcoholic beverage (beer, wine, or liquor)-- more than just a few sips?

8. Never	10.5	8.5	12.5		8.0	7.7	13.3	14.0		20.6	.4	2.5	1.2	-
1. Grade 6 or below	9.7	13.0	6.6		10.4	10.0	7.9	12.1		7.5	9.3	8.5	13.2	25.2
2. Grade 7 or 8	17.3	22.0	13.0		22.1	18.1	11.1	22.2		7.9	20.9	24.9	32.3	44.3
3. Grade 9 (Freshman)	22.9	23.7	21.8		26.5	22.8	21.2	21.2		18.0	30.2	28.1	30.2	16.8
4. Grade 10 (Sophomore)	18.2	15.9	20.5		14.6	18.0	22.7	13.9		17.2	20.3	21.6	16.4	8.4
5. Grade 11 (Junior)	15.4	12.0	18.5		14.7	16.8	16.3	11.2		18.5	16.5	12.6	6.1	3.6
6. Grade 12 (Senior)	6.1	5.0	7.1		3.8	6.6	7.5	5.4		10.1	2.4	1.8	.5	1.6
Item 5580 N(Wtd)	2915	1386	1501		664	904	932	414		1289	524	224	520	38

A028: On how many different occasions have you had alcohol to drink...‡

A028A: ...in your lifetime?

1. 0 occasions	11.0	9.0	13.1		8.5	8.0	14.1	15.0		21.4	.4	2.6	1.3	-
2. 1-2	8.1	6.2	9.9		4.1	7.1	13.3	4.8		12.7	2.3	6.1	1.0	-
3. 3-5	8.6	7.0	10.2		6.3	8.1	11.2	7.8		13.8	5.7	4.5	2.2	5.6
4. 6-9	8.7	6.5	10.7		7.4	9.7	7.5	11.0		12.1	6.7	6.2	2.2	-
5. 10-19	13.7	12.3	15.0		14.7	14.5	12.1	13.8		14.4	15.8	12.6	8.8	7.6
6. 20-39	12.8	11.4	14.2		12.2	15.0	11.8	11.2		11.3	14.1	18.2	12.6	19.3
7. 40 or more	37.1	47.6	26.8		46.8	37.5	30.0	36.4		14.2	55.1	49.9	72.0	67.5
Item 810 N(Wtd)	2757	1305	1430		627	862	882	386		1241	501	217	494	34

A028B: ...during the last 12 months?

1. 0 occasions	17.6	15.4	19.8		11.8	14.1	23.9	20.6		31.6	3.6	8.4	2.5	2.6
2. 1-2	13.0	10.8	15.1		10.3	12.3	16.1	12.0		19.3	7.6	10.7	3.9	5.2
3. 3-5	14.2	10.5	17.7		13.4	13.8	15.8	12.9		18.7	13.0	9.1	5.8	17.0
4. 6-9	11.2	10.6	11.9		11.3	12.4	9.9	11.4		10.4	15.2	10.0	8.7	8.2
5. 10-19	16.4	17.9	15.2		17.7	18.9	14.2	14.0		11.2	21.7	21.6	20.1	17.8
6. 20-39	11.6	12.8	10.4		14.3	10.6	10.3	12.1		4.6	17.6	17.7	20.2	21.8
7. 40 or more	16.0	22.1	9.9		21.2	17.9	9.9	17.0		4.2	21.2	22.5	38.9	27.4
Item 820 N(Wtd)	2739	1300	1417		624	862	863	389		1230	500	215	486	34

A028C: ...during the last 30 days?

1. 0 occasions	34.7	30.8	38.8		26.9	30.7	42.9	37.9		55.2	15.7	26.4	8.8	11.0
2. 1-2	24.5	21.2	27.9		25.9	24.1	24.8	22.5		25.5	29.8	20.9	17.3	24.4
3. 3-5	15.9	16.9	14.8		17.4	18.9	12.2	15.1		10.5	23.3	19.6	19.3	9.0
4. 6-9	11.3	13.3	9.3		12.1	11.7	11.0	9.9		4.9	15.4	14.1	22.3	10.8
5. 10-19	10.0	13.2	7.0		12.7	11.3	6.8	10.0		2.9	13.2	14.7	22.5	29.8
6. 20-39	2.3	3.3	1.2		3.5	2.3	1.3	2.2		.6	1.9	2.8	6.5	11.9
7. 40 or more	1.3	1.5	1.0		1.4	1.0	.9	2.3		.3	.7	1.5	3.4	3.1
Item 830 N(Wtd)	2766	1313	1427		626	875	868	396		1228	499	215	499	37

‡=Wording changed in subsequent years.
CAUTION: Items were rearranged after 1975; changes in context may produce spurious "trends" (see page 12).

QUESTIONNAIRE FORM 1 1975	TOTAL	SEX			REGION					ILLICIT DRUG USE: LIFETIME				
		M	F		NE	NC	S	W		None	Mari-juana Only	Few Pills	More Pills	Any Her-oin
Weighted No. of Cases:	3038	1437	1568		688	943	979	428		1374	528	225	523	39
% of Weighted Total:	100.0	47.3	51.6		22.7	31.0	32.2	14.1		45.2	17.4	7.4	17.2	1.3

IF YOU HAVE NOT HAD ANY BEER, WINE, OR LIQUOR IN THE LAST TWELVE MONTHS, GO TO Q.A040.

A032: What have been the most important reasons for your drinking alcoholic beverages? (Mark all that apply.)

	TOTAL	M	F		NE	NC	S	W		None	Mari-juana Only	Few Pills	More Pills	Any Her-oin
To experiment--to see what it's like@	-	-	-		-	-	-	-		-	-	-	-	-
A. To relax or relieve tension	26.5	26.2	26.7		31.5	25.9	23.4	26.9		13.9	37.8	39.2	44.4	50.7
B. To feel good or get high	37.0	40.6	33.2		43.8	40.7	26.5	42.1		15.4	58.3	61.5	68.3	73.8
C. To seek deeper insights and understanding	3.1	3.7	2.5		3.3	2.3	3.0	4.8		1.3	3.1	8.3	4.6	10.6
D. To have a good time with my friends	51.3	54.4	48.1		56.9	57.5	40.4	53.4		34.6	72.0	67.4	71.0	66.0
E. To fit in with a group I like	9.3	10.8	8.0		6.9	11.8	8.6	9.0		8.4	10.2	11.8	7.8	3.4
F. To get away from my problems or troubles	10.5	10.0	11.0		12.4	10.6	8.6	11.8		4.5	14.7	19.6	18.3	28.7
G. Because of boredom, nothing else to do	17.9	18.9	17.1		20.2	20.6	13.8	17.7		10.2	21.1	30.6	28.8	25.8
H. Because of anger or frustration	9.6	9.5	9.8		10.4	9.1	9.2	10.4		4.4	11.6	18.0	17.8	16.1
J. To get through the day	.6	.8	.4		.6	.8	.2	.8		.1	.3	1.1	1.6	3.2
K. To increase the effects of some other drug(s)	4.6	5.6	3.5		5.8	5.1	3.3	4.6		-	1.3	6.2	20.0	25.3
L. To decrease (offset) the effects of some other drug(s)	.9	1.4	.5		.7	.7	1.4	.7		-	.4	3.1	3.4	-
To get to sleep@	-	-	-		-	-	-	-		-	-	-	-	-
N. Because it tastes good	44.2	45.8	42.6		51.4	48.0	35.3	44.7		28.8	58.8	57.2	66.3	44.9
M. Because I am "hooked"--I feel I have to drink	.2	.4	.1		.3	.2	.2	.3		-	.3	-	.7	3.4
Item 1820-1960 N(Wtd) ★	2861	1357	1478		644	895	922	401		1374	478	194	490	34

A033: When you drink alcoholic beverages, how high do you usually get?

	TOTAL	M	F		NE	NC	S	W		None	Mari-juana Only	Few Pills	More Pills	Any Her-oin
1. Not at all high	23.6	20.6	26.9		20.0	23.0	29.1	19.7		43.5	11.2	12.0	4.4	14.1
2. A little high	33.8	31.1	36.6		34.8	32.4	37.6	27.4		35.2	37.9	33.6	26.1	23.1
3. Moderately high	35.9	39.6	32.1		39.7	37.2	28.6	41.8		19.0	45.5	44.1	55.5	49.4
4. Very high	6.6	8.7	4.4		5.5	7.4	4.6	11.0		2.2	5.3	10.2	14.0	13.4
Item 1970 N(Wtd) ★	2321	1131	1165		568	751	684	318		853	490	201	490	36

A034: When you drink alcoholic beverages, how long do you usually stay high?

	TOTAL	M	F		NE	NC	S	W		None	Mari-juana Only	Few Pills	More Pills	Any Her-oin
1. Usually don't get high	25.7	23.3	28.6		22.2	23.7	33.0	21.3		46.0	13.5	17.3	5.5	14.1
2. One to two hours	40.5	38.5	42.5		40.0	41.7	43.4	32.6		38.0	47.5	43.8	38.8	26.0
3. Three to six hours	30.1	34.1	25.7		32.8	30.4	21.6	42.5		15.0	35.5	33.0	48.7	48.6
4. Seven to 24 hours	3.4	3.9	3.1		4.2	4.2	2.0	3.6		.9	3.3	5.9	6.5	9.4
5. More than 24 hours	.2	.3	.1		.8	-	.1	-		.1	.2	-	.5	1.9
Item 1980 N(Wtd) ★	2305	1123	1156		563	746	677	319		837	492	201	494	36

The following questions ask about how much you have to drink on the occasions when you drink alcoholic beverages. For these questions, a ' drink" means any of the following: A 12-ounce can (or bottle) of beer, a 4-ounce glass of wine, a mixed drink or shot glass of liquor.

A035: Think back over the last two weeks. How many times have you had five or more drinks in a row?

	TOTAL	M	F		NE	NC	S	W		None	Mari-juana Only	Few Pills	More Pills	Any Her-oin
1. None	61.0	48.4	73.6		57.2	58.7	68.7	56.8		78.2	54.1	53.8	38.9	52.9
2. Once	11.9	14.5	9.2		12.6	12.6	10.3	12.2		10.0	15.0	14.0	12.2	9.3
3. Twice	9.9	12.5	7.1		10.8	10.0	8.7	10.2		6.1	12.8	10.1	14.6	-
4. 3 to 5 times	11.2	15.4	7.1		13.0	12.1	7.7	13.1		3.9	13.8	11.7	21.7	11.8
5. 6 to 9 times	3.4	4.8	1.9		3.6	3.4	3.1	3.3		1.0	2.5	3.6	7.9	14.8
6. 10 or more times	2.7	4.4	1.1		2.7	3.1	1.4	4.5		.9	1.7	6.8	4.7	11.2
Item 850 N(Wtd) ★	2262	1090	1146		553	734	665	309		834	472	195	484	35

@ = category eliminated in this data collection.   ★ = excludes respondents for whom question was inappropriate.

CAUTION: Items were rearranged after 1975; changes in context may produce spurious "trends" (see page 12).

QUESTIONNAIRE FORM 1 1975	TOTAL	SEX			REGION					ILLICIT DRUG USE: LIFETIME				
		M	F		NE	NC	S	W		None	Marijuana Only	Few Pills	More Pills	Any Heroin
Weighted No. of Cases:	3038	1437	1568		688	943	979	428		1374	528	225	523	39
% of Weighted Total:	100.0	47.3	51.6		22.7	31.0	32.2	14.1		45.2	17.4	7.4	17.2	1.3

A036: During the last two weeks, how many times have you had 3 or 4 drinks in a row?

1. None	53.3	43.3	63.3		48.8	51.9	58.5	53.1		71.4	45.1	47.9	29.5	42.5
2. Once	16.2	15.8	16.2		16.3	15.6	17.2	15.3		15.1	17.5	15.3	17.4	15.3
3. Twice	12.0	14.9	9.3		12.0	12.7	11.7	11.1		7.5	16.5	11.7	16.9	5.0
4. 3 to 5 times	11.1	15.4	6.9		14.6	12.0	7.1	11.9		3.9	14.7	17.5	18.2	12.1
5. 6 to 9 times	5.0	6.7	3.3		5.9	5.7	4.1	3.6		1.3	4.7	4.6	13.4	12.0
6. 10 or more times	2.4	3.8	1.0		2.4	2.1	1.4	5.0		.8	1.6	3.0	4.7	13.0
Item 1990　N(Wtd) ★	2288	1108	1155		556	740	675	317		848	478	195	488	36

A037: During the last two weeks, how many times have you had two drinks in a row?

1. None	44.2	35.8	52.3		39.6	43.7	48.7	44.0		60.6	36.5	36.2	24.0	33.8
2. Once	19.9	19.2	20.5		19.7	19.3	21.4	18.4		21.3	22.3	15.8	15.8	21.5
3. Twice	12.9	13.9	12.0		14.3	13.8	10.6	13.1		8.2	15.8	19.9	16.7	6.0
4. 3 to 5 times	13.0	16.1	10.0		14.6	12.8	11.3	14.3		7.6	15.4	14.5	20.9	10.2
5. 6 to 9 times	6.1	9.3	3.0		7.4	5.7	5.5	6.0		1.2	7.0	8.0	14.2	8.6
6. 10 to 19 times	3.1	4.5	1.6		3.8	3.8	2.1	2.4		.9	2.2	4.5	7.0	16.7
7. 20 or more times	.8	1.1	.5		.7	1.0	.3	1.7		.1	.9	1.1	1.4	3.2
Item 2000　N(Wtd) ★	2228	1074	1130		543	716	659	310		826	461	187	479	36

A038: During the last two weeks, how many times have you had just one drink?

1. None	43.3	39.4	47.3		44.2	42.6	42.4	45.0		54.6	39.7	39.6	29.8	22.3
2. Once	26.3	22.8	29.9		22.7	28.9	26.6	25.9		26.9	26.7	23.2	26.7	21.1
3. Twice	13.1	14.4	11.6		14.4	11.1	14.8	12.1		10.6	15.4	17.7	12.9	26.2
4. 3 to 5 times	9.8	12.3	7.4		9.0	10.7	10.3	8.4		5.3	11.6	9.7	15.8	8.4
5. 6 to 9 times	4.3	6.3	2.2		6.0	3.7	3.7	3.7		1.9	3.6	5.2	8.7	10.7
6. 10 to 19 times	2.2	3.4	1.2		2.6	2.2	1.4	3.4		.2	2.6	3.5	3.8	7.7
7. 20 or more times	.9	1.5	.3		.9	.8	.8	1.5		.5	.3	1.2	2.3	3.6
Item 2010　N(Wtd) ★	2128	1024	1079		523	690	612	303		774	443	183	474	32

A039: Have you ever tried to stop using alcoholic beverages and found that you couldn't stop?

1. Yes	2.8	3.9	1.7		2.6	2.9	2.6	3.5		2.5	1.9	3.4	3.2	1.3
2. No	97.2	96.1	98.3		97.4	97.1	97.4	96.5		97.5	98.1	96.6	96.8	98.7
Item 2020　N(Wtd) ★	2285	1121	1139		558	739	672	316		824	489	199	496	36

A040: Do you think you will be drinking alcoholic beverages five years from now?

1. I definitely will	13.9	18.0	10.2		20.1	15.6	7.3	15.5		7.4	20.2	18.5	22.2	40.6
2. I probably will	54.4	52.4	56.0		57.0	59.1	49.1	51.9		45.1	64.5	61.4	67.2	36.5
3. I probably will not	14.7	13.0	16.4		12.3	12.5	18.7	14.2		20.0	9.9	9.1	6.3	15.0
4. I definitely will not	17.0	16.6	17.5		10.7	12.8	24.9	18.4		27.4	5.3	10.9	4.3	7.9
Item 2030　N(Wtd)	2960	1399	1533		676	920	951	413		1340	522	225	519	38

The next questions are about MARIJUANA and HASHISH.

Marijuana is sometimes called: grass, pot, dope.

Hashish is sometimes called: hash, hash oil.

A043: When did you first try marijuana or hashish?

8. Never	53.7	50.7	57.2		43.9	53.1	64.0	47.2		100.0	-	16.6	6.1	2.6
1. Grade 6 or below	.6	1.1	.2		1.2	.4	.3	.9		-	.3	1.5	1.6	5.8
2. Grade 7 or 8	5.8	7.4	4.1		8.4	4.5	3.7	9.1		-	4.5	6.5	20.4	56.2
3. Grade 9 (Freshman)	10.5	9.7	10.3		13.3	10.5	6.7	14.5		-	12.8	24.5	30.0	10.4
4. Grade 10 (Sophomore)	13.1	13.6	12.8		14.3	14.2	10.9	13.8		-	28.6	23.3	26.9	20.7
5. Grade 11 (Junior)	11.5	12.5	10.7		14.2	11.4	10.0	10.8		-	35.7	22.5	11.5	4.3
6. Grade 12 (Senior)	4.8	5.1	4.7		4.8	5.9	4.5	3.6		-	18.0	5.1	3.6	-
Item 5590　N(Wtd)	2963	1392	1543		670	916	956	422		1374	528	223	521	39

★=excludes respondents for whom question was inappropriate.

CAUTION: Items were rearranged after 1975; changes in context may produce spurious "trends" (see page 12).

QUESTIONNAIRE FORM 1 1975	TOTAL	SEX			REGION					ILLICIT DRUG USE: LIFETIME				
		M	F		NE	NC	S	W		None	Mari-juana Only	Few Pills	More Pills	Any Her-oin
Weighted No. of Cases:	3038	1437	1568		688	943	979	428		1374	528	225	523	39
% of Weighted Total:	100.0	47.3	51.6		22.7	31.0	32.2	14.1		45.2	17.4	7.4	17.2	1.3

A044: On how many different occasions have you used marijuana or hashish...‡

A044A: ...in your lifetime?

	TOTAL	M	F		NE	NC	S	W		None	Mar. Only	Few Pills	More Pills	Any Her.
1. 0 occasions	55.0	51.9	58.8		44.8	54.3	66.0	48.2		100.0	-	17.1	6.3	2.6
2. 1-2	6.8	7.7	6.2		8.1	7.2	6.1	5.6		-	29.6	5.2	2.1	2.5
3. 3-5	4.8	5.0	4.5		4.6	4.9	4.8	5.0		-	18.3	8.6	2.7	1.8
4. 6-9	4.0	4.2	3.9		6.4	2.7	3.3	4.7		-	12.9	8.5	3.7	-
5. 10-19	4.7	4.7	4.8		5.3	5.9	3.3	4.1		-	11.7	11.8	6.6	-
6. 20-39	5.7	5.0	6.3		7.2	6.3	3.4	7.1		-	11.7	15.9	11.3	9.7
7. 40 or more	18.9	21.6	15.6		23.6	18.6	13.1	25.2		-	15.7	32.9	67.3	83.4
Item 860 N(Wtd)	2890	1362	1501		656	895	926	413		1374	528	217	506	39

A044B: ...during the last 12 months?

	TOTAL	M	F		NE	NC	S	W		None	Mar. Only	Few Pills	More Pills	Any Her.
1. 0 occasions	62.0	59.0	65.8		53.6	59.3	73.2	56.5		100.0	25.5	26.1	11.1	13.3
2. 1-2	7.4	8.2	6.7		8.9	7.9	6.8	5.5		-	26.1	8.9	7.4	7.3
3. 3-5	4.5	4.5	4.5		5.7	4.4	2.7	7.1		-	14.5	9.0	4.4	-
4. 6-9	4.0	3.9	4.2		4.1	4.1	3.9	3.6		-	9.2	11.2	6.1	1.1
5. 10-19	5.6	5.3	5.7		7.9	7.6	2.1	5.3		-	10.3	17.9	11.7	11.1
6. 20-39	5.8	5.4	6.1		5.6	6.7	4.3	7.7		-	7.0	11.1	19.0	14.5
7. 40 or more	10.6	13.6	6.9		14.2	10.0	7.1	14.3		-	7.4	15.8	40.4	52.7
Item 870 N(Wtd)	2873	1352	1494		653	894	920	406		1374	515	214	507	37

A044C: ...during the last 30 days?

	TOTAL	M	F		NE	NC	S	W		None	Mar. Only	Few Pills	More Pills	Any Her.
1. 0 occasions	73.6	71.4	76.6		67.7	71.1	82.9	67.3		100.0	61.9	48.5	24.4	20.3
2. 1-2	7.4	7.6	7.1		7.6	9.6	5.0	7.5		-	17.8	17.1	12.4	6.3
3. 3-5	4.5	4.5	4.5		6.8	5.6	2.2	3.8		-	9.2	13.6	8.2	9.2
4. 6-9	4.2	4.5	3.6		4.4	3.7	3.5	6.7		-	5.2	8.4	14.4	3.8
5. 10-19	4.7	4.7	4.7		5.8	4.7	3.6	5.7		-	3.3	5.8	19.4	11.4
6. 20-39	3.3	4.1	2.4		4.4	3.7	1.8	4.4		-	1.7	2.4	13.0	33.8
7. 40 or more	2.2	3.2	1.1		3.4	1.6	.9	4.6		-	.9	4.1	8.0	15.3
Item 880 N(Wtd)	2880	1356	1498		655	894	922	409		1374	515	214	509	37

IF YOU HAVE NOT USED MARIJUANA OR HASHISH IN THE LAST TWELVE MONTHS, GO TO Q.A053.

A049: What have been the most important reasons for your using marijuana or hashish? (Mark all that apply.)

	TOTAL	M	F		NE	NC	S	W		None	Mar. Only	Few Pills	More Pills	Any Her.
A. To experiment--to see what it's like	60.3	57.6	63.4		60.8	61.3	64.8	51.1		-	74.7	58.8	49.4	27.3
B. To relax or relieve tension	35.2	33.4	37.3		39.1	28.9	34.3	42.4		-	22.9	33.9	46.9	68.7
C. To feel good or get high	71.7	72.1	70.4		74.6	73.5	63.9	74.5		-	59.2	70.7	85.1	79.5
D. To seek deeper insights and understanding	13.1	13.6	12.4		13.3	12.5	14.1	12.6		-	7.3	13.7	18.3	27.3
E. To have a good time with my friends	62.4	60.9	63.2		60.1	66.0	54.9	69.2		-	56.6	58.4	69.6	62.0
F. To fit in with a group I like	10.5	12.8	8.2		7.9	12.4	8.8	13.3		-	9.9	11.5	10.2	-
G. To get away from my problems or troubles	14.8	12.6	17.1		16.5	15.0	14.5	12.0		-	11.6	16.3	17.1	27.7
H. Because of boredom, nothing else to do	23.4	23.8	23.2		21.6	24.0	22.0	26.8		-	13.8	23.8	31.8	33.4
I. Because of anger or frustration	10.6	8.9	12.4		11.5	7.6	13.9	10.7		-	7.5	12.2	13.3	13.6
K. To get through the day	4.0	5.5	2.5		4.1	4.3	3.8	3.6		-	.7	3.9	6.8	11.6
L. To increase the effects of some other drug(s)	11.4	11.7	10.9		10.3	12.4	13.6	8.4		-	2.1	2.9	21.7	27.5
M. To decrease (offset) the effects of some other drug(s)	2.5	2.2	2.8		2.0	1.2	2.8	5.2		-	.1	-	5.7	2.1
Because I am "hooked"--I have to have it @	-	-	-		-	-	-	-		-	-	-	-	-
Item 2210-2330 N(Wtd) ★	1090	548	520		300	358	252	181		-	375	160	452	33

‡=Wording changed in subsequent years.   @ = category eliminated in this data collection.   ★=excludes respondents for whom question was inappropriate.

CAUTION: Items were rearranged after 1975; changes in context may produce spurious "trends" (see page 12).

	TOTAL	SEX			REGION				ILLICIT DRUG USE: LIFETIME				
QUESTIONNAIRE FORM 1 **1975**		M	F		NE	NC	S	W	None	Mari- juana Only	Few Pills	More Pills	Any Her- oin
Weighted No. of Cases:	3038	1437	1568		688	943	979	428	1374	528	225	523	39
% of Weighted Total:	100.0	47.3	51.6		22.7	31.0	32.2	14.1	45.2	17.4	7.4	17.2	1.3

A050: When you use marijuana or hashish how high do you usually get?

1. Not at all high	6.9	7.5	6.5		5.0	7.3	9.4	5.7	-	14.4	1.9	1.6	5.0
2. A little high	22.1	21.0	23.6		21.2	20.0	24.4	24.7	-	30.9	26.9	11.9	5.2
3. Moderately high	45.5	44.4	45.9		44.4	50.0	41.8	43.7	-	42.8	47.2	50.1	41.9
4. Very high	25.5	27.0	24.0		29.4	22.6	24.4	25.8	-	12.0	24.0	36.5	47.8
Item 2340 N(Wtd) ★	1096	554	521		304	359	250	183	-	381	159	449	33

A051: When you use marijuana or hashish how long do you usually stay high?

1. Usually don't get high	8.5	8.3	9.0		5.4	7.8	12.5	9.3	-	15.8	5.9	1.3	5.0
2. One to two hours	39.7	39.4	40.2		38.8	39.9	43.0	36.4	-	44.8	45.7	34.8	23.7
3. Three to six hours	45.4	46.9	43.4		50.4	44.7	40.3	45.5	-	37.1	40.4	55.1	50.7
4. Seven to 24 hours	5.9	5.1	6.7		4.7	7.5	3.2	8.4	-	2.2	6.9	8.2	18.4
5. More than 24 hours	.5	.4	.6		.7	-	1.0	.3	-	-	1.1	.6	2.1
Item 2350 N(Wtd) ★	1095	551	522		303	359	249	184	-	377	159	453	33

A052: Have you ever tried to stop using marijuana or hashish and found that you couldn't stop?

1. Yes	3.1	3.5	2.8		2.1	3.4	1.7	6.4	-	2.1	4.6	2.3	4.4
2. No	96.9	96.5	97.2		97.9	96.6	98.3	93.6	-	97.9	95.4	97.7	95.6
Item 2380 N(Wtd) ★	1091	548	520		305	359	251	176	-	378	158	454	33

A053: Do you think you will be using marijuana or hashish five years from now?

1. I definitely will	4.8	5.8	3.5		8.9	3.6	3.0	4.9	.3	3.5	5.0	17.5	32.6
2. I probably will	14.3	15.2	13.2		17.3	15.0	8.7	20.6	1.1	20.8	26.8	39.9	34.8
3. I probably will not	22.0	23.4	20.7		24.2	24.0	17.9	23.9	14.0	34.3	32.8	26.3	18.9
4. I definitely will not	58.8	55.5	62.6		49.5	57.3	70.5	50.6	84.6	41.4	35.3	16.3	13.7
Item 2390 N(Wtd)	2949	1386	1541		671	908	955	415	1350	519	223	513	39

The next questions are about LSD, the psychedelic drug which is sometimes called "acid".

A056: When did you first try LSD?

8. Never	89.1	89.1	89.8		87.7	87.9	92.6	85.9	100.0	99.9	84.2	49.4	21.5
1. Grade 6 or below	.1	.2	-		-	.1	.2	-	-	.1	-	.3	1.8
2. Grade 7 or 8	.7	.8	.7		.8	.3	.6	1.9	-	-	-	3.2	15.3
3. Grade 9 (Freshman)	2.3	2.1	2.3		2.6	2.5	1.6	2.7	-	-	1.7	10.3	28.7
4. Grade 10 (Sophomore)	2.8	3.1	2.4		3.4	3.0	2.0	3.5	-	-	3.8	13.5	16.0
5. Grade 11 (Junior)	3.1	2.9	3.1		3.8	3.6	1.9	3.6	-	-	4.4	15.3	14.1
6. Grade 12 (Senior)	1.8	1.9	1.7		1.7	2.6	1.0	2.4	-	-	5.9	8.0	2.6
Item 5600 N(Wtd)	2904	1360	1523		666	880	948	409	1356	524	217	496	38

A057: On how many different occasions have you taken LSD...‡

A057A: ...in your lifetime?

1. 0 occasions	89.3	89.2	90.0		88.0	88.0	92.8	85.9	100.0	100.0	84.4	49.5	23.1
2. 1-2	3.7	3.0	4.0		3.3	5.0	2.5	4.1	-	-	15.6	14.3	3.9
3. 3-5	2.7	3.0	2.3		3.6	2.4	1.5	4.9	-	-	-	15.6	3.7
4. 6-9	1.3	1.1	1.5		1.7	.9	.8	2.7	-	-	-	6.8	15.9
5. 10-19	1.1	1.5	.6		1.2	1.3	.9	1.0	-	-	-	5.4	14.7
6. 20-39	1.1	1.0	1.1		1.5	1.0	1.0	.6	-	-	-	5.1	16.6
7. 40 or more	.8	1.2	.4		.6	1.4	.5	.8	-	-	-	3.4	22.1
Item 890 N(Wtd)	2898	1358	1519		664	879	946	409	1356	523	216	494	35

★=excludes respondents for whom question was inappropriate.   *=less than .05 per cent.   ‡=Wording changed in subsequent years.

CAUTION: Items were rearranged after 1975; changes in context may produce spurious "trends" (see page 12).

QUESTIONNAIRE FORM 1 1975	TOTAL	SEX			REGION					ILLICIT DRUG USE: LIFETIME				
		M	F		NE	NC	S	W		None	Mari-juana Only	Few Pills	More Pills	Any Her-oin
Weighted No. of Cases:	3038	1437	1568		688	943	979	428		1374	528	225	523	39
% of Weighted Total:	100.0	47.3	51.6		22.7	31.0	32.2	14.1		45.2	17.4	7.4	17.2	1.3
A057B: ...during the last 12 months?														
1. 0 occasions	92.9	92.7	93.8		92.1	91.7	95.7	90.6		100.0	100.0	93.1	65.7	40.8
2. 1-2	3.4	3.2	3.2		4.0	4.3	1.7	4.4		-	-	6.9	16.5	8.6
3. 3-5	1.8	2.0	1.4		1.9	1.4	1.6	2.7		-	-	-	9.3	13.9
4. 6-9	.9	.8	.9		.8	1.2	.3	1.8		-	-	-	4.3	16.3
5. 10-19	.7	.7	.6		1.1	.9	.4	.3		-	-	-	3.2	13.2
6. 20-39	*	.1	-		-	.1	-	-		-	-	-	.2	-
7. 40 or more	.2	.4	.1		-	.4	.3	.2		-	-	-	.9	7.2
Item 900 N(Wtd)	2890	1351	1518		661	876	945	408		1356	523	211	489	37
A057C: ...during the last 30 days?														
1. 0 occasions	97.2	96.4	98.1		96.9	96.7	98.3	96.1		100.0	100.0	98.9	86.4	65.2
2. 1-2	1.9	2.6	1.2		2.6	2.4	.8	2.4		-	-	1.1	9.9	14.1
3. 3-5	.6	.6	.6		.4	.5	.6	1.5		-	-	-	2.7	15.1
4. 6-9	.1	.1	-		.2	.1	-	-		-	-	-	.4	-
5. 10-19	*	.1	*		-	.1	*	-		-	-	-	-	3.6
6. 20-39	*	.1	-		-	.1	-	-		-	-	-	.2	-
7. 40 or more	.1	.2	-		-	-	.3	-		-	-	-	.3	2.0
Item 910 N(Wtd)	2887	1351	1516		661	876	943	408		1356	523	211	489	35

IF YOU HAVE NOT TAKEN LSD IN THE LAST TWELVE MONTHS, GO TO Q.A067.

	TOTAL	M	F		NE	NC	S	W		None	Mari-juana Only	Few Pills	More Pills	Any Her-oin
A062: What have been the most important reasons for your taking LSD? (Mark all that apply.)														
A. To experiment--to see what it's like	81.1	70.7	92.2		79.8	88.2	73.3	77.3		-	-	100.0	79.2	81.9
B. To relax or relieve tension	10.5	6.0	15.2		15.0	4.5	19.8	6.3		-	-	-	9.8	24.1
C. To feel good or get high	63.9	63.9	62.1		59.2	68.3	58.6	67.7		-	-	8.8	69.9	58.2
D. To seek deeper insights and understanding	32.4	35.8	29.8		25.2	29.8	41.0	38.5		-	-	25.3	32.9	33.6
E. To have a good time with my friends	45.8	47.4	45.6		43.8	46.8	43.0	49.6		-	-	6.1	49.1	50.2
F. To fit in with a group I like	4.8	7.8	2.3		6.4	4.1	6.1	2.8		-	-	-	5.9	-
G. To get away from my problems or troubles	10.8	5.4	16.8		7.4	13.4	13.2	7.8		-	-	18.2	8.8	20.3
H. Because of boredom, nothing else to do	16.3	19.2	15.3		8.0	26.6	7.5	17.4		-	-	15.5	17.7	6.1
I. Because of anger or frustration	2.6	2.5	3.1		3.6	2.0	2.4	2.7		-	-	2.7	1.8	9.0
K. To get through the day	2.3	2.6	2.2		1.9	2.0	2.9	2.5		-	-	-	1.5	9.7
L. To increase the effects of some other drug(s)	7.2	7.7	6.2		5.6	6.6	13.7	3.9		-	-	4.8	5.9	19.3
M. To decrease (offset) the effects of some other drug(s)	2.2	2.5	2.3		4.0	3.3	-	-		-	-	-	2.7	-
Because I am "hooked"--I have to have it @	-	-	-		-	-	-	-		-	-	-	-	-
Item 2520-2640 N(Wtd) ★	205	99	94		53	74	39	38		-	-	16	167	21
A063: When you take LSD how high do you usually get?														
1. Not at all high	.2	.4	-		-	-	-	1.0		-	-	-	-	1.7
2. A little high	4.8	7.1	3.0		1.7	2.6	15.2	2.9		-	-	-	5.9	-
3. Moderately high	16.2	12.1	20.1		18.9	10.3	13.3	26.7		-	-	9.2	17.1	14.1
4. Very high	78.8	80.5	76.9		79.4	87.0	71.4	69.4		-	-	90.8	76.9	84.2
Item 2650 N(Wtd) ★	204	99	93		54	74	38	38		-	-	16	166	22
A064: When you take LSD how long do you usually stay high?														
1. Usually don't get high	1.6	2.3	1.1		1.8	2.6	-	1.0		-	-	6.2	1.2	1.7
2. One to two hours	1.3	1.7	1.0		1.7	-	4.3	-		-	-	-	1.6	-
3. Three to six hours	22.7	19.4	25.5		18.6	21.7	28.1	24.9		-	-	30.7	23.5	11.2
4. Seven to 24 hours	69.8	73.0	66.2		69.3	72.7	63.8	71.0		-	-	49.4	69.8	84.0
5. More than 24 hours	4.6	3.6	6.3		8.5	3.0	3.8	3.1		-	-	13.6	4.0	3.2
Item 2660 N(Wtd) ★	206	100	94		54	74	40	38		-	-	16	168	22

* = less than .05 per cent.   @ = category eliminated in this data collection.   ★ = excludes respondents for whom question was inappropriate.

CAUTION: Items were rearranged after 1975; changes in context may produce spurious "trends" (see page 12).

QUESTIONNAIRE FORM 1 1975	TOTAL	SEX			REGION					ILLICIT DRUG USE: LIFETIME				
		M	F		NE	NC	S	W		None	Mari- juana Only	Few Pills	More Pills	Any Her- oin
Weighted No. of Cases:	3038	1437	1568		688	943	979	428		1374	528	225	523	39
% of Weighted Total:	100.0	47.3	51.6		22.7	31.0	32.2	14.1		45.2	17.4	7.4	17.2	1.3
A065: Have you ever had a ''bad trip'' on LSD?														
1. No	68.0	68.2	65.8		69.9	72.3	55.4	69.8		-	-	90.4	69.2	40.8
2. Yes, once	27.2	25.0	32.3		23.7	22.5	40.1	28.0		-	-	9.6	26.9	43.8
3. Yes, more than once	4.8	6.8	1.9		6.4	5.2	4.5	2.2		-	-	-	3.9	15.4
Item 2670 N(Wtd) ★	208	100	96		55	74	40	39		-	-	16	169	22
A066: Have you ever tried to stop using LSD and found that you couldn't stop?														
1. Yes	1.6	1.5	1.8		-	4.4	-	-		-	-	-	1.9	-
2. No	98.4	98.5	98.2		100.0	95.6	99.9	99.9		-	-	100.0	98.1	100.0
Item 2680 N(Wtd) ★	206	100	94		53	74	41	38		-	-	16	167	22
A067: Do you think you will be using LSD five years from now?														
1. I definitely will	.8	.9	.7		1.0	.6	.6	1.4		.4	1.1	-	2.1	2.8
2. I probably will	2.0	2.3	1.6		2.5	1.9	1.8	2.1		.2	.1	.3	9.6	21.1
3. I probably will not	11.3	11.9	10.6		14.9	10.8	8.5	13.5		5.0	10.0	16.2	28.2	37.0
4. I definitely will not	85.9	84.9	87.1		81.6	86.7	89.1	83.0		94.4	88.8	83.5	60.1	39.1
Item 2690 N(Wtd)	2844	1324	1496		637	878	935	394		1335	492	212	477	37

The next questions are about PSYCHEDELICS OTHER THAN LSD.

This group would include the following drugs: mescaline, peyote, psilocybin, THC. ‡

	TOTAL	M	F		NE	NC	S	W		None	Mari- juana Only	Few Pills	More Pills	Any Her- oin
A070: When did you first try any of them? ‡														
8. Never	84.7	85.3	85.0		79.9	83.3	88.9	85.7		100.0	99.7	67.8	30.7	17.1
1. Grade 6 or below	*	*	-		-	.1	-	-		-	.1	-	-	-
2. Grade 7 or 8	.7	.7	.6		1.5	.2	.2	1.5		-	-	.8	3.1	6.5
3. Grade 9 (Freshman)	2.7	2.9	2.3		2.6	3.4	1.9	3.5		-	-	2.3	12.7	31.5
4. Grade 10 (Sophomore)	4.5	3.6	5.1		7.9	3.9	3.0	3.9		-	-	7.1	21.6	25.4
5. Grade 11 (Junior)	4.3	3.8	4.5		4.8	4.9	3.7	3.5		-	-	8.4	20.5	13.4
6. Grade 12 (Senior)	3.1	3.6	2.5		3.3	4.2	2.3	1.9		-	.2	13.5	11.4	6.0
Item 5610 N(Wtd)	2872	1354	1496		657	886	937	392		1347	517	209	488	38
A071: On how many different occasions have you taken psychedelics other than LSD...‡														
A071A: ...in your lifetime?														
1. 0 occasions	85.2	85.8	85.4		80.5	84.3	89.2	85.1		100.0	100.0	69.3	31.1	17.9
2. 1-2	5.3	4.1	6.3		5.3	6.4	3.2	8.1		-	-	30.7	17.5	14.0
3. 3-5	2.9	2.6	2.9		3.6	2.5	3.4	1.3		-	-	-	15.6	18.7
4. 6-9	1.5	1.4	1.6		2.2	1.3	1.2	1.5		-	-	-	8.4	8.7
5. 10-19	2.1	2.8	1.3		3.5	2.2	1.4	1.2		-	-	-	11.9	9.0
6. 20-39	1.3	1.4	1.0		2.5	.8	1.1	1.2		-	-	-	7.0	13.0
7. 40 or more	1.7	1.9	1.4		2.4	2.5	.4	1.6		-	-	-	8.4	18.6
Item 920 N(Wtd)	2856	1346	1488		652	876	933	394		1347	516	205	481	36
A071B: ...during the last 12 months?														
1. 0 occasions	89.1	88.6	90.3		84.3	88.4	92.1	91.5		100.0	100.0	84.9	47.2	30.0
2. 1-2	4.6	4.4	4.4		6.4	4.8	3.2	4.6		-	-	14.6	19.1	26.0
3. 3-5	2.2	2.3	2.2		2.0	2.3	2.7	1.4		-	-	.5	11.4	21.5
4. 6-9	1.4	1.5	1.3		3.1	.8	1.0	.9		-	-	-	7.8	7.0
5. 10-19	1.4	2.0	.7		2.1	2.2	.7	.5		-	-	-	8.2	4.5
6. 20-39	.7	.6	.8		1.5	.6	.3	.7		-	-	-	4.2	-
7. 40 or more	.5	.6	.4		.6	.9	.1	.5		-	-	-	2.1	10.9
Item 930 N(Wtd)	2854	1343	1489		649	874	936	394		1347	516	200	481	38

★ = excludes respondents for whom question was inappropriate.   ‡ = Wording changed in subsequent years.   * = less than .05 per cent.

CAUTION: Items were rearranged after 1975; changes in context may produce spurious ''trends'' (see page 12).

QUESTIONNAIRE FORM 1 1975	TOTAL	SEX			REGION					ILLICIT DRUG USE: LIFETIME				
		M	F		NE	NC	S	W		None	Mari-juana Only	Few Pills	More Pills	Any Her-oin
Weighted No. of Cases:	3038	1437	1568		688	943	979	428		1374	528	225	523	39
% of Weighted Total:	100.0	47.3	51.6		22.7	31.0	32.2	14.1		45.2	17.4	7.4	17.2	1.3
A071C: ...during the last 30 days?														
1. 0 occasions	94.9	93.8	96.3		91.7	94.5	96.9	96.0		100.0	100.0	98.1	72.8	71.0
2. 1-2	3.0	3.4	2.5		4.5	2.8	2.2	2.7		-	-	1.9	15.8	15.4
3. 3-5	.9	1.5	.3		2.3	.6	.4	.5		-	-	-	5.2	3.8
4. 6-9	.7	.9	.4		1.0	1.1	.4	.3		-	-	-	4.4	-
5. 10-19	.3	.2	.4		.2	.8	-	.2		-	-	-	1.1	6.7
6. 20-39	.1	.1	.1		.2	.1	*	.2		-	-	-	.6	1.2
7. 40 or more	.1	.1	-		.1	-	.1	.2		-	-	-	.3	1.9
Item 940 N(Wtd)	2851	1343	1486		648	876	933	394		1347	516	200	479	36

IF YOU HAVE NOT TAKEN ANY PSYCHEDELICS OTHER THAN LSD IN THE LAST TWELVE MONTHS, GO TO Q.A082.

	TOTAL	M	F		NE	NC	S	W		None	Mari-juana Only	Few Pills	More Pills	Any Her-oin
A077: When you take psychedelics other than LSD how high do you usually get?														
1. Not at all high	2.4	3.5	1.5		3.6	2.5	1.3	1.1		-	-	11.8	.4	9.2
2. A little high	7.9	6.8	9.5		7.9	6.5	11.0	6.0		-	-	28.3	5.4	5.1
3. Moderately high	35.5	35.1	33.4		35.3	37.9	29.9	40.9		-	-	20.3	38.4	28.0
4. Very high	54.1	54.6	55.6		53.2	53.1	57.8	51.9		-	-	39.5	55.8	57.7
Item 2700 N(Wtd) ★	309	153	142		101	105	71	32		-	-	34	249	26
A078: When you take psychedelics other than LSD how long do you usually stay high?														
1. Usually don't get high	2.0	2.7	1.5		2.6	2.5	1.3	-		-	-	9.3	.4	7.8
2. One to two hours	8.5	8.7	9.1		8.9	7.7	9.8	7.0		-	-	25.0	6.6	5.6
3. Three to six hours	41.3	43.9	38.0		42.1	38.1	41.4	49.1		-	-	29.4	44.4	26.3
4. Seven to 24 hours	45.6	42.5	48.0		42.4	48.7	47.5	40.9		-	-	21.9	47.3	59.0
5. More than 24 hours	2.7	2.2	3.4		4.1	3.0	-	3.1		-	-	14.4	1.2	1.4
Item 2710 N(Wtd) ★	309	153	142		100	106	72	31		-	-	33	250	26
A079: What psychedelics other than LSD have you taken during the last year? (Mark all that apply.)														
A. Mescaline	64.1	66.3	60.8		53.2	73.0	58.5	82.5		-	-	31.3	67.0	78.3
B. Peyote	13.7	18.0	9.0		15.9	10.1	9.6	28.6		-	-	-	15.0	19.0
C. Psilocybin	17.0	21.7	10.7		9.7	13.1	29.0	26.6		-	-	3.1	18.1	24.3
PCP @	-	-	-		-	-	-	-		-	-	-	-	-
D. THC ‡	79.3	86.5	72.5		92.7	77.6	74.6	52.8		-	-	75.4	80.2	76.6
E. Other	42.2	42.8	42.6		40.7	45.6	40.1	41.1		-	-	14.5	46.6	35.8
F. Don't know the names of some I have used	11.1	9.2	13.8		8.5	12.2	16.2	3.8		-	-	6.4	10.8	19.6
Item 2720-2780 N(Wtd) ★	308	152	141		101	104	72	31		-	-	33	248	26

The next questions are about AMPHETAMINES, which doctors sometimes prescribe to help people lose weight or to give people more energy. Drugstores are not supposed to sell them without a prescription.

Amphetamines are sometimes called: uppers, ups, speed, bennies, dexies, pep pills, diet pills. They include the following drugs: Benzedrine, Dexedrine, Methedrine, Ritalin, Preludin, Dexamyl, Methamphetamine.

	TOTAL	M	F		NE	NC	S	W		None	Mari-juana Only	Few Pills	More Pills	Any Her-oin
A085: Have you ever taken amphetamines because a doctor told you to use them?														
1. No	87.1	89.4	85.2		87.8	85.6	86.8	89.7		93.9	91.9	85.0	71.4	63.0
2. Yes, but I had already tried them on my own	4.4	3.3	5.4		3.4	5.1	4.6	4.1		-	.2	2.8	21.2	32.4
3. Yes, and it was the first time I took any	8.5	7.3	9.5		8.8	9.3	8.6	6.2		6.1	7.9	12.1	7.4	4.6
Item 2790 N(Wtd)	2827	1319	1486		660	855	916	395		1357	517	207	496	38

* = less than .05 per cent.   ★ = excludes respondents for whom question was inappropriate.   @ = category eliminated in this data collection.   ‡ = Wording changed in subsequent years.

CAUTION: Items were rearranged after 1975; changes in context may produce spurious "trends" (see page 12).

QUESTIONNAIRE FORM 1 1975	TOTAL	SEX			REGION					ILLICIT DRUG USE: LIFETIME				
		M	F		NE	NC	S	W		None	Mari- juana Only	Few Pills	More Pills	Any Her- oin
Weighted No. of Cases:	3038	1437	1568		688	943	979	428		1374	528	225	523	39
% of Weighted Total:	100.0	47.3	51.6		22.7	31.0	32.2	14.1		45.2	17.4	7.4	17.2	1.3

A086: When did you first try amphetamines without a doctor's orders? ‡

8. Never	81.3	84.2	79.5		80.9	77.3	87.9	75.4		100.0	99.4	62.7	16.1	22.4
1. Grade 6 or below	.1	.1	.2		.2	.1	.1	.3		-	.1	-	.3	4.3
2. Grade 7 or 8	.8	.7	.7		.4	.5	.6	2.2		-	-	1.1	2.7	15.3
3. Grade 9 (Freshman)	3.6	3.0	3.9		3.1	4.6	2.0	6.1		-	.2	4.7	16.4	28.4
4. Grade 10 (Sophomore)	4.8	3.5	5.7		6.5	4.9	2.9	6.3		-	-	8.7	22.3	17.1
5. Grade 11 (Junior)	6.2	5.5	6.6		5.4	8.2	4.5	7.3		-	-	11.4	29.7	8.5
6. Grade 12 (Senior)	3.1	2.9	3.4		3.5	4.4	2.0	2.4		-	.2	11.4	12.6	4.0
Item 5620 N(Wtd)	2824	1318	1485		657	856	917	396		1356	517	207	498	38

A087: On how many different occasions have you taken amphetamines on your own--that is, without a doctor telling you to take them...‡

A087A: ...in your lifetime?

1. 0 occasions	81.8	84.6	80.0		81.6	77.8	88.0	76.1		100.0	100.0	63.5	16.4	23.5
2. 1-2	4.1	3.2	4.8		4.4	5.0	2.6	5.2		-	-	36.5	8.0	4.8
3. 3-5	3.1	2.4	3.6		2.0	4.4	3.1	2.5		-	-	-	17.6	4.7
4. 6-9	2.4	2.2	2.5		2.0	3.1	1.4	3.8		-	-	-	13.2	8.0
5. 10-19	3.0	3.1	2.9		3.3	3.2	1.8	5.0		-	-	-	16.9	6.6
6. 20-39	2.1	1.4	2.4		2.3	1.9	1.4	3.6		-	-	-	10.6	17.8
7. 40 or more	3.5	3.0	3.8		4.3	4.5	1.7	3.8		-	-	-	17.4	34.6
Item 980 N(Wtd)	2808	1312	1475		651	851	915	392		1356	515	204	490	36

A087B: ...during the last 12 months?

1. 0 occasions	85.5	87.3	84.7		84.8	82.3	90.9	81.3		100.0	100.0	84.4	27.8	40.7
2. 1-2	3.5	3.0	3.9		2.7	4.2	3.3	3.9		-	-	15.6	13.2	6.8
3. 3-5	3.4	3.3	3.2		3.1	4.7	2.0	4.4		-	-	-	18.8	10.9
4. 6-9	2.8	2.4	2.9		3.1	3.2	1.6	4.0		-	-	-	15.4	8.2
5. 10-19	1.6	1.8	1.3		1.9	2.3	.6	1.9		-	-	-	8.6	9.5
6. 20-39	2.0	1.0	2.8		2.6	1.7	1.1	3.7		-	-	-	10.4	14.7
7. 40 or more	1.1	1.1	1.2		1.7	1.6	.4	.8		-	-	-	5.9	9.3
Item 990 N(Wtd)	2805	1307	1478		650	850	911	394		1356	515	202	487	37

A087C: ...during the last 30 days?

1. 0 occasions	92.0	92.8	91.7		90.9	89.6	95.6	90.8		100.0	100.0	97.3	58.0	60.4
2. 1-2	3.7	3.9	3.4		3.4	5.6	1.8	4.8		-	-	2.7	19.7	9.9
3. 3-5	1.8	2.0	1.5		2.6	2.1	1.1	1.7		-	-	-	10.1	6.9
4. 6-9	1.1	.4	1.8		1.6	1.5	.4	1.4		-	-	-	6.6	-
5. 10-19	.9	.7	1.2		1.3	1.0	.9	.6		-	-	-	4.2	15.7
6. 20-39	.2	.2	.3		.2	.3	.2	.5		-	-	-	1.0	5.1
7. 40 or more	.1	*	.1		.1	-	.1	.2		-	-	-	.3	1.9
Item 1000 N(Wtd)	2804	1307	1477		650	850	911	394		1356	515	203	487	37

‡ = Wording changed in subsequent years.   * = less than .05 per cent.

CAUTION: Items were rearranged after 1975; changes in context may produce spurious "trends" (see page 12).

QUESTIONNAIRE FORM 1 1975	TOTAL	SEX			REGION					ILLICIT DRUG USE: LIFETIME				
		M	F		NE	NC	S	W		None	Mari-juana Only	Few Pills	More Pills	Any Her-oin
Weighted No. of Cases:	3038	1437	1568		688	943	979	428		1374	528	225	523	39
% of Weighted Total:	100.0	47.3	51.6		22.7	31.0	32.2	14.1		45.2	17.4	7.4	17.2	1.3

IF YOU HAVE NOT TAKEN AMPHETAMINES IN THE LAST TWELVE MONTHS, GO TO Q.A097.

THE FOLLOWING QUESTIONS REFER ONLY TO TAKING AMPHETAMINES WITHOUT A DOCTOR'S ORDERS. ‡

A092: What have been the most important reasons for your taking amphetamines without a doctor's orders? (Mark all that apply.)

	TOTAL	M	F		NE	NC	S	W		None	Mari-juana Only	Few Pills	More Pills	Any Heroin
A. To experiment--to see what it's like	55.4	54.4	56.6		50.0	56.5	66.7	47.1		-	-	67.4	54.7	46.5
B. To relax or relieve tension	19.6	15.3	22.9		19.8	17.5	27.2	14.8		-	-	3.5	20.8	23.9
C. To feel good or get high	61.6	58.5	62.8		67.8	56.7	67.4	56.0		-	-	27.5	63.9	76.0
D. To seek deeper insights and understanding	8.2	7.6	8.3		11.7	7.8	4.9	8.3		-	-	3.6	9.0	4.3
E. To have a good time with my friends	38.5	36.8	39.5		40.6	34.6	40.3	41.8		-	-	18.8	40.1	43.3
F. To fit in with a group I like	3.6	5.1	2.7		3.2	5.1	2.9	1.8		-	-	-	4.2	-
G. To get away from my problems or troubles	10.3	7.2	13.3		12.0	7.1	16.4	7.6		-	-	-	11.6	6.3
H. Because of boredom, nothing else to do	16.1	17.1	16.4		12.3	18.9	18.1	13.2		-	-	6.3	16.9	18.5
I. Because of anger or frustration	5.5	5.2	5.8		6.8	5.6	7.7	1.0		-	-	1.9	5.6	9.6
K. To get through the day	13.3	14.8	12.3		10.6	14.4	14.0	13.7		-	-	7.8	13.8	11.4
L. To increase the effects of some other drug(s)	8.2	7.3	9.4		8.1	11.8	4.3	5.1		-	-	2.1	8.3	15.4
M. To decrease (offset) the effects of some other drug(s)	2.7	3.1	2.5		4.2	2.3	-	4.7		-	-	-	3.1	-
N. To stay awake	55.1	57.1	54.4		55.0	57.7	47.4	59.1		-	-	46.2	55.7	60.1
O. To get more energy	53.7	49.0	59.0		48.0	51.5	58.3	61.3		-	-	23.6	55.8	68.5
P. To help me lose weight	31.6	10.0	48.9		29.3	32.5	32.9	31.6		-	-	28.4	31.8	34.3
Q. Because I am "hooked"--I feel I have to have them	.7	-	1.3		-	.8	2.0	-		-	-	-	.8	-
Item 2940-3090 N(Wtd) ★	397	163	220		98	147	83	69		-	-	33	342	21

A093: When you take amphetamines, how high do you usually get?

	TOTAL	M	F		NE	NC	S	W		None	Mari-juana Only	Few Pills	More Pills	Any Heroin
1. Not at all high	4.6	2.9	5.9		5.7	5.1	2.9	4.1		-	-	20.5	3.3	-
2. A little high	26.4	30.1	25.1		13.3	36.0	26.0	24.8		-	-	30.9	26.7	14.4
3. Moderately high	44.6	43.0	43.1		45.1	40.5	51.3	44.5		-	-	24.3	46.6	43.0
4. Very high	15.1	14.8	15.9		24.9	11.6	12.2	12.5		-	-	8.4	14.3	39.2
5. I don't take them to get high	9.3	9.2	9.9		11.0	6.9	7.6	14.1		-	-	15.8	9.0	3.4
Item 3100 N(Wtd) ★	393	161	218		95	145	83	70		-	-	33	339	21

A094: When you take amphetamines how long do you usually stay high?

	TOTAL	M	F		NE	NC	S	W		None	Mari-juana Only	Few Pills	More Pills	Any Heroin
1. Usually don't get high	10.7	6.2	14.5		11.0	11.7	4.1	16.4		-	-	32.9	9.1	2.4
2. One to two hours	11.4	12.4	10.8		5.8	15.1	14.6	7.7		-	-	21.2	11.2	-
3. Three to six hours	37.0	40.4	35.3		24.4	42.5	40.1	39.2		-	-	25.0	38.5	29.4
4. Seven to 24 hours	37.0	37.0	36.1		53.4	26.7	38.0	34.7		-	-	13.7	38.1	58.1
5. More than 24 hours	3.8	4.0	3.3		5.4	3.9	3.1	1.9		-	-	7.3	3.0	10.1
Item 3110 N(Wtd)	395	161	221		97	147	82	69		-	-	33	341	21

A095: What amphetamines have you taken during the last year without a doctor's orders? (Mark all that apply.)

	TOTAL	M	F		NE	NC	S	W		None	Mari-juana Only	Few Pills	More Pills	Any Heroin
A. Benzedrine	31.1	35.8	26.7		36.6	26.1	30.1	35.5		-	-	1.5	32.0	59.4
B. Dexedrine	29.0	34.5	25.8		40.7	25.0	30.7	18.6		-	-	6.0	28.4	71.3
C. Methedrine	33.9	32.0	34.9		38.0	33.5	41.2	19.3		-	-	30.0	32.9	53.0
D. Ritalin	7.4	7.2	7.4		5.6	9.3	3.2	11.3		-	-	-	7.5	16.5
E. Preludin	6.0	7.5	4.6		1.7	8.3	9.1	3.4		-	-	-	5.7	18.8
F. Dexamyl	13.5	10.3	16.0		12.9	12.5	16.5	12.7		-	-	5.2	14.3	12.0
G. Methamphetamine	17.7	18.2	16.0		18.7	16.2	27.6	6.9		-	-	12.7	17.3	31.4
H. Other	28.7	27.9	28.6		26.4	31.3	30.2	24.3		-	-	3.1	30.9	29.7
I. Don't know the names of some amphetamines I have used	44.7	41.1	48.6		45.6	42.7	52.0	38.4		-	-	48.0	44.4	44.6
Item 3120-3200 N(Wtd) ★	389	155	221		96	144	83	66		-	-	30	337	22

‡ = Wording changed in subsequent years.   ★ = excludes respondents for whom question was inappropriate.

CAUTION: Items were rearranged after 1975; changes in context may produce spurious "trends" (see page 12).

QUESTIONNAIRE FORM 1 1975	TOTAL	SEX			REGION					ILLICIT DRUG USE: LIFETIME				
		M	F		NE	NC	S	W		None	Mari- juana Only	Few Pills	More Pills	Any Her- oin
Weighted No. of Cases:	3038	1437	1568		688	943	979	428		1374	528	225	523	39
% of Weighted Total:	100.0	47.3	51.6		22.7	31.0	32.2	14.1		45.2	17.4	7.4	17.2	1.3

A096: Have you ever tried to stop using amphetamines and found that you couldn't stop?

	TOTAL	M	F		NE	NC	S	W		None	Mari- juana Only	Few Pills	More Pills	Any Her- oin
1. Yes	2.2	.8	3.4		3.2	1.9	2.8	1.0		-	-	-	2.4	3.2
2. No	97.8	99.2	96.6		96.8	98.1	97.2	99.0		100.0	-	100.0	97.6	96.8
Item 3240 N(Wtd) ★	398	164	221		100	143	86	69		3	-	32	339	22

A097: Do you think you will be using amphetamines without a doctor's orders five years from now?

	TOTAL	M	F		NE	NC	S	W		None	Mari- juana Only	Few Pills	More Pills	Any Her- oin
1. I definitely will	1.1	1.2	.8		1.2	1.9	.4	.6		.2	.7	-	3.4	10.6
2. I probably will	5.4	4.7	5.9		5.8	4.9	3.2	11.0		.2	1.6	3.9	26.3	18.8
3. I probably will not	19.2	19.8	18.2		23.7	19.7	15.5	19.2		10.2	18.8	29.3	39.5	36.4
4. I definitely will not	74.4	74.3	75.1		69.3	73.5	80.9	69.2		89.4	78.9	66.8	30.7	34.2
Item 3250 N(Wtd)	2868	1340	1509		654	874	940	400		1338	501	210	481	37

The next questions are about QUAALUDES (Methaqualone), which are sometimes prescribed by doctors. Drugstores are not supposed to sell them without a prescription.

Quaaludes are sometimes called: soapers, quads.

A101: When did you first try quaaludes without a doctor's orders? ‡

	TOTAL	M	F		NE	NC	S	W		None	Mari- juana Only	Few Pills	More Pills	Any Her- oin
8. Never	93.9	94.2	94.1		92.9	93.1	93.7	97.6		100.0	100.0	92.4	69.4	41.5
1. Grade 6 or below	*	.1	-		.1	-	-	-		-	-	-	.2	-
2. Grade 7 or 8	.1	.2	.1		.2	.1	.2	-		-	-	-	.6	2.5
3. Grade 9 (Freshman)	.7	.6	.6		.2	1.2	.6	.4		-	-	-	3.4	10.4
4. Grade 10 (Sophomore)	1.8	1.7	1.9		2.0	2.2	1.6	1.0		-	-	2.8	8.8	18.4
5. Grade 11 (Junior)	2.0	1.9	1.9		2.4	1.9	2.4	.7		-	-	2.8	10.6	13.4
6. Grade 12 (Senior)	1.4	1.4	1.4		2.2	1.4	1.4	.4		-	-	2.0	7.0	13.7
Item 5630 N(Wtd)	2782	1310	1452		637	843	925	377		1353	516	205	439	34

A102: On how many different occasions have you taken quaaludes on your own--that is, without a doctor telling you to take them...‡

A102A: ...in your lifetime?

	TOTAL	M	F		NE	NC	S	W		None	Mari- juana Only	Few Pills	More Pills	Any Her- oin
1. 0 occasions	94.1	94.3	94.3		93.2	93.1	94.1	97.6		100.0	100.0	92.4	70.2	41.5
2. 1-2	2.0	1.8	2.2		1.6	3.0	1.9	.6		-	-	7.6	8.3	10.9
3. 3-5	1.4	1.2	1.5		2.8	.6	1.5	.2		-	-	-	8.3	5.5
4. 6-9	.8	.7	.8		.9	.7	.6	1.0		-	-	-	4.3	9.6
5. 10-19	.8	1.0	.6		.8	.5	1.3	.5		-	-	-	4.1	14.7
6. 20-39	.5	.5	.2		.4	.6	.6	.1		-	-	-	2.5	6.8
7. 40 or more	.5	.5	.5		.3	1.3	*	-		-	-	-	2.3	10.8
Item 1010 N(Wtd)	2777	1308	1449		636	843	921	377		1353	516	205	434	34

A102B: ...during the last 12 months?

	TOTAL	M	F		NE	NC	S	W		None	Mari- juana Only	Few Pills	More Pills	Any Her- oin
1. 0 occasions	95.9	95.8	96.4		94.5	95.4	96.5	98.3		100.0	100.0	96.6	79.4	51.6
2. 1-2	1.9	2.2	1.5		3.1	2.1	1.2	1.1		-	-	3.4	9.1	17.7
3. 3-5	.7	.5	.9		1.3	.4	.9	.2		-	-	-	4.0	9.8
4. 6-9	.8	1.0	.5		.6	.6	1.1	.4		-	-	-	3.9	11.8
5. 10-19	.3	.2	.3		.3	.4	.2	.1		-	-	-	1.7	1.9
6. 20-39	.2	.2	.3		.1	.6	.1	-		-	-	-	1.2	4.7
7. 40 or more	.1	.2	.1		-	.4	-	-		-	-	-	.7	2.5
Item 1020 N(Wtd)	2775	1307	1448		634	843	921	377		1353	516	205	432	34

★=excludes respondents for whom question was inappropriate.   ‡=Wording changed in subsequent years.   *=less than .05 per cent.
CAUTION: Items were rearranged after 1975; changes in context may produce spurious "trends" (see page 12).

QUESTIONNAIRE FORM 1 1975	TOTAL	SEX			REGION					ILLICIT DRUG USE: LIFETIME				
		M	F		NE	NC	S	W		None	Mari-juana Only	Few Pills	More Pills	Any Her-oin
Weighted No. of Cases:	3038	1437	1568		688	943	979	428		1374	528	225	523	39
% of Weighted Total:	100.0	47.3	51.6		22.7	31.0	32.2	14.1		45.2	17.4	7.4	17.2	1.3
A102C: ...during the last 30 days?														
1. 0 occasions	98.3	98.7	98.1		98.2	98.0	98.1	99.9		100.0	100.0	99.5	91.8	70.7
2. 1-2	.9	.7	1.0		1.1	.5	1.3	.1		-	-	.5	3.8	18.9
3. 3-5	.3	.3	.3		.2	.3	.6	.1		-	-	-	2.2	.6
4. 6-9	.1	.1	.1		.3	.2	-	-		-	-	-	.4	5.0
5. 10-19	.3	.1	.5		.1	.8	.1	-		-	-	-	1.6	4.8
6. 20-39	*	-	*		-	.1	-	-		-	-	-	.1	-
7. 40 or more	-	-	-		-	-	-	-		-	-	-	-	-
Item 1030 N(Wtd)	2773	1306	1447		632	843	921	377		1353	516	205	431	33

IF YOU HAVE NOT TAKEN QUAALUDES IN THE LAST TWELVE MONTHS, GO TO Q.A111.

THE FOLLOWING QUESTIONS REFER ONLY TO TAKING QUAALUDES WITHOUT A DOCTOR'S ORDERS. ‡

	TOTAL	M	F		NE	NC	S	W		None	Mari-juana Only	Few Pills	More Pills	Any Her-oin
A108: When you take quaaludes how high do you usually get?														
1. Not at all high	2.3	1.7	3.1		5.6	-	1.3	-		-	-	17.4	-	-
2. A little high	15.9	17.2	15.6		10.7	15.8	19.8	26.7		-	-	10.3	18.5	10.6
3. Moderately high	33.1	36.6	27.6		39.9	22.0	35.1	41.1		-	-	28.1	39.0	17.4
4. Very high	43.4	38.2	49.3		41.5	60.3	31.4	32.2		-	-	44.1	41.0	69.5
5. I don't take them to get high	5.3	6.3	4.5		2.4	2.0	12.3	-		-	-	-	1.5	2.6
Item 3260 N(Wtd) ★	110	57	50		37	33	35	6		-	-	6	82	17
A109: When you take quaaludes how long do you usually stay high?														
1. Usually don't get high	6.3	7.2	5.7		6.6	2.0	9.4	10.7		-	-	17.4	1.5	8.5
2. One to two hours	18.3	17.9	20.2		13.4	16.9	20.0	47.8		-	-	19.5	21.4	5.9
3. Three to six hours	48.7	48.8	50.7		42.7	60.9	48.9	14.8		-	-	42.9	48.2	61.9
4. Seven to 24 hours	24.9	24.9	20.8		35.5	18.2	21.7	15.6		-	-	9.8	27.2	23.7
5. More than 24 hours	1.8	1.2	2.7		1.8	2.0	-	11.1		-	-	10.3	1.6	-
Item 3270 N(Wtd) ★	107	55	48		36	33	33	6		-	-	6	81	17

The next questions are about BARBITURATES, which doctors sometimes prescribe to help people relax or get to sleep. Drugstores are not supposed to sell them without a prescription.

Barbiturates are sometimes called: downs, downers, goofballs, yellows, reds, blues, rainbows.

They include the following drugs: Phenobarbitol, Seconal, Tuinal, Nembutal, Luminal, Desbutal, Amytal.

	TOTAL	M	F		NE	NC	S	W		None	Mari-juana Only	Few Pills	More Pills	Any Her-oin
A114: Have you ever taken barbiturates because a doctor told you to use them?														
1. No	89.4	91.2	88.1		91.4	88.0	89.1	89.9		94.7	94.5	89.6	73.4	69.1
2. Yes, but I had already tried them on my own	2.6	2.1	3.1		2.1	3.1	2.4	2.9		-	.2	1.5	13.6	21.0
3. Yes, and it was the first time I took any	8.0	6.7	8.8		6.4	8.9	8.5	7.3		5.3	5.3	8.8	13.0	9.9
Item 3280 N(Wtd)	2774	1293	1465		638	837	908	392		1356	514	201	448	37

---

* = less than .05 per cent.   ‡ = Wording changed in subsequent years.   ★ = excludes respondents for whom question was inappropriate.

CAUTION: Items were rearranged after 1975; changes in context may produce spurious "trends" (see page 12).

QUESTIONNAIRE FORM 1 1975	TOTAL	SEX			REGION					ILLICIT DRUG USE: LIFETIME				
		M	F		NE	NC	S	W		None	Mari- juana Only	Few Pills	More Pills	Any Her- oin
Weighted No. of Cases:	3038	1437	1568		688	943	979	428		1374	528	225	523	39
% of Weighted Total:	100.0	47.3	51.6		22.7	31.0	32.2	14.1		45.2	17.4	7.4	17.2	1.3

A115: When did you first try barbiturates without a doctor's orders? ‡

	TOTAL	M	F		NE	NC	S	W		None	Mari- juana Only	Few Pills	More Pills	Any Her- oin
8. Never	88.7	89.8	88.2		86.1	89.1	90.5	87.9		100.0	100.0	84.7	43.1	24.2
1. Grade 6 or below	.1	.1	.1		.3	-	-	.1		-	-	.2	.2	2.4
2. Grade 7 or 8	.7	.8	.5		.9	.4	.4	1.5		-	-	.6	2.6	15.2
3. Grade 9 (Freshman)	2.0	1.8	2.0		2.9	2.2	1.3	1.4		-	-	.9	9.7	22.3
4. Grade 10 (Sophomore)	3.8	2.9	4.3		4.3	4.4	3.0	3.5		-	-	3.1	20.4	19.0
5. Grade 11 (Junior)	3.1	2.8	3.3		4.1	2.4	3.1	3.3		-	-	4.6	16.8	7.8
6. Grade 12 (Senior)	1.7	1.8	1.6		1.5	1.6	1.7	2.2		-	-	5.9	7.1	9.1
Item 5640 N(Wtd)	2770	1292	1461		637	832	909	392		1355	514	202	445	37

A116: On how many different occasions have you taken barbiturates on your own-- that is, without a doctor telling you to take them...‡

A116A: ...in your lifetime?

	TOTAL	M	F		NE	NC	S	W		None	Mari- juana Only	Few Pills	More Pills	Any Her- oin
1. 0 occasions	88.9	90.0	88.5		86.6	89.4	90.5	88.1		100.0	100.0	84.7	43.7	24.8
2. 1-2	3.3	3.7	3.0		3.9	3.4	3.0	2.8		-	-	15.3	13.2	6.0
3. 3-5	2.4	1.5	2.9		3.1	1.8	2.4	2.1		-	-	-	14.1	9.2
4. 6-9	1.2	.9	1.5		1.1	1.2	1.2	1.6		-	-	-	7.3	5.3
5. 10-19	1.4	1.2	1.6		2.1	.9	.8	3.0		-	-	-	8.3	8.5
6. 20-39	1.2	1.2	1.2		1.4	1.1	1.0	1.7		-	-	-	6.5	15.2
7. 40 or more	1.5	1.5	1.4		1.8	2.2	1.1	.7		-	-	-	7.0	30.9
Item 1040 N(Wtd)	2762	1289	1456		633	829	909	391		1355	513	202	439	36

A116B: ...during the last 12 months?

	TOTAL	M	F		NE	NC	S	W		None	Mari- juana Only	Few Pills	More Pills	Any Her- oin
1. 0 occasions	92.8	93.4	92.6		91.8	92.7	93.7	92.6		100.0	100.0	92.8	62.3	45.9
2. 1-2	2.8	2.4	2.8		2.3	3.3	2.8	2.5		-	-	7.2	13.5	9.4
3. 3-5	1.5	1.5	1.4		2.3	.9	1.2	1.9		-	-	-	8.1	13.8
4. 6-9	.9	.7	1.1		1.2	.6	.6	2.1		-	-	-	5.5	4.1
5. 10-19	1.0	.8	1.2		1.4	1.5	.6	.6		-	-	-	5.3	15.0
6. 20-39	.6	.6	.5		.7	.5	.8	.3		-	-	-	3.6	4.7
7. 40 or more	.4	.5	.2		.3	.6	.3	.2		-	-	-	1.7	7.1
Item 1050 N(Wtd)	2760	1287	1456		633	828	908	391		1355	513	202	437	36

A116C: ...during the last 30 days?

	TOTAL	M	F		NE	NC	S	W		None	Mari- juana Only	Few Pills	More Pills	Any Her- oin
1. 0 occasions	96.3	96.7	96.2		95.4	96.2	97.0	96.2		100.0	100.0	100.0	79.2	64.5
2. 1-2	1.8	1.8	1.7		2.6	1.5	1.5	1.7		-	-	-	10.7	10.4
3. 3-5	.8	.5	1.0		.6	.7	.7	1.4		-	-	-	4.2	8.2
4. 6-9	.7	.7	.6		.5	1.3	.2	.5		-	-	-	3.6	8.4
5. 10-19	.4	.2	.4		.6	.2	.4	.2		-	-	-	1.7	6.6
6. 20-39	.1	.1	.1		.1	.1	.1	-		-	-	-	.5	-
7. 40 or more	*	*	*		.1	-	.1	-		-	-	-	.1	2.0
Item 1060 N(Wtd)	2757	1288	1453		633	826	908	391		1355	513	202	436	35

‡=Wording changed in subsequent years.   *=less than .05 per cent.

CAUTION: Items were rearranged after 1975; changes in context may produce spurious "trends" (see page 12).

QUESTIONNAIRE FORM 1 1975	TOTAL	SEX			REGION					ILLICIT DRUG USE: LIFETIME				
		M	F		NE	NC	S	W		None	Mari-juana Only	Few Pills	More Pills	Any Her-oin
Weighted No. of Cases:	3038	1437	1568		688	943	979	428		1374	528	225	523	39
% of Weighted Total:	100.0	47.3	51.6		22.7	31.0	32.2	14.1		45.2	17.4	7.4	17.2	1.3

IF YOU HAVE NOT TAKEN BARBITURATES IN THE LAST TWELVE MONTHS, GO TO Q.A126.

THE FOLLOWING QUESTIONS REFER ONLY TO TAKING BARBITURATES WITHOUT A DOCTOR'S ORDERS. ‡

A121: What are the most important reasons for your taking barbiturates without a doctor's orders? (Mark all that apply.)

	TOTAL	M	F		NE	NC	S	W		None	Mari-juana Only	Few Pills	More Pills	Any Heroin
A. To experiment--to see what it's like	57.7	52.0	62.6		55.9	59.5	60.2	52.8		-	-	66.5	56.9	57.9
B. To relax or relieve tension	50.7	35.1	61.9		50.6	54.8	51.8	41.3		-	-	4.1	52.2	67.4
C. To feel good or get high	56.4	54.1	58.2		53.5	63.1	52.3	56.8		-	-	24.5	57.4	68.8
D. To seek deeper insights and understanding	5.6	5.4	4.6		4.2	6.5	8.3	1.6		-	-	-	5.7	8.1
E. To have a good time with my friends	42.2	39.9	43.5		40.9	50.4	41.1	31.7		-	-	25.9	42.3	51.7
F. To fit in with a group I like	2.4	3.7	.6		5.4	.9	.9	2.2		-	-	-	2.8	-
G. To get away from my problems or troubles	14.7	5.6	21.5		13.6	13.1	15.1	18.7		-	-	5.3	14.7	20.0
H. Because of boredom, nothing else to do	13.5	12.0	15.3		12.0	16.1	14.7	9.3		-	-	-	13.6	21.0
I. Because of anger or frustration	10.6	5.6	15.0		9.9	8.6	14.9	8.0		-	-	-	9.8	23.1
K. To get through the day	3.1	.8	5.1		5.0	3.0	1.8	2.2		-	-	-	3.2	4.7
L. To increase the effects of some other drug(s)	10.9	10.1	10.7		13.2	12.7	8.3	8.2		-	-	-	12.2	7.9
M. To decrease (offset) the effects of some other drug(s)	4.9	4.5	5.3		3.3	8.2	4.5	1.9		-	-	-	5.9	-
N. To get to sleep	29.5	21.9	36.6		31.9	26.7	30.4	28.5		-	-	11.1	32.4	17.9
O. Because I am "hooked"--I have to have them	-	-	-		-	-	-	-		-	-	-	-	-
Item 3450-3580 N(Wtd) ★	178	77	97		49	51	50	28		-	-	12	147	19

A122: When you take barbiturates how high do you usually get?

	TOTAL	M	F		NE	NC	S	W		None	Mari-juana Only	Few Pills	More Pills	Any Heroin
1. Not at all high	6.3	8.9	4.6		3.4	9.1	10.0	-		-	-	26.0	4.7	4.2
2. A little high	24.7	19.0	28.6		20.3	24.7	26.4	29.7		-	-	17.5	27.9	5.0
3. Moderately high	37.1	33.4	40.6		36.4	37.6	31.5	47.4		-	-	20.9	40.3	24.3
4. Very high	23.6	28.1	19.7		36.6	17.3	24.1	11.9		-	-	27.6	19.6	53.0
5. I don't take them to get high	8.2	10.6	6.6		3.4	11.3	8.0	11.0		-	-	8.0	7.5	13.5
Item 3590 N(Wtd) ★	178	77	97		49	51	50	28		-	-	14	146	18

A123: When you take barbiturates how long do you usually stay high?

	TOTAL	M	F		NE	NC	S	W		None	Mari-juana Only	Few Pills	More Pills	Any Heroin
1. Usually don't get high	13.1	16.6	10.9		6.7	18.0	17.5	8.0		-	-	39.1	12.0	6.3
2. One to two hours	20.0	20.3	19.8		21.6	24.2	19.4	10.3		-	-	26.9	19.1	22.6
3. Three to six hours	42.4	41.6	43.8		45.0	43.7	39.7	40.2		-	-	22.3	44.5	38.4
4. Seven to 24 hours	23.7	21.5	24.1		25.3	14.1	23.4	38.9		-	-	11.7	23.5	32.8
5. More than 24 hours	.8	-	1.4		1.3	-	-	2.6		-	-	-	.9	-
Item 3600 N(Wtd) ★	177	75	98		49	51	48	28		-	-	12	146	19

A124: What barbiturates have you taken during the last year without a doctor's orders? (Mark all that apply.)

	TOTAL	M	F		NE	NC	S	W		None	Mari-juana Only	Few Pills	More Pills	Any Heroin
A. Phenobarbital	47.4	44.6	48.3		57.9	49.5	48.6	23.3		-	-	25.2	46.5	66.7
B. Seconal	51.7	48.5	53.1		51.5	46.2	66.4	37.5		-	-	11.8	50.8	81.9
C. Tuinal	31.1	30.9	30.4		39.5	31.6	31.7	14.4		-	-	9.5	30.9	45.2
D. Nembutal	22.1	17.9	23.9		22.6	19.6	21.4	26.7		-	-	6.2	20.2	45.1
E. Luminal	8.0	2.0	10.5		6.5	8.1	2.9	18.7		-	-	-	8.0	12.1
F. Desbutal	3.7	3.8	2.4		8.9	1.1	3.1	-		-	-	-	3.8	4.6
G. Amytal	7.0	6.9	6.1		6.3	11.2	3.7	6.3		-	-	-	6.4	15.5
H. Adrenocal	3.8	2.9	3.3		6.5	4.4	2.6	-		-	-	-	3.4	9.0
I. Other	33.4	32.3	34.2		34.0	37.0	28.5	34.0		-	-	14.1	34.3	37.6
J. Don't know the names of some that I have used	45.6	47.1	46.2		54.3	38.6	49.1	37.1		-	-	44.7	46.6	38.5
Item 3610-3700 N(Wtd) ★	176	73	99		49	51	47	29		-	-	11	145	20

‡=Wording changed in subsequent years.   ★=excludes respondents for whom question was inappropriate.

CAUTION: Items were rearranged after 1975; changes in context may produce spurious "trends" (see page 12).

QUESTIONNAIRE FORM 1 1975	TOTAL	SEX			REGION					ILLICIT DRUG USE: LIFETIME				
		M	F		NE	NC	S	W		None	Mari- juana Only	Few Pills	More Pills	Any Her- oin
Weighted No. of Cases:	3038	1437	1568		688	943	979	428		1374	528	225	523	39
% of Weighted Total:	100.0	47.3	51.6		22.7	31.0	32.2	14.1		45.2	17.4	7.4	17.2	1.3

A125: Have you ever tried to stop using barbiturates and found that you couldn't stop?

	TOTAL	M	F		NE	NC	S	W		None	Marijuana Only	Few Pills	More Pills	Any Heroin
1. Yes	4.5	5.3	3.3		11.1	2.0	-	4.7		-	-	8.2	4.4	3.0
2. No	95.5	94.7	96.7		88.9	98.0	99.9	95.3		-	-	91.8	95.6	97.0
Item 3710 N(Wtd) ★	178	75	100		51	51	49	28		-	-	12	146	20

A126: Do you think you will be using barbiturates without a doctor's prescription five years from now?

	TOTAL	M	F		NE	NC	S	W		None	Marijuana Only	Few Pills	More Pills	Any Heroin
1. I definitely will	.6	.5	.5		.7	.6	.4	.6		-	1.0	.3	.9	9.4
2. I probably will	3.1	2.8	3.3		3.9	2.9	2.1	4.8		.1	.7	1.9	15.9	14.1
3. I probably will not	19.0	19.2	18.8		22.0	19.3	15.4	22.1		10.4	18.8	25.1	41.1	45.5
4. I definitely will not	77.3	77.5	77.4		73.4	77.2	82.1	72.5		89.5	79.5	72.7	42.1	31.0
Item 3720 N(Wtd)	2799	1305	1483		635	850	917	396		1329	496	204	435	36

The next questions are about TRANQUILIZERS, which doctors sometimes prescribe to calm people down, quiet their nerves, or relax their muscles.

They include the following drugs: Librium, Valium, Miltown ‡

A129: Have you ever taken tranquilizers because a doctor told you to use them?

	TOTAL	M	F		NE	NC	S	W		None	Marijuana Only	Few Pills	More Pills	Any Heroin
1. No	86.3	89.5	83.5		88.1	86.7	84.9	85.6		91.1	89.8	81.6	75.1	60.7
2. Yes, but I had already tried them on my own.	1.7	1.1	2.3		1.5	1.0	2.0	3.0		-	-	1.5	8.7	19.3
3. Yes, and it was the first time I took any	12.0	9.4	14.2		10.4	12.2	13.1	11.4		8.9	10.2	16.9	16.2	20.0
Item 3730 N(Wtd)	2730	1267	1453		631	819	896	383		1346	510	201	434	33

A130: When did you first try tranquilizers without a doctor's orders?

	TOTAL	M	F		NE	NC	S	W		None	Marijuana Only	Few Pills	More Pills	Any Heroin
8. Never	91.2	93.1	89.6		90.7	92.7	91.0	89.2		100.0	100.0	77.9	59.4	43.6
1. Grade 6 or below	.1	.2	.1		-	.1	.2	.2		-	-	-	.9	-
2. Grade 7 or 8	.5	.7	.4		.5	.1	.5	1.4		-	-	1.2	2.2	7.1
3. Grade 9 (Freshman)	1.5	1.0	2.0		1.4	1.5	1.6	1.7		-	-	3.4	7.0	15.0
4. Grade 10 (Sophomore)	2.0	1.5	2.4		2.6	1.9	2.3	1.0		*	-	3.8	10.3	9.5
5. Grade 11 (Junior)	2.8	2.3	3.3		3.2	2.6	2.8	2.8		-	-	5.1	13.5	19.9
6. Grade 12 (Senior)	1.8	1.1	2.3		1.7	1.1	1.6	3.8		-	-	8.6	6.8	4.8
Item 5650 N(Wtd)	2725	1263	1452		629	816	895	385		1346	509	201	431	33

A131: On how many different occasions have you taken tranquilizers on your own-- that is, without a doctor telling you to take them...‡

A131A: ...in your lifetime?

	TOTAL	M	F		NE	NC	S	W		None	Marijuana Only	Few Pills	More Pills	Any Heroin
1. 0 occasions	91.3	93.4	89.7		90.7	92.6	91.5	89.2		100.0	100.0	77.8	59.6	45.0
2. 1-2	3.1	2.7	3.6		2.4	2.9	3.2	4.7		-	-	22.2	9.3	2.2
3. 3-5	2.0	1.5	2.6		2.2	1.3	2.3	2.7		-	-	-	12.3	8.1
4. 6-9	1.0	.8	1.2		1.5	1.1	.7	1.0		-	-	-	6.4	2.0
5. 10-19	.8	.5	.9		.6	.6	.9	1.0		-	-	-	3.5	17.5
6. 20-39	.6	.5	.8		1.0	.3	.5	.7		-	-	-	2.5	19.2
7. 40 or more	1.1	.7	1.3		1.5	1.2	.8	.7		-	-	-	6.3	6.1
Item 1070 N(Wtd)	2720	1260	1450		629	816	890	385		1345	509	201	429	32

★=excludes respondents for whom question was inappropriate.   ‡=Wording changed in subsequent years.   *=less than .05 per cent.

CAUTION: Items were rearranged after 1975; changes in context may produce spurious "trends" (see page 12).

QUESTIONNAIRE FORM 1 1975	TOTAL	SEX			REGION					ILLICIT DRUG USE: LIFETIME				
		M	F		NE	NC	S	W		None	Mari-juana Only	Few Pills	More Pills	Any Her-oin
Weighted No. of Cases:	3038	1437	1568		688	943	979	428		1374	528	225	523	39
% of Weighted Total:	100.0	47.3	51.6		22.7	31.0	32.2	14.1		45.2	17.4	7.4	17.2	1.3
A131B: ...during the last 12 months?														
1. 0 occasions	93.9	95.9	92.2		92.6	94.4	94.7	93.1		100.0	100.0	91.6	68.7	57.0
2. 1-2	3.0	2.0	3.8		3.6	3.0	2.4	3.5		-	-	8.4	14.0	12.5
3. 3-5	1.2	1.1	1.3		1.8	.6	1.1	1.8		-	-	-	6.7	8.4
4. 6-9	.6	.4	.7		.3	.6	.7	.6		-	-	-	3.4	3.2
5. 10-19	.5	*	.9		.4	.5	.6	.5		-	-	-	2.1	14.1
6. 20-39	.5	.5	.5		.5	.6	.5	.3		-	-	-	3.3	-
7. 40 or more	.3	.1	.5		.8	.4	.1	.2		-	-	-	1.8	4.8
Item 1080 N(Wtd)	2718	1261	1447		628	815	890	385		1345	509	199	428	32
A131C: ...during the last 30 days?														
1. 0 occasions	97.4	98.7	96.4		96.9	97.6	97.5	97.5		100.0	100.0	98.4	86.1	79.1
2. 1-2	1.3	.9	1.7		1.8	.9	1.2	1.7		-	-	1.6	7.2	2.0
3. 3-5	.4	-	.7		-	.5	.5	.5		-	-	-	1.6	10.3
4. 6-9	.3	*	.5		.8	.2	.1	.2		-	-	-	1.8	3.8
5. 10-19	.4	.3	.4		.2	.6	.4	-		-	-	-	2.1	2.6
6. 20-39	.2	.1	.2		.1	.2	.1	.2		-	-	-	1.0	-
7. 40 or more	.1	.1	-		.2	-	.1	-		-	-	-	.3	2.2
Item 1090 N(Wtd)	2714	1259	1445		628	815	888	384		1345	509	198	426	32

IF YOU HAVE NOT TAKEN TRANQUILIZERS IN THE LAST TWELVE MONTHS, GO TO Q.A140.

THE FOLLOWING QUESTIONS REFER ONLY TO TAKING TRANQUILIZERS WITHOUT A DOCTOR'S ORDERS. ‡

	TOTAL	M	F		NE	NC	S	W		None	Mari-juana Only	Few Pills	More Pills	Any Her-oin
A136: What have been the most important reasons for your taking tranquilizers without a doctor's orders? (Mark all that apply.)														
A. To experiment--to see what it's like	38.7	30.4	43.2		31.4	42.0	40.1	43.1		-	-	41.8	38.0	45.5
B. To relax or relieve tension	66.1	53.1	72.0		57.6	69.0	76.7	54.8		-	-	65.9	63.8	88.0
C. To feel good or get high	42.5	44.9	40.6		56.8	48.0	24.2	42.3		-	-	12.3	44.7	58.8
D. To seek deeper insights and understanding	4.9	2.6	4.8		4.2	8.2	4.8	-		-	-	-	6.0	-
E. To have a good time with my friends	25.1	28.4	22.6		31.3	23.2	25.4	16.6		-	-	12.4	24.1	52.1
F. To fit in with a group I like	.7	.9	.6		-	1.1	-	2.9		-	-	-	.9	-
G. To get away from my problems or troubles	15.9	4.7	21.5		16.5	22.4	14.5	4.6		-	-	5.0	18.1	6.6
H. Because of boredom, nothing else to do	8.9	7.3	9.8		8.2	12.0	6.9	8.3		-	-	-	7.8	31.8
I. Because of anger or frustration	7.4	3.3	9.5		6.0	11.9	5.8	4.6		-	-	17.6	6.1	10.2
K. To get through the day	4.8	1.3	6.5		6.2	3.6	5.4	2.9		-	-	-	5.8	-
L. To increase the effects of some other drug(s)	5.6	1.2	6.6		3.1	10.1	3.8	5.5		-	-	5.0	6.3	-
M. To decrease (offset) the effects of some other drug(s)	2.0	.9	2.6		1.6	4.7	1.0	-		-	-	-	2.5	-
N. To get to sleep	32.0	16.3	40.1		42.1	11.8	38.2	40.1		-	-	21.9	34.5	21.7
O. Because I am "hooked"--I have to have them	.3	-	.4		1.1	-	-	-		-	-	-	.4	-
Item 3910-4040 N(Wtd) ★	151	49	101		41	43	45	22		-	-	14	124	12
A137: When you take tranquilizers how high do you usually get?														
1. Not at all high	11.1	8.6	12.4		8.6	15.4	11.8	7.0		-	-	35.3	8.1	7.9
2. A little high	30.1	32.6	29.4		20.9	27.8	40.5	30.0		-	-	30.5	33.0	6.2
3. Moderately high	28.9	34.9	25.4		38.2	26.9	22.9	27.9		-	-	5.1	29.4	53.5
4. Very high	11.9	10.4	12.7		10.0	19.5	6.2	13.1		-	-	15.6	10.4	23.7
5. I don't take them to get high	17.9	13.4	20.2		22.4	10.4	18.6	21.9		-	-	13.6	19.1	8.7
Item 4050 N(Wtd) ★	153	47	105		42	41	47	23		-	-	14	124	13

*=less than .05 per cent.   ‡=Wording changed in subsequent years.   ★=excludes respondents for whom question was inappropriate.

CAUTION: Items were rearranged after 1975; changes in context may produce spurious "trends" (see page 12).

QUESTIONNAIRE FORM 1 1975	TOTAL	SEX				REGION					ILLICIT DRUG USE: LIFETIME				
		M	F			NE	NC	S	W		None	Mari- juana Only	Few Pills	More Pills	Any Her- oin
Weighted No. of Cases:	3038	1437	1568			688	943	979	428		1374	528	225	523	39
% of Weighted Total:	100.0	47.3	51.6			22.7	31.0	32.2	14.1		45.2	17.4	7.4	17.2	1.3
A138: When you take tranquilizers how long do you usually stay high?															
1. Usually don't get high	29.9	25.0	32.5			28.2	25.1	36.5	27.7		-	-	53.8	27.6	16.6
2. One to two hours	17.6	17.9	17.8			14.4	17.1	20.9	18.0		-	-	16.1	18.3	15.9
3. Three to six hours	42.9	47.5	41.3			42.1	54.6	37.9	34.5		-	-	30.1	43.8	54.3
4. Seven to 24 hours	9.5	9.5	8.4			15.3	3.2	4.8	19.8		-	-	-	10.4	13.3
5. More than 24 hours	-	-	-			-	-	-	-		-	-	-	-	-
Item 4060 N(Wtd) ★	152	48	103			42	40	47	23		-	-	14	124	13
A139: Have you ever tried to stop using tranquilizers and found that you couldn't stop?															
1. Yes	2.8	-	2.9			4.0	4.6	-	3.0		-	-	-	3.4	-
2. No	97.2	100.0	97.1			96.0	95.4	99.9	97.0		-	-	100.0	96.6	100.0
Item 4170 N(Wtd) ★	156	49	106			43	41	49	24		-	-	14	126	13
A140: Do you think you will be using tranquilizers without a doctor's orders five years from now?															
1. I definitely will	.4	.3	.4			.7	.2	.4	.4		.2	.7	-	.7	2.6
2. I probably will	3.4	2.8	4.0			2.8	3.3	2.9	5.8		.2	.9	5.1	14.1	18.5
3. I probably will not	25.5	25.4	25.4			28.4	27.0	20.1	30.1		15.9	25.4	31.4	47.8	44.9
4. I definitely will not	70.7	71.5	70.2			68.1	69.5	76.6	63.7		83.7	73.0	63.5	37.4	34.0
Item 4180 N(Wtd)	2819	1313	1498			634	850	929	405		1340	504	209	431	34
The next questions are about COCAINE, which is sometimes called "coke".															
A143: When did you first try cocaine?															
8. Never	93.1	91.2	95.0			91.0	94.2	94.6	90.5		100.0	99.9	79.8	70.0	37.9
1. Grade 6 or below	*	.1	-			.1	-	-	-		-	-	-	.2	-
2. Grade 7 or 8	.2	.2	.2			.5	-	.1	.4		-	-	.3	.7	5.9
3. Grade 9 (Freshman)	.6	.7	.5			.7	.5	.3	1.2		-	-	.8	2.2	14.5
4. Grade 10 (Sophomore)	1.2	1.1	1.2			1.8	1.0	1.0	1.3		-	-	1.4	6.4	11.1
5. Grade 11 (Junior)	2.8	3.8	1.7			3.1	2.6	2.0	4.3		-	-	9.1	12.0	17.4
6. Grade 12 (Senior)	2.2	2.9	1.5			2.8	1.7	2.0	2.4		-	.1	8.6	8.6	13.2
Item 5660 N(Wtd)	2805	1308	1489			647	852	914	391		1345	514	207	434	35
A144: On how many different occasions have you taken cocaine...‡															
A144A: ...in your lifetime?															
1. 0 occasions	93.3	91.5	95.2			91.3	94.4	94.9	90.6		100.0	100.0	80.3	70.7	39.0
2. 1-2	3.8	5.3	2.4			4.3	3.5	3.0	5.3		-	-	19.7	14.1	13.0
3. 3-5	1.1	1.6	.8			1.7	.8	1.0	1.2		-	-	-	7.0	4.9
4. 6-9	.5	.3	.6			1.2	.4	.2	.3		-	-	-	2.8	6.9
5. 10-19	.5	.5	.6			.6	.1	.6	1.2		-	-	-	2.5	12.3
6. 20-39	.3	.4	.2			.2	.4	.1	.6		-	-	-	1.1	10.8
7. 40 or more	.4	.5	.3			.7	.5	.1	.7		-	-	-	1.8	13.1
Item 950 N(Wtd)	2797	1304	1485			645	850	912	390		1345	513	206	430	34
A144B: ...during the last 12 months?															
1. 0 occasions	95.4	94.2	96.5			93.8	96.2	96.5	93.4		100.0	100.0	90.7	78.5	46.0
2. 1-2	3.0	4.1	2.0			4.0	2.5	2.5	3.3		-	-	9.3	14.3	7.3
3. 3-5	.8	.8	.7			1.2	.4	.9	.8		-	-	-	3.2	22.7
4. 6-9	.3	.3	.2			.1	.4	*	1.0		-	-	-	1.5	5.0
5. 10-19	.3	.1	.3			.5	.2	*	.5		-	-	-	1.0	10.8
6. 20-39	.1	.3	.1			.3	.1	-	.4		-	-	-	.7	3.6
7. 40 or more	.2	.2	.1			.1	.2	-	.5		-	-	-	.7	4.6
Item 960 N(Wtd)	2796	1304	1484			644	850	912	390		1345	513	205	429	34

★=excludes respondents for whom question was inappropriate.   *=less than .05 per cent.   ‡=Wording changed in subsequent years.

CAUTION: Items were rearranged after 1975; changes in context may produce spurious "trends" (see page 12).

QUESTIONNAIRE FORM 1 1975	TOTAL	SEX			REGION					ILLICIT DRUG USE: LIFETIME				
		M	F		NE	NC	S	W		None	Mari-juana Only	Few Pills	More Pills	Any Her-oin
Weighted No. of Cases:	3038	1437	1568		688	943	979	428		1374	528	225	523	39
% of Weighted Total:	100.0	47.3	51.6		22.7	31.0	32.2	14.1		45.2	17.4	7.4	17.2	1.3

A144C: ...during the last 30 days?

	TOTAL	M	F		NE	NC	S	W		None	Mari-juana Only	Few Pills	More Pills	Any Her-oin
1. 0 occasions	98.2	98.0	98.4		97.4	98.7	98.7	97.1		100.0	100.0	98.8	91.4	66.7
2. 1-2	1.1	1.4	.8		1.4	.9	1.2	1.0		-	-	1.2	5.5	14.3
3. 3-5	.3	.1	.4		.5	-	.1	.9		-	-	-	1.5	4.3
4. 6-9	.2	.2	.1		.3	-	-	.9		-	-	-	.9	4.5
5. 10-19	.1	.1	.2		.3	.3	-	-		-	-	-	.1	10.2
6. 20-39	-	-	-		-	-	-	-		-	-	-	-	-
7. 40 or more	.1	.1	.1		.1	.1	-	.2		-	-	-	.5	-
Item 970 N(Wtd)	2793	1303	1483		645	847	912	389		1345	513	203	428	34

IF YOU HAVE NOT TAKEN COCAINE IN THE LAST TWELVE MONTHS, GO TO Q.A154.

A149: What have been the most important reasons for your taking cocaine? (Mark all that apply.)

	TOTAL	M	F		NE	NC	S	W		None	Mari-juana Only	Few Pills	More Pills	Any Her-oin
A. To experiment--to see what it's like	68.0	60.6	78.2		45.1	81.3	83.4	64.4		-	-	87.1	65.2	60.5
B. To relax or relieve tension	22.2	16.5	29.5		15.1	25.0	32.1	16.2		-	-	2.3	20.3	51.7
C. To feel good or get high	71.7	66.3	79.9		81.7	51.3	72.7	82.4		-	-	10.5	84.4	84.8
D. To seek deeper insights and understanding	6.4	9.8	1.5		3.6	4.4	13.0	5.0		-	-	-	8.1	6.6
E. To have a good time with my friends	38.6	30.5	49.9		44.7	32.3	41.2	34.8		-	-	11.6	41.3	56.4
F. To fit in with a group I like	1.8	1.3	2.6		-	3.9	3.0	-		-	-	2.3	2.1	-
G. To get away from my problems or troubles	2.2	2.1	2.6		4.3	-	-	5.0		-	-	2.1	1.5	5.7
H. Because of boredom, nothing else to do	4.5	5.3	3.5		-	9.7	4.3	4.8		-	-	-	3.3	15.6
I. Because of anger or frustration	2.7	4.5	-		-	8.7	-	1.9		-	-	2.1	3.4	-
K. To get through the day	3.1	3.6	2.3		-	7.6	-	5.4		-	-	-	4.0	-
L. To increase the effects of some other drug(s)	4.1	4.0	4.5		2.4	2.3	2.4	11.3		-	-	-	4.2	8.7
M. To decrease (offset) the effects of some other drug(s)	1.1	1.0	1.2		-	2.3	-	2.3		-	-	-	1.6	-
To stay awake @	-	-	-		-	-	-	-		-	-	-	-	-
N. To get more energy	13.0	8.2	20.7		8.8	12.2	15.7	16.9		-	-	3.8	11.6	30.5
O. Because I am "hooked"--I have to have it	-	-	-		-	-	-	-		-	-	-	-	-
Item 4370-4510 N(Wtd) ★	116	69	46		33	30	29	23		-	-	20	78	17

A150: When you take cocaine how high do you usually get?

	TOTAL	M	F		NE	NC	S	W		None	Mari-juana Only	Few Pills	More Pills	Any Her-oin
1. Not at all high	3.5	2.9	4.5		6.1	3.4	3.1	-		-	-	14.9	.6	2.4
2. A little high	18.8	20.7	16.3		16.1	25.4	16.1	17.4		-	-	30.6	18.7	5.5
3. Moderately high	40.1	40.2	38.1		38.5	36.5	48.7	36.9		-	-	32.8	41.6	40.8
4. Very high	36.6	34.3	41.1		39.2	34.7	32.1	40.3		-	-	17.7	39.1	48.9
5. I don't take it to get high	1.1	1.8	-		-	-	-	5.4		-	-	4.0	-	2.5
Item 4520 N(Wtd) ★	119	72	46		36	31	28	24		-	-	22	79	18

A151: When you take cocaine how long do you usually stay high?

	TOTAL	M	F		NE	NC	S	W		None	Mari-juana Only	Few Pills	More Pills	Any Her-oin
1. Usually don't get high	3.4	2.9	4.5		6.1	3.4	3.1	-		-	-	14.9	.6	2.4
2. One to two hours	31.0	36.6	22.9		25.1	26.9	33.3	41.7		-	-	43.0	29.6	20.9
3. Three to six hours	47.5	42.2	54.3		41.0	54.2	53.2	41.7		-	-	32.4	48.1	63.9
4. Seven to 24 hours	14.4	16.0	12.3		23.4	11.6	5.9	14.8		-	-	7.8	16.7	12.8
5. More than 24 hours	3.7	2.3	6.0		4.4	3.8	4.4	1.7		-	-	2.0	5.0	-
Item 4530 N(Wtd) ★	120	73	46		36	31	28	25		-	-	22	79	18

A152: Have you ever tried to stop using cocaine and found that you couldn't stop?

	TOTAL	M	F		NE	NC	S	W		None	Mari-juana Only	Few Pills	More Pills	Any Her-oin
1. Yes	1.1	.6	1.8		-	-	4.4	-		-	-	2.2	1.0	-
2. No	98.9	99.4	98.2		100.0	99.9	95.6	99.9		-	-	97.8	99.0	100.0
Item 4540 N(Wtd) ★	118	72	44		35	29	29	24		-	-	21	78	18

@ = category eliminated in this data collection.   ★ = excludes respondents for whom question was inappropriate.

CAUTION: Items were rearranged after 1975; changes in context may produce spurious "trends" (see page 12).

QUESTIONNAIRE FORM 1 1975	TOTAL	SEX			REGION					ILLICIT DRUG USE: LIFETIME				
		M	F		NE	NC	S	W		None	Mari- juana Only	Few Pills	More Pills	Any Her- oin
Weighted No. of Cases:	3038	1437	1568		688	943	979	428		1374	528	225	523	39
% of Weighted Total:	100.0	47.3	51.6		22.7	31.0	32.2	14.1		45.2	17.4	7.4	17.2	1.3

A153: What methods have you used for taking cocaine? (Mark all that apply.)

A. Sniffing or "snorting"	84.8	85.8	82.9		78.4	86.8	80.4	96.8		-	-	80.8	87.2	78.7
B. Smoking	21.9	24.2	18.9		16.8	34.1	21.9	13.8		-	-	9.0	28.5	8.8
C. Injection	3.1	3.2	3.1		5.1	2.2	1.5	3.5		-	-	-	.9	17.0
D. By mouth	23.5	20.1	27.6		16.4	30.0	33.8	13.4		-	-	28.2	19.6	35.9
E. Other	1.9	2.1	1.5		-	5.0	-	2.8		-	-	-	1.9	3.9
Item 4550-4590 N(Wtd) ★	121	73	46		36	31	29	25		-	-	22	80	18

A154: Do you think you will be using cocaine five years from now?

1. I definitely will	.7	1.0	.4		.9	.7	.4	1.3		-	.8	-	2.0	14.1
2. I probably will	3.0	2.8	3.1		3.9	2.3	2.1	5.2		.1	.5	4.2	14.9	19.2
3. I probably will not	15.1	17.8	12.7		17.9	14.6	11.7	19.7		6.6	16.1	22.3	36.3	38.9
4. I definitely will not	81.2	78.4	83.8		77.3	82.4	85.8	73.8		93.3	82.6	73.5	46.8	27.8
Item 4600 N(Wtd)	2798	1305	1487		629	848	921	400		1335	497	210	424	36

The next questions are about HEROIN.

Heroin is sometimes called: smack, horse, skag.

A157: When did you first try heroin?

8. Never	98.6	98.4	98.8		98.2	99.0	98.7	98.2		100.0	100.0	100.0	100.0	-
1. Grade 6 or below	.1	.1	-		.2	.1	-	-		-	-	-	-	4.7
2. Grade 7 or 8	.1	.1	.1		.2	-	-	.3		-	-	-	-	5.7
3. Grade 9 (Freshman)	.1	.1	.1		.2	.1	.1	-		-	-	-	-	5.9
4. Grade 10 (Sophomore)	.5	.4	.5		.4	.7	.4	.3		-	-	-	-	35.1
5. Grade 11 (Junior)	.2	.2	.3		.3	.1	.4	.2		-	-	-	-	17.9
6. Grade 12 (Senior)	.4	.6	.3		.7	.1	.3	1.0		-	-	-	-	30.6
Item 5670 N(Wtd)	2786	1292	1486		638	836	918	394		1339	510	206	421	39

A158: On how many different occasions have you taken heroin...‡

A158A: ...in your lifetime?

1. 0 occasions	98.6	98.4	98.8		98.2	99.0	98.7	98.2		100.0	100.0	100.0	100.0	-
2. 1-2	.8	.8	.6		.9	.6	.6	1.3		-	-	-	-	53.8
3. 3-5	.3	.1	.4		.3	.3	.3	.2		-	-	-	-	18.9
4. 6-9	.1	.1	.1		.2	-	.1	-		-	-	-	-	5.2
5. 10-19	.1	.2	*		.1	-	.1	.1		-	-	-	-	5.8
6. 20-39	.1	.1	*		.2	.1	-	.2		-	-	-	-	6.4
7. 40 or more	.1	.2	.1		.2	-	.2	.2		-	-	-	-	10.0
Item 1100 N(Wtd)	2786	1292	1485		638	836	918	394		1339	510	206	421	39

A158B: ...during the last 12 months?

1. 0 occasions	99.1	98.9	99.3		98.6	99.5	99.4	98.7		100.0	100.0	100.0	100.0	38.6
2. 1-2	.6	.8	.4		1.1	.2	.4	1.0		-	-	-	-	43.0
3. 3-5	.1	.1	.2		.3	.2	-	-		-	-	-	-	8.2
4. 6-9	*	.1	-		-	.1	-	.1		-	-	-	-	3.1
5. 10-19	*	-	*		-	-	.1	.1		-	-	-	-	1.8
6. 20-39	*	*	*		-	-	*	.1		-	-	-	-	2.2
7. 40 or more	*	.1	-		-	-	.1	-		-	-	-	-	2.9
Item 1110 N(Wtd)	2786	1292	1485		638	836	918	394		1339	510	206	421	39

A158C: ...during the last 30 days?

1. 0 occasions	99.7	99.7	99.7		99.9	99.7	99.6	99.5		100.0	100.0	100.0	100.0	76.8
2. 1-2	.2	.1	.3		.1	.2	.2	.4		-	-	-	-	14.8
3. 3-5	*	.1	-		-	.1	-	.1		-	-	-	-	3.1
4. 6-9	*	-	*		-	-	.1	-		-	-	-	-	1.3
5. 10-19	*	-	*		-	-	*	-		-	-	-	-	1.1
6. 20-39	-	-	-		-	-	-	-		-	-	-	-	-
7. 40 or more	*	.1	-		-	-	.1	-		-	-	-	-	2.9
Item 1120 N(Wtd)	2786	1292	1485		638	836	918	394		1339	510	206	421	39

★ = excludes respondents for whom question was inappropriate.   ‡ = Wording changed in subsequent years.   * = less than .05 per cent.

CAUTION: Items were rearranged after 1975; changes in context may produce spurious "trends" (see page 12).

QUESTIONNAIRE FORM 1 1975	TOTAL	SEX			REGION					ILLICIT DRUG USE: LIFETIME				
		M	F		NE	NC	S	W		None	Mari- juana Only	Few Pills	More Pills	Any Her- oin
Weighted No. of Cases:	3038	1437	1568		688	943	979	428		1374	528	225	523	39
% of Weighted Total:	100.0	47.3	51.6		22.7	31.0	32.2	14.1		45.2	17.4	7.4	17.2	1.3

IF YOU HAVE NOT TAKEN HEROIN IN THE LAST TWELVE MONTHS, GO TO Q.A168.

A163: What have been the most important reasons for your taking heroin? (Mark all that apply.)

	TOTAL	M	F		NE	NC	S	W		None	Mari- juana Only	Few Pills	More Pills	Any Her- oin
A. To experiment--to see what it's like	73.2	67.1	80.4		78.0	99.9	75.2	36.3		-	-	-	-	73.2
B. To relax or relieve tension	27.9	21.5	35.5		24.3	44.0	37.8	9.2		-	-	-	-	27.9
C. To feel good or get high	43.9	24.2	67.1		43.0	67.4	47.2	20.4		-	-	-	-	43.9
D. To seek deeper insights and understanding	7.3	13.4	-		-	23.4	-	15.8		-	-	-	-	7.3
E. To have a good time with my friends	18.7	21.9	15.0		9.9	23.4	-	54.4		-	-	-	-	18.7
F. To fit in with a group I like	7.6	14.1	-		-	-	-	39.3		-	-	-	-	7.6
G. To get away from my problems or troubles	4.5	-	9.7		11.1	-	-	-		-	-	-	-	4.5
H. Because of boredom, nothing else to do	-	-	-		-	-	-	-		-	-	-	-	-
I. Because of anger or frustration	-	-	-		-	-	-	-		-	-	-	-	-
K. To get through the day	-	-	-		-	-	-	-		-	-	-	-	-
L. To increase the effects of some other drug(s)	4.0	-	8.6		9.9	-	-	-		-	-	-	-	4.0
M. To decrease (offset) the effects of some other drug(s)	-	-	-		-	-	-	-		-	-	-	-	-
N. Because I am "hooked"--I have to have it	5.7	10.5	-		-	-	25.4	-		-	-	-	-	5.7
Item 4800-4920 N(Wtd) ★	20	11	9		8	4	5	4		-	-	-	-	20

A164: When you take heroin how high do you usually get?

	TOTAL	M	F		NE	NC	S	W		None	Mari- juana Only	Few Pills	More Pills	Any Her- oin
1. Not at all high	5.3	9.7	-		-	-	13.8	9.2		-	-	-	-	5.3
2. A little high	-	-	-		-	-	-	-		-	-	-	-	-
3. Moderately high	29.2	49.0	4.8		38.1	-	17.5	54.6		-	-	-	-	29.2
4. Very high	65.5	41.3	95.2		61.9	99.9	68.7	36.2		-	-	-	-	65.5
5. I don't take it to get high	-	-	-		-	-	-	-		-	-	-	-	-
Item 4930 N(Wtd) ★	20	11	9		7	4	5	4		-	-	-	-	20

A165: When you take heroin how long do you usually stay high?

	TOTAL	M	F		NE	NC	S	W		None	Mari- juana Only	Few Pills	More Pills	Any Her- oin
1. Usually don't get high	5.3	9.7	-		-	-	13.8	9.3		-	-	-	-	5.3
2. One to two hours	15.2	27.6	-		24.4	-	24.7	-		-	-	-	-	15.2
3. Three to six hours	45.1	44.4	45.9		63.1	67.4	10.0	36.3		-	-	-	-	45.1
4. Seven to 24 hours	34.4	18.3	54.1		12.5	32.6	51.5	54.4		-	-	-	-	34.4
5. More than 24 hours	-	-	-		-	-	-	-		-	-	-	-	-
Item 4940 N(Wtd) ★	20	11	9		7	4	5	4		-	-	-	-	20

A166: Have you ever tried to stop using heroin and found that you couldn't stop?

	TOTAL	M	F		NE	NC	S	W		None	Mari- juana Only	Few Pills	More Pills	Any Her- oin
1. Yes	5.5	10.5	-		-	-	22.8	-		-	-	-	-	5.5
2. No	94.5	89.5	100.0		100.0	99.9	77.2	99.9		-	-	-	-	94.5
Item 4950 N(Wtd) ★	21	11	10		8	4	5	4		-	-	-	-	21

A167: What methods have you used for taking heroin? (Mark all that apply.)

	TOTAL	M	F		NE	NC	S	W		None	Mari- juana Only	Few Pills	More Pills	Any Her- oin
A. Sniffing or "snorting"	54.0	45.7	63.2		79.0	44.0	58.7	5.3		-	-	-	-	54.0
B. Smoking	7.8	7.4	8.2		19.7	-	-	-		-	-	-	-	7.8
C. Injection	34.4	34.8	34.0		22.2	23.4	27.5	78.9		-	-	-	-	34.4
D. By mouth	16.4	5.7	28.2		-	76.6	-	15.8		-	-	-	-	16.4
E. Other	3.4	6.4	-		-	-	13.8	-		-	-	-	-	3.4
Item 4960-5000 N(Wtd) ★	21	11	10		8	4	5	4		-	-	-	-	21

★=excludes respondents for whom question was inappropriate.

CAUTION: Items were rearranged after 1975; changes in context may produce spurious "trends" (see page 12).

QUESTIONNAIRE FORM 1 1975	TOTAL	SEX				REGION					ILLICIT DRUG USE: LIFETIME				
		M	F			NE	NC	S	W		None	Mari- juana Only	Few Pills	More Pills	Any Her- oin
Weighted No. of Cases:	3038	1437	1568			688	943	979	428		1374	528	225	523	39
% of Weighted Total:	100.0	47.3	51.6			22.7	31.0	32.2	14.1		45.2	17.4	7.4	17.2	1.3

A168: Do you think you will be using heroin five years from now?

	TOTAL	M	F			NE	NC	S	W		None	Mari- juana Only	Few Pills	More Pills	Any Heroin
1. I definitely will	.6	.7	.4			.4	.5	.6	.8		.1	.8	–	1.3	2.9
2. I probably will	.3	.3	.3			.4	.4	.2	.3		–	.1	–	.9	13.1
3. I probably will not	8.2	9.1	7.3			9.3	7.5	8.3	8.0		5.0	7.7	8.0	15.4	46.6
4. I definitely will not	90.9	89.9	92.0			89.8	91.6	90.9	90.8		94.8	91.3	92.0	82.4	37.5
Item 5010 N(Wtd)	2770	1289	1475			621	838	916	396		1331	498	202	407	37

The next questions are about NARCOTICS OTHER THAN HEROIN which are sometimes prescribed by doctors. Drugstores are not supposed to sell them without a prescription.

These include: methadone, opium, morphine, codeine, demerol, paregoric, talwin, laudanum.

A171: Have you ever taken any narcotics other than heroin because a doctor told you to use them?

	TOTAL	M	F			NE	NC	S	W		None	Mari- juana Only	Few Pills	More Pills	Any Heroin
1. No	89.0	90.1	88.0			89.7	90.8	88.5	85.3		92.0	91.3	86.9	80.8	71.3
2. Yes, but I had already tried them on my own	1.1	1.1	1.0			.6	1.3	.8	2.1		–	–	1.3	5.0	20.6
3. Yes, and it was the first time I took any	9.9	8.7	11.0			9.7	8.0	10.7	12.6		8.0	8.7	11.8	14.2	8.1
Item 5020 N(Wtd)	2674	1247	1422			610	799	892	373		1331	510	195	383	34

A172: When did you first try narcotics other than heroin without a doctor's orders? ‡

	TOTAL	M	F			NE	NC	S	W		None	Mari- juana Only	Few Pills	More Pills	Any Heroin
8. Never	95.1	94.7	95.4			93.1	95.3	96.3	94.8		100.0	100.0	94.3	74.9	26.8
1. Grade 6 or below	.1	.1	*			.2	.1	*	–		–	–	–	.6	–
2. Grade 7 or 8	.2	.1	.4			.4	–	.3	.5		–	–	–	.4	15.3
3. Grade 9 (Freshman)	.7	.9	.6			.8	.9	.7	.5		–	–	.4	3.8	15.2
4. Grade 10 (Sophomore)	1.3	1.0	1.5			1.5	1.7	.8	1.5		–	–	1.6	6.8	18.1
5. Grade 11 (Junior)	1.7	2.1	1.4			2.9	1.1	1.4	1.9		–	–	2.0	9.4	19.4
6. Grade 12 (Senior)	.8	1.0	.6			1.1	.8	.5	.9		–	–	1.8	4.2	5.3
Item 5680 N(Wtd)	2668	1244	1419			609	795	890	373		1330	510	195	381	33

A173: On how many different occasions have you taken narcotics other than heroin on your own--that is, without a doctor telling you to take them...‡

A173A: ...in your lifetime?

	TOTAL	M	F			NE	NC	S	W		None	Mari- juana Only	Few Pills	More Pills	Any Heroin
1. 0 occasions	95.0	94.6	95.4			93.3	95.0	96.3	94.8		100.0	100.0	94.0	74.6	26.8
2. 1-2	2.1	2.7	1.5			2.4	2.2	1.3	3.0		–	–	6.0	10.4	11.3
3. 3-5	1.2	.9	1.4			1.5	1.0	1.0	1.5		–	–	–	6.4	20.0
4. 6-9	.5	.7	.2			.8	.5	.3	.6		–	–	–	3.1	5.1
5. 10-19	.4	.3	.5			.6	.3	.5	.2		–	–	–	1.8	12.5
6. 20-39	.4	.2	.5			1.0	.2	.2	–		–	–	–	1.5	13.4
7. 40 or more	.5	.5	.4			.5	.7	.4	–		–	–	–	2.2	10.8
Item 1130 N(Wtd)	2669	1246	1419			608	798	890	373		1330	510	196	382	33

A173B: ...during the last 12 months?

	TOTAL	M	F			NE	NC	S	W		None	Mari- juana Only	Few Pills	More Pills	Any Heroin
1. 0 occasions	97.1	96.9	97.2			95.3	97.2	98.1	97.3		100.0	100.0	99.3	84.1	53.3
2. 1-2	1.5	1.6	1.4			2.7	1.4	.6	1.8		–	–	.7	8.9	13.0
3. 3-5	.6	.7	.6			.7	.5	.7	.7		–	–	–	3.1	16.5
4. 6-9	.3	.4	.2			.8	.2	.1	.2		–	–	–	2.0	2.4
5. 10-19	.1	*	.2			.2	.1	.1	–		–	–	–	.4	4.0
6. 20-39	.2	.1	.3			.2	.4	.1	–		–	–	–	1.0	4.8
7. 40 or more	.1	.2	.1			.1	.1	.3	–		–	–	–	.5	6.0
Item 1140 N(Wtd)	2665	1242	1418			608	795	889	373		1330	510	193	381	33

‡ = Wording changed in subsequent years.   * = less than .05 per cent.

CAUTION: Items were rearranged after 1975; changes in context may produce spurious "trends" (see page 12).

QUESTIONNAIRE FORM 1 1975	TOTAL	SEX			REGION					ILLICIT DRUG USE: LIFETIME				
		M	F		NE	NC	S	W		None	Marijuana Only	Few Pills	More Pills	Any Heroin
Weighted No. of Cases:	3038	1437	1568		688	943	979	428		1374	528	225	523	39
% of Weighted Total:	100.0	47.3	51.6		22.7	31.0	32.2	14.1		45.2	17.4	7.4	17.2	1.3
A173C: ...during the last 30 days?														
1. 0 occasions	98.8	98.7	98.9		98.4	98.9	98.9	99.1		100.0	100.0	100.0	93.9	74.5
2. 1-2	.6	.8	.5		1.0	.5	.5	.7		-	-	-	4.0	4.7
3. 3-5	.1	.1	.1		-	.1	.2	-		-	-	-	.2	5.4
4. 6-9	.2	.1	.3		.4	.2	.1	.2		-	-	-	.9	4.1
5. 10-19	.2	.3	.2		.2	.3	.3	-		-	-	-	1.0	9.0
6. 20-39	-	-	-		-	-	-	-		-	-	-	-	-
7. 40 or more	*	.1	-		-	-	.1	-		-	-	-	-	2.2
Item 1150 N(Wtd)	2663	1243	1415		608	794	888	373		1330	510	193	379	32

IF YOU HAVE NOT TAKEN NARCOTICS OTHER THAN HEROIN IN THE LAST TWELVE MONTHS, GO TO Q.A184.

THE FOLLOWING QUESTIONS REFER ONLY TO TAKING NARCOTICS OTHER THAN HEROIN WITHOUT A DOCTOR'S ORDERS. ‡

	TOTAL	M	F		NE	NC	S	W		None	Marijuana Only	Few Pills	More Pills	Any Heroin
A178: What have been the most important reasons for your using narcotics other than heroin without a doctor's orders? (Mark all that apply.)														
A. To experiment--to see what it's like	63.0	60.8	65.3		58.3	72.2	64.5	50.2		-	-	100.0	55.6	85.7
B. To relax or relieve tension	28.5	20.1	37.4		33.1	16.6	34.2	33.7		-	-	-	30.7	25.7
C. To feel good or get high	60.9	62.7	59.0		67.0	55.5	55.3	68.4		-	-	-	64.3	60.6
D. To seek deeper insights and understanding	4.6	8.9	-		-	3.9	14.1	-		-	-	-	4.4	6.3
E. To have a good time with my friends	33.0	36.2	29.7		39.2	50.6	-	38.0		-	-	-	37.2	23.0
F. To fit in with a group I like	1.4	2.6	-		-	2.1	-	6.0		-	-	-	1.8	-
G. To get away from my problems or troubles	1.1	-	2.2		-	-	-	9.0		-	-	-	1.4	-
H. Because of boredom, nothing else to do	10.2	10.3	10.2		12.0	6.8	7.1	20.1		-	-	-	12.1	4.8
I. Because of anger or frustration	4.9	4.7	5.0		7.3	-	6.5	6.7		-	-	-	6.3	-
K. To get through the day	4.4	-	9.1		9.2	2.3	2.4	-		-	-	-	4.9	3.2
L. To increase the effects of some other drug(s)	5.9	3.4	8.6		8.7	7.2	-	6.7		-	-	-	6.2	6.0
M. To decrease (offset) the effects of some other drug(s)	1.8	1.8	1.8		2.6	3.1	-	-		-	-	-	2.3	-
To get to sleep @	-	-	-		-	-	-	-		-	-	-	-	-
O. As a substitute for heroin	4.0	5.6	2.3		3.2	3.9	7.1	-		-	-	-	3.7	6.0
N. Because I am "hooked"--I have to have it	.9	1.8	-		-	-	3.9	-		-	-	-	-	5.2
Item 5230-5370 N(Wtd) ★	74	38	36		25	22	18	9		-	-	3	57	14
A179: When you take narcotics other than heroin how high do you usually get?														
1. Not at all high	3.6	5.6	1.5		-	6.6	3.7	6.0		-	-	-	4.7	-
2. A little high	8.8	12.0	5.3		5.2	9.9	13.5	6.7		-	-	-	11.4	-
3. Moderately high	45.0	45.4	44.5		40.2	53.5	35.7	55.4		-	-	100.0	42.1	44.8
4. Very high	38.5	34.4	43.0		51.0	27.0	39.1	31.9		-	-	-	37.3	52.1
5. I don't take it to get high	4.1	2.6	5.7		3.6	3.1	8.0	-		-	-	-	4.5	3.1
Item 5380 N(Wtd) ★	75	39	36		25	23	18	9		-	-	3	58	14
A180: When you take narcotics other than heroin how long do you usually stay high?														
1. Usually don't get high	6.8	5.8	7.9		4.9	5.5	11.7	5.4		-	-	-	8.1	3.1
2. One to two hours	8.8	12.7	4.5		-	21.6	2.4	12.2		-	-	78.3	7.1	-
3. Three to six hours	56.5	56.3	56.8		55.2	57.2	49.6	70.8		-	-	21.7	55.8	67.5
4. Seven to 24 hours	24.5	20.2	29.0		37.2	15.6	25.6	11.6		-	-	-	25.8	24.4
5. More than 24 hours	3.4	5.0	1.8		2.7	-	10.7	-		-	-	-	3.3	5.0
Item 5390 N(Wtd) ★	75	39	36		24	23	18	10		-	-	3	58	14

*=less than .05 per cent.   ‡=Wording changed in subsequent years.   @=category eliminated in this data collection.   ★=excludes respondents for whom question was inappropriate.

CAUTION: Items were rearranged after 1975; changes in context may produce spurious "trends" (see page 12).

QUESTIONNAIRE FORM 1 1975	TOTAL	SEX			REGION					ILLICIT DRUG USE: LIFETIME				
		M	F		NE	NC	S	W		None	Mari- juana Only	Few Pills	More Pills	Any Her- oin
Weighted No. of Cases:	3038	1437	1568		688	943	979	428		1374	528	225	523	39
% of Weighted Total:	100.0	47.3	51.6		22.7	31.0	32.2	14.1		45.2	17.4	7.4	17.2	1.3

A181: What narcotics other than heroin have you taken during the last year without a doctor's orders? (Mark all that apply.)

	TOTAL	M	F		NE	NC	S	W		None	Mari- juana Only	Few Pills	More Pills	Any Her- oin
A. Methadone	21.7	21.0	22.5		27.6	24.0	22.6	-		-	-	-	19.1	38.3
B. Opium	57.3	64.9	49.2		69.6	64.9	37.0	46.1		-	-	66.2	49.9	85.8
C. Morphine	25.2	20.7	29.9		26.1	30.3	26.6	8.6		-	-	-	18.3	60.4
D. Codeine	57.1	47.4	67.4		62.4	51.7	55.6	58.9		-	-	18.3	59.5	57.7
E. Demerol	24.4	12.6	36.8		36.2	21.1	19.7	10.7		-	-	-	22.5	39.0
F. Paregoric	11.6	9.7	13.7		5.8	7.8	30.8	-		-	-	15.5	10.7	14.7
G. Talwin	2.0	-	4.1		-	2.0	2.8	5.4		-	-	-	1.7	3.6
H. Laudanum	2.2	-	4.4		4.1	-	-	6.0		-	-	-	2.8	-
I. Other	28.6	18.8	38.8		18.3	39.1	32.0	24.2		-	-	-	29.0	34.1
J. Don't know the names of some I have used	13.9	14.0	13.7		10.7	21.9	3.8	22.0		-	-	-	12.7	22.2
Item 5400-5490 N(Wtd) ★	76	39	37		25	23	18	10		-	-	4	58	14

A182: Have you ever tried to stop using some narcotics other than heroin and found that you couldn't stop?

	TOTAL	M	F		NE	NC	S	W		None	Mari- juana Only	Few Pills	More Pills	Any Her- oin
1. Yes	1.4	-	2.8		-	4.6	-	-		-	-	-	1.8	-
2. No	98.6	100.0	97.2		100.0	95.4	99.9	99.9		-	-	100.0	98.2	100.0
Item 5500 N(Wtd) ★	77	40	37		26	23	18	10		-	-	3	59	15

A183: What methods have you used for taking any of these narcotics other than heroin? (Mark all that apply.)

	TOTAL	M	F		NE	NC	S	W		None	Mari- juana Only	Few Pills	More Pills	Any Her- oin
A. Sniffing or "snorting"	35.5	39.0	31.8		43.8	40.8	16.5	36.9		-	-	-	38.0	33.1
B. Smoking	59.6	69.9	48.4		57.1	84.8	34.6	53.5		-	-	78.3	57.3	64.4
C. Injection	5.6	2.1	9.3		7.2	3.7	5.1	6.5		-	-	-	1.8	21.8
D. By mouth	64.3	55.7	73.7		64.7	52.3	80.2	62.0		-	-	21.7	68.7	55.8
E. Other	6.5	6.3	6.8		3.5	7.1	10.7	5.4		-	-	-	7.4	4.7
Item 5510-5550 N(Wtd) ★	77	40	37		26	23	18	10		-	-	3	59	15

A184: Do you think you will be using any narcotics other than heroin without a doctor's orders five years from now?

	TOTAL	M	F		NE	NC	S	W		None	Mari- juana Only	Few Pills	More Pills	Any Her- oin
1. I definitely will	.5	.7	.3		.6	.4	.3	1.5		-	.7	.2	1.1	4.9
2. I probably will	1.9	1.8	2.0		3.0	1.6	.9	2.8		.3	.2	3.4	7.0	17.7
3. I probably will not	16.6	17.9	15.4		19.2	16.8	13.2	19.8		8.1	14.4	18.8	40.7	44.5
4. I definitely will not	81.0	79.6	82.3		77.2	81.2	85.6	75.9		91.6	84.7	77.6	51.2	32.9
Item 5560 N(Wtd)	2792	1305	1481		632	836	920	404		1332	502	205	418	36

★ = excludes respondents for whom question was inappropriate.

CAUTION: Items were rearranged after 1975; changes in context may produce spurious "trends" (see page 12).

QUESTIONNAIRE FORM 2 1975	TOTAL	SEX			REGION					ILLICIT DRUG USE: LIFETIME				
		M	F		NE	NC	S	W		None	Mari-juana Only	Few Pills	More Pills	Any Her-oin
Weighted No. of Cases:	2972	1404	1475		678	926	934	434		1109	484	270	494	47
% of Weighted Total:	100.0	47.2	49.6		22.8	31.2	31.4	14.6		37.3	16.3	9.1	16.6	1.6

A06: Some people think a lot about the social problems of the nation and the world, and about how they might be solved. Others spend little time thinking about these issues. How much do you think about such things?

1. Never	2.3	3.1	1.4		2.0	2.6	2.0	2.8		1.7	2.3	1.9	2.7	13.0
2. Seldom	16.0	19.0	13.2		15.3	18.6	15.0	13.9		13.5	17.0	18.1	18.2	6.5
3. Sometimes	48.6	45.2	51.5		53.6	48.0	45.1	49.9		49.9	51.6	46.4	45.2	32.6
4. Quite often	26.7	26.2	27.8		24.5	25.4	28.3	29.3		27.3	24.7	28.3	28.8	32.6
5. A great deal	6.3	6.3	6.2		4.7	5.4	9.6	3.8		7.6	4.4	4.9	5.3	13.0
Item 6880 N(Wtd)	2891	1372	1452		661	900	906	423		1092	477	265	489	46

A10: Do you think that you would prefer having a mate for most of your life, or would you prefer not having a mate?

5. Definitely prefer to have a mate	53.0	47.2	58.8		52.7	52.0	55.0	51.8		55.2	52.7	56.7	54.7	42.6
4. Probably prefer to have a mate	29.4	32.4	26.2		31.2	31.1	25.8	30.7		27.5	34.3	29.3	27.8	31.9
3. Not sure	13.2	15.5	11.1		11.0	12.9	15.1	12.9		12.2	8.9	8.9	13.4	17.0
2. Probably prefer not to have a mate	3.4	3.9	3.1		3.4	3.0	3.7	3.7		3.7	3.7	4.1	3.7	10.6
1. Definitely prefer not to have a mate	1.0	1.1	.8		1.5	1.2	.5	.7		1.4	.6	.7	.4	-
Item 6120 N(Wtd)	2937	1397	1472		670	914	926	427		1106	484	270	492	47

A11: Which do you think you are most likely to choose in the long run?

3. Getting married	76.5	71.5	81.1		74.3	78.3	76.3	76.3		78.4	80.6	82.6	74.8	59.6
2. I have no idea	17.0	20.4	13.7		17.9	16.1	16.8	17.6		14.4	14.0	12.2	19.5	23.4
1. Not getting married	6.6	8.1	5.2		7.8	5.6	7.0	5.9		7.2	5.2	4.8	5.7	17.0
8. Am already married@	-	-	-		-	-	-	-		-	-	-	-	-
Item 6130 N(Wtd)	2938	1399	1470		670	913	928	427		1106	484	270	493	47

A12: If you did get married,

A12A: How likely do you think it is that you would stay married to the same person for life?

5. Very likely	64.9	60.4	69.5		60.4	64.6	67.9	65.9		74.3	61.2	64.8	52.6	56.5
4. Fairly likely	20.5	23.3	17.8		23.4	21.5	17.9	19.3		16.6	24.3	20.7	25.6	23.9
3. Uncertain	12.3	13.3	11.1		13.5	11.9	11.9	12.0		7.8	11.8	10.7	18.8	15.2
2. Fairly unlikely	1.3	1.6	1.1		1.7	1.1	1.3	1.4		.6	2.3	2.2	1.4	2.2
1. Very unlikely	1.0	1.4	.6		.9	.9	.9	1.6		.6	.4	1.1	1.6	4.3
Item 6140 N(Wtd)	2921	1388	1464		666	907	923	425		1100	482	270	489	46

A12B: How likely is it that you would want to have children?

5. Very likely	58.5	56.7	60.2		58.0	57.6	60.8	56.0		63.0	60.6	56.5	52.0	27.7
4. Fairly likely	20.5	22.7	18.4		23.0	20.2	18.1	22.6		17.7	21.2	22.7	21.2	36.2
3. Uncertain	14.8	15.1	14.5		12.8	15.1	15.4	16.2		12.7	13.5	13.4	19.4	19.1
2. Fairly unlikely	3.3	3.3	3.1		2.9	4.7	2.3	2.8		3.4	3.5	4.5	4.1	4.3
1. Very unlikely	2.9	2.2	3.8		3.5	2.3	3.4	2.4		3.4	1.2	3.0	3.3	14.9
8. Already have child(ren)@	-	-	-		-	-	-	-		-	-	-	-	-
Item 6150 N(Wtd)	2919	1387	1464		666	906	922	425		1099	482	269	490	47

These next questions ask you to imagine that you are married. ‡

We want you to think about different ways you might share responsibilities for working, taking care of the home, and taking care of children. Please indicate how acceptable for you each of the different arrangements would be.

@ = category eliminated in this data collection.   ‡ = Wording changed in subsequent years.

CAUTION: Items were rearranged after 1975; changes in context may produce spurious "trends" (see page 12).

QUESTIONNAIRE FORM 2 1975	TOTAL	SEX			REGION					ILLICIT DRUG USE: LIFETIME				
		M	F		NE	NC	S	W		None	Mari-juana Only	Few Pills	More Pills	Any Her-oin
Weighted No. of Cases:	2972	1404	1475		678	926	934	434		1109	484	270	494	47
% of Weighted Total:	100.0	47.2	49.6		22.8	31.2	31.4	14.6		37.3	16.3	9.1	16.6	1.6

A15: Suppose you were married and had no children - how would you feel about each of the following working arrangements? ‡

A15A: Husband works full-time, wife doesn't work

	TOTAL	M	F		NE	NC	S	W		None	Marijuana Only	Few Pills	More Pills	Any Heroin
1. Not at all acceptable	31.7	16.5	46.2		34.5	31.3	33.2	24.5		31.5	33.2	34.8	33.1	31.8
2. Somewhat acceptable	33.2	32.8	33.1		33.3	34.7	31.4	33.6		34.0	30.5	34.5	36.8	25.0
3. Acceptable	25.2	35.4	15.8		24.4	23.5	24.8	31.4		24.5	25.6	21.3	21.6	34.1
4. Desirable	9.9	15.2	4.9		7.8	10.5	10.5	10.5		10.0	10.7	9.0	8.4	11.4
Item 6160 N(Wtd)	2903	1380	1458		664	903	916	420		1100	476	267	487	44

A15B: Husband works full-time, wife works about half-time

1. Not at all acceptable	4.8	5.1	4.5		5.7	4.6	4.8	3.6		4.4	4.2	3.7	5.1	6.5
2. Somewhat acceptable	23.0	19.6	26.0		24.2	21.6	25.1	19.7		21.4	24.5	20.2	22.8	19.6
3. Acceptable	51.1	54.0	48.3		52.7	50.9	51.0	49.1		53.0	46.6	50.9	51.3	45.7
4. Desirable	21.1	21.3	21.1		17.4	22.8	19.0	27.7		21.3	24.7	25.1	20.9	28.3
Item 6170 N(Wtd)	2912	1385	1461		666	906	919	422		1101	481	267	487	46

A15C: Both work full-time

1. Not at all acceptable	17.0	23.7	10.5		15.5	18.6	15.0	20.0		16.9	17.8	10.8	13.0	9.3
2. Somewhat acceptable	19.4	23.1	15.9		20.2	17.6	19.9	21.2		17.5	20.3	19.7	21.9	7.0
3. Acceptable	38.4	34.8	41.4		39.7	36.7	39.1	38.6		41.1	35.0	43.1	34.0	48.8
4. Desirable	25.2	18.4	32.1		24.7	27.2	26.0	20.0		24.5	26.8	26.4	31.1	32.6
Item 6180 N(Wtd)	2902	1378	1461		665	903	915	420		1100	477	269	485	43

A15D: Both work about half-time

1. Not at all acceptable	58.4	62.3	54.8		61.9	58.7	59.8	49.4		59.1	63.7	54.1	55.3	41.9
2. Somewhat acceptable	24.0	21.4	26.6		20.9	24.2	22.9	31.3		24.3	19.3	26.7	25.5	39.5
3. Acceptable	12.6	11.7	13.3		12.3	13.3	12.0	13.1		12.7	13.2	13.5	13.4	7.0
4. Desirable	5.0	4.6	5.3		5.0	3.9	5.4	6.4		4.0	3.8	5.6	5.8	14.0
Item 6190 N(Wtd)	2882	1364	1455		661	894	907	419		1090	471	266	486	43

A15E: Husband works about half-time, wife works full-time

1. Not at all acceptable	75.9	78.9	73.6		75.7	75.2	78.1	73.1		77.4	78.6	71.1	72.6	67.4
2. Somewhat acceptable	16.1	14.0	17.7		15.7	17.3	14.0	19.0		16.0	14.5	18.8	16.7	23.3
3. Acceptable	6.0	5.0	6.9		7.1	5.9	5.1	6.2		5.7	6.3	7.5	7.4	7.0
4. Desirable	2.0	2.1	1.8		1.7	1.6	2.9	1.4		1.0	.6	2.6	3.5	4.7
Item 6200 N(Wtd)	2894	1373	1456		662	901	910	420		1097	476	266	485	43

A15F: Husband doesn't work, wife works full-time

1. Not at all acceptable	89.2	90.1	88.7		87.2	90.5	89.4	89.5		90.8	92.2	86.1	88.3	83.7
2. Somewhat acceptable	6.2	5.2	6.8		8.1	5.4	5.0	7.2		5.7	5.0	7.1	6.4	9.3
3. Acceptable	2.8	2.5	3.0		3.2	2.6	2.9	2.4		2.6	1.5	4.1	3.1	2.3
4. Desirable	1.8	2.2	1.4		1.5	1.6	2.7	1.0		.9	1.1	2.6	2.3	7.0
Item 6210 N(Wtd)	2897	1377	1457		664	901	912	419		1099	476	266	486	43

A16: Suppose you were married and had one or more pre-school children. How would you feel about each of the following working arrangements? ‡

‡ = Wording changed in subsequent years.

CAUTION: Items were rearranged after 1975; changes in context may produce spurious "trends" (see page 12).

QUESTIONNAIRE FORM 2 1975	TOTAL	SEX			REGION					ILLICIT DRUG USE: LIFETIME				
		M	F		NE	NC	S	W		None	Mari- juana Only	Few Pills	More Pills	Any Her- oin
Weighted No. of Cases:	2972	1404	1475		678	926	934	434		1109	484	270	494	47
% of Weighted Total:	100.0	47.2	49.6		22.8	31.2	31.4	14.6		37.3	16.3	9.1	16.6	1.6
A16A: Husband works full-time, wife doesn't work														
1. Not at all acceptable	5.0	4.1	5.9		4.1	4.1	6.6	5.0		3.7	4.4	2.6	5.7	2.2
2. Somewhat acceptable	12.7	10.7	14.1		10.5	11.7	15.3	12.4		10.4	12.1	10.4	14.6	13.3
3. Acceptable	32.1	31.4	32.5		37.6	31.0	30.8	28.3		30.8	29.6	34.7	33.7	33.3
4. Desirable	50.2	53.8	47.4		47.7	53.2	47.3	54.3		55.2	54.0	52.6	46.0	51.1
Item 6220 N(Wtd)	2909	1381	1463		665	903	922	420		1102	480	268	487	45
A16B: Husband works full-time, wife works about half-time														
1. Not at all acceptable	21.6	27.9	15.8		28.5	20.9	17.6	20.8		22.2	23.3	19.9	18.8	11.4
2. Somewhat acceptable	31.4	31.6	31.0		30.9	30.6	31.9	32.8		30.7	32.5	32.0	29.7	34.1
3. Acceptable	38.3	33.1	43.2		33.2	39.4	41.5	36.6		39.1	35.4	40.2	39.8	38.6
4. Desirable	8.8	7.4	10.0		7.4	9.1	9.1	9.8		8.0	9.0	7.9	11.8	15.9
Item 6230 N(Wtd)	2899	1373	1460		663	903	915	418		1099	477	266	485	44
A16C: Both work full-time														
1. Not at all acceptable	76.8	77.6	76.6		81.0	81.7	68.5	77.7		80.3	76.2	78.9	75.6	67.4
2. Somewhat acceptable	13.4	12.5	13.8		9.9	10.7	18.4	14.1		12.0	14.1	12.4	13.5	25.6
3. Acceptable	6.6	7.0	6.0		7.0	4.8	8.6	5.3		5.4	5.9	6.4	6.6	4.7
4. Desirable	3.2	2.8	3.6		2.1	2.9	4.4	3.1		2.2	3.8	1.9	4.3	2.3
Item 6240 N(Wtd)	2883	1363	1455		659	898	908	417		1094	474	266	483	43
A16D: Both work about half-time														
1. Not at all acceptable	64.6	69.2	60.6		65.8	68.2	61.7	61.3		64.9	71.1	63.4	62.9	46.5
2. Somewhat acceptable	23.8	19.5	27.7		21.7	21.3	26.8	26.2		25.1	20.5	25.7	23.2	32.6
3. Acceptable	8.6	8.4	8.9		9.1	8.7	8.2	8.2		8.2	6.3	6.8	10.4	9.3
4. Desirable	3.0	2.9	2.8		3.3	1.9	3.3	4.4		1.8	2.3	4.5	3.7	14.0
Item 6250 N(Wtd)	2873	1365	1443		660	893	907	413		1087	474	265	482	43
A16E: Husband works about half-time, wife works full-time														
1. Not at all acceptable	85.6	86.3	85.1		87.1	87.1	85.4	80.8		89.0	87.6	82.0	84.3	86.0
2. Somewhat acceptable	9.3	8.3	10.1		8.8	9.0	7.7	13.9		6.8	8.4	15.0	9.7	9.3
3. Acceptable	4.0	4.1	3.6		3.6	3.1	5.2	3.6		3.7	3.8	1.9	4.8	2.3
4. Desirable	1.2	1.2	1.2		.6	.9	1.8	1.7		.5	.2	.8	1.2	4.7
Item 6260 N(Wtd)	2886	1368	1453		661	898	908	417		1095	476	266	483	43
A16F: Husband doesn't work, wife works full-time														
1. Not at all acceptable	88.4	89.8	87.2		87.5	89.0	89.8	85.3		89.0	91.2	86.5	88.4	88.4
2. Somewhat acceptable	6.4	5.5	7.4		6.8	7.4	4.8	7.5		5.9	5.5	7.5	6.8	2.3
3. Acceptable	3.6	2.9	4.1		4.2	2.7	3.3	5.3		3.9	2.9	3.4	2.9	4.7
4. Desirable	1.5	1.8	1.3		1.5	.9	2.1	1.7		1.3	.4	2.6	1.9	4.7
Item 6270 N(Wtd)	2884	1367	1453		662	897	910	416		1094	475	266	484	43
A17: Suppose you were married and had one or more pre-school children. Suppose also that the husband were working full-time and the wife did not have a job outside the home. How would you feel about each of these arrangements for the day-to-day care of the child(ren)? ‡														
A17A: Wife does all child care														
1. Not at all acceptable	23.4	22.6	23.8		24.9	23.8	23.1	21.3		24.0	24.8	20.2	22.4	27.3
2. Somewhat acceptable	26.3	27.2	25.4		26.6	26.9	24.9	28.2		24.1	23.8	30.0	29.2	25.0
3. Acceptable	32.0	29.3	34.7		31.6	33.1	31.7	30.8		34.0	32.0	28.5	31.7	27.3
4. Desirable	18.2	20.9	16.0		17.0	16.1	20.4	19.7		18.0	19.2	21.3	16.6	20.5
Item 6280 N(Wtd)	2892	1370	1457		659	900	911	422		1098	475	267	483	44

‡ = Wording changed in subsequent years.

CAUTION: Items were rearranged after 1975; changes in context may produce spurious "trends" (see page 12).

QUESTIONNAIRE FORM 2 1975	TOTAL	SEX			REGION					ILLICIT DRUG USE: LIFETIME				
		M	F		NE	NC	S	W		None	Mari- juana Only	Few Pills	More Pills	Any Her- oin
Weighted No. of Cases:	2972	1404	1475		678	926	934	434		1109	484	270	494	47
% of Weighted Total:	100.0	47.2	49.6		22.8	31.2	31.4	14.6		37.3	16.3	9.1	16.6	1.6

A17B: Wife does most of it

1. Not at all acceptable	7.1	7.9	6.4		9.2	5.6	7.5	6.6		6.8	8.4	5.9	6.6	13.3
2. Somewhat acceptable	21.9	23.4	19.8		21.8	24.1	20.9	19.4		20.7	23.0	21.9	18.9	20.0
3. Acceptable	45.5	45.1	46.5		43.7	41.9	48.9	48.3		46.6	42.5	46.7	48.3	33.3
4. Desirable	25.5	23.6	27.3		25.3	28.4	22.7	25.6		25.9	26.4	25.2	26.3	33.3
Item 6290 N(Wtd)	2910	1379	1467		664	904	920	422		1102	478	270	487	45

A17C: Both do it equally

1. Not at all acceptable	14.1	14.5	13.6		16.9	10.2	16.3	13.1		14.3	13.1	13.9	12.4	16.7
2. Somewhat acceptable	33.1	35.3	31.6		30.4	34.2	32.0	37.6		30.9	35.7	36.7	33.5	31.0
3. Acceptable	30.6	29.9	31.0		31.0	32.2	31.0	25.5		32.1	28.7	27.7	30.2	33.3
4. Desirable	22.2	20.2	24.0		21.7	23.5	20.5	24.0		22.7	22.6	21.7	24.0	21.4
Item 6300 N(Wtd)	2888	1368	1457		658	903	906	420		1098	474	267	484	42

A17D: Husband does most of it

1. Not at all acceptable	71.7	67.7	75.5		73.2	69.3	73.3	70.8		74.1	70.4	74.5	70.7	62.8
2. Somewhat acceptable	23.5	26.1	20.8		22.6	25.6	21.3	25.4		22.3	25.2	21.7	25.6	30.2
3. Acceptable	3.7	4.8	2.7		3.3	4.2	3.9	2.6		3.1	3.6	3.0	3.1	9.3
4. Desirable	1.1	1.4	1.0		.8	1.0	1.5	1.0		.5	.8	.7	.6	-
Item 6310 N(Wtd)	2884	1366	1455		660	898	905	421		1096	473	267	481	43

A17E: Husband does all of it

1. Not at all acceptable	94.0	92.5	95.5		92.6	93.8	94.8	94.8		95.5	93.7	95.1	94.2	88.4
2. Somewhat acceptable	3.9	4.9	2.9		5.9	4.1	2.2	3.8		3.5	5.1	3.7	4.6	4.7
3. Acceptable	1.1	1.5	.6		1.1	1.6	.8	.7		.4	.8	-	1.0	7.0
4. Desirable	1.1	1.1	1.1		.3	.7	2.1	.7		.6	.4	.7	.2	2.3
Item 6320 N(Wtd)	2887	1367	1457		660	898	908	421		1098	474	267	483	43

A19: These next questions ask you to guess how well you might do in several different situations. How good do you think you would be...

A19A: As a husband or wife?

1. Poor	.4	.6	.3		.7	.1	.7	.5		.2	.4	.4	.6	4.3
2. Not so good	1.2	1.2	1.2		1.0	1.1	1.1	1.7		1.2	1.5	.7	1.6	-
3. Fairly good	9.7	10.2	9.1		9.3	10.9	9.1	9.3		8.8	8.4	10.8	11.7	13.0
4. Good	45.4	47.1	44.4		46.5	45.9	43.9	46.1		45.4	46.3	49.6	43.4	28.3
5. Very good	33.0	29.6	36.0		32.7	31.2	34.6	34.2		34.6	33.6	31.3	31.1	34.8
8. Don't know	10.2	11.2	9.0		9.7	10.9	10.6	8.3		9.8	9.8	6.3	11.7	17.4
Item 6850 N(Wtd)	2908	1379	1465		667	908	912	421		1099	479	268	486	46

A19B: As a parent?

1. Poor	1.1	.8	1.3		.8	1.1	1.3	.9		1.1	.8	1.1	1.6	6.5
2. Not so good	2.6	2.3	2.7		2.6	2.5	2.3	4.3		2.5	2.3	2.6	3.1	10.9
3. Fairly good	13.9	14.4	13.5		12.9	15.1	13.4	13.7		13.2	14.2	15.7	16.1	13.0
4. Good	38.9	41.0	37.7		36.8	40.5	37.5	42.4		40.5	35.3	42.5	35.5	21.7
5. Very good	31.2	30.6	31.4		34.4	29.7	32.3	26.5		31.1	35.9	27.2	29.7	23.9
8. Don't know	12.3	10.9	13.2		12.6	11.1	13.4	11.8		11.6	11.7	10.4	14.0	23.9
Item 6860 N(Wtd)	2907	1377	1466		666	907	913	422		1099	479	268	485	46

A19C: As a worker on a job?

1. Poor	.1	.2	-		-	.2	.2	-		-	-	.4	.6	-
2. Not so good	.3	.5	.2		.5	.4	.2	.5		.1	.6	.4	.6	2.2
3. Fairly good	6.5	4.9	8.0		5.1	6.7	7.9	5.2		5.6	5.4	4.5	7.2	6.5
4. Good	43.1	39.4	47.0		45.0	44.0	41.1	42.6		43.4	40.3	50.7	42.1	41.3
5. Very good	47.7	53.1	42.5		47.3	45.9	49.1	49.4		49.2	51.1	42.2	46.8	47.8
8. Don't know	2.2	1.9	2.3		2.3	2.8	1.6	2.1		1.7	2.5	1.9	2.9	-
Item 6870 N(Wtd)	2908	1378	1465		666	909	911	423		1100	479	268	485	46

CAUTION: Items were rearranged after 1975; changes in context may produce spurious "trends" (see page 12).

QUESTIONNAIRE FORM 2 1975	TOTAL	SEX			REGION					ILLICIT DRUG USE: LIFETIME				
		M	F		NE	NC	S	W		None	Marijuana Only	Few Pills	More Pills	Any Heroin
Weighted No. of Cases:	2972	1404	1475		678	926	934	434		1109	484	270	494	47
% of Weighted Total:	100.0	47.2	49.6		22.8	31.2	31.4	14.6		37.3	16.3	9.1	16.6	1.6

A20: Now we'd like you to make some ratings of how honest and moral the people are who run the following organizations. To what extent are there problems or dishonesty and immorality in the leadership of...

A20A: Large corporations

	TOTAL	M	F		NE	NC	S	W		None	Marijuana Only	Few Pills	More Pills	Any Heroin
1. Not at all	2.4	3.4	1.5		2.4	2.6	2.4	2.2		1.7	2.7	1.5	2.9	4.3
2. Slight	9.2	10.0	8.5		9.7	8.1	9.9	8.9		8.9	9.7	4.9	7.7	15.2
3. Moderate	28.1	29.1	27.4		28.2	32.4	24.4	26.0		29.0	31.1	30.4	23.5	17.4
4. Considerable	32.8	31.6	33.8		31.9	32.7	32.7	34.4		36.9	31.7	33.5	34.9	28.3
5. Great	13.1	13.6	12.7		16.2	11.3	12.7	12.7		11.2	13.7	17.5	16.6	15.2
8. No opinion	14.5	12.3	16.0		11.7	12.8	17.7	15.6		12.2	11.3	12.5	14.1	17.4
Item 6890 N(Wtd)	2879	1370	1448		659	897	908	416		1095	476	263	481	46

A20B: Major labor unions

	TOTAL	M	F		NE	NC	S	W		None	Marijuana Only	Few Pills	More Pills	Any Heroin
1. Not at all	2.3	3.2	1.7		2.6	1.9	2.8	1.9		2.1	2.9	.4	3.3	-
2. Slight	12.7	14.7	11.1		15.5	10.9	13.3	11.1		12.3	14.9	8.4	9.1	19.6
3. Moderate	27.9	26.6	29.5		27.1	29.4	26.5	29.2		28.4	29.0	28.5	29.7	21.7
4. Considerable	27.4	27.7	26.6		28.0	29.6	25.3	26.0		27.7	26.9	31.2	29.3	17.4
5. Great	12.1	14.5	10.0		10.8	11.9	11.8	15.4		12.6	12.2	14.4	11.6	21.7
8. No opinion	17.5	13.3	21.0		16.1	16.2	20.4	16.4		16.9	14.1	16.7	16.6	19.6
Item 6900 N(Wtd)	2868	1363	1445		658	894	902	415		1091	476	263	481	46

A20C: The nation's colleges and universities

	TOTAL	M	F		NE	NC	S	W		None	Marijuana Only	Few Pills	More Pills	Any Heroin
1. Not at all	5.4	5.7	5.1		4.0	5.5	6.1	5.8		6.7	3.4	5.3	4.2	8.7
2. Slight	29.1	30.9	28.0		31.4	30.3	28.0	25.7		31.5	30.7	30.8	27.3	21.7
3. Moderate	28.1	28.4	27.7		27.7	30.3	25.4	29.8		27.7	29.4	29.3	29.4	41.3
4. Considerable	17.4	14.9	19.7		16.4	15.6	19.6	18.2		16.5	16.7	18.6	17.3	13.0
5. Great	6.0	7.2	5.1		6.4	5.4	6.7	5.3		5.5	6.3	3.4	6.7	4.3
8. No opinion	14.0	12.8	14.4		14.2	13.0	14.2	15.3		12.2	13.5	12.2	14.8	6.5
Item 6910 N(Wtd)	2862	1358	1442		653	892	904	413		1087	473	263	479	46

A20D: The nation's public schools

	TOTAL	M	F		NE	NC	S	W		None	Marijuana Only	Few Pills	More Pills	Any Heroin
1. Not at all	7.0	7.2	7.0		5.2	6.5	8.9	7.0		6.6	7.8	8.4	5.6	15.2
2. Slight	29.3	33.4	25.6		31.6	31.4	25.0	30.4		31.2	29.4	28.6	28.9	21.7
3. Moderate	27.0	25.3	28.5		25.6	30.5	25.6	24.3		27.3	29.8	28.2	25.2	23.9
4. Considerable	19.0	16.7	21.1		18.5	16.8	21.1	20.2		19.5	17.1	17.9	21.2	26.1
5. Great	8.4	7.7	9.1		8.2	6.8	10.6	7.2		7.2	5.7	9.5	10.8	6.5
8. No opinion	9.3	9.6	8.6		10.8	8.0	8.8	10.8		8.3	10.1	7.3	8.1	4.3
Item 6920 N(Wtd)	2868	1360	1448		655	892	907	415		1093	473	262	481	46

A20E: Churches and religious organizations

	TOTAL	M	F		NE	NC	S	W		None	Marijuana Only	Few Pills	More Pills	Any Heroin
1. Not at all	17.4	19.1	15.9		15.7	19.5	18.6	13.0		20.8	14.3	14.1	16.1	21.7
2. Slight	34.5	33.8	35.6		36.1	35.5	32.1	35.3		37.3	34.3	39.9	33.4	23.9
3. Moderate	14.8	13.5	16.1		17.2	13.4	12.3	19.5		12.5	16.6	18.3	16.5	15.2
4. Considerable	11.9	11.3	12.7		12.0	11.7	13.0	9.6		11.9	11.2	10.6	12.3	13.0
5. Great	9.5	11.1	8.0		8.2	7.9	11.5	10.3		7.9	10.3	9.5	10.0	10.9
8. No opinion	12.0	11.2	11.7		10.7	12.1	12.5	12.7		9.6	13.3	7.6	11.7	15.2
Item 6930 N(Wtd)	2872	1359	1451		656	894	907	416		1094	475	263	479	46

A20F: The national news media (TV, magazines, news services)

	TOTAL	M	F		NE	NC	S	W		None	Marijuana Only	Few Pills	More Pills	Any Heroin
1. Not at all	4.6	6.4	3.0		4.4	4.4	5.1	3.8		4.1	5.7	3.8	3.3	4.3
2. Slight	18.3	19.4	17.3		19.6	17.8	18.8	15.9		19.2	18.0	17.2	16.0	28.3
3. Moderate	28.4	29.4	27.5		27.7	30.0	25.7	32.0		28.2	28.5	31.7	28.8	13.0
4. Considerable	23.7	22.8	24.3		21.7	25.8	22.5	24.5		24.4	24.4	26.0	21.5	26.1
5. Great	16.3	14.3	18.3		17.3	14.5	17.4	15.6		15.2	15.1	16.0	21.7	19.6
8. No opinion	8.9	7.5	9.6		9.0	7.5	10.5	7.9		8.9	8.1	5.3	8.8	6.5
Item 6940 N(Wtd)	2865	1355	1448		653	888	908	416		1092	471	262	480	46

CAUTION: Items were rearranged after 1975; changes in context may produce spurious "trends" (see page 12).

QUESTIONNAIRE FORM 2 1975	TOTAL	SEX			REGION					ILLICIT DRUG USE: LIFETIME				
		M	F		NE	NC	S	W		None	Mari-juana Only	Few Pills	More Pills	Any Her-oin
Weighted No. of Cases:	2972	1404	1475		678	926	934	434		1109	484	270	494	47
% of Weighted Total:	100.0	47.2	49.6		22.8	31.2	31.4	14.6		37.3	16.3	9.1	16.6	1.6

A20G: The President and his administration ‡

1. Not at all	6.0	7.5	4.8		4.8	6.0	6.7	6.5		4.6	8.0	3.0	5.6	19.6
2. Slight	14.0	16.6	11.4		12.7	13.1	16.4	12.7		15.6	14.0	11.8	10.8	13.0
3. Moderate	19.4	21.6	17.6		20.3	19.9	18.7	18.7		21.7	18.8	20.2	15.6	15.2
4. Considerable	24.3	22.1	26.6		24.4	24.2	22.9	27.8		26.3	24.7	27.4	22.9	19.6
5. Great	25.4	22.7	28.0		26.1	26.7	24.5	23.7		21.6	25.8	29.3	35.8	28.3
8. No opinion	10.8	9.5	11.5		11.8	10.1	10.8	10.8		10.3	8.7	8.0	9.2	4.3
Item 6950 N(Wtd)	2867	1359	1446		651	893	905	417		1092	473	263	480	46

A20H: Congress-that is, the U.S. Senate and House of Representatives

1. Not at all	3.8	4.8	3.0		3.2	3.8	4.1	4.3		2.6	5.1	1.9	4.2	8.7
2. Slight	14.0	16.5	11.5		11.3	15.5	14.8	13.3		13.6	14.3	14.8	13.3	15.2
3. Moderate	23.5	24.7	22.7		25.4	22.4	22.2	26.0		25.7	23.4	24.0	20.6	15.2
4. Considerable	26.3	25.8	26.8		28.3	26.1	25.4	25.3		27.8	25.1	28.5	27.7	30.4
5. Great	18.5	18.2	18.8		17.6	19.8	19.7	14.0		17.7	18.9	19.0	22.1	19.6
8. No opinion	13.9	10.1	17.2		14.2	12.3	13.9	17.1		12.6	13.1	11.8	11.9	10.9
Item 6960 N(Wtd)	2870	1361	1448		654	894	907	415		1095	475	263	480	46

A20I: The U.S. Supreme Court

1. Not at all	8.2	11.7	4.9		7.2	8.8	8.2	8.5		9.2	10.0	6.1	7.1	8.7
2. Slight	22.7	25.9	19.7		22.4	23.0	22.1	23.7		24.1	24.6	22.8	20.5	21.7
3. Moderate	22.5	20.8	24.2		22.8	24.2	20.2	23.2		23.6	18.4	28.1	24.4	15.2
4. Considerable	17.9	17.3	18.4		16.5	17.2	19.4	18.4		17.2	15.7	18.3	19.2	28.3
5. Great	10.6	10.5	11.1		11.8	10.9	10.9	8.0		9.3	12.5	9.5	13.8	10.9
8. No opinion	18.0	13.8	21.6		19.3	16.0	19.1	18.4		16.4	18.9	15.2	15.2	13.0
Item 6970 N(Wtd)	2857	1358	1438		653	890	899	414		1091	472	263	479	46

A20J: All the courts and the justice system in general

1. Not at all	4.4	6.1	2.8		4.3	4.1	4.2	5.3		3.5	4.8	3.0	4.2	8.7
2. Slight	20.7	23.0	18.4		17.7	22.2	19.6	24.3		22.9	21.6	17.9	18.8	8.7
3. Moderate	29.1	30.8	27.6		29.7	31.4	26.7	28.6		29.9	30.9	35.7	27.1	28.3
4. Considerable	20.1	18.1	22.2		19.9	19.3	21.0	20.0		19.9	17.2	20.5	24.6	19.6
5. Great	10.3	10.2	10.4		13.0	9.6	11.0	5.8		9.5	11.1	8.7	12.7	17.4
8. No opinion	15.5	11.7	18.6		15.4	13.2	17.5	16.1		14.2	14.3	14.4	12.5	15.2
Item 6980 N(Wtd)	2865	1360	1444		654	892	904	416		1092	476	263	479	46

A20K: The police and other law enforcement agencies

1. Not at all	4.3	4.9	3.7		3.2	3.6	5.7	4.3		3.1	5.9	1.5	6.3	8.7
2. Slight	20.6	22.0	19.4		15.3	20.3	23.6	22.8		24.3	19.4	18.3	11.9	19.6
3. Moderate	29.6	28.0	31.8		30.8	30.6	26.3	33.2		32.8	28.2	34.6	26.9	19.6
4. Considerable	22.7	23.2	22.3		26.0	23.3	20.8	20.4		21.2	26.1	24.0	24.3	21.7
5. Great	14.9	15.4	14.4		16.7	15.5	14.6	12.0		11.2	12.4	15.6	23.1	21.7
8. No opinion	7.8	6.6	8.4		8.0	6.6	9.2	7.2		7.3	8.2	6.5	5.7	6.5
Item 6990 N(Wtd)	2865	1355	1448		653	890	906	416		1095	475	263	477	46

A20L: The U.S. military

1. Not at all	7.6	8.1	7.2		7.5	7.4	8.4	6.3		7.7	8.0	6.5	7.3	6.5
2. Slight	24.4	26.8	22.3		25.3	26.1	22.2	24.0		26.1	24.3	24.7	20.0	23.9
3. Moderate	24.7	25.7	24.0		26.8	23.8	23.6	26.2		24.5	24.7	30.4	30.9	19.6
4. Considerable	17.3	15.9	18.8		14.5	17.1	19.9	16.8		18.0	16.5	19.4	14.2	32.6
5. Great	8.6	12.0	5.5		8.6	10.1	6.8	9.4		6.8	9.9	5.7	11.7	2.2
8. No opinion	17.3	11.6	22.3		17.3	15.6	19.1	17.3		16.9	16.5	13.7	15.9	13.0
Item 7000 N(Wtd)	2865	1356	1448		653	890	906	416		1094	474	263	479	46

‡ = Wording changed in subsequent years.

CAUTION: Items were rearranged after 1975; changes in context may produce spurious "trends" (see page 12).

QUESTIONNAIRE FORM 2 1975	TOTAL	SEX			REGION					ILLICIT DRUG USE: LIFETIME				
		M	F		NE	NC	S	W		None	Marijuana Only	Few Pills	More Pills	Any Heroin
Weighted No. of Cases:	2972	1404	1475		678	926	934	434		1109	484	270	494	47
% of Weighted Total:	100.0	47.2	49.6		22.8	31.2	31.4	14.6		37.3	16.3	9.1	16.6	1.6

A21: Below are several ways that people have used to protest about serious social issues. How much do you approve or disapprove of these actions?

A21A: Signing petitions

	TOTAL	M	F		NE	NC	S	W		None	Mari. Only	Few Pills	More Pills	Any Heroin
4. Strongly approve	28.9	31.7	26.3		30.8	29.4	25.3	33.0		31.1	27.3	34.3	28.9	39.1
3. Approve	43.4	42.6	44.3		42.3	46.7	42.7	39.7		42.8	46.6	43.8	46.4	32.6
2. Disapprove	5.4	6.3	4.7		6.0	6.1	4.2	5.5		5.2	4.8	3.0	6.0	8.7
1. Strongly disapprove	1.5	1.8	1.2		1.2	1.3	1.9	1.4		1.5	1.3	1.1	.4	4.3
8. Don't know, or it depends	20.8	17.5	23.6		19.5	16.6	25.9	20.7		19.4	20.0	17.4	18.1	15.2
Item 6040 N(Wtd)	2881	1364	1455		655	896	909	421		1099	476	265	481	46

A21B: Boycotting certain products or stores

	TOTAL	M	F		NE	NC	S	W		None	Mari. Only	Few Pills	More Pills	Any Heroin
4. Strongly approve	22.2	26.0	19.0		30.0	20.3	20.4	18.1		21.5	23.5	20.5	29.6	37.8
3. Approve	36.5	36.0	36.9		40.5	38.9	31.9	35.6		34.0	39.0	39.5	37.3	33.3
2. Disapprove	15.3	14.7	16.2		9.6	15.6	17.5	18.8		16.5	15.9	15.2	13.3	11.1
1. Strongly disapprove	3.6	4.0	3.4		2.3	2.8	4.7	5.2		4.2	2.3	3.0	2.5	11.1
8. Don't know, or it depends	22.3	19.3	24.6		17.4	22.5	25.6	22.6		23.9	19.3	21.7	17.5	8.9
Item 6050 N(Wtd)	2881	1364	1455		656	893	910	421		1098	477	263	480	45

A21C: Lawful demonstrations

	TOTAL	M	F		NE	NC	S	W		None	Mari. Only	Few Pills	More Pills	Any Heroin
4. Strongly approve	20.8	24.5	17.5		24.7	19.4	20.1	19.1		17.4	22.2	24.2	30.5	26.7
3. Approve	41.9	43.3	40.2		40.9	45.6	38.2	43.9		41.4	42.4	42.3	44.1	48.9
2. Disapprove	13.6	13.1	14.6		12.9	13.6	14.7	12.6		15.7	14.1	12.8	10.4	6.7
1. Strongly disapprove	4.5	4.3	4.8		4.0	5.4	4.6	3.6		5.9	3.8	2.6	1.3	6.7
8. Don't know, or it depends	19.1	14.7	22.9		17.7	16.1	22.5	20.5		19.5	17.7	18.5	13.6	11.1
Item 6060 N(Wtd)	2866	1356	1449		651	895	901	419		1093	474	265	479	45

A21D: Occupying buildings or factories

	TOTAL	M	F		NE	NC	S	W		None	Mari. Only	Few Pills	More Pills	Any Heroin
4. Strongly approve	3.0	3.6	2.5		2.9	3.6	3.0	2.1		1.9	3.4	4.2	4.0	4.3
3. Approve	13.8	13.8	13.9		12.5	14.8	13.4	14.8		10.3	11.6	13.6	16.6	2.2
2. Disapprove	38.0	39.0	37.5		41.7	39.6	34.0	37.5		39.3	40.0	44.2	38.7	45.7
1. Strongly disapprove	19.3	24.5	14.7		16.5	17.8	22.8	19.1		23.4	21.1	16.6	16.6	17.4
8. Don't know, or it depends	25.9	19.2	31.5		26.4	24.1	26.9	26.7		25.1	24.0	21.9	23.8	28.3
Item 6070 N(Wtd)	2860	1349	1451		648	891	903	419		1092	475	265	475	46

A21E: Wildcat strikes

	TOTAL	M	F		NE	NC	S	W		None	Mari. Only	Few Pills	More Pills	Any Heroin
4. Strongly approve	2.8	4.1	1.5		2.8	3.8	2.4	1.7		1.9	3.6	2.3	3.8	6.5
3. Approve	9.7	12.7	6.7		13.6	11.0	7.1	6.2		6.8	7.3	7.3	11.3	13.0
2. Disapprove	34.0	35.1	33.4		34.5	35.5	31.3	35.9		34.0	35.4	39.8	32.6	26.1
1. Strongly disapprove	23.2	23.6	23.2		18.3	23.2	25.7	25.8		28.4	19.2	20.7	22.3	26.1
8. Don't know, or it depends	30.3	24.5	35.0		30.8	26.4	33.6	30.6		28.9	29.6	29.9	30.0	26.1
Item 6080 N(Wtd)	2845	1345	1438		646	889	891	418		1091	469	261	476	46

A21F: Blocking traffic

	TOTAL	M	F		NE	NC	S	W		None	Mari. Only	Few Pills	More Pills	Any Heroin
4. Strongly approve	2.1	3.4	.9		2.6	2.2	2.2	1.0		1.6	2.9	1.5	3.1	4.3
3. Approve	3.2	4.4	2.1		4.3	2.9	3.0	2.6		2.2	2.1	2.3	5.6	2.2
2. Disapprove	40.2	37.5	42.5		45.4	39.6	37.7	38.6		37.5	43.2	42.6	39.5	34.8
1. Strongly disapprove	43.9	44.4	43.6		38.2	44.6	45.5	47.6		50.1	42.3	42.6	39.7	39.1
8. Don't know, or it depends	10.6	10.2	10.9		9.5	10.7	11.7	10.2		8.6	9.5	10.9	12.1	17.4
Item 6090 N(Wtd)	2875	1359	1455		654	895	907	420		1097	475	265	479	46

A21G: Damaging things

	TOTAL	M	F		NE	NC	S	W		None	Mari. Only	Few Pills	More Pills	Any Heroin
4. Strongly approve	2.0	2.8	1.3		2.0	2.0	2.3	1.4		1.8	1.9	.8	2.7	4.3
3. Approve	1.1	1.2	1.0		1.5	1.6	.3	1.0		.5	1.3	-	2.1	-
2. Disapprove	16.9	19.6	14.4		20.1	15.7	16.4	15.2		12.3	14.9	15.5	20.9	15.2
1. Strongly disapprove	74.3	70.1	78.3		72.0	76.9	72.8	76.0		81.5	78.2	77.7	66.6	67.4
8. Don't know, or it depends	5.7	6.3	5.0		4.3	3.9	8.1	6.4		3.8	3.8	5.7	7.9	13.0
Item 6100 N(Wtd)	2877	1361	1454		656	896	905	420		1098	476	265	479	46

CAUTION: Items were rearranged after 1975; changes in context may produce spurious "trends" (see page 12).

QUESTIONNAIRE FORM 2 1975	TOTAL	SEX			REGION					ILLICIT DRUG USE: LIFETIME				
		M	F		NE	NC	S	W		None	Marijuana Only	Few Pills	More Pills	Any Heroin
Weighted No. of Cases:	2972	1404	1475		678	926	934	434		1109	484	270	494	47
% of Weighted Total:	100.0	47.2	49.6		22.8	31.2	31.4	14.6		37.3	16.3	9.1	16.6	1.6
A21H: Personal violence														
4. Strongly approve	1.9	2.9	1.0		2.1	2.3	1.5	1.7		1.5	2.3	1.1	2.7	4.3
3. Approve	2.3	3.1	1.5		1.8	2.8	2.3	1.7		1.6	2.1	.4	4.0	2.2
2. Disapprove	14.5	17.5	11.5		18.3	13.5	13.2	13.3		10.9	12.2	14.0	14.8	13.0
1. Strongly disapprove	74.4	69.3	79.3		71.5	76.5	74.4	74.5		80.7	76.7	78.5	69.2	71.7
8. Don't know, or it depends	6.9	7.1	6.6		6.2	5.0	8.5	8.8		5.3	6.9	6.4	9.6	8.7
Item 6110 N(Wtd)	2877	1359	1456		657	896	904	420		1098	476	265	480	46
A23: How much do you agree or disagree with each of the following statements?														
A23A: People should do their own thing, even if other people think it's strange														
1. Disagree	2.7	3.0	2.3		.6	1.7	4.6	4.1		2.8	2.2	2.0	1.3	2.4
2. Mostly disagree	3.9	3.9	4.1		3.9	4.4	3.1	4.8		4.8	2.4	5.6	1.7	2.4
3. Neither	11.1	13.3	9.1		10.0	12.9	7.8	15.7		12.1	10.6	9.9	9.6	2.4
4. Mostly agree	41.3	40.9	41.6		38.9	42.2	41.6	42.2		46.2	42.5	39.7	38.0	33.3
5. Agree	41.0	39.0	43.0		46.5	38.8	42.9	33.3		34.2	42.1	42.1	49.5	59.5
Item 7040 N(Wtd)	2761	1302	1403		660	879	807	415		1048	461	252	469	42
A23C: There is too much competition in this society														
1. Disagree	7.9	9.9	6.0		5.7	8.9	9.9	5.1		8.3	8.3	7.1	4.5	7.5
2. Mostly disagree	10.1	13.4	6.9		6.3	11.8	11.7	9.9		10.7	11.5	6.3	8.4	7.5
3. Neither	16.2	19.6	13.1		16.9	13.7	17.2	18.4		15.9	16.1	19.4	12.7	17.5
4. Mostly agree	29.0	29.0	28.9		30.1	30.2	26.5	29.5		30.4	28.5	26.6	30.5	22.5
5. Agree	36.8	28.1	45.1		41.0	35.5	34.8	37.2		34.5	35.5	40.5	43.7	45.0
Item 7010 N(Wtd)	2732	1288	1389		651	870	797	414		1042	459	252	465	40
A23H: Too many young people are sloppy about their grooming and clothing, and just don't care how they look														
1. Disagree	25.0	25.9	24.6		28.0	26.9	21.8	22.5		16.9	28.9	28.2	34.2	61.9
2. Mostly disagree	25.2	24.5	25.4		26.4	24.7	23.1	28.6		23.2	27.2	29.0	27.1	16.7
3. Neither	18.0	19.1	17.1		18.1	20.3	15.5	18.2		18.6	18.0	18.3	19.0	2.4
4. Mostly agree	17.1	17.5	16.7		14.4	16.5	19.1	18.6		22.0	15.4	14.7	11.5	11.9
5. Agree	14.7	13.0	16.3		13.1	11.5	20.3	12.3		19.1	10.7	10.3	8.1	9.5
Item 7020 N(Wtd)	2737	1284	1399		651	867	806	413		1046	460	252	468	42
A23I: There is too much hard rock music on the radio these days														
1. Disagree	50.5	51.9	49.4		52.1	51.0	52.1	43.8		36.2	58.0	55.2	68.5	73.2
2. Mostly disagree	21.5	21.1	22.1		20.9	24.2	18.7	22.5		24.8	22.2	23.8	14.0	12.2
3. Neither	15.3	15.3	14.9		15.8	14.2	15.2	17.2		21.2	12.2	9.5	9.4	7.3
4. Mostly agree	6.9	6.9	6.9		4.9	6.7	7.5	9.7		9.2	3.3	8.3	5.1	4.9
5. Agree	5.7	4.6	6.7		6.5	4.0	6.6	6.5		8.6	4.1	3.2	2.8	4.9
Item 7030 N(Wtd)	2735	1284	1396		651	869	801	413		1042	459	252	470	41
A23J: In the United States, we put too much emphasis on making profits and not enough on human well-being														
1. Disagree	3.2	4.4	2.3		4.3	2.8	3.3	2.4		2.7	3.9	3.6	2.4	9.5
2. Mostly disagree	6.2	8.9	3.9		4.6	7.6	6.4	5.6		6.2	6.3	5.2	4.3	4.8
3. Neither	12.3	15.8	9.3		12.1	11.8	11.0	16.2		11.1	14.1	9.1	12.8	21.4
4. Mostly agree	35.7	34.1	36.8		33.2	40.0	31.2	39.5		38.0	36.4	39.3	34.2	11.9
5. Agree	42.6	37.0	47.8		45.8	38.0	48.1	36.3		42.0	39.3	42.9	46.4	52.4
Item 5990 N(Wtd)	2731	1280	1396		651	868	799	413		1044	461	252	468	42

CAUTION: Items were rearranged after 1975; changes in context may produce spurious "trends" (see page 12).

QUESTIONNAIRE FORM 2 1975	TOTAL	SEX			REGION					ILLICIT DRUG USE: LIFETIME				
		M	F		NE	NC	S	W		None	Mari-juana Only	Few Pills	More Pills	Any Her-oin
Weighted No. of Cases:	2972	1404	1475		678	926	934	434		1109	484	270	494	47
% of Weighted Total:	100.0	47.2	49.6		22.8	31.2	31.4	14.6		37.3	16.3	9.1	16.6	1.6

A23K: People are too much concerned with material things these days

1. Disagree	2.5	2.9	2.2		2.8	1.7	4.0	.7		2.0	2.2	.8	2.8	4.8
2. Mostly disagree	4.9	7.4	2.7		5.0	5.2	4.8	3.9		4.6	3.7	5.2	4.9	4.8
3. Neither	14.9	18.6	11.6		13.8	13.8	14.8	18.7		13.0	15.6	14.7	14.1	19.0
4. Mostly agree	33.9	35.9	31.7		36.5	36.9	27.9	35.3		32.9	36.6	33.9	36.4	28.6
5. Agree	43.9	35.2	51.8		41.8	42.3	48.4	41.4		47.4	41.7	45.4	41.8	42.9
Item 6000 N(Wtd)	2716	1271	1389		643	868	795	411		1039	456	251	467	42

A23L: Since it helps the economy to grow, people should be encouraged to buy more

1. Disagree	16.8	13.1	20.4		16.3	13.0	20.3	18.8		14.6	18.1	15.5	18.5	26.2
2. Mostly disagree	21.2	18.3	23.6		20.7	23.7	16.8	25.4		20.6	21.7	24.3	21.0	28.6
3. Neither	37.7	37.2	38.5		39.1	36.5	36.7	39.8		39.3	36.1	40.2	36.5	31.0
4. Mostly agree	17.0	21.2	13.1		15.2	18.8	19.2	11.7		18.8	14.8	15.1	16.3	16.7
5. Agree	7.3	10.2	4.4		8.5	8.1	7.0	4.4		6.8	9.5	4.8	7.9	-
Item 6010 N(Wtd)	2717	1271	1394		644	861	803	410		1044	452	251	466	42

A23M: There is nothing wrong with advertising that gets people to buy things they don't really need

1. Disagree	37.4	33.0	41.4		38.3	32.8	41.5	37.5		37.7	35.8	37.3	40.7	42.9
2. Mostly disagree	26.8	25.6	28.1		26.1	32.8	22.9	23.2		27.5	26.2	32.9	26.2	23.8
3. Neither	20.1	20.9	19.3		18.5	20.9	18.1	24.5		21.0	18.9	17.5	18.8	16.7
4. Mostly agree	9.9	13.2	7.0		11.6	8.7	10.1	9.7		8.5	11.7	9.5	10.4	11.9
5. Agree	5.8	7.2	4.3		5.4	5.0	7.3	5.1		5.2	7.4	3.2	3.6	7.1
Item 6020 N(Wtd)	2733	1285	1395		647	867	805	413		1042	461	252	469	42

A23N: There will probably be more shortages in the future, so Americans will have to learn how to be happy with fewer "things"

1. Disagree	4.0	4.7	3.4		5.2	3.7	3.8	2.9		3.2	4.3	2.0	5.1	7.1
2. Mostly disagree	6.9	7.9	5.8		6.0	7.7	7.3	5.8		6.2	7.8	4.0	6.6	7.1
3. Neither	14.0	13.7	14.4		14.5	15.8	11.5	14.5		13.9	13.7	12.7	13.9	9.5
4. Mostly agree	33.6	33.4	33.7		34.3	34.9	29.3	38.0		33.7	32.1	32.1	37.4	26.2
5. Agree	41.5	40.4	42.7		40.1	37.8	48.1	38.7		43.1	42.3	49.6	37.0	50.0
Item 6030 N(Wtd)	2735	1286	1398		648	866	808	413		1045	461	252	468	42

The next section of this questionnaire is about government and public affairs.

A31: Some people think about what's going on in government very often, and others are not that interested. How much of an interest do you take in government and current events?

1. No interest at all	5.4	5.6	5.1		6.8	5.8	4.8	3.8		3.9	4.7	4.9	6.4	11.9
2. Very little interest	17.4	14.1	20.4		20.0	17.4	15.0	17.5		14.2	18.4	19.7	21.6	9.5
3. Some interest	47.5	45.1	49.7		48.6	48.3	46.0	46.8		48.7	46.7	44.3	44.3	45.2
4. A lot of interest	23.6	26.9	20.5		18.9	23.5	26.5	25.3		26.5	22.9	25.8	20.5	26.2
5. A very great interest	6.2	8.3	4.5		5.8	5.0	7.5	6.6		6.6	7.3	5.7	7.3	9.5
Item 6330 N(Wtd)	2602	1221	1341		619	817	771	395		1034	450	244	454	42

A32: Do you think some of the people running the government are crooked or dishonest?

1. Most of them are crooked or dishonest	16.3	16.0	16.6		17.8	16.2	17.4	12.2		13.7	15.4	16.7	20.2	23.8
2. Quite a few are	40.3	39.6	41.0		41.6	39.9	40.5	39.0		38.6	41.3	43.7	42.8	42.9
3. Some are	40.9	41.2	40.6		38.5	41.5	41.1	43.4		44.7	41.1	36.3	35.7	31.0
4. Hardly any are	2.1	2.6	1.7		1.8	1.8	1.3	5.1		2.7	2.0	2.4	.9	-
5. None at all are crooked or dishonest	.3	.6	.2		.3	.5	-	.5		.2	.2	.4	.2	2.4
Item 6340 N(Wtd)	2584	1216	1328		611	814	766	392		1026	448	245	451	42

CAUTION: Items were rearranged after 1975; changes in context may produce spurious "trends" (see page 12).

QUESTIONNAIRE FORM 2 1975	TOTAL	SEX			REGION					ILLICIT DRUG USE: LIFETIME				
		M	F		NE	NC	S	W		None	Marijuana Only	Few Pills	More Pills	Any Heroin
Weighted No. of Cases:	2972	1404	1475		678	926	934	434		1109	484	270	494	47
% of Weighted Total:	100.0	47.2	49.6		22.8	31.2	31.4	14.6		37.3	16.3	9.1	16.6	1.6

A33: Do you think the government wastes much of the money we pay in taxes?

	TOTAL	M	F		NE	NC	S	W		None	Marijuana Only	Few Pills	More Pills	Any Heroin
1. Nearly all tax money is wasted	7.7	8.6	6.7		7.0	7.5	8.7	7.4		6.2	7.8	8.2	8.4	9.5
2. A lot of tax money is wasted	50.2	50.4	50.0		55.0	50.7	46.9	48.1		47.7	52.0	54.1	56.5	61.9
3. Some tax money is wasted	36.7	35.3	38.3		34.1	37.1	37.6	38.6		40.2	35.3	30.7	31.7	21.4
4. A little tax money wasted	4.8	5.2	4.4		3.6	4.3	6.2	5.1		5.3	4.2	6.1	2.9	4.8
5. No tax money is wasted	.5	.5	.6		.3	.5	.8	.8		.6	.7	.4	.2	-
Item 6350 N(Wtd)	2579	1215	1325		613	812	763	391		1025	448	244	451	42

A34: How much of the time do you think you can trust the government in Washington to do what is right?

	TOTAL	M	F		NE	NC	S	W		None	Marijuana Only	Few Pills	More Pills	Any Heroin
1. Almost always	4.9	6.2	3.8		3.8	4.3	6.7	4.7		5.6	6.3	2.5	4.5	2.4
2. Often	28.4	31.0	26.3		23.7	29.6	28.9	31.8		31.5	27.1	27.0	26.8	16.7
3. Sometimes	48.2	44.3	51.3		50.5	47.1	47.1	48.8		48.9	46.9	52.5	46.4	50.0
4. Seldom	15.5	15.1	15.8		17.6	16.2	13.7	14.0		11.7	16.4	16.4	19.4	28.6
5. Never	3.0	3.4	2.8		4.3	2.8	3.4	.8		2.4	3.1	1.2	2.9	2.4
Item 6360 N(Wtd)	2568	1205	1323		608	813	760	387		1020	446	244	448	42

A35: Do you feel that the people running the government are smart people who usually know what they are doing?

	TOTAL	M	F		NE	NC	S	W		None	Marijuana Only	Few Pills	More Pills	Any Heroin
1. They almost always know what they are doing	8.6	10.2	7.3		7.3	8.6	9.0	10.5		7.8	10.3	5.4	8.7	4.8
2. They usually know what they are doing	43.3	42.5	43.9		38.9	43.9	44.5	46.9		47.1	42.4	45.5	41.9	26.2
3. They sometimes know what they are doing	36.6	34.8	38.0		39.8	36.1	35.7	34.1		36.0	37.4	40.9	33.2	40.5
4. They seldom know what they are doing	9.3	9.8	9.2		12.0	8.4	9.3	7.2		7.3	7.6	7.9	14.5	26.2
5. They never know what they are doing	2.1	2.7	1.5		2.1	3.2	1.3	1.5		1.8	2.5	.4	2.0	2.4
Item 6370 N(Wtd)	2567	1205	1322		606	807	764	390		1026	446	242	449	42

A36: Would you say the government is pretty much run for a few big interests looking out for themselves, or is it run for the benefit of all the people?

	TOTAL	M	F		NE	NC	S	W		None	Marijuana Only	Few Pills	More Pills	Any Heroin
1. Nearly always run for a few big interests	10.5	13.1	8.4		11.6	10.7	10.5	8.9		8.8	12.2	8.5	11.3	16.7
2. Usually run for a few big interests	24.0	25.4	22.6		26.1	23.3	22.4	25.5		22.0	23.1	29.7	24.8	28.6
3. Run some for the big interests, some for the people	46.6	43.7	49.5		47.1	47.0	46.0	46.5		47.4	48.4	41.9	48.9	42.9
4. Usually run for the benefit of all the people	16.0	14.6	17.0		12.6	16.5	17.9	17.1		17.8	13.8	18.2	14.0	9.5
5. Nearly always run for the benefit of all the people	2.8	3.2	2.4		2.8	2.6	3.3	2.1		4.0	2.7	1.7	1.1	2.4
Item 6380 N(Wtd)	2528	1180	1308		597	795	755	381		1012	442	236	444	42

A37: Have you ever done, or do you plan to do, the following things?

A37A: Vote in a public election

	TOTAL	M	F		NE	NC	S	W		None	Marijuana Only	Few Pills	More Pills	Any Heroin
1. I probably won't do this	4.6	4.4	4.6		6.8	4.6	3.6	3.3		3.8	3.2	4.6	4.4	6.5
2. Don't know	8.1	8.8	7.4		9.9	7.3	7.3	9.0		6.5	8.9	3.5	9.1	19.6
3. I probably will do this	81.7	79.7	83.7		79.8	80.9	84.0	80.8		83.9	81.5	84.2	82.2	76.1
4. I have already done this	5.6	7.1	4.3		3.6	7.2	5.2	6.7		5.8	6.4	7.7	4.2	-
Item 6390 N(Wtd)	2709	1260	1403		619	833	868	390		1091	470	259	473	46

CAUTION: Items were rearranged after 1975; changes in context may produce spurious "trends" (see page 12).

QUESTIONNAIRE FORM 2 1975	TOTAL	SEX			REGION					ILLICIT DRUG USE: LIFETIME				
		M	F		NE	NC	S	W		None	Mari- juana Only	Few Pills	More Pills	Any Her- oin
Weighted No. of Cases:	*2972*	*1404*	*1475*		*678*	*926*	*934*	*434*		*1109*	*484*	*270*	*494*	*47*
% of Weighted Total:	*100.0*	*47.2*	*49.6*		*22.8*	*31.2*	*31.4*	*14.6*		*37.3*	*16.3*	*9.1*	*16.6*	*1.6*
A37B: Write to public officials														
1. I probably won't do this	20.0	17.5	22.2		24.1	19.1	19.4	16.5		17.5	18.6	17.1	23.5	32.6
2. Don't know	45.1	43.2	46.5		42.5	44.7	46.6	46.6		46.0	44.3	45.1	41.3	28.3
3. I probably will do this	22.0	25.7	19.0		22.7	22.4	20.8	22.9		22.7	23.9	22.2	21.6	30.4
4. I have already done this	12.9	13.5	12.3		10.7	13.8	13.2	13.9		13.8	13.1	15.6	13.8	8.7
Item 6400 N(Wtd)	*2702*	*1258*	*1399*		*617*	*832*	*864*	*388*		*1087*	*472*	*257*	*472*	*46*
A37C: Give money to a political candidate or cause														
1. I probably won't do this	39.8	39.9	39.6		43.9	41.7	35.9	38.3		35.9	39.5	39.3	44.6	56.5
2. Don't know	36.8	35.5	37.9		39.1	33.5	37.3	39.4		40.6	36.9	30.0	32.6	19.6
3. I probably will do this	16.6	16.6	16.7		12.0	17.8	19.0	16.3		17.4	17.4	19.8	15.2	15.2
4. I have already done this	6.7	8.0	5.8		5.0	7.1	8.0	6.0		6.0	6.2	10.9	7.6	8.7
Item 6410 N(Wtd)	*2697*	*1252*	*1400*		*617*	*828*	*867*	*386*		*1089*	*471*	*257*	*473*	*46*
A37D: Work in a political campaign														
1. I probably won't do this	45.6	46.4	44.7		48.7	47.6	41.7	45.1		45.1	43.3	44.5	43.8	56.5
2. Don't know	36.0	36.0	35.9		37.2	33.3	37.6	36.0		36.2	36.7	35.9	36.8	26.1
3. I probably will do this	9.7	9.9	9.9		8.3	8.1	12.4	9.6		10.5	10.6	9.4	9.3	10.9
4. I have already done this	8.7	7.8	9.6		5.8	11.1	8.3	9.3		8.2	9.1	10.2	9.9	6.5
Item 6420 N(Wtd)	*2698*	*1255*	*1399*		*618*	*829*	*866*	*386*		*1089*	*471*	*256*	*473*	*46*
A37E: Participate in a lawful demonstration														
1. I probably won't do this	40.6	33.7	47.0		38.9	41.9	40.3	41.1		49.4	35.6	39.3	26.5	17.4
2. Don't know	40.1	41.8	38.3		40.5	38.6	41.5	39.5		39.0	45.1	35.8	40.9	37.0
3. I probably will do this	15.0	18.6	11.6		14.4	14.9	15.9	14.5		10.3	15.0	19.8	24.8	21.7
4. I have already done this	4.3	5.9	2.9		6.1	4.6	2.3	4.9		1.3	4.2	4.7	7.8	23.9
Item 6430 N(Wtd)	*2701*	*1255*	*1401*		*619*	*832*	*863*	*387*		*1091*	*472*	*257*	*472*	*46*
A37F: Boycott certain products or stores														
1. I probably won't do this	32.4	27.9	36.4		23.6	33.5	36.2	36.0		36.3	29.1	32.3	23.1	20.5
2. Don't know	38.3	40.8	36.3		36.7	39.1	37.1	41.5		37.8	37.2	35.0	42.2	29.5
3. I probably will do this	19.9	21.3	18.6		29.8	18.9	17.5	11.9		18.6	23.4	22.2	21.6	27.3
4. I have already done this	9.3	10.0	8.8		9.9	8.5	9.2	10.6		7.3	10.2	10.1	13.1	22.7
Item 6440 N(Wtd)	*2697*	*1251*	*1401*		*618*	*831*	*862*	*386*		*1090*	*470*	*257*	*472*	*44*
A38: How much do you agree or disagree with each of the following statements?														
A38A: The U.S. should begin a gradual program of disarming whether other countries do or not														
1. Disagree	30.5	42.4	19.9		27.2	28.7	35.8	27.6		31.1	33.4	27.0	32.0	40.0
2. Mostly disagree	21.2	22.6	20.1		20.0	24.0	19.3	21.7		22.5	22.2	21.8	18.4	15.6
3. Neither	31.9	22.1	40.9		32.5	31.2	30.1	36.7		32.3	28.7	32.5	30.5	24.4
4. Mostly agree	11.1	8.5	13.5		13.7	11.4	9.0	11.0		9.3	11.4	13.5	14.7	15.6
5. Agree	5.2	4.4	5.6		6.5	4.6	5.7	3.2		4.8	4.5	5.2	4.3	4.4
Item 6450 N(Wtd)	*2623*	*1231*	*1348*		*600*	*807*	*843*	*373*		*1070*	*464*	*252*	*462*	*45*
A38B: There may be times when the U.S. should go to war to protect the rights of other countries														
1. Disagree	15.2	15.8	14.7		17.3	15.9	14.0	12.8		14.9	13.5	15.7	18.1	13.3
2. Mostly disagree	21.4	20.9	21.7		21.8	22.6	20.4	20.8		19.6	23.6	24.8	21.6	40.0
3. Neither	27.1	24.8	29.0		29.8	26.8	23.3	32.3		26.0	28.1	26.0	26.3	17.8
4. Mostly agree	25.8	25.5	26.2		22.5	27.4	27.9	23.2		28.4	24.8	23.2	27.4	15.6
5. Agree	10.5	12.9	8.3		8.5	7.5	14.4	10.9		11.1	10.1	10.6	6.5	13.3
Item 5690 N(Wtd)	*2641*	*1237*	*1358*		*601*	*811*	*853*	*375*		*1077*	*467*	*254*	*463*	*45*

CAUTION: Items were rearranged after 1975; changes in context may produce spurious "trends" (see page 12).

QUESTIONNAIRE FORM 2 1975	TOTAL	SEX			REGION					ILLICIT DRUG USE: LIFETIME				
		M	F		NE	NC	S	W		None	Mari- juana Only	Few Pills	More Pills	Any Her- oin
Weighted No. of Cases:	2972	1404	1475		678	926	934	434		1109	484	270	494	47
% of Weighted Total:	100.0	47.2	49.6		22.8	31.2	31.4	14.6		37.3	16.3	9.1	16.6	1.6

A38C: The U.S. should be willing to go to war to protect its own economic interests

	TOTAL	M	F		NE	NC	S	W		None	Mari- juana Only	Few Pills	More Pills	Any Her- oin
1. Disagree	7.4	7.4	7.5		9.3	8.4	5.1	7.8		6.4	7.6	7.1	9.2	13.3
2. Mostly disagree	10.7	11.0	10.0		11.3	11.1	7.9	14.7		9.4	9.7	11.8	11.8	22.2
3. Neither	26.0	24.2	27.7		29.8	28.4	20.2	27.9		25.9	28.1	26.0	25.8	15.6
4. Mostly agree	32.2	31.5	33.2		32.1	31.3	34.6	28.7		34.8	27.9	31.5	31.0	35.6
5. Agree	23.7	25.9	21.7		17.6	20.8	32.2	20.6		23.5	26.6	23.6	22.2	15.6
Item 6460 N(Wtd)	2631	1230	1356		601	811	846	373		1075	462	254	465	45

A38D: The only good reason for the U.S. to go to war is to defend against an attack on our own country

	TOTAL	M	F		NE	NC	S	W		None	Mari- juana Only	Few Pills	More Pills	Any Her- oin
1. Disagree	6.5	7.5	5.6		5.7	4.4	9.5	5.3		7.1	7.7	5.9	5.6	4.4
2. Mostly disagree	12.2	13.2	11.5		11.4	13.0	12.6	11.2		13.9	12.3	14.9	9.9	4.4
3. Neither	14.9	13.7	15.7		16.2	14.6	13.9	15.8		13.7	16.8	12.5	14.3	15.6
4. Mostly agree	33.4	31.2	35.5		31.6	34.0	33.3	35.0		33.8	32.9	31.8	35.2	28.9
5. Agree	33.0	34.4	31.7		35.1	34.1	30.6	32.6		31.4	30.1	34.9	34.8	48.9
Item 6470 N(Wtd)	2631	1228	1359		598	810	849	374		1078	465	255	463	45

A38E: The U.S. does not need to have greater military power than the soviet union

	TOTAL	M	F		NE	NC	S	W		None	Mari- juana Only	Few Pills	More Pills	Any Her- oin
1. Disagree	26.7	28.7	25.1		21.7	22.3	37.5	19.4		28.0	23.4	30.6	24.8	20.0
2. Mostly disagree	24.9	26.0	23.9		24.4	26.4	25.7	20.8		26.8	22.9	20.0	24.6	28.9
3. Neither	28.2	24.5	32.0		29.0	30.6	22.2	35.8		26.1	30.7	28.6	31.3	35.6
4. Mostly agree	11.5	11.2	11.3		14.1	11.1	7.7	16.4		10.9	14.1	11.0	11.6	8.9
5. Agree	8.7	9.7	7.7		10.9	9.7	6.9	7.5		8.4	9.1	9.4	8.0	8.9
Item 6480 N(Wtd)	2618	1228	1345		594	808	845	371		1068	462	255	464	45

A38F: The U.S. ought to have much more military power than any other nation in the world

	TOTAL	M	F		NE	NC	S	W		None	Mari- juana Only	Few Pills	More Pills	Any Her- oin
1. Disagree	12.1	11.0	12.8		13.5	12.8	11.1	10.8		11.7	12.1	11.1	13.9	15.6
2. Mostly disagree	18.3	19.1	17.5		19.2	21.5	13.8	20.1		19.6	18.8	17.0	17.4	22.2
3. Neither	34.7	29.5	39.9		37.4	35.3	29.3	41.2		33.1	33.6	36.4	38.2	37.8
4. Mostly agree	18.6	20.2	16.7		15.0	17.1	23.1	17.1		19.1	18.5	19.8	16.7	8.9
5. Agree	16.4	20.3	13.1		14.8	13.4	22.8	11.1		16.5	17.2	15.8	13.9	15.6
Item 6490 N(Wtd)	2607	1223	1340		593	805	839	369		1064	464	253	461	45

A38G: Our present foreign policy is based on our own narrow economic and power interests

	TOTAL	M	F		NE	NC	S	W		None	Mari- juana Only	Few Pills	More Pills	Any Her- oin
1. Disagree	3.2	3.7	2.8		2.8	2.9	4.6	1.7		4.3	2.4	.8	2.2	2.3
2. Mostly disagree	10.6	11.8	9.4		11.2	13.2	9.0	7.3		10.3	9.8	7.3	11.0	14.0
3. Neither	50.2	43.3	56.5		49.7	49.7	49.4	54.5		49.8	52.7	49.4	50.6	32.6
4. Mostly agree	23.9	27.3	20.8		21.6	23.9	24.4	26.5		24.7	23.7	29.1	22.5	37.2
5. Agree	12.1	13.8	10.4		14.8	10.3	12.5	10.3		10.9	11.1	13.4	13.5	14.0
Item 6500 N(Wtd)	2552	1202	1306		580	795	818	358		1047	459	247	453	43

A38H: Servicemen should obey orders without question

	TOTAL	M	F		NE	NC	S	W		None	Mari- juana Only	Few Pills	More Pills	Any Her- oin
1. Disagree	16.5	16.3	16.5		17.3	17.3	16.8	13.0		14.4	15.7	18.8	20.1	13.3
2. Mostly disagree	23.0	21.0	25.1		24.7	23.8	21.3	22.5		22.0	25.6	28.9	21.6	28.9
3. Neither	27.8	25.9	29.8		27.6	28.3	24.6	34.7		27.6	27.5	21.5	29.4	24.4
4. Mostly agree	22.0	23.8	20.4		21.2	22.7	22.7	20.1		24.3	21.3	19.9	21.4	17.8
5. Agree	10.6	13.1	8.3		9.1	7.9	14.4	9.8		11.6	9.9	10.9	7.4	15.6
Item 6510 N(Wtd)	2618	1218	1356		595	810	845	369		1075	465	256	462	45

CAUTION: Items were rearranged after 1975; changes in context may produce spurious "trends" (see page 12).

QUESTIONNAIRE FORM 2 1975	TOTAL	SEX			REGION					ILLICIT DRUG USE: LIFETIME				
		M	F		NE	NC	S	W		None	Mari-juana Only	Few Pills	More Pills	Any Her-oin
Weighted No. of Cases:	2972	1404	1475		678	926	934	434		1109	484	270	494	47
% of Weighted Total:	100.0	47.2	49.6		22.8	31.2	31.4	14.6		37.3	16.3	9.1	16.6	1.6

A39: This section deals with activities which may be against the rules or against the law. We hope you will answer all of these questions. However, if you find a question which you cannot answer honestly, we would prefer that you leave it blank. Remember, only the research staff will see your answers. Your answers will never be connected with your name. In the last year how often have you...‡

A39A: Argued or had a fight with either of your parents

	TOTAL	M	F		NE	NC	S	W		None	Mari-juana Only	Few Pills	More Pills	Any Her-oin
1. Not at all	12.1	14.4	10.1		8.6	9.5	16.5	13.4		15.6	10.3	5.4	5.7	8.7
2. Once	8.0	8.7	7.0		6.2	8.7	8.8	7.0		10.9	4.9	6.6	4.0	6.5
3. Twice	9.6	11.0	8.5		8.4	10.3	9.3	10.7		10.8	8.2	9.3	6.6	6.5
4. 3 or 4 times	22.6	23.5	21.4		23.8	22.9	20.3	24.9		22.9	25.2	22.6	21.1	21.7
5. 5 or more times	47.7	42.4	52.8		53.0	48.4	45.1	43.9		39.9	51.2	56.0	62.6	54.3
Item 6520 N(Wtd)	2613	1198	1372		596	802	841	374		1078	465	257	470	46

A39B: Hit an instructor or supervisor

	TOTAL	M	F		NE	NC	S	W		None	Mari-juana Only	Few Pills	More Pills	Any Her-oin
1. Not at all	96.9	94.5	99.1		96.5	95.9	97.4	98.1		98.9	95.5	96.5	95.1	91.1
2. Once	2.1	3.6	.8		2.0	2.5	2.1	1.6		.7	3.4	2.7	3.2	6.7
3. Twice	.4	.7	.1		.7	.6	.2	-		.1	.6	.8	.6	2.2
4. 3 or 4 times	.4	.7	.1		.5	.5	.2	.3		.1	.2	-	1.1	-
5. 5 or more times	.2	.4	-		.2	.5	-	.3		.1	.2	-	.2	2.2
Item 6530 N(Wtd)	2638	1211	1384		603	811	847	377		1089	471	257	471	45

A39C: Gotten into a serious fight in school or at work

	TOTAL	M	F		NE	NC	S	W		None	Mari-juana Only	Few Pills	More Pills	Any Her-oin
1. Not at all	85.4	80.0	90.5		84.2	83.6	88.4	84.1		90.7	81.3	84.3	79.2	80.0
2. Once	9.1	11.6	6.3		9.5	10.1	6.5	11.6		6.5	11.9	10.2	10.4	15.6
3. Twice	3.3	5.0	2.0		3.3	3.2	3.6	3.2		1.9	4.0	1.6	6.2	2.2
4. 3 or 4 times	1.7	2.3	1.0		2.0	2.2	1.3	.8		.4	2.3	3.5	3.2	-
5. 5 or more times	.6	1.1	.1		.8	.9	.2	-		.4	.2	.4	1.1	2.2
Item 6540 N(Wtd)	2634	1206	1384		603	810	844	378		1089	470	255	471	45

A39D: Taken part in a fight where a group of your friends were against another group

	TOTAL	M	F		NE	NC	S	W		None	Mari-juana Only	Few Pills	More Pills	Any Her-oin
1. Not at all	82.6	76.8	87.6		78.8	82.1	84.5	85.3		90.9	78.9	79.7	74.5	76.1
2. Once	10.8	13.6	8.6		12.4	11.4	9.2	10.4		6.1	15.1	12.1	13.8	10.9
3. Twice	3.6	5.1	2.2		3.8	3.5	3.9	2.7		1.8	2.3	6.6	5.5	8.7
4. 3 or 4 times	1.8	2.6	1.2		2.6	1.9	1.2	1.6		.9	2.3	1.2	3.8	2.2
5. 5 or more times	1.2	1.9	.4		2.3	1.1	.9	.3		.4	1.3	.8	2.1	2.2
Item 6550 N(Wtd)	2630	1208	1379		604	806	845	375		1084	470	256	470	46

A39E: Hurt someone badly enough to need bandages or a doctor

	TOTAL	M	F		NE	NC	S	W		None	Mari-juana Only	Few Pills	More Pills	Any Her-oin
1. Not at all	90.5	82.5	97.8		90.9	90.1	90.6	90.7		94.7	87.2	88.7	86.6	82.6
2. Once	6.1	11.1	1.5		5.1	6.3	6.3	6.3		4.3	7.9	7.0	7.7	8.7
3. Twice	2.0	3.8	.5		1.3	2.0	2.7	1.6		.6	3.0	2.7	3.4	6.5
4. 3 or 4 times	.8	1.7	.1		1.7	1.0	.2	.8		.4	.9	1.2	1.1	-
5. 5 or more times	.5	1.0	-		1.0	.6	.1	.5		.1	.6	.4	1.1	2.2
Item 6560 N(Wtd)	2629	1203	1382		602	806	843	378		1089	469	256	470	46

A39F: Used a knife or gun or some other thing (like a club) to get something from a person

	TOTAL	M	F		NE	NC	S	W		None	Mari-juana Only	Few Pills	More Pills	Any Her-oin
1. Not at all	97.3	95.2	99.2		97.0	97.9	96.4	98.4		99.3	95.5	99.2	94.5	91.3
2. Once	1.3	2.4	.3		.8	1.4	1.8	.5		.4	2.6	-	2.3	2.2
3. Twice	.6	1.2	.1		1.0	.4	.6	.8		.2	1.3	.4	1.3	-
4. 3 or 4 times	.4	.7	.1		.2	.2	.7	.3		.1	.4	-	1.3	-
5. 5 or more times	.4	.5	.4		.8	.2	.5	-		.1	.2	.4	.8	8.7
Item 6570 N(Wtd)	2634	1207	1383		603	808	845	378		1089	470	256	473	46

‡=Wording changed in subsequent years.

CAUTION: Items were rearranged after 1975; changes in context may produce spurious "trends" (see page 12).

QUESTIONNAIRE FORM 2 1975	TOTAL	SEX			REGION					ILLICIT DRUG USE: LIFETIME				
		M	F		NE	NC	S	W		None	Marijuana Only	Few Pills	More Pills	Any Heroin
Weighted No. of Cases:	2972	1404	1475		678	926	934	434		1109	484	270	494	47
% of Weighted Total:	100.0	47.2	49.6		22.8	31.2	31.4	14.6		37.3	16.3	9.1	16.6	1.6

A39G: Taken something not belonging to you worth under $50

1. Not at all	67.6	56.9	76.7		67.6	65.2	70.8	65.6		80.8	59.8	59.8	50.5	60.0
2. Once	13.2	15.6	11.1		11.6	14.4	12.9	14.1		9.9	15.5	13.4	16.9	15.6
3. Twice	7.3	9.8	5.2		6.4	7.3	7.2	9.2		3.4	10.5	13.0	11.3	2.2
4. 3 or 4 times	5.6	7.5	4.0		6.9	5.0	5.3	5.7		3.0	6.8	5.1	10.1	4.4
5. 5 or more times	6.3	10.1	2.9		7.6	8.0	3.9	5.4		3.0	7.6	9.1	11.1	17.8
Item 6580 N(Wtd)	2599	1185	1372		595	799	837	369		1083	458	254	467	45

A39H: Taken something not belonging to you worth over $50

1. Not at all	94.4	89.3	99.0		94.6	93.7	95.5	93.0		98.3	94.6	95.7	87.7	77.8
2. Once	2.7	5.1	.6		2.2	3.4	2.1	3.2		.8	3.0	1.6	5.9	11.1
3. Twice	1.0	2.0	.1		.8	1.0	.7	1.6		.1	2.0	1.2	1.7	4.4
4. 3 or 4 times	.8	1.4	.1		.5	.9	.6	1.1		-	.2	1.2	1.5	2.2
5. 5 or more times	1.2	2.2	.3		1.7	1.1	1.0	1.1		.8	.2	.4	3.2	4.4
Item 6590 N(Wtd)	2608	1190	1374		598	798	840	373		1087	460	253	471	45

A39I: Taken something from a store without paying for it

1. Not at all	64.9	55.3	72.9		61.3	63.7	67.9	66.8		81.1	57.5	55.5	47.4	40.0
2. Once	13.7	16.0	11.8		12.8	13.7	15.1	12.0		8.9	16.8	13.8	18.8	13.3
3. Twice	7.1	9.2	5.3		8.1	8.0	5.0	8.0		3.2	9.7	11.4	9.8	6.7
4. 3 or 4 times	6.7	7.5	6.2		7.2	6.1	6.2	8.6		3.2	8.8	7.5	9.8	8.9
5. 5 or more times	7.6	12.0	3.9		10.6	8.6	5.9	4.5		3.5	7.3	11.8	14.1	28.9
Item 6600 N(Wtd)	2604	1187	1375		595	798	837	374		1085	464	254	468	45

A39J: Taken a car that didn't belong to someone in your family without permission of the owner

1. Not at all	96.1	94.1	97.9		95.2	95.1	97.7	96.3		98.6	96.0	96.5	92.6	91.3
2. Once	2.2	3.0	1.5		2.3	3.1	1.2	2.1		.7	1.7	1.6	4.7	6.5
3. Twice	.6	.9	.4		1.2	.6	.4	.3		.2	1.1	1.2	.9	2.2
4. 3 or 4 times	.4	.8	.1		.5	.4	.1	.8		.1	.4	-	.9	-
5. 5 or more times	.6	1.3	.1		.7	.6	.6	.8		.4	.9	.4	1.1	-
Item 6610 N(Wtd)	2619	1198	1381		602	801	841	375		1086	470	257	470	46

A39K: Taken part of a car without permission of the owner

1. Not at all	94.4	89.4	98.8		94.3	93.9	95.1	94.4		97.7	91.9	96.5	89.2	87.0
2. Once	3.2	6.1	.7		3.8	3.4	2.3	3.7		1.1	6.2	2.0	5.7	6.5
3. Twice	1.2	2.3	.1		.3	1.4	1.8	.8		.4	1.1	.4	2.5	8.7
4. 3 or 4 times	.6	.9	.3		.8	.6	.4	.3		.3	.4	.8	.8	-
5. 5 or more times	.6	1.3	.1		.5	.7	.6	.5		.5	.2	.4	1.7	-
Item 6620 N(Wtd)	2620	1198	1379		600	802	843	374		1087	469	256	471	46

A39L: Gone into some house or building when you weren't supposed to be there

1. Not at all	71.9	60.5	81.7		72.3	68.8	73.7	74.1		79.9	69.1	65.6	58.9	54.3
2. Once	13.2	16.6	10.3		10.9	14.4	13.5	13.5		11.4	11.1	19.1	16.0	17.4
3. Twice	7.5	11.8	3.7		8.0	9.0	6.7	5.4		4.9	11.7	7.8	10.2	10.9
4. 3 or 4 times	3.8	5.5	2.1		4.0	4.4	3.0	3.8		2.3	3.4	3.5	6.8	10.9
5. 5 or more times	3.6	5.5	2.1		4.8	3.5	3.1	3.2		1.6	4.7	3.5	7.9	4.3
Item 6630 N(Wtd)	2604	1191	1372		603	800	832	370		1080	469	256	470	46

CAUTION: Items were rearranged after 1975; changes in context may produce spurious "trends" (see page 12).

QUESTIONNAIRE FORM 2 1975	TOTAL	SEX			REGION					ILLICIT DRUG USE: LIFETIME				
		M	F		NE	NC	S	W		None	Marijuana Only	Few Pills	More Pills	Any Heroin
Weighted No. of Cases:	2972	1404	1475		678	926	934	434		1109	484	270	494	47
% of Weighted Total:	100.0	47.2	49.6		22.8	31.2	31.4	14.6		37.3	16.3	9.1	16.6	1.6

A39M: Set fire to someone's property on purpose

1. Not at all	98.3	96.7	99.7		97.7	98.0	98.7	98.7		99.7	98.1	98.8	96.4	97.8
2. Once	1.0	1.8	.1		1.3	1.1	.5	1.1		.2	1.1	.8	2.6	2.2
3. Twice	.4	.8	-		.3	.5	.5	.5		.1	.4	.4	.6	-
4. 3 or 4 times	.2	.3	.1		.3	.2	.1	-		-	.2	.4	.2	-
5. 5 or more times	.2	.3	-		.2	.1	.2	-		.1	-	-	.4	-
Item 6640 N(Wtd)	2616	1196	1379		601	802	840	374		1086	470	256	470	46

A39N: Damaged school property on purpose

1. Not at all	87.2	79.0	94.2		84.6	85.2	90.4	88.2		94.6	80.8	88.3	77.1	62.2
2. Once	6.3	10.2	3.1		6.8	7.8	4.7	6.2		3.2	9.4	5.9	10.6	8.9
3. Twice	3.6	6.1	1.5		4.2	3.5	3.2	3.5		1.3	6.6	2.0	5.7	11.1
4. 3 or 4 times	1.5	2.1	.9		2.5	1.8	.7	.8		.2	2.1	2.0	3.4	4.4
5. 5 or more times	1.5	2.7	.3		1.8	1.9	1.0	1.1		.6	.9	1.6	3.2	11.1
Item 6650 N(Wtd)	2604	1189	1373		599	799	833	373		1077	469	256	472	45

A39O: Damaged property at work on purpose

1. Not at all	94.9	90.4	98.9		93.5	94.9	95.9	94.4		97.7	95.1	95.3	89.2	88.9
2. Once	2.3	4.2	.5		2.2	2.4	1.7	3.5		1.4	1.7	3.1	4.0	2.2
3. Twice	1.4	2.6	.4		1.0	1.8	1.2	1.6		.6	1.7	-	3.6	4.4
4. 3 or 4 times	.7	1.3	.1		1.2	.6	.5	.3		.1	.6	1.2	1.7	2.2
5. 5 or more times	.8	1.6	.2		2.0	.4	.6	.3		.4	1.1	.4	1.5	-
Item 6660 N(Wtd)	2609	1194	1373		600	800	836	374		1079	470	257	471	45

A39P: Gotten into trouble with police because of something you did

1. Not at all	79.9	68.5	89.8		80.3	75.2	85.3	77.5		91.7	79.3	77.0	59.9	52.2
2. Once	11.7	17.6	6.9		10.7	14.6	8.5	14.7		6.3	12.6	12.1	20.3	23.9
3. Twice	4.8	7.7	2.2		4.3	6.0	3.9	5.1		1.5	4.7	7.4	9.8	4.3
4. 3 or 4 times	2.1	3.6	.7		2.2	3.0	1.2	2.1		.2	3.0	2.3	5.3	8.7
5. 5 or more times	1.5	2.7	.4		2.7	1.4	1.2	.5		.3	.4	1.2	4.5	10.9
Item 6670 N(Wtd)	2606	1189	1375		598	797	836	374		1082	468	256	469	46

A40: The following questions concern cigarettes, alcohol, and a number of other drugs. How difficult do you think it would be for you to get each of the following types of drugs, if you wanted some?

A40A: Marijuana (pot, grass)

1. Probably impossible	4.1	2.8	5.2		2.3	2.2	6.9	4.5		6.1	1.0	2.7	.2	-
2. Very difficult	3.4	2.3	4.2		1.6	3.5	5.4	1.9		5.8	.6	1.1	.4	2.2
3. Fairly difficult	4.8	4.5	4.8		3.0	4.6	6.2	4.5		8.3	2.3	.4	1.0	2.2
4. Fairly easy	29.4	29.1	30.2		28.4	29.0	28.9	33.0		38.1	26.9	30.3	16.3	15.2
5. Very easy	58.3	61.2	55.6		64.7	60.7	52.5	56.1		41.6	69.0	65.2	82.3	80.4
Item 6750 N(Wtd)	2628	1211	1373		609	806	836	376		1078	480	264	485	46

A40B: LSD

1. Probably impossible	11.4	10.3	12.1		9.6	8.1	16.0	11.2		13.6	11.0	9.5	2.7	2.1
2. Very difficult	15.1	16.3	13.9		12.9	16.6	15.0	15.6		17.5	13.4	17.2	10.4	6.4
3. Fairly difficult	27.3	26.9	27.7		29.9	26.3	26.8	26.8		28.6	34.0	26.3	22.8	19.1
4. Fairly easy	35.8	34.4	37.4		33.1	39.2	35.0	34.8		33.6	32.9	38.5	45.4	44.7
5. Very easy	10.4	12.0	8.9		14.8	9.8	7.1	11.8		6.6	8.9	8.0	18.5	27.7
Item 6760 N(Wtd)	2581	1187	1352		596	794	826	365		1058	471	262	482	47

CAUTION: Items were rearranged after 1975; changes in context may produce spurious "trends" (see page 12).

QUESTIONNAIRE FORM 2 1975	TOTAL	SEX			REGION					ILLICIT DRUG USE: LIFETIME				
		M	F		NE	NC	S	W		None	Mari-juana Only	Few Pills	More Pills	Any Her-oin
Weighted No. of Cases:	2972	1404	1475		678	926	934	434		1109	484	270	494	47
% of Weighted Total:	100.0	47.2	49.6		22.8	31.2	31.4	14.6		37.3	16.3	9.1	16.6	1.6

A40C: Some other psychedelic (mescaline, peyote, psilocybin, THC, etc.) ‡

	TOTAL	M	F		NE	NC	S	W		None	Marijuana Only	Few Pills	More Pills	Any Heroin
1. Probably impossible	13.1	12.0	13.6		10.0	11.0	18.2	11.2		17.6	12.1	7.6	3.9	-
2. Very difficult	15.8	15.2	16.7		13.5	16.6	16.7	15.9		18.6	16.3	16.3	8.0	8.5
3. Fairly difficult	23.3	23.0	24.0		23.8	22.4	21.9	27.7		28.0	23.4	21.7	18.3	17.0
4. Fairly easy	34.8	33.9	35.5		36.5	37.2	31.9	33.7		30.0	37.2	41.1	43.4	36.2
5. Very easy	13.0	16.0	10.1		16.2	12.7	11.4	11.5		6.0	11.0	12.9	26.3	36.2
Item 6770 N(Wtd)	2560	1185	1335		592	790	813	365		1035	471	263	486	47

A40D: Amphetamines (uppers, pep pills, bennies, speed)

	TOTAL	M	F		NE	NC	S	W		None	Marijuana Only	Few Pills	More Pills	Any Heroin
1. Probably impossible	7.7	6.9	8.2		6.4	5.7	11.0	6.9		10.5	7.1	3.0	1.0	-
2. Very difficult	8.7	8.3	8.6		7.0	8.0	10.9	8.0		11.1	7.5	7.2	3.5	4.3
3. Fairly difficult	15.9	16.9	15.0		16.9	14.3	16.6	15.9		17.6	22.9	13.2	8.7	4.3
4. Fairly easy	41.8	43.0	41.1		39.8	48.1	36.4	43.4		41.6	41.5	47.2	41.4	46.8
5. Very easy	26.0	24.9	27.1		29.9	24.0	25.2	25.5		19.3	21.0	29.1	45.3	44.7
Item 6780 N(Wtd)	2572	1186	1345		598	792	819	364		1054	467	265	483	47

A40F: Barbiturates (downers, goofballs, reds, yellows, etc.)

	TOTAL	M	F		NE	NC	S	W		None	Marijuana Only	Few Pills	More Pills	Any Heroin
1. Probably impossible	9.9	8.5	11.1		7.9	8.4	13.8	7.5		13.3	9.2	3.8	2.7	-
2. Very difficult	11.7	11.5	11.6		10.1	9.7	13.1	15.0		12.6	11.8	12.9	8.5	2.2
3. Fairly difficult	18.4	19.4	17.6		19.0	19.4	16.9	18.6		18.2	24.1	16.7	14.9	17.4
4. Fairly easy	38.4	39.6	37.2		38.9	44.1	32.1	39.4		39.4	38.5	40.5	38.3	34.8
5. Very easy	21.6	20.9	22.6		24.0	18.3	24.1	19.4		16.5	16.2	26.1	35.6	43.5
Item 6790 N(Wtd)	2556	1183	1333		596	783	817	360		1045	468	264	483	46

A40G: Tranquilizers

	TOTAL	M	F		NE	NC	S	W		None	Marijuana Only	Few Pills	More Pills	Any Heroin
1. Probably impossible	6.8	6.6	7.0		5.2	5.0	10.3	5.3		8.4	6.9	1.5	3.1	-
2. Very difficult	6.7	7.4	6.2		6.6	6.6	6.6	7.5		6.7	6.2	6.5	3.7	2.1
3. Fairly difficult	14.7	15.1	14.0		14.2	15.3	13.8	16.1		14.3	15.6	15.2	13.5	10.6
4. Fairly easy	37.8	37.7	37.8		37.8	40.4	35.7	37.5		41.2	42.0	32.7	34.7	34.0
5. Very easy	34.0	33.1	35.1		36.3	32.8	33.8	33.3		29.5	29.3	44.1	45.1	51.1
Item 6800 N(Wtd)	2555	1182	1337		593	783	819	360		1049	467	263	481	47

A40H: Cocaine

	TOTAL	M	F		NE	NC	S	W		None	Marijuana Only	Few Pills	More Pills	Any Heroin
1. Probably impossible	14.6	13.4	15.7		12.3	14.3	17.8	11.9		17.7	13.5	13.4	6.7	-
2. Very difficult	18.8	19.9	17.5		16.9	19.8	19.5	18.1		22.0	17.2	21.1	13.4	8.5
3. Fairly difficult	29.7	28.9	31.0		34.2	30.0	27.0	27.5		29.3	35.6	32.2	27.8	21.3
4. Fairly easy	26.9	26.2	27.3		24.4	27.5	26.5	30.0		24.2	24.9	24.5	35.5	40.4
5. Very easy	10.1	11.6	8.6		12.4	8.4	9.1	12.5		6.9	9.0	8.4	16.9	29.8
Item 6810 N(Wtd)	2539	1176	1321		587	777	815	360		1036	466	261	479	47

A40I: Heroin (smack, horse)

	TOTAL	M	F		NE	NC	S	W		None	Marijuana Only	Few Pills	More Pills	Any Heroin
1. Probably impossible	23.8	24.7	23.3		20.2	23.0	27.6	23.1		24.3	23.3	28.4	19.5	6.4
2. Very difficult	26.6	27.4	25.8		27.0	25.8	26.3	28.3		25.3	28.2	26.8	30.0	17.0
3. Fairly difficult	25.3	24.0	26.6		27.3	25.3	23.2	26.9		25.5	25.2	26.1	26.0	27.7
4. Fairly easy	17.8	17.0	18.5		16.8	19.5	17.1	17.2		19.7	17.3	13.4	18.0	25.5
5. Very easy	6.4	6.9	5.8		8.5	6.2	5.9	4.4		5.2	6.0	5.0	6.5	23.4
Item 6820 N(Wtd)	2542	1177	1327		589	778	815	360		1040	468	261	477	47

A40J: Some other narcotic (methadone, opium, codeine, paregoric, etc.)

	TOTAL	M	F		NE	NC	S	W		None	Marijuana Only	Few Pills	More Pills	Any Heroin
1. Probably impossible	16.9	16.6	17.0		14.2	16.1	20.0	15.8		18.5	17.8	14.4	9.2	2.1
2. Very difficult	22.8	23.7	22.1		20.5	22.7	24.1	23.7		24.2	24.0	26.6	19.9	10.6
3. Fairly difficult	25.8	26.8	25.3		30.3	25.3	23.1	25.7		24.9	27.9	21.3	29.8	17.0
4. Fairly easy	25.8	23.1	27.9		25.4	27.6	24.2	26.3		26.6	22.7	28.9	27.9	38.3
5. Very easy	8.7	9.9	7.7		9.5	8.3	8.6	8.5		5.8	7.5	9.1	13.2	29.8
Item 6830 N(Wtd)	2532	1171	1322		590	775	814	354		1031	466	263	477	47

‡ = Wording changed in subsequent years.

CAUTION: Items were rearranged after 1975; changes in context may produce spurious "trends" (see page 12).

QUESTIONNAIRE FORM 2 1975	TOTAL	SEX			REGION					ILLICIT DRUG USE: LIFETIME				
		M	F		NE	NC	S	W		None	Mari- juana Only	Few Pills	More Pills	Any Her- oin
Weighted No. of Cases:	2972	1404	1475		678	926	934	434		1109	484	270	494	47
% of Weighted Total:	100.0	47.2	49.6		22.8	31.2	31.4	14.6		37.3	16.3	9.1	16.6	1.6

A41: How many of your friends would you estimate...

A41A: Smoke cigarettes

1. None	4.8	4.4	5.0		2.4	4.7	4.9	8.7		7.5	1.7	4.1	2.1	-
2. A few	19.3	19.0	20.0		14.0	18.5	19.9	28.8		27.9	15.1	15.3	8.6	6.4
3. Some	34.3	35.7	32.8		32.3	34.5	34.0	37.8		40.0	35.5	32.1	25.7	25.5
4. Most	37.5	36.9	38.1		46.1	38.0	37.4	22.5		23.0	43.6	45.1	56.0	57.4
5. All	4.0	3.9	4.2		5.2	4.2	3.9	2.1		1.4	4.4	3.0	7.6	10.6
Item 7070 N(Wtd)	2650	1216	1392		616	811	845	378		1102	482	268	486	47

A41B: Smoke marijuana (pot, grass) or hashish

1. None	17.0	13.1	20.5		10.7	18.1	20.0	18.4		31.6	1.9	10.1	3.5	-
2. A few	26.9	27.9	26.4		20.3	26.1	34.6	22.1		38.8	25.9	22.0	7.4	2.1
3. Some	25.7	25.7	25.5		30.7	25.3	22.3	26.3		22.1	35.1	30.2	22.0	14.9
4. Most	24.3	26.7	22.2		30.7	25.3	18.3	25.0		7.0	31.7	32.8	49.3	51.1
5. All	6.0	6.6	5.5		7.5	5.2	4.7	8.5		.5	5.2	4.5	17.9	29.8
Item 7080 N(Wtd)	2639	1212	1388		610	807	846	376		1098	482	268	487	47

A41C: Take LSD

1. None	63.6	62.9	64.1		61.4	62.2	66.7	62.4		78.9	70.2	58.0	28.4	13.0
2. A few	23.6	24.1	23.1		23.2	24.9	22.5	23.4		16.8	23.8	29.2	36.5	32.6
3. Some	10.2	9.8	10.7		12.2	10.4	8.7	9.8		4.0	5.8	12.5	25.7	37.0
4. Most	2.1	2.8	1.4		2.5	2.1	1.4	3.0		.1	-	.4	7.9	8.7
5. All	.6	.5	.8		.7	.4	.7	1.1		.2	-	-	1.2	8.7
Item 7090 N(Wtd)	2602	1197	1369		598	799	839	367		1085	480	264	482	46

A41D: Take other psychedelics (mescaline, peyote, THC , etc.) ‡

1. None	58.8	54.9	62.5		54.1	58.0	63.5	57.7		80.6	58.3	48.7	22.2	2.1
2. A few	25.9	27.7	24.0		27.3	25.8	25.4	25.4		15.5	34.8	35.1	34.6	40.4
3. Some	10.5	11.6	9.5		13.1	11.0	7.1	12.6		3.4	5.8	14.0	27.0	31.9
4. Most	3.9	4.5	3.3		4.0	4.5	3.3	3.6		.3	.8	2.6	13.6	17.0
5. All	.9	1.2	.6		1.5	.5	.8	.8		.2	.2	-	2.7	8.5
Item 7100 N(Wtd)	2595	1195	1366		604	798	828	366		1077	480	265	486	47

A41E: Take amphetamines (uppers, pep pills, bennies, speed)

1. None	49.0	45.7	51.7		45.4	48.4	53.0	47.3		68.8	49.7	34.1	14.7	8.5
2. A few	30.5	33.3	28.0		32.3	29.4	31.1	28.6		24.4	41.3	43.9	28.0	27.7
3. Some	14.6	14.4	15.0		15.4	16.3	11.2	17.6		6.0	8.8	20.5	35.7	31.9
4. Most	4.6	5.0	4.1		5.3	4.4	4.0	4.9		.4	.2	1.1	18.0	19.1
5. All	1.3	1.6	1.1		1.7	1.4	.8	1.6		.3	.2	.4	3.5	12.8
Item 7110 N(Wtd)	2584	1190	1362		603	789	827	364		1076	477	264	482	47

A41F: Take quaaludes (quads, methaqualone)

1. None	68.3	64.9	71.5		66.3	70.0	67.8	69.9		84.5	70.9	62.2	39.1	17.4
2. A few	20.4	22.4	18.3		22.1	19.1	19.6	22.5		12.1	25.2	25.1	30.3	37.0
3. Some	8.3	8.7	7.9		8.1	8.1	9.3	6.5		2.8	3.6	12.0	20.8	28.3
4. Most	2.2	2.9	1.6		3.0	1.8	2.6	.8		.2	.2	1.2	8.0	13.0
5. All	.8	1.0	.7		.7	1.0	.9	.6		.3	.2	-	1.9	4.3
Item 7120 N(Wtd)	2542	1176	1336		594	776	816	355		1060	468	259	476	46

‡ = Wording changed in subsequent years.

CAUTION: Items were rearranged after 1975; changes in context may produce spurious "trends" (see page 12).

	TOTAL	SEX			REGION					ILLICIT DRUG USE: LIFETIME				
QUESTIONNAIRE FORM 2 **1975**		M	F		NE	NC	S	W		None	Mari- juana Only	Few Pills	More Pills	Any Her- oin
Weighted No. of Cases:	2972	1404	1475		678	926	934	434		1109	484	270	494	47
% of Weighted Total:	100.0	47.2	49.6		22.8	31.2	31.4	14.6		37.3	16.3	9.1	16.6	1.6

A41G: Take barbiturates (downers, goofballs, reds, yellows, etc.)

1. None	55.0	53.6	56.3		53.1	54.1	58.1	53.3		71.5	59.5	45.5	20.1	13.0
2. A few	28.8	29.7	28.1		31.1	27.4	27.4	31.4		22.8	35.7	35.7	36.4	28.3
3. Some	11.9	12.0	11.8		11.5	14.0	9.8	12.8		5.0	5.1	16.2	29.2	39.1
4. Most	3.3	3.7	3.1		3.5	3.4	3.7	1.9		.3	-	2.3	12.0	13.0
5. All	.9	1.2	.7		1.0	1.0	.8	.6		.3	-	.4	2.3	6.5
Item 7130 N(Wtd)	2577	1187	1358		601	788	828	360		1074	474	266	483	46

A41H: Take tranquilizers

1. None	54.4	55.3	53.8		54.7	54.3	54.4	54.2		66.1	61.3	41.7	29.6	10.6
2. A few	29.2	27.8	30.3		29.7	29.1	30.2	26.4		25.6	31.1	39.8	33.8	40.4
3. Some	12.8	12.6	13.1		12.2	13.5	11.3	15.8		7.6	7.0	16.3	26.1	27.7
4. Most	2.6	2.9	2.3		2.9	2.0	2.9	2.8		.3	.4	1.9	8.8	14.9
5. All	.9	1.3	.5		.5	1.1	1.1	.6		.3	.4	.4	1.7	6.4
Item 7140 N(Wtd)	2568	1187	1350		596	787	825	360		1074	473	264	479	47

A41I: Take cocaine

1. None	66.4	63.4	69.0		65.8	67.9	69.0	58.2		83.1	71.9	61.0	32.8	4.3
2. A few	21.4	22.5	20.5		22.2	20.7	20.1	25.2		13.6	23.7	25.8	34.5	34.0
3. Some	8.7	9.7	8.0		8.7	9.0	7.5	11.1		2.9	3.8	11.4	21.8	31.9
4. Most	2.3	2.8	1.9		2.5	1.4	2.1	4.4		-	.4	.8	8.3	21.3
5. All	1.1	1.6	.7		.8	.9	1.3	1.4		.3	.2	.8	2.5	8.5
Item 7150 N(Wtd)	2574	1189	1351		600	786	826	361		1076	473	264	481	47

A41J: Take heroin (smack, horse)

1. None	84.8	85.1	85.0		82.6	84.2	86.4	86.5		88.9	88.0	86.8	75.4	36.2
2. A few	12.4	11.9	12.2		13.4	13.0	11.4	11.5		8.5	10.9	11.7	20.9	46.8
3. Some	2.1	2.1	2.1		3.7	2.2	1.2	1.4		2.2	1.1	1.1	2.3	10.6
4. Most	.3	.1	.5		.3	.5	.1	.3		.3	.2	-	.4	4.3
5. All	.4	.8	.1		.2	.1	.7	.3		.2	-	.8	.6	2.1
Item 7160 N(Wtd)	2572	1184	1356		597	787	824	364		1078	476	266	484	47

A41K: Take other narcotics (methadone, opium, codeine, paregoric, etc.)

1. None	71.2	69.6	72.7		67.5	71.6	72.4	73.3		81.8	77.0	66.9	47.7	13.0
2. A few	21.1	22.4	19.9		22.4	21.1	20.2	20.9		13.9	19.9	27.4	34.9	37.0
3. Some	5.6	5.4	5.8		7.7	5.7	4.9	3.9		3.1	3.0	4.5	12.2	32.6
4. Most	1.7	1.8	1.5		2.0	1.1	1.9	1.4		1.0	.2	.4	3.9	15.2
5. All	.4	.8	.1		.3	.4	.5	.3		.1	-	.8	1.2	4.3
Item 7170 N(Wtd)	2559	1176	1352		594	786	821	359		1078	473	266	482	46

A41L: Use inhalants (sniffing glue, laughing gas, snappers, etc.) ‡

1. None	75.7	74.8	77.0		76.3	76.7	73.0	79.4		80.1	74.5	71.7	69.7	68.1
2. A few	17.8	17.6	17.4		15.7	17.6	21.0	14.4		14.7	22.8	19.6	20.1	21.3
3. Some	5.4	6.1	4.9		6.9	5.0	4.8	5.6		4.6	2.3	7.2	7.7	8.5
4. Most	.7	.9	.5		.7	.5	1.0	.6		.5	.2	.4	1.7	2.1
5. All	.4	.7	.1		.3	.4	.5	-		.2	.4	.8	.8	-
Item 7180 N(Wtd)	2552	1171	1348		591	780	821	360		1073	474	265	482	47

A41M: Drink alcoholic beverages (liquor, beer, wine)

1. None	3.3	2.4	4.1		1.8	2.5	4.6	4.9		5.3	.4	1.1	1.4	2.1
2. A few	10.3	8.2	12.0		5.8	9.5	13.0	13.3		16.9	3.5	10.1	2.5	2.1
3. Some	17.9	14.2	21.1		14.1	17.3	21.0	18.7		27.7	10.0	13.5	7.2	6.4
4. Most	38.5	41.3	36.1		38.5	39.1	39.3	35.8		35.6	48.8	46.4	32.6	38.3
5. All	29.8	33.8	26.7		39.9	31.7	22.0	27.4		14.4	37.3	29.2	56.1	51.1
Item 7190 N(Wtd)	2598	1188	1374		602	793	833	369		1093	480	267	485	47

‡ = Wording changed in subsequent years.

CAUTION: Items were rearranged after 1975; changes in context may produce spurious "trends" (see page 12).

QUESTIONNAIRE FORM 2 1975	TOTAL	SEX			REGION					ILLICIT DRUG USE: LIFETIME				
		M	F		NE	NC	S	W		None	Mari- juana Only	Few Pills	More Pills	Any Her- oin
Weighted No. of Cases:	*2972*	*1404*	*1475*		*678*	*926*	*934*	*434*		*1109*	*484*	*270*	*494*	*47*
% of Weighted Total:	*100.0*	*47.2*	*49.6*		*22.8*	*31.2*	*31.4*	*14.6*		*37.3*	*16.3*	*9.1*	*16.6*	*1.6*
A41N: Get drunk at least once a week														
1. None	17.5	13.2	21.3		14.7	14.6	19.6	24.1		27.8	8.1	12.4	7.4	6.4
2. A few	23.6	21.2	25.7		17.9	25.3	27.3	20.9		29.8	21.8	22.8	15.2	8.5
3. Some	28.8	30.0	28.1		30.3	28.8	27.5	29.3		27.6	33.2	29.6	25.9	17.0
4. Most	20.4	22.9	17.9		22.2	22.5	19.1	15.4		11.6	25.1	28.5	29.8	38.3
5. All	9.7	12.7	7.0		14.9	8.7	6.5	10.3		3.1	11.6	6.4	21.4	27.7
Item 7200 N(Wtd)	*2600*	*1190*	*1374*		*604*	*794*	*833*	*369*		*1093*	*482*	*267*	*486*	*47*

CAUTION: Items were rearranged after 1975; changes in context may produce spurious "trends" (see page 12).

QUESTIONNAIRE FORM 3 1975	TOTAL	SEX			REGION					ILLICIT DRUG USE: LIFETIME				
		M	F		NE	NC	S	W		None	Mari-juana Only	Few Pills	More Pills	Any Her-oin
Weighted No. of Cases:	3049	1356	1559		681	961	975	432		1125	438	268	507	57
% of Weighted Total:	100.0	44.5	51.1		22.3	31.5	32.0	14.2		36.9	14.4	8.8	16.6	1.9

A06: Some people think a lot about the social problems of the nation and the world, and about how they might be solved. Others spend little time thinking about these issues. How much do you think about such things?

	TOTAL	M	F		NE	NC	S	W		None	Mari-juana Only	Few Pills	More Pills	Any Her-oin
1. Never	1.3	1.2	1.4		1.5	1.1	1.3	1.2		1.3	1.4	.8	1.6	1.9
2. Seldom	10.4	12.0	9.0		13.2	10.5	8.4	10.5		9.2	11.7	12.4	10.4	11.1
3. Sometimes	47.2	47.9	46.8		49.8	48.8	44.7	45.2		47.7	48.8	50.0	44.4	51.9
4. Quite often	32.4	30.1	34.3		27.8	30.9	37.1	32.4		33.9	29.3	28.9	35.5	27.8
5. A great deal	8.7	8.7	8.4		7.6	8.7	8.6	10.7		7.9	8.5	8.6	8.0	7.4
Item 6880　N(Wtd)	2960	1330	1541		658	933	949	420		1115	426	266	498	54

A08: In the following list you will find some statements about leisure time and work. Please show whether you agree or disagree with each statement.

A08D: I like the kind of work you can forget about after the work day is over

	TOTAL	M	F		NE	NC	S	W		None	Mari-juana Only	Few Pills	More Pills	Any Her-oin
1. Disagree	19.5	19.1	19.7		19.3	18.2	22.2	16.8		20.5	19.8	18.2	15.2	16.4
2. Mostly disagree	14.0	13.4	14.4		13.8	15.8	11.4	16.4		15.5	11.8	14.4	17.0	7.3
3. Neither	18.5	19.1	18.0		20.1	19.3	15.5	20.6		18.1	22.4	16.3	18.8	16.4
4. Mostly agree	19.2	17.9	20.2		19.0	19.0	19.6	19.2		18.0	19.6	17.8	19.8	14.5
5. Agree	28.8	30.5	27.7		27.9	27.7	31.3	27.1		28.0	26.5	33.3	29.3	45.5
Item 8050　N(Wtd)	2977	1338	1546		653	936	960	428		1118	434	264	501	55

A08E: To me, work is nothing more than making a living

	TOTAL	M	F		NE	NC	S	W		None	Mari-juana Only	Few Pills	More Pills	Any Her-oin
1. Disagree	46.3	40.7	50.8		42.3	45.6	49.8	45.9		51.7	40.8	48.3	42.9	36.4
2. Mostly disagree	23.7	23.3	24.4		24.9	26.0	20.4	24.2		24.5	26.1	20.4	26.6	21.8
3. Neither	10.8	11.8	10.3		10.3	11.8	10.4	10.0		9.3	13.1	10.9	10.3	18.2
4. Mostly agree	9.8	12.0	7.6		12.3	9.1	9.4	8.2		8.1	10.3	9.4	10.3	12.7
5. Agree	9.4	12.2	7.0		10.2	7.4	10.0	11.4		6.4	9.6	10.9	9.9	10.9
Item 8060　N(Wtd)	2986	1342	1551		659	937	961	429		1118	436	265	503	55

A08G: I expect my work to be a very central part of my life

	TOTAL	M	F		NE	NC	S	W		None	Mari-juana Only	Few Pills	More Pills	Any Her-oin
1. Disagree	6.7	6.1	7.2		7.8	5.9	6.5	7.2		5.8	8.3	6.4	9.3	7.0
2. Mostly disagree	10.9	9.6	11.9		9.5	10.4	10.5	15.0		11.4	8.7	9.8	11.9	15.8
3. Neither	17.6	17.4	18.2		18.0	18.1	16.6	18.0		16.2	20.9	15.8	21.5	15.8
4. Mostly agree	33.7	33.4	33.3		35.8	36.9	30.6	29.9		34.6	33.6	36.5	32.6	35.1
5. Agree	31.1	33.6	29.4		28.7	28.8	35.8	29.7		32.0	28.3	31.6	24.5	26.3
Item 8070　N(Wtd)	2983	1344	1546		656	937	962	428		1114	435	266	503	57

A08H: I want to do my best in my job, even if this sometimes means working overtime

	TOTAL	M	F		NE	NC	S	W		None	Mari-juana Only	Few Pills	More Pills	Any Her-oin
1. Disagree	2.6	3.3	1.9		3.5	2.2	2.3	3.1		1.8	2.8	2.3	4.2	8.8
2. Mostly disagree	3.8	3.7	3.8		5.5	3.1	3.0	4.5		2.9	3.9	5.3	5.0	5.3
3. Neither	9.0	10.0	8.3		8.6	9.7	7.4	12.0		7.1	11.0	7.5	11.2	10.5
4. Mostly agree	33.1	32.2	33.7		34.4	35.3	31.4	30.1		32.9	32.6	30.9	36.3	29.8
5. Agree	51.4	50.7	52.3		48.1	49.7	55.9	50.4		55.3	49.7	53.6	43.2	43.9
Item 8080　N(Wtd)	2988	1344	1551		659	941	963	425		1119	435	265	502	57

A08I: I would like to stay in the same job for most of my adult life

	TOTAL	M	F		NE	NC	S	W		None	Mari-juana Only	Few Pills	More Pills	Any Her-oin
1. Disagree	20.7	18.7	22.1		22.0	19.9	19.0	24.4		14.8	20.6	23.8	29.4	19.3
2. Mostly disagree	11.5	10.4	12.6		12.3	11.6	10.8	11.8		10.6	10.6	13.2	12.5	8.8
3. Neither	19.0	18.7	19.6		20.3	19.3	16.6	21.3		20.4	21.8	15.1	18.1	21.1
4. Mostly agree	21.9	21.9	21.7		21.6	22.8	22.3	19.2		23.0	17.9	20.0	21.5	22.8
5. Agree	26.9	30.2	23.9		23.5	26.5	31.3	23.5		31.3	29.1	27.5	18.5	28.1
Item 8090　N(Wtd)	2978	1340	1545		656	937	963	422		1114	436	265	503	57

CAUTION: Items were rearranged after 1975; changes in context may produce spurious "trends" (see page 12).

QUESTIONNAIRE FORM 3 1975	TOTAL	SEX			REGION					ILLICIT DRUG USE: LIFETIME				
		M	F		NE	NC	S	W		None	Mari-juana Only	Few Pills	More Pills	Any Her-oin
Weighted No. of Cases:	3049	1356	1559		681	961	975	432		1125	438	268	507	57
% of Weighted Total:	100.0	44.5	51.1		22.3	31.5	32.0	14.2		36.9	14.4	8.8	16.6	1.9
A10: If you were to get enough money to live as comfortably as you'd like for the rest of your life, would you want to work?														
1. I would want to work	78.9	78.1	79.8		77.0	79.5	80.1	78.0		82.8	79.3	82.6	69.3	71.4
2. I would not want to work	21.1	21.9	20.2		23.0	20.5	19.9	22.0		17.2	21.0	17.4	30.7	28.6
Item 8100 N(Wtd)	2970	1331	1544		660	937	951	422		1113	434	265	498	56
A17: The next questions ask your opinions about a number of different topics. How much do you agree or disagree with each statement below?														
A17A: Men and women should be paid the same money if they do the same work														
1. Disagree	3.2	5.4	1.4		3.3	3.3	3.4	2.4		3.1	2.8	2.6	2.6	3.6
2. Mostly disagree	2.0	3.2	.9		2.3	1.8	2.2	1.4		1.5	2.8	2.3	1.8	1.8
3. Neither	3.1	5.2	1.2		3.3	4.0	2.3	2.8		2.7	2.3	3.4	4.0	1.8
4. Mostly agree	14.3	19.2	9.9		14.1	17.9	10.7	14.7		14.4	19.0	10.5	12.5	12.7
5. Agree	77.3	67.0	86.7		77.0	72.9	81.4	78.7		78.3	73.2	81.2	79.0	81.8
Item 7930 N(Wtd)	2988	1344	1552		661	942	961	423		1120	436	266	504	55
A17B: Women should be considered as seriously as men for jobs as executives or politicians														
1. Disagree	5.8	9.3	2.8		5.7	7.0	5.2	4.5		6.1	3.2	6.0	5.2	9.1
2. Mostly disagree	5.7	9.1	2.8		6.1	5.5	5.5	6.1		5.4	7.8	2.6	5.0	3.6
3. Neither	9.2	13.3	5.6		9.1	10.7	7.2	10.8		8.8	8.5	9.4	7.3	7.3
4. Mostly agree	22.4	26.8	18.8		20.6	21.6	25.4	20.0		22.1	26.0	20.7	21.0	25.5
5. Agree	56.9	41.5	70.0		58.7	55.2	56.7	58.5		57.6	54.5	61.3	61.7	54.5
Item 7940 N(Wtd)	2986	1342	1552		661	941	959	424		1121	435	266	504	55
A17C: A woman should have exactly the same job opportunities as a man														
1. Disagree	9.8	15.1	5.0		10.3	9.1	10.4	9.0		9.3	6.2	12.0	8.7	5.6
2. Mostly disagree	9.9	13.6	6.3		9.9	11.6	8.7	9.0		9.9	11.2	9.4	8.1	14.8
3. Neither	9.2	11.7	7.0		8.2	10.0	8.0	11.3		9.0	9.9	6.4	9.3	11.1
4. Mostly agree	26.0	26.4	26.1		24.1	26.8	24.0	31.4		25.6	29.6	25.9	22.8	24.1
5. Agree	45.2	33.1	55.4		47.6	42.5	48.7	39.2		46.3	43.1	45.9	51.0	44.4
Item 7950 N(Wtd)	2981	1341	1549		659	938	961	423		1120	436	266	504	54
A17D: A woman should have exactly the same educational opportunities as a man														
1. Disagree	1.0	1.6	.6		1.2	.6	1.5	.7		1.2	.2	.8	.2	3.6
2. Mostly disagree	1.0	1.4	.6		.9	1.5	.8	.5		.9	.7	1.1	.6	3.6
3. Neither	2.9	4.1	1.7		3.2	2.9	2.3	4.0		3.1	2.8	2.3	2.6	3.6
4. Mostly agree	13.2	18.0	8.9		12.5	16.1	11.2	13.1		10.5	13.8	9.8	14.9	9.1
5. Agree	81.8	74.9	88.1		82.2	78.9	84.2	81.9		84.3	82.5	85.7	81.7	78.2
Item 7960 N(Wtd)	2976	1337	1548		658	939	958	421		1123	435	265	503	55
A17H: It is usually better for everyone involved if the man is the achiever outside the home and the woman takes care of the home and family														
1. Disagree	15.3	7.9	21.9		19.2	13.7	14.7	14.6		14.6	14.1	20.7	19.5	10.9
2. Mostly disagree	16.2	11.3	20.4		16.2	19.2	14.8	13.0		15.9	18.3	15.0	19.3	7.3
3. Neither	23.6	25.9	22.1		23.2	25.3	20.0	28.8		21.2	22.9	24.8	26.8	36.4
4. Mostly agree	24.1	28.6	19.7		23.3	22.6	27.4	20.8		24.6	24.8	23.3	20.7	30.9
5. Agree	20.8	26.1	16.0		18.1	19.1	23.1	22.9		23.7	19.9	16.2	13.5	16.4
Item 7970 N(Wtd)	2973	1335	1547		656	936	957	424		1118	432	266	503	55

CAUTION: Items were rearranged after 1975; changes in context may produce spurious "trends" (see page 12).

QUESTIONNAIRE FORM 3 1975	TOTAL	SEX			REGION					ILLICIT DRUG USE: LIFETIME				
		M	F		NE	NC	S	W		None	Mari- juana Only	Few Pills	More Pills	Any Her- oin
Weighted No. of Cases:	3049	1356	1559		681	961	975	432		1125	438	268	507	57
% of Weighted Total:	100.0	44.5	51.1		22.3	31.5	32.0	14.2		36.9	14.4	8.8	16.6	1.9

A17I: A preschool child is likely to suffer if the mother works

1. Disagree	9.0	6.7	10.7		9.6	9.2	8.5	9.0		8.6	7.2	8.6	10.1	7.3
2. Mostly disagree	11.4	7.2	15.0		11.5	9.8	13.0	10.9		9.9	11.4	12.0	14.9	14.5
3. Neither	14.1	12.5	15.6		15.1	15.7	11.6	14.7		11.3	16.2	15.8	15.5	14.5
4. Mostly agree	29.9	31.2	28.5		27.9	29.9	32.0	27.5		31.4	30.4	30.1	27.2	29.1
5. Agree	35.7	42.3	30.2		35.9	35.4	34.9	37.7		38.8	34.8	33.5	32.0	34.5
Item 7980 N(Wtd)	2967	1334	1544		655	939	952	422		1122	431	266	503	55

A17J: A working mother can establish just as warm and secure a relationship with her children as a mother who does not work

1. Disagree	19.7	26.4	13.9		19.6	19.0	19.7	21.6		20.9	21.8	18.4	17.3	11.1
2. Mostly disagree	24.0	27.3	21.1		24.7	24.3	23.2	23.9		25.4	22.7	23.3	21.9	33.3
3. Neither	14.2	16.1	12.6		14.5	15.0	13.6	13.5		15.3	11.2	13.2	14.1	18.5
4. Mostly agree	21.3	17.4	24.7		19.9	21.7	21.9	20.6		20.9	24.8	22.2	22.7	16.7
5. Agree	20.9	12.8	27.8		21.3	20.0	21.5	20.4		17.5	19.5	22.6	24.3	20.4
Item 7990 N(Wtd)	2977	1334	1553		657	941	958	422		1121	436	266	503	54

The next questions are about living or working with people of different races. Please rate each of the statements below using the following terms:

Not at all acceptable: I'd avoid this if I possibly could.

Somewhat acceptable: I could live with this, but not be happy about it.

Acceptable: This would be O.K., or I'd be neutral about this.

Desirable: I'd really like this.

A19: How would you feel about...

A19A: Having close personal friends of another race?

1. Not at all acceptable	4.5	5.7	3.5		3.9	4.9	5.9	1.2		5.5	3.7	2.6	2.8	7.3
2. Somewhat acceptable	8.3	10.4	6.3		7.0	9.0	10.8	2.8		8.1	8.0	7.5	6.4	3.6
3. Acceptable	54.3	59.4	50.0		55.4	53.3	57.4	48.5		53.8	53.8	52.1	55.3	61.8
4. Desirable	32.9	24.5	40.3		33.7	32.8	25.9	47.5		32.4	34.6	37.8	35.6	27.3
Item 8110 N(Wtd)	2981	1341	1552		661	935	961	423		1122	437	267	503	55

A19B: Having a job with a supervisor of a different race?

1. Not at all acceptable	3.5	5.8	1.6		3.9	3.5	4.2	.9		3.8	4.1	1.5	3.0	7.3
2. Somewhat acceptable	11.5	15.5	8.1		10.3	12.6	14.7	3.8		11.7	13.5	12.4	9.1	9.1
3. Acceptable	68.2	66.4	69.5		70.2	68.4	67.7	65.3		68.3	63.2	72.3	68.4	60.0
4. Desirable	16.9	12.3	20.8		15.6	15.5	13.4	29.7		16.2	19.2	13.9	19.5	23.6
Item 8120 N(Wtd)	2979	1340	1551		662	935	958	424		1121	437	267	503	55

A19C: A family of a different race (but same level of education and income) moving next door to you? ‡

1. Not at all acceptable	5.9	8.4	3.9		4.9	5.6	8.9	1.2		6.1	6.9	4.5	5.2	9.1
2. Somewhat acceptable	11.9	14.4	9.6		11.2	11.7	15.3	5.9		12.3	12.1	10.5	10.1	21.8
3. Acceptable	55.4	59.4	51.8		52.7	56.3	57.4	53.4		54.3	52.4	55.3	56.0	43.6
4. Desirable	26.8	17.8	34.8		31.1	26.5	18.4	39.5		27.4	28.6	30.1	28.6	27.3
Item 8130 N(Wtd)	2973	1338	1548		659	935	956	423		1118	437	266	504	55

‡=Wording changed in subsequent years.

CAUTION: Items were rearranged after 1975; changes in context may produce spurious "trends" (see page 12).

QUESTIONNAIRE FORM 3 1975	TOTAL	SEX			REGION					ILLICIT DRUG USE: LIFETIME				
		M	F		NE	NC	S	W		None	Mari-juana Only	Few Pills	More Pills	Any Her-oin
Weighted No. of Cases:	3049	1356	1559		681	961	975	432		1125	438	268	507	57
% of Weighted Total:	100.0	44.5	51.1		22.3	31.5	32.0	14.2		36.9	14.4	8.8	16.6	1.9

A19D: Having your (future) children's friends be all of your race?

1. Not at all acceptable	19.3	16.3	22.4		18.2	18.4	18.7	24.4		18.1	19.2	25.7	21.4	27.3
2. Somewhat acceptable	22.6	21.5	23.1		22.6	23.4	19.2	28.5		22.8	20.6	21.5	24.8	18.2
3. Acceptable	40.0	43.1	36.9		43.1	40.8	39.1	35.4		39.4	41.6	37.0	39.7	32.7
4. Desirable	18.1	19.1	17.6		16.1	17.4	23.0	11.7		19.7	18.7	16.2	14.0	23.6
Item 8140 N(Wtd)	2946	1322	1537		654	926	948	418		1108	433	265	499	55

A19E: Having some of your (future) children's friends be of other races?

1. Not at all acceptable	4.0	5.3	2.8		3.3	4.3	5.3	1.7		3.7	4.4	4.9	3.2	7.3
2. Somewhat acceptable	9.4	12.5	6.9		9.9	9.7	11.1	3.8		9.1	9.4	8.3	8.2	14.5
3. Acceptable	48.3	51.9	44.9		48.1	48.5	50.6	42.8		49.6	48.3	41.4	44.9	43.6
4. Desirable	38.4	30.3	45.4		38.8	37.4	33.0	51.8		37.6	37.9	45.5	43.9	34.5
Item 8150 N(Wtd)	2960	1328	1545		659	928	952	421		1114	435	266	499	55

A19: How would you feel about having a job where...

A19F: ...all the employees are of your race?

1. Not at all acceptable	7.4	6.1	8.7		6.4	6.3	7.4	11.1		5.4	6.9	9.4	8.2	5.6
2. Somewhat acceptable	14.8	12.4	16.7		13.1	14.6	13.6	20.4		14.8	13.9	12.4	13.9	14.8
3. Acceptable	54.0	54.9	52.6		58.5	55.3	49.5	54.3		53.1	55.9	56.6	58.2	42.6
4. Desirable	23.9	26.6	22.0		22.0	23.7	29.4	14.2		26.6	23.3	21.7	19.7	37.0
Item 8160 N(Wtd)	2969	1333	1549		658	931	958	422		1120	433	267	502	54

A19G: ...some employees are of a different race?

1. Not at all acceptable	1.5	2.2	.8		1.2	1.4	2.3	.2		1.5	1.1	1.5	1.2	-
2. Somewhat acceptable	6.1	8.5	3.9		7.3	6.3	5.9	3.5		4.9	5.5	8.2	5.0	10.9
3. Acceptable	65.7	68.7	63.2		66.6	65.1	69.3	57.9		67.1	66.6	61.0	64.7	63.6
4. Desirable	26.7	20.7	32.0		25.0	27.1	22.6	38.1		26.5	26.8	29.2	29.1	27.3
Item 8170 N(Wtd)	2978	1340	1551		661	933	961	423		1122	437	267	502	55

A19H: ...most employees are of a different race?

1. Not at all acceptable	12.6	14.1	11.7		12.8	14.5	14.1	4.7		13.2	14.1	12.0	12.2	14.5
2. Somewhat acceptable	32.3	34.3	30.0		29.2	32.5	36.6	26.5		35.7	30.7	33.3	29.4	27.3
3. Acceptable	46.7	44.4	49.2		50.5	45.9	41.2	55.5		42.6	47.6	50.2	49.0	45.5
4. Desirable	8.4	7.2	9.1		7.6	7.2	8.0	13.3		8.4	7.9	4.1	9.4	12.7
Item 8180 N(Wtd)	2966	1333	1546		658	931	955	422		1118	433	267	500	55

A19: How would you feel about living in an area where...

A19I: ...all the neighbors are of your race?

1. Not at all acceptable	5.6	4.7	6.5		5.5	4.5	5.5	8.8		4.4	4.8	7.5	5.2	5.6
2. Somewhat acceptable	10.6	8.6	12.4		11.5	11.3	7.0	15.8		10.5	10.9	11.6	9.6	7.4
3. Acceptable	51.9	53.9	50.1		54.9	53.3	46.2	56.6		47.9	53.8	52.4	58.2	59.3
4. Desirable	31.9	33.0	31.1		27.9	31.1	41.2	18.9		37.2	30.5	28.1	27.2	29.6
Item 8190 N(Wtd)	2966	1331	1546		659	933	956	419		1119	433	267	500	54

A19J: ...some of the neighbors are of other races?

1. Not at all acceptable	3.2	4.0	2.3		2.7	2.8	5.0	.7		3.0	2.8	4.1	3.0	1.8
2. Somewhat acceptable	9.9	11.8	8.2		9.1	11.0	12.1	3.6		9.5	10.6	5.6	8.6	16.4
3. Acceptable	65.0	68.5	62.0		64.1	64.3	67.9	61.4		65.0	65.1	66.3	64.3	61.8
4. Desirable	21.9	15.7	27.6		24.1	21.9	15.0	34.4		22.5	21.8	23.6	24.0	21.8
Item 8200 N(Wtd)	2970	1336	1546		660	931	957	422		1120	436	267	501	55

CAUTION: Items were rearranged after 1975; changes in context may produce spurious "trends" (see page 12).

QUESTIONNAIRE FORM 3 1975	TOTAL	SEX			REGION					ILLICIT DRUG USE: LIFETIME				
		M	F		NE	NC	S	W		None	Marijuana Only	Few Pills	More Pills	Any Heroin
Weighted No. of Cases:	3049	1356	1559		681	961	975	432		1125	438	268	507	57
% of Weighted Total:	100.0	44.5	51.1		22.3	31.5	32.0	14.2		36.9	14.4	8.8	16.6	1.9

A19K: ...most of the neighbors are of other races?

1. Not at all acceptable	21.7	24.0	19.7		19.3	21.8	28.4	10.2		23.8	24.9	16.9	21.0	23.6
2. Somewhat acceptable	33.7	35.8	31.7		31.3	36.9	35.0	27.3		32.6	28.2	39.5	32.6	32.7
3. Acceptable	38.4	35.5	41.4		42.7	37.0	30.7	52.1		37.1	41.3	40.2	39.0	30.9
4. Desirable	6.2	4.7	7.3		6.5	4.2	6.0	10.4		6.5	5.8	3.8	7.2	10.9
Item 8210 N(Wtd)	2964	1332	1543		658	930	955	422		1119	433	266	500	55

A19: How would you feel about having your (future) children go to schools where...

A19L: ...all the children are of your race?

1. Not at all acceptable	10.2	7.4	12.8		7.9	7.9	11.8	15.0		8.6	9.3	12.8	11.0	5.6
2. Somewhat acceptable	13.8	13.4	14.0		13.9	12.0	12.2	21.0		12.3	12.7	13.2	14.7	18.5
3. Acceptable	47.4	48.6	46.1		52.1	50.8	40.4	48.4		47.1	49.5	49.6	49.6	40.7
4. Desirable	28.7	30.5	27.0		26.0	29.2	35.8	15.8		32.1	28.5	24.4	24.7	37.0
Item 8220 N(Wtd)	2958	1328	1543		655	931	953	419		1118	432	266	498	54

A19M: ...some of the children are of other races?

1. Not at all acceptable	1.5	1.9	1.2		1.7	1.5	2.0	.2		1.3	1.4	1.9	1.4	-
2. Somewhat acceptable	8.3	10.8	6.3		8.8	8.8	9.0	4.3		7.7	7.4	7.1	6.6	14.5
3. Acceptable	61.8	65.6	58.0		61.3	61.3	64.9	56.7		62.9	63.0	56.8	61.0	67.3
4. Desirable	28.4	21.7	34.6		28.3	28.3	24.1	38.8		28.1	28.3	34.6	31.0	18.2
Item 8230 N(Wtd)	2966	1334	1545		657	933	956	420		1118	435	266	497	55

A19N: ...most of the children are of other races?

1. Not at all acceptable	24.5	28.8	21.0		23.4	26.8	29.1	11.0		26.1	24.0	20.3	25.1	40.0
2. Somewhat acceptable	34.6	34.2	34.7		31.6	36.3	35.5	33.3		33.8	33.9	40.2	34.5	25.5
3. Acceptable	34.8	32.6	37.0		38.5	32.8	29.6	45.5		34.1	35.3	36.1	34.3	27.3
4. Desirable	6.1	4.4	7.3		6.6	4.1	5.8	10.2		6.0	6.9	3.8	6.0	7.3
Item 8240 N(Wtd)	2960	1328	1544		655	930	955	420		1115	434	266	498	55

A20: What race are the students in your school? ‡

1. All my race	17.9	16.6	19.0		21.2	35.0	4.5	5.2		19.0	23.7	17.3	16.7	18.5
2. Almost all my race	38.4	40.7	36.7		48.9	44.3	26.7	35.6		36.8	39.3	43.6	42.6	40.7
3. Mostly my race	23.3	24.2	22.7		18.6	12.0	33.9	31.4		23.4	18.6	19.9	26.7	22.2
4. About half my race	13.1	11.2	14.4		4.9	5.8	25.1	14.7		13.9	10.8	13.2	10.2	13.0
5. Mostly other race(s)	4.7	4.8	4.5		3.4	2.9	7.0	5.5		4.5	4.4	3.4	3.0	5.6
6. Almost all other race(s)	2.7	2.4	2.7		3.2	.1	2.8	7.6		2.3	3.4	2.6	1.2	1.9
Item 8280 N(Wtd)	2971	1334	1547		655	935	959	421		1119	435	266	502	54

A21: What race were the students in the elementary school where you spent the most time?

1. All my race	49.9	48.7	51.1		54.7	60.4	48.5	22.4		55.2	53.2	44.5	48.7	31.5
2. Almost all my race	28.2	28.4	28.3		24.3	27.4	28.2	36.4		25.9	26.5	33.6	30.5	38.9
3. Mostly my race	12.3	12.9	11.6		9.6	7.4	15.4	20.0		11.3	12.0	11.3	12.8	11.1
4. About half my race	5.1	5.6	4.4		6.9	2.8	4.3	9.0		3.8	4.4	6.0	6.2	9.3
5. Mostly other race(s)	2.6	2.7	2.5		2.4	1.4	2.8	5.2		2.0	2.1	2.3	1.2	5.6
6. Almost all other race(s)	1.8	1.7	2.0		2.1	.5	.7	6.7		1.7	1.8	2.3	.6	1.9
Item 8270 N(Wtd)	2961	1328	1543		654	932	955	420		1119	434	265	499	54

‡ = Wording changed in subsequent years.
CAUTION: Items were rearranged after 1975; changes in context may produce spurious "trends" (see page 12).

QUESTIONNAIRE FORM 3 1975	TOTAL	SEX			REGION					ILLICIT DRUG USE: LIFETIME				
		M	F		NE	NC	S	W		None	Mari-juana Only	Few Pills	More Pills	Any Her-oin
Weighted No. of Cases:	3049	1356	1559		681	961	975	432		1125	438	268	507	57
% of Weighted Total:	100.0	44.5	51.1		22.3	31.5	32.0	14.2		36.9	14.4	8.8	16.6	1.9

A22: What race are your close friends?

	TOTAL	M	F		NE	NC	S	W		None	Mar.	Few	More	Her.
1. All my race	57.1	54.9	59.6		62.8	67.6	53.2	34.1		60.9	61.0	60.5	52.9	42.6
2. Almost all my race	22.0	22.9	21.5		20.0	18.9	24.5	26.7		21.4	21.1	23.0	24.0	29.6
3. Mostly my race	11.9	13.9	9.8		9.7	9.2	14.2	16.1		11.0	8.1	7.7	14.8	16.7
4. About half my race	5.8	5.8	5.5		4.9	2.9	5.8	13.9		4.1	5.3	6.1	7.0	1.9
5. Mostly other race(s)	1.8	1.4	2.2		.9	.9	1.3	6.3		1.3	2.8	1.1	.8	-
6. Almost all other race(s)	1.3	1.3	1.2		1.7	.5	1.2	2.9		1.1	1.6	1.1	.6	5.6
Item 8250 N(Wtd)	2945	1321	1536		650	927	951	416		1113	431	261	499	54

A23: What race are the people in your neighborhood?

	TOTAL	M	F		NE	NC	S	W		None	Mar.	Few	More	Her.
1. All my race	63.4	61.6	65.1		60.7	74.0	66.7	36.0		68.6	62.5	61.3	62.4	63.0
2. Almost all my race	18.9	20.0	18.4		19.4	17.0	16.4	27.9		15.5	20.6	22.9	18.6	13.0
3. Mostly my race	9.1	10.1	7.8		10.0	4.2	9.1	18.3		8.3	6.9	7.5	11.8	13.0
4. About half my race	4.4	3.8	4.7		4.3	2.9	4.9	6.7		4.3	3.2	5.3	4.2	1.9
5. Mostly other race(s)	2.2	2.4	2.0		2.3	1.0	1.9	5.2		2.1	3.5	1.1	1.2	1.9
6. Almost all other race(s)	2.1	2.1	1.9		3.4	.7	1.0	5.7		1.3	3.2	1.9	1.6	9.3
Item 8260 N(Wtd)	2958	1329	1542		651	934	954	420		1118	432	266	500	54

A24: How often do you do things (like having a conversation, eating together, playing sports) with people of other races?

	TOTAL	M	F		NE	NC	S	W		None	Mar.	Few	More	Her.
1. Not at all	16.8	14.7	18.6		21.8	24.2	10.1	7.4		19.1	15.9	16.2	15.1	17.9
2. A little	31.4	32.1	30.8		32.2	35.8	28.9	25.7		32.7	33.0	33.5	30.1	25.0
3. Some	34.7	34.1	35.2		33.8	29.2	40.1	35.9		34.1	32.3	30.5	37.6	37.5
4. A lot	17.2	19.2	15.3		12.2	10.7	20.8	31.1		14.1	18.9	19.9	16.9	19.6
Item 8300 N(Wtd)	2969	1333	1547		656	932	960	421		1122	433	266	502	56

A25: Generally, how do you feel about the experiences you have had with people of other races?

	TOTAL	M	F		NE	NC	S	W		None	Mar.	Few	More	Her.
5. Very good	18.2	13.6	22.2		18.3	19.2	13.6	26.2		19.4	17.7	19.7	17.9	23.6
4. Mostly good	40.7	37.6	43.9		41.2	41.1	40.5	39.7		40.2	38.4	42.1	43.3	29.1
3. Mixed	35.9	41.0	30.9		36.2	33.2	40.2	31.5		35.7	38.4	34.7	32.9	38.2
2. Mostly bad	3.8	5.6	2.3		2.6	4.2	5.0	2.2		3.4	4.0	3.5	4.0	7.3
1. Very bad	1.4	2.1	.8		1.7	2.3	.7	.5		1.4	1.4	.4	1.8	3.6
Item 8310 N(Wtd)	2914	1319	1507		646	901	953	413		1099	430	259	496	55

A27: Now we'd like you to make some ratings of how good or bad a job you feel each of the following organizations is doing for the country as a whole. For each one, mark the circle that best describes how you feel. How good or bad a job is being done for the country as a whole by...

A27A: Large corporations?

	TOTAL	M	F		NE	NC	S	W		None	Mar.	Few	More	Her.
1. Very poor	8.5	10.6	6.5		11.6	7.5	6.3	11.0		8.8	7.9	9.0	8.7	9.1
2. Poor	17.4	20.5	14.7		18.1	20.2	13.3	19.8		16.0	17.8	24.8	19.6	20.0
3. Fair	35.0	32.7	37.0		31.9	34.0	37.9	35.3		34.8	34.6	32.3	34.5	32.7
4. Good	22.4	24.1	20.9		21.6	20.8	25.4	20.3		23.3	25.2	20.7	20.4	29.1
5. Very good	4.5	4.1	4.5		4.3	5.5	4.6	2.0		4.1	4.6	3.0	4.2	5.5
8. No opinion	12.3	7.8	16.2		12.3	11.9	12.6	11.8		13.0	9.9	9.8	12.5	3.6
Item 8380 N(Wtd)	2904	1307	1515		648	914	942	400		1108	433	266	495	55

A27B: Major labor unions?

	TOTAL	M	F		NE	NC	S	W		None	Mar.	Few	More	Her.
1. Very poor	6.2	8.7	3.9		6.0	6.9	4.9	8.0		7.7	6.5	3.4	4.9	3.6
2. Poor	14.6	16.4	12.8		15.8	17.1	12.2	12.5		14.5	13.6	17.5	14.1	27.3
3. Fair	35.8	35.6	36.4		33.3	32.8	40.0	37.0		36.9	34.9	35.4	39.7	32.7
4. Good	22.8	23.0	22.6		25.4	23.2	20.6	22.8		20.9	23.3	22.8	23.0	21.8
5. Very good	7.2	7.6	6.8		6.8	6.9	7.6	7.3		6.5	9.9	5.7	6.5	7.3
8. No opinion	13.4	8.6	17.5		12.4	13.1	14.8	12.5		13.6	11.8	15.6	11.8	9.1
Item 8390 N(Wtd)	2890	1303	1504		645	908	937	400		1103	433	263	491	55

CAUTION: Items were rearranged after 1975; changes in context may produce spurious "trends" (see page 12).

QUESTIONNAIRE FORM 3 1975	TOTAL	SEX			REGION					ILLICIT DRUG USE: LIFETIME				
		M	F		NE	NC	S	W		None	Mari- juana Only	Few Pills	More Pills	Any Her- oin
Weighted No. of Cases:	3049	1356	1559		681	961	975	432		1125	438	268	507	57
% of Weighted Total:	100.0	44.5	51.1		22.3	31.5	32.0	14.2		36.9	14.4	8.8	16.6	1.9

A27C: The nation's colleges and universities?

	TOTAL	M	F		NE	NC	S	W		None	Mari- juana Only	Few Pills	More Pills	Any Her- oin
1. Very poor	1.3	1.8	.9		2.2	.8	1.5	.7		1.6	.9	.4	.6	3.6
2. Poor	3.3	4.4	2.3		3.5	4.4	2.7	2.0		2.5	3.2	4.2	3.8	5.5
3. Fair	17.4	17.4	17.1		19.8	17.4	15.7	17.3		16.9	15.2	17.4	16.8	34.5
4. Good	42.2	41.2	43.4		41.8	40.7	42.1	46.5		42.6	44.3	45.3	45.5	25.5
5. Very good	30.8	30.7	31.2		27.2	32.2	32.9	29.0		31.8	33.0	27.9	29.1	23.6
8. No opinion	5.0	4.4	5.2		5.4	4.7	5.1	4.2		4.6	3.2	5.3	4.2	7.3
Item 8400 N(Wtd)	2908	1308	1516		650	914	941	404		1113	433	265	499	55

A27D: The nation's public schools?

	TOTAL	M	F		NE	NC	S	W		None	Mari- juana Only	Few Pills	More Pills	Any Her- oin
1. Very poor	4.0	4.1	4.0		3.9	2.8	5.0	4.5		4.0	3.2	3.0	3.8	9.1
2. Poor	12.3	12.2	12.1		15.7	9.0	11.9	15.6		11.4	10.9	14.7	15.3	14.5
3. Fair	31.4	31.1	31.2		32.4	30.7	32.0	29.7		30.0	32.6	29.3	31.9	34.5
4. Good	34.7	36.0	34.1		32.1	38.7	32.9	33.7		37.7	36.5	32.7	32.1	16.4
5. Very good	13.5	12.7	14.1		10.3	14.3	15.0	13.1		13.2	14.3	16.5	12.0	14.5
8. No opinion	4.2	3.8	4.6		5.7	4.5	3.3	3.5		3.7	2.8	3.4	4.6	10.9
Item 8410 N(Wtd)	2902	1304	1514		648	915	934	404		1110	433	266	498	55

A27E: Churches and religious organizations?

	TOTAL	M	F		NE	NC	S	W		None	Mari- juana Only	Few Pills	More Pills	Any Her- oin
1. Very poor	3.2	4.5	2.0		4.5	2.5	2.7	4.3		2.0	4.8	3.0	4.1	9.1
2. Poor	6.2	7.6	5.0		9.4	5.5	4.5	7.0		5.9	7.2	6.4	7.7	3.6
3. Fair	25.7	26.8	25.0		27.9	26.7	23.3	25.3		24.4	22.6	27.8	26.6	21.8
4. Good	34.7	33.2	35.7		33.4	35.2	35.1	34.5		36.3	36.3	33.5	32.1	25.5
5. Very good	21.3	20.5	22.4		15.3	20.8	27.0	19.3		25.3	20.3	18.8	16.5	21.8
8. No opinion	8.9	7.4	10.0		9.6	9.3	7.4	10.0		6.2	8.5	10.9	13.2	18.2
Item 8420 N(Wtd)	2902	1303	1515		649	913	940	400		1111	433	266	492	55

A27F: The national news media (TV, magazines, news services)?

	TOTAL	M	F		NE	NC	S	W		None	Mari- juana Only	Few Pills	More Pills	Any Her- oin
1. Very poor	4.4	5.0	3.9		3.5	4.6	4.8	4.0		5.5	4.6	3.8	3.4	3.6
2. Poor	8.6	9.7	7.7		7.4	10.1	7.8	9.2		9.5	7.2	9.4	7.8	9.1
3. Fair	26.8	26.4	27.1		25.2	26.6	28.0	27.2		26.5	29.6	22.6	26.6	20.0
4. Good	32.8	33.7	32.3		37.5	33.1	28.5	34.9		33.0	32.6	33.8	33.0	41.8
5. Very good	22.3	21.1	23.2		21.9	21.3	24.8	19.6		20.6	22.9	25.2	23.3	18.2
8. No opinion	5.1	4.2	5.9		4.5	4.4	6.2	5.2		5.0	3.0	5.3	5.6	7.3
Item 8430 N(Wtd)	2905	1305	1515		648	915	938	404		1109	433	266	497	55

A27G: The President and his administration?

	TOTAL	M	F		NE	NC	S	W		None	Mari- juana Only	Few Pills	More Pills	Any Her- oin
1. Very poor	14.1	15.3	12.7		19.6	14.6	11.2	11.4		11.5	13.4	15.0	17.7	29.1
2. Poor	18.3	19.7	17.2		17.6	18.3	18.5	19.2		17.1	21.5	19.5	20.0	21.8
3. Fair	36.8	35.5	38.0		39.7	37.4	35.0	34.8		36.3	36.3	35.7	37.5	23.6
4. Good	16.6	17.4	16.0		11.9	16.6	18.1	20.4		20.5	17.6	15.8	12.1	10.9
5. Very good	3.3	4.1	2.7		2.6	3.0	4.7	2.5		3.5	2.1	3.8	3.0	3.6
8. No opinion	10.9	7.9	13.5		8.6	10.3	12.6	11.9		11.1	9.0	10.2	9.7	12.7
Item 8440 N(Wtd)	2903	1303	1516		648	914	939	402		1109	432	266	496	55

A27H: Congress--that is, the U.S. Senate and House of Representatives?

	TOTAL	M	F		NE	NC	S	W		None	Mari- juana Only	Few Pills	More Pills	Any Her- oin
1. Very poor	10.8	13.8	8.0		11.5	11.6	10.2	9.0		9.1	8.6	12.5	12.1	20.0
2. Poor	19.3	21.5	17.1		19.4	21.3	17.6	18.6		18.2	19.7	21.5	24.2	27.3
3. Fair	37.0	35.6	38.1		38.8	35.6	38.0	35.2		37.8	39.6	36.6	32.7	21.8
4. Good	16.3	15.5	17.3		14.0	15.7	16.7	20.4		19.3	16.2	14.0	15.6	12.7
5. Very good	2.9	3.4	2.4		3.0	2.5	3.2	2.8		2.1	3.9	2.3	3.0	1.8
8. No opinion	13.8	10.2	17.2		13.4	13.4	14.4	14.1		13.5	12.3	13.2	12.1	16.4
Item 8450 N(Wtd)	2899	1302	1513		644	916	940	398		1106	432	265	495	55

CAUTION: Items were rearranged after 1975; changes in context may produce spurious "trends" (see page 12).

QUESTIONNAIRE FORM 3 1975	TOTAL	SEX			REGION					ILLICIT DRUG USE: LIFETIME				
		M	F		NE	NC	S	W		None	Mari- juana Only	Few Pills	More Pills	Any Her- oin
Weighted No. of Cases:	3049	1356	1559		681	961	975	432		1125	438	268	507	57
% of Weighted Total:	100.0	44.5	51.1		22.3	31.5	32.0	14.2		36.9	14.4	8.8	16.6	1.9
A27I: The U.S. Supreme Court?														
1. Very poor	6.5	8.5	4.8		7.8	7.3	6.0	4.3		4.8	5.6	6.0	8.3	10.9
2. Poor	12.0	14.2	10.1		14.3	12.9	11.5	7.6		11.1	11.3	14.3	13.2	23.6
3. Fair	34.0	31.8	35.7		33.6	34.1	33.9	34.9		33.8	36.1	31.2	35.2	29.1
4. Good	23.6	25.6	21.8		22.3	23.7	21.9	29.1		26.7	24.1	22.9	21.7	16.4
5. Very good	5.2	6.4	4.2		5.9	4.1	6.0	4.8		4.5	7.9	3.0	4.9	1.8
8. No opinion	18.7	13.5	23.4		16.0	18.1	20.8	19.2		18.9	15.0	22.6	16.5	18.2
Item 8460 N(Wtd)	2890	1300	1507		645	913	937	395		1103	432	266	492	55
A27J: All the courts and the justice system in general?														
1. Very poor	8.2	10.7	6.0		10.3	9.4	6.5	6.0		6.5	8.6	6.4	10.2	20.4
2. Poor	18.9	21.2	17.2		23.2	19.2	16.3	16.9		17.1	20.1	23.0	22.7	24.1
3. Fair	37.2	36.4	37.9		34.6	38.4	37.8	37.0		40.4	37.0	35.5	37.1	24.1
4. Good	19.3	19.7	18.8		17.3	18.2	20.0	23.4		20.0	20.8	17.0	18.2	9.3
5. Very good	2.9	3.0	2.6		3.7	2.3	3.1	2.5		3.2	2.8	1.9	1.6	3.7
8. No opinion	13.6	9.1	17.5		10.9	12.5	16.2	14.1		12.8	10.6	16.2	10.2	18.5
Item 8470 N(Wtd)	2891	1299	1510		642	913	939	397		1108	432	265	490	54
A27K: The police and other law enforcement agencies?														
1. Very poor	8.5	9.9	7.1		9.3	10.5	7.4	5.0		4.9	6.7	10.9	14.9	25.5
2. Poor	14.9	15.5	14.6		15.3	16.0	14.4	12.9		12.6	16.2	16.2	17.1	18.2
3. Fair	34.5	32.3	36.3		37.7	34.4	32.6	34.0		35.4	35.6	28.7	37.6	30.9
4. Good	29.1	29.6	28.8		25.7	27.6	31.4	32.3		34.5	28.0	29.4	21.1	18.2
5. Very good	8.2	8.6	7.8		6.5	6.7	9.2	11.4		7.9	10.6	6.8	5.2	9.1
8. No opinion	4.9	4.3	5.5		5.3	4.8	4.9	4.5		4.5	3.0	7.5	4.0	1.8
Item 8480 N(Wtd)	2905	1306	1516		645	916	942	403		1109	432	265	497	55
A27L: The U.S. military?														
1. Very poor	4.9	6.9	3.1		5.3	5.6	3.3	6.2		3.0	6.3	6.4	5.7	14.5
2. Poor	5.4	7.5	3.6		5.1	5.1	5.3	6.7		4.1	6.6	4.9	7.5	5.5
3. Fair	26.3	25.2	27.5		24.3	31.3	22.8	26.1		27.0	24.4	22.9	29.9	18.2
4. Good	34.4	33.3	35.2		36.0	31.7	37.4	31.3		37.0	31.8	35.7	30.5	29.1
5. Very good	17.8	20.3	15.5		16.7	15.4	21.5	16.1		17.2	22.0	18.0	17.0	18.2
8. No opinion	11.2	6.9	15.0		12.6	10.8	9.7	13.6		11.7	9.3	12.0	9.5	14.5
Item 8490 N(Wtd)	2898	1299	1515		641	913	941	403		1106	431	266	495	55
A28: All things considered, do you think the armed services presently have too much or too little influence on the way this country is run?														
1. Far too little	2.7	2.9	2.3		1.6	2.9	3.3	2.3		3.0	2.4	1.9	.8	7.7
2. Too little	14.4	14.4	14.6		14.9	13.6	16.2	11.4		14.0	15.5	12.4	15.3	15.4
3. About right	62.8	59.2	66.1		59.1	61.0	66.4	64.1		65.6	64.2	61.8	61.7	48.1
4. Too much	15.2	16.6	14.0		17.8	17.1	10.9	16.7		13.9	12.2	18.1	17.0	19.2
5. Far too much	4.9	6.9	3.0		6.5	5.4	3.4	5.3		3.4	5.7	5.4	5.2	7.7
Item 8500 N(Wtd)	2821	1292	1448		619	888	920	395		1082	419	259	483	52
A29: Do you think the U.S. spends too much or too little on the armed services?														
1. Far too little	3.1	4.9	1.4		1.9	2.2	5.1	2.3		2.8	4.3	2.3	2.5	7.5
2. Too little	15.5	19.2	12.3		12.9	12.4	19.8	16.1		17.5	15.0	13.7	13.8	26.4
3. About right	47.0	41.0	52.4		43.8	47.6	48.7	46.9		49.1	42.8	48.5	45.8	34.0
4. Too much	25.2	24.2	25.9		30.4	27.8	20.0	23.4		24.1	25.7	28.2	26.9	15.1
5. Far too much	9.3	10.8	7.9		11.0	10.0	6.6	11.3		6.6	12.4	7.3	11.1	18.9
Item 8510 N(Wtd)	2835	1299	1460		619	890	929	397		1083	421	262	487	53

CAUTION: Items were rearranged after 1975; changes in context may produce spurious "trends" (see page 12).

QUESTIONNAIRE FORM 3 1975	TOTAL	SEX			REGION					ILLICIT DRUG USE: LIFETIME				
		M	F		NE	NC	S	W		None	Mari-juana Only	Few Pills	More Pills	Any Her-oin
Weighted No. of Cases:	3049	1356	1559		681	961	975	432		1125	438	268	507	57
% of Weighted Total:	100.0	44.5	51.1		22.3	31.5	32.0	14.2		36.9	14.4	8.8	16.6	1.9

A31: The next questions are about pollution and the environment. How much do you agree or disagree with each statement below?

A31A: Pollution of most types has increased in the U.S. in the last ten years

1. Disagree	2.0	2.6	1.6		1.7	1.8	2.9	1.0		1.5	2.5	.8	1.0	3.6
2. Mostly disagree	3.8	4.2	3.4		3.1	4.5	3.9	3.2		3.5	3.0	3.8	2.6	3.6
3. Neither	6.3	7.6	5.1		7.7	6.1	5.3	7.2		6.5	6.9	7.5	4.8	3.6
4. Mostly agree	33.1	31.2	34.3		30.8	37.9	31.7	29.4		32.1	29.4	35.1	32.7	32.7
5. Agree	54.7	54.3	55.6		56.7	49.7	56.3	59.3		56.5	58.1	52.5	58.7	56.4
Item 8000 N(Wtd)	2898	1296	1522		640	911	942	405		1116	432	265	499	55

A31D: Government should take steps to deal with our environmental problems, even if it means that most of us pay higher prices or taxes

1. Disagree	10.3	10.7	9.7		11.2	9.0	11.8	8.0		9.1	7.4	9.8	11.7	7.3
2. Mostly disagree	14.0	13.4	14.0		14.6	14.2	14.7	10.7		13.4	12.3	14.0	13.7	20.0
3. Neither	26.6	23.9	29.2		27.2	27.9	23.5	30.1		25.7	30.0	27.9	26.0	23.6
4. Mostly agree	30.0	30.8	29.4		26.5	31.4	31.4	29.1		31.4	32.3	26.4	28.0	36.4
5. Agree	19.1	21.1	17.6		20.5	17.4	18.6	22.1		20.5	18.1	21.9	20.7	12.7
Item 8010 N(Wtd)	2873	1284	1510		635	901	936	402		1110	430	265	497	55

A31E: I would prefer to pay more money for things that will last a long time, rather than have them cost less and break sooner

1. Disagree	1.1	1.0	1.1		1.1	1.3	1.0	.5		1.1	.7	.8	.8	-
2. Mostly disagree	2.1	2.8	1.5		1.6	1.7	2.9	2.5		1.9	2.8	1.1	1.4	5.5
3. Neither	6.7	8.0	5.6		7.4	8.1	5.1	6.4		5.1	6.5	5.7	8.8	10.9
4. Mostly agree	28.8	27.9	29.3		25.0	32.0	29.6	25.7		26.9	30.3	29.1	29.1	30.9
5. Agree	61.3	60.2	62.5		65.0	56.9	61.4	64.9		65.0	60.0	63.4	60.1	52.7
Item 8020 N(Wtd)	2878	1283	1515		635	900	938	405		1113	432	265	499	55

A31F: I would probably be willing to use a bicycle or mass transit (if available) rather than a car to get to work

1. Disagree	10.9	11.4	10.4		11.3	10.9	12.4	6.7		8.7	9.7	13.9	10.0	12.7
2. Mostly disagree	14.5	15.7	13.1		13.6	14.8	16.8	10.1		12.7	17.1	14.3	13.6	21.8
3. Neither	18.6	20.9	16.9		16.9	17.6	21.5	16.8		18.4	20.1	16.5	18.4	16.4
4. Mostly agree	28.0	26.0	29.9		28.3	29.6	26.0	28.7		31.2	22.5	27.8	31.3	18.2
5. Agree	28.0	25.9	29.8		29.7	27.1	23.3	37.9		29.0	30.8	27.8	26.7	32.7
Item 8030 N(Wtd)	2878	1284	1514		639	899	936	404		1111	432	266	499	55

A31G: I would be willing to eat less meat and more grains and vegetables, if it would help provide food for starving people

1. Disagree	8.4	13.2	4.4		8.5	11.4	6.3	6.7		7.5	8.4	8.3	10.2	12.7
2. Mostly disagree	9.9	12.6	7.2		10.7	9.8	9.8	9.4		9.6	13.0	9.8	7.4	3.6
3. Neither	21.3	25.6	17.7		20.3	22.9	21.7	18.8		21.1	21.6	14.7	23.5	25.5
4. Mostly agree	32.3	27.5	36.9		33.0	31.4	34.2	29.0		33.2	30.5	34.6	33.5	27.3
5. Agree	28.0	21.1	33.9		27.6	24.4	28.2	36.4		28.6	26.3	32.7	25.5	32.7
Item 8040 N(Wtd)	2879	1285	1514		637	901	937	404		1113	430	266	498	55

A32: The questions in this section deal with population problems. How much do you agree or disagree with each statement?

CAUTION: Items were rearranged after 1975; changes in context may produce spurious "trends" (see page 12).

QUESTIONNAIRE FORM 3 1975	TOTAL	SEX			REGION				ILLICIT DRUG USE: LIFETIME				
		M	F		NE	NC	S	W	None	Marijuana Only	Few Pills	More Pills	Any Heroin
Weighted No. of Cases:	3049	1356	1559		681	961	975	432	1125	438	268	507	57
% of Weighted Total:	100.0	44.5	51.1		22.3	31.5	32.0	14.2	36.9	14.4	8.8	16.6	1.9

A32A: Governments should avoid making policy about population and let the individual decide

	TOTAL	M	F		NE	NC	S	W	None	Mari-juana Only	Few Pills	More Pills	Any Her-oin
1. Disagree	12.8	15.0	10.5		10.9	11.5	13.7	16.8	12.5	12.4	11.8	14.2	5.4
2. Mostly disagree	19.1	20.6	18.0		16.3	19.0	19.6	23.0	17.6	21.7	20.6	20.1	21.4
3. Neither	26.2	26.3	26.4		25.2	27.4	25.2	27.5	25.3	25.2	28.2	26.4	25.0
4. Mostly agree	24.8	23.2	26.3		25.7	26.5	25.2	18.8	26.6	25.5	21.8	25.4	23.2
5. Agree	17.0	14.8	18.7		21.9	15.6	16.2	14.1	18.0	15.4	17.6	14.0	25.0
Item 9770 N(Wtd)	2839	1266	1496		626	890	919	404	1104	428	262	492	56

A32B: I feel strongly enough about preventing overpopulation that I'd be willing to limit my family to two children

1. Disagree	12.5	9.7	14.4		14.0	11.6	12.9	11.6	14.1	10.8	9.9	11.0	17.9
2. Mostly disagree	10.1	8.6	11.2		11.4	10.7	8.9	9.7	10.0	11.9	7.9	7.7	5.4
3. Neither	16.5	19.1	14.6		18.1	17.0	15.7	14.9	17.7	15.7	11.4	16.2	14.3
4. Mostly agree	24.6	25.3	24.2		24.3	27.1	23.6	22.0	25.0	22.5	22.4	24.9	23.2
5. Agree	36.2	37.3	35.6		32.1	33.8	39.0	42.1	33.3	38.9	43.3	40.0	39.3
Item 9780 N(Wtd)	2848	1267	1504		629	890	924	404	1110	427	263	493	56

A32C: To help prevent overpopulation, I might decide not to have any children of my own

1. Disagree	48.6	42.9	53.4		48.2	46.6	51.6	47.0	51.4	49.2	49.0	43.6	39.3
2. Mostly disagree	17.2	19.9	15.0		20.1	18.8	16.0	12.3	17.4	19.8	13.7	18.3	17.9
3. Neither	15.1	19.7	11.5		15.6	15.3	13.8	16.8	13.5	16.2	14.8	16.0	10.7
4. Mostly agree	8.1	8.3	7.7		7.5	8.4	7.7	9.8	8.3	5.4	9.1	8.7	10.7
5. Agree	10.9	9.1	12.3		8.8	10.9	10.9	14.3	9.4	9.6	13.3	13.4	19.6
Item 9790 N(Wtd)	2836	1262	1498		628	888	921	400	1106	425	263	493	56

A32E: High schools should offer instruction in birth control methods

1. Disagree	5.9	5.8	6.1		5.8	4.0	7.0	7.8	7.7	4.0	5.8	2.9	5.5
2. Mostly disagree	4.5	4.8	4.3		5.6	4.4	3.4	5.8	6.8	3.0	1.5	2.9	1.8
3. Neither	14.8	17.2	12.9		11.9	15.8	14.9	16.8	16.8	11.2	13.5	11.8	10.9
4. Mostly agree	26.8	27.1	26.2		27.8	27.0	25.7	26.8	26.1	29.0	26.9	23.7	25.5
5. Agree	48.1	45.1	50.5		49.0	48.9	48.7	43.0	42.6	52.5	52.7	58.6	56.4
Item 9800 N(Wtd)	2826	1258	1491		623	886	917	400	1103	427	260	490	55

A32I: I personally consider most methods of birth control to be immoral

1. Disagree	46.0	40.5	50.5		44.7	48.2	43.6	48.3	39.3	51.5	56.5	60.2	50.0
2. Mostly disagree	18.1	19.9	16.8		16.9	19.2	17.6	18.6	18.0	17.8	18.5	16.6	18.5
3. Neither	21.5	23.8	19.6		22.2	21.4	22.0	19.6	24.9	17.8	16.2	14.8	16.7
4. Mostly agree	6.6	7.6	5.7		6.4	5.3	8.4	5.6	8.0	6.7	4.2	3.7	7.4
5. Agree	7.9	8.2	7.5		10.0	5.8	8.4	8.1	9.8	6.4	4.2	4.7	9.3
Item 9810 N(Wtd)	2795	1242	1480		622	879	901	393	1097	421	260	493	54

A32M: The government should make birth control information and services available without cost to anyone who wants them

1. Disagree	5.3	4.9	5.5		4.5	5.5	5.3	6.1	7.6	4.5	5.0	1.0	1.9
2. Mostly disagree	4.1	3.9	4.2		4.5	3.9	4.0	4.3	4.5	3.1	5.3	3.0	1.9
3. Neither	13.3	14.8	12.2		12.8	15.2	12.0	12.5	14.4	14.1	11.1	11.3	20.4
4. Mostly agree	24.2	25.3	23.4		22.7	26.5	23.0	24.3	25.2	21.9	22.1	25.7	22.2
5. Agree	53.1	51.1	54.6		55.4	49.0	55.8	52.4	48.2	56.2	56.5	58.9	53.7
Item 9820 N(Wtd)	2810	1239	1495		626	879	914	391	1101	425	262	494	54

CAUTION: Items were rearranged after 1975; changes in context may produce spurious "trends" (see page 12).

	TOTAL	SEX			REGION				ILLICIT DRUG USE: LIFETIME				
QUESTIONNAIRE FORM 3 1975		M	F		NE	NC	S	W	None	Mari-juana Only	Few Pills	More Pills	Any Her-oin
Weighted No. of Cases:	3049	1356	1559		681	961	975	432	1125	438	268	507	57
% of Weighted Total:	100.0	44.5	51.1		22.3	31.5	32.0	14.2	36.9	14.4	8.8	16.6	1.9
A32N: Our government should help other countries to control their population													
1. Disagree	13.3	14.9	11.7		16.2	11.7	11.9	15.4	14.1	14.2	13.4	12.0	20.4
2. Mostly disagree	10.7	10.6	10.6		11.1	11.1	10.6	9.5	10.6	11.1	8.4	11.2	11.1
3. Neither	25.5	25.1	26.0		27.0	24.6	25.8	23.9	26.0	22.7	25.7	25.4	29.6
4. Mostly agree	23.0	21.5	24.5		23.0	25.1	21.6	21.9	22.9	26.1	20.7	23.7	11.1
5. Agree	27.5	27.8	27.3		22.7	27.5	30.0	29.3	26.3	25.8	32.6	28.0	29.6
Item 9760 N(Wtd)	2805	1237	1492		622	877	916	389	1107	422	261	493	54
A33: How do you feel about giving food to foreign countries?													
1. I would share only or mostly with those countries that work on birth control	21.9	24.5	20.4		16.4	24.6	21.7	25.4	20.9	25.5	25.3	21.8	7.5
2. I would share with all needy countries	47.8	38.9	55.1		49.6	44.9	50.4	45.4	51.3	42.3	47.1	44.3	43.4
3. I feel we have no obligation to foreign countries	18.6	24.8	13.3		21.6	17.4	17.4	19.2	17.2	21.4	18.3	17.9	30.2
4. I don't care one way or the other	11.7	11.8	11.2		12.3	13.2	10.5	10.0	10.7	11.1	8.9	16.0	18.9
Item 9840 N(Wtd)	2720	1212	1436		603	856	891	370	1079	416	257	476	53
A34: What do you think would be the ideal population size for the united states?													
1. Much smaller than it is now	12.5	12.9	12.1		14.1	10.0	11.5	18.1	10.1	10.0	15.4	17.1	18.5
2. Somewhat smaller than it is now	43.0	42.9	43.5		42.3	47.7	39.3	42.0	44.3	46.8	41.3	45.9	31.5
3. About the same as it is now	37.8	36.7	38.8		37.8	37.0	40.5	33.3	39.7	37.5	35.1	32.9	35.2
4. Somewhat larger than it is now	4.9	5.7	4.1		4.8	3.9	5.9	5.2	4.3	3.8	6.9	3.7	11.1
5. Much larger than it is now	1.7	1.8	1.5		1.0	1.3	2.8	1.3	1.6	1.9	1.2	.2	1.9
Item 9830 N(Wtd)	2744	1221	1452		608	851	904	381	1084	421	259	486	54
A35: What do you think would be the ideal population size for the entire world?													
1. Much smaller than it is now	37.5	39.0	36.3		38.1	41.5	30.9	42.9	37.4	38.0	41.9	41.4	49.1
2. Somewhat smaller than it is now	41.1	40.8	41.6		39.2	40.5	43.2	40.3	40.6	44.1	40.0	43.5	27.3
3. About the same as it is now	15.9	14.9	16.7		17.4	14.7	18.1	11.0	16.8	13.7	13.1	13.2	18.2
4. Somewhat larger than it is now	3.4	3.3	3.3		3.4	2.6	4.1	3.4	3.0	3.1	2.3	1.6	1.8
5. Much larger than it is now	2.1	2.0	2.1		1.8	.6	3.7	2.4	2.2	1.4	3.1	.4	3.6
Item 9850 N(Wtd)	2750	1224	1456		609	857	903	382	1088	424	260	485	55
A41: The next questions are about some of your own plans. are you married or engaged?													
1. Married --SKIP TO Q.A43	1.8	1.2	2.0		.7	1.6	2.9	1.3	1.4	2.6	1.6	2.5	-
2. Engaged	9.6	5.2	13.1		6.5	11.0	11.3	7.8	8.5	7.5	8.2	12.9	16.1
3. Neither	88.6	93.6	84.8		92.9	87.5	85.6	90.8	90.1	90.1	90.2	84.6	82.1
Item 8320 N(Wtd)	2653	1160	1429		602	831	849	371	1074	416	245	474	56
A42: If it were just up to you, what would be the ideal time for you to get married													
1. Within the next year or so	10.8	5.1	15.3		6.9	11.2	14.0	8.8	10.8	8.2	9.6	11.7	21.8
2. Two or three years from now	25.1	18.8	30.1		21.6	25.2	28.0	23.9	26.0	22.5	27.9	22.6	14.5
3. Four or five years from now	34.1	35.7	33.2		36.1	34.3	32.0	35.4	37.7	37.6	32.5	28.8	25.5
4. Over five years from now	24.7	34.7	16.3		29.2	25.2	20.2	25.5	20.9	28.0	26.3	29.6	32.7
5. I don't want to marry	5.4	5.7	5.2		6.1	4.0	5.7	6.6	4.7	3.7	3.8	7.5	5.5
Item 8330 N(Wtd) ★	2596	1138	1397		592	820	820	364	1050	404	240	469	55

★=excludes respondents for whom question was inappropriate.

CAUTION: Items were rearranged after 1975; changes in context may produce spurious "trends" (see page 12).

QUESTIONNAIRE FORM 3 1975	TOTAL	SEX			REGION					ILLICIT DRUG USE: LIFETIME				
		M	F		NE	NC	S	W		None	Mari-juana Only	Few Pills	More Pills	Any Her-oin
Weighted No. of Cases:	3049	1356	1559		681	961	975	432		1125	438	268	507	57
% of Weighted Total:	100.0	44.5	51.1		22.3	31.5	32.0	14.2		36.9	14.4	8.8	16.6	1.9
A43: Have you thought at all about whether you'd like to have children or how many you'd like to have?														
3. I've thought about it a lot	48.9	31.8	62.8		42.8	47.3	53.9	50.4		48.3	50.2	51.5	51.1	51.8
2. I've thought about it a little	43.3	54.4	34.2		48.5	44.5	38.6	43.5		43.5	44.4	42.4	41.7	37.5
1. I haven't thought about it at all	7.8	13.7	3.0		8.8	8.1	7.5	6.1		8.2	5.4	5.7	7.2	10.7
Item 8340 N(Wtd)	2735	1202	1467		615	852	891	377		1106	428	262	489	56
A44: All things considered, if you could have exactly the number of children you want, what number would you choose to have?														
1. None	5.1	4.6	5.6		4.4	5.1	5.1	5.7		4.6	3.5	5.7	5.5	16.1
2. One	5.5	5.6	5.5		3.6	4.4	8.0	5.5		5.3	6.9	8.1	5.4	5.4
3. Two	46.8	49.9	44.0		43.2	46.8	49.1	47.5		43.6	49.7	44.7	49.7	39.3
4. Three	18.3	17.7	19.3		19.7	19.5	17.9	14.9		20.1	20.0	21.8	14.6	14.3
5. Four	10.7	7.3	13.3		11.6	11.0	9.8	10.4		12.0	12.8	5.7	9.1	10.7
6. Five	2.5	2.2	2.8		3.1	2.8	1.5	3.1		2.0	2.3	4.2	2.2	1.8
7. Six or more	2.8	2.2	3.1		3.1	2.7	2.2	3.4		3.2	2.8	3.4	1.4	7.1
8. Don't know	8.3	10.5	6.4		11.6	7.6	6.4	9.4		9.3	6.3	7.3	9.1	3.6
Item 8350 N(Wtd)	2747	1207	1474		614	855	895	383		1112	431	262	493	56
A45: If the "population explosion" were not a problem, would you choose to have a larger number of children?														
4. Yes, I'm sure I would want more	9.8	8.5	11.0		9.3	8.5	10.0	13.2		10.4	11.8	11.1	7.1	19.3
3. I probably would want more	15.1	13.2	16.6		15.0	17.7	12.4	16.3		15.3	15.7	18.4	14.2	8.8
2. I probably would not want more	31.2	33.7	29.4		35.1	29.7	31.3	27.9		32.7	31.9	29.5	30.7	17.5
1. I'm sure I would not want more	25.7	21.9	28.9		20.5	25.9	28.6	26.3		23.8	26.6	23.8	30.3	35.1
8. Don't know, no idea	18.2	22.6	14.2		20.2	18.2	17.6	16.6		17.9	13.7	17.6	17.9	15.8
Item 8360 N(Wtd)	2740	1206	1469		615	851	894	380		1107	432	261	492	57
A46: If it were just up to you, how soon after getting married would you want to have your first child?														
1. I don't want to have children (or get married)	4.1	3.4	4.8		4.3	3.6	4.4	4.2		3.4	2.8	5.7	5.1	10.5
2. I wouldn't wait at all	4.5	6.9	2.5		5.4	3.6	3.8	6.6		4.5	3.2	3.8	4.1	5.3
3. I would wait one year	21.2	22.2	20.2		23.7	23.9	17.1	21.1		18.9	25.4	20.6	22.0	19.3
4. I would wait two years	29.8	25.8	33.4		26.8	32.2	31.0	25.9		32.4	29.1	33.2	27.2	21.1
5. I would wait three years	13.3	11.2	14.8		12.9	12.5	13.8	15.0		13.8	12.2	15.3	13.4	14.0
6. I would wait four or five years	8.5	5.5	11.3		7.4	8.6	9.7	7.1		8.4	9.9	6.5	9.8	8.8
7. I would wait more than five years	1.7	1.6	1.8		.7	1.2	2.7	2.1		1.1	1.4	2.3	2.4	1.8
8. Don't know, no idea ‡	16.9	23.5	11.2		19.0	14.2	17.4	18.2		17.5	13.8	12.6	15.9	19.3
Item 8370 N(Wtd)	2733	1205	1463		611	850	894	379		1110	426	262	492	57
A48: Next are some questions which ask about your experiences and attitudes concerning particular drugs. First we want your answers about some drugs that can be bought at a drugstore without a doctor's prescription--sometimes called over-the-counter or non-prescription drugs. During the last 12 months, on how many occasions have you...														
A48A: ...used non-prescription drugs which are supposed to relieve pain (such as aspirin, Anacin, Bufferin, or Excedrin)?														
1. 0 occasions	8.8	11.6	6.5		7.8	8.6	9.3	9.8		10.2	10.0	6.9	4.2	5.3
2. 1-2 occasions	19.1	20.8	17.6		19.3	17.0	18.7	23.7		20.8	18.8	18.3	12.4	15.8
3. 3-5 occasions	16.6	18.3	15.4		19.3	15.8	15.6	16.6		18.9	17.2	17.2	12.2	10.5
4. 6-9 occasions	15.7	17.5	14.4		16.4	15.8	14.8	16.4		15.9	16.5	16.8	15.7	5.3
5. 10-19 occasions	17.7	14.0	20.8		17.2	19.9	16.0	17.4		16.3	18.4	21.0	20.7	21.1
6. 20-39 occasions	11.2	8.8	13.0		10.1	12.2	12.4	8.4		9.8	10.9	9.9	17.1	17.5
7. 40 or more	10.9	9.1	12.2		9.9	10.6	13.3	7.4		8.2	8.1	9.9	17.9	22.8
Item 8520 N(Wtd)	2695	1177	1454		605	829	881	379		1113	430	262	498	57

‡=Wording changed in subsequent years.

CAUTION: Items were rearranged after 1975; changes in context may produce spurious "trends" (see page 12).

QUESTIONNAIRE FORM 3 1975	TOTAL	SEX			REGION					ILLICIT DRUG USE: LIFETIME				
		M	F		NE	NC	S	W		None	Mari- juana Only	Few Pills	More Pills	Any Her- oin
Weighted No. of Cases:	3049	1356	1559		681	961	975	432		1125	438	268	507	57
% of Weighted Total:	100.0	44.5	51.1		22.3	31.5	32.0	14.2		36.9	14.4	8.8	16.6	1.9

A48B: ...used non-prescription drugs that are supposed to help people get to sleep (such as Sleep-Eze, Sominex, or Nytol)?

	TOTAL	M	F		NE	NC	S	W		None	Mari-juana Only	Few Pills	More Pills	Any Heroin
1. 0 occasions	89.1	89.3	89.2		91.4	88.3	88.5	89.1		95.4	92.6	86.3	77.4	61.4
2. 1-2 occasions	5.7	5.3	5.9		4.6	5.8	6.3	5.6		2.7	3.0	11.0	10.4	17.5
3. 3-5 occasions	2.1	2.0	2.2		1.7	2.5	2.4	.8		.5	1.9	1.5	4.8	7.0
4. 6-9 occasions	1.7	2.4	1.2		1.3	1.9	1.0	3.7		.5	2.6	.8	4.0	3.5
5. 10-19 occasions	.7	.6	.8		.5	.7	1.0	.5		.3	-	-	2.8	3.5
6. 20-39 occasions	.3	.1	.3		.2	.4	.3	.3		.5	-	-	.2	1.8
7. 40 or more	.4	.5	.3		.5	.5	.5	-		.2	-	.4	.4	5.3
Item 8530 N(Wtd)	2684	1173	1449		605	826	877	375		1107	430	263	499	57

A48C: ...used non-prescription drugs that are supposed to help people stay awake (such as No-Doz, Wake, or Vivarin)?

	TOTAL	M	F		NE	NC	S	W		None	Mari-juana Only	Few Pills	More Pills	Any Heroin
1. 0 occasions	89.0	88.0	90.2		92.4	85.9	89.0	90.4		96.3	92.3	90.8	74.7	46.4
2. 1-2 occasions	5.3	5.8	4.6		3.5	6.1	5.7	5.3		2.3	5.3	4.2	9.8	21.4
3. 3-5 occasions	1.7	1.9	1.3		1.5	2.6	1.0	1.6		.5	1.2	3.1	4.2	1.8
4. 6-9 occasions	1.5	1.5	1.5		1.0	2.2	1.6	.8		.4	1.2	.4	4.4	7.1
5. 10-19 occasions	1.0	1.1	1.0		.7	1.8	.8	.5		.1	.2	-	3.6	5.4
6. 20-39 occasions	.8	.8	.8		.3	.7	1.1	.8		.3	-	.4	2.6	5.4
7. 40 or more	.7	.9	.6		.7	.9	.7	.5		.3	-	.8	.6	14.3
Item 8540 N(Wtd)	2675	1169	1444		605	823	873	374		1105	430	262	499	56

A48D: ...used non-prescription drugs that are supposed to calm people down--keep them from being nervous or in a bad mood (such as Cope, Compoz, Devarex, or Miles Nervine)?

	TOTAL	M	F		NE	NC	S	W		None	Mari-juana Only	Few Pills	More Pills	Any Heroin
1. 0 occasions	91.5	94.1	90.1		94.5	90.9	88.9	94.1		96.8	96.3	87.8	81.2	66.1
2. 1-2 occasions	4.0	2.6	4.7		2.7	3.5	5.6	3.2		1.1	1.4	7.6	9.2	14.3
3. 3-5 occasions	1.8	1.0	2.5		.8	2.6	2.2	1.1		.9	1.4	2.7	3.4	3.6
4. 6-9 occasions	1.0	.9	1.0		.5	.9	1.7	.8		.5	.5	1.1	2.6	3.6
5. 10-19 occasions	.9	.7	.8		.7	1.1	.9	.3		.5	-	.4	1.4	5.4
6. 20-39 occasions	.3	.2	.5		.2	.5	.2	.3		.1	-	-	1.6	1.8
7. 40 or more	.4	.5	.4		.5	.6	.5	.3		.2	.2	.4	.6	5.4
Item 8550 N(Wtd)	2671	1164	1446		602	823	875	371		1105	430	262	499	56

A53: Individuals differ in whether or not they disapprove of people doing certain things. Do you disapprove of people who are in their twenties or older doing each of the following? ‡

A53A: Smoking one or more packs of cigarettes per day

	TOTAL	M	F		NE	NC	S	W		None	Mari-juana Only	Few Pills	More Pills	Any Heroin
1. Don't disapprove	32.6	34.7	30.6		32.3	34.7	33.6	25.8		20.7	34.9	39.1	48.9	62.5
2. Disapprove	36.5	35.4	37.2		40.9	33.0	37.5	34.2		39.0	35.6	31.6	31.9	26.8
3. Strongly disapprove	31.0	29.9	32.1		26.8	32.3	28.7	39.7		40.4	29.2	29.3	19.0	12.5
Item 8560 N(Wtd)	2638	1155	1426		597	813	863	365		1108	435	266	499	56

A53B: Trying marijuana (pot, grass) once or twice

	TOTAL	M	F		NE	NC	S	W		None	Mari-juana Only	Few Pills	More Pills	Any Heroin
1. Don't disapprove	53.1	59.9	47.3		64.0	52.2	45.2	55.9		23.2	79.5	67.0	84.7	96.4
2. Disapprove	21.4	18.9	23.6		19.3	22.2	23.3	18.4		30.1	14.1	15.4	10.2	3.6
3. Strongly disapprove	25.6	21.2	29.2		16.6	25.6	31.5	25.8		46.6	6.5	17.2	5.2	1.8
Item 8570 N(Wtd)	2641	1157	1427		597	816	863	365		1111	434	267	502	56

‡=Wording changed in subsequent years.

CAUTION: Items were rearranged after 1975; changes in context may produce spurious "trends" (see page 12).

QUESTIONNAIRE FORM 3 1975	TOTAL	SEX			REGION					ILLICIT DRUG USE: LIFETIME				
		M	F		NE	NC	S	W		None	Mari-juana Only	Few Pills	More Pills	Any Her-oin
Weighted No. of Cases:	*3049*	*1356*	*1559*		*681*	*961*	*975*	*432*		*1125*	*438*	*268*	*507*	*57*
% of Weighted Total:	*100.0*	*44.5*	*51.1*		*22.3*	*31.5*	*32.0*	*14.2*		*36.9*	*14.4*	*8.8*	*16.6*	*1.9*
A53C: Smoking marijuana occasionally														
1. Don't disapprove	45.2	52.3	39.3		54.5	44.6	37.6	49.6		14.7	68.6	55.1	80.6	94.6
2. Disapprove	23.3	22.2	24.7		26.2	24.0	22.7	18.1		29.7	22.6	21.7	11.4	5.4
3. Strongly disapprove	31.5	25.6	36.1		19.3	31.4	39.7	32.3		55.5	8.8	23.2	8.2	1.8
Item 8580 N(Wtd)	*2635*	*1153*	*1425*		*595*	*813*	*862*	*365*		*1110*	*433*	*267*	*500*	*56*
A53D: Smoking marijuana regularly														
1. Don't disapprove	28.1	35.0	22.0		34.9	27.7	24.4	27.1		7.4	34.3	30.5	59.2	89.3
2. Disapprove	26.4	26.6	26.8		29.3	26.6	24.1	26.3		21.1	41.4	29.3	23.4	7.1
3. Strongly disapprove	45.5	38.3	51.2		35.8	45.6	51.5	46.6		71.5	24.3	39.8	17.4	3.6
Item 8590 N(Wtd)	*2629*	*1153*	*1419*		*593*	*811*	*858*	*365*		*1109*	*432*	*266*	*500*	*56*
A53E: Trying LSD once or twice														
1. Don't disapprove	17.1	22.0	13.2		21.8	17.8	12.8	18.0		5.5	11.9	16.5	42.1	67.9
2. Disapprove	22.8	21.3	23.9		24.8	24.5	20.9	20.8		17.8	26.6	27.0	25.7	21.4
3. Strongly disapprove	60.0	56.7	62.9		53.4	57.6	66.3	61.2		76.7	61.2	56.6	32.1	10.7
Item 8600 N(Wtd)	*2635*	*1154*	*1424*		*597*	*811*	*861*	*366*		*1108*	*436*	*267*	*501*	*56*
A53F: Taking LSD regularly														
1. Don't disapprove	6.0	9.0	3.4		5.7	7.3	5.5	4.7		3.1	4.4	2.2	12.0	33.9
2. Disapprove	19.7	20.2	19.4		24.0	20.2	15.9	20.1		11.4	15.7	22.1	33.4	42.9
3. Strongly disapprove	74.4	70.7	77.1		70.2	72.5	78.6	75.5		85.4	79.9	75.7	54.6	23.2
Item 8610 N(Wtd)	*2628*	*1151*	*1422*		*597*	*810*	*859*	*363*		*1110*	*433*	*267*	*500*	*56*
A53G: Trying heroin (smack, horse) once or twice														
1. Don't disapprove	8.5	11.3	6.3		9.9	8.4	8.8	5.8		3.7	6.7	6.0	14.8	64.3
2. Disapprove	17.9	16.4	19.1		21.0	19.6	14.5	16.9		13.8	15.6	21.1	23.8	16.1
3. Strongly disapprove	73.6	72.3	74.7		69.1	71.9	76.6	77.6		82.5	77.8	72.9	61.4	19.6
Item 8620 N(Wtd)	*2628*	*1155*	*1417*		*596*	*810*	*860*	*362*		*1108*	*436*	*266*	*500*	*56*
A53H: Taking heroin occasionally														
1. Don't disapprove	5.2	7.5	3.4		5.0	5.7	5.7	3.6		2.8	5.3	1.5	7.6	35.7
2. Disapprove	15.1	15.3	15.1		18.0	15.7	13.0	13.8		11.0	12.0	14.7	21.0	41.1
3. Strongly disapprove	79.7	77.2	81.6		77.0	78.6	81.4	82.9		86.3	82.7	84.2	71.1	23.2
Item 8630 N(Wtd)	*2623*	*1152*	*1415*		*595*	*805*	*861*	*362*		*1109*	*434*	*266*	*499*	*56*
A53I: Taking heroin regularly														
1. Don't disapprove	3.2	5.1	1.6		2.9	3.6	3.6	2.2		2.6	3.2	.8	3.2	17.9
2. Disapprove	13.1	13.8	12.7		15.9	13.3	12.3	10.2		9.6	11.1	10.6	18.7	37.5
3. Strongly disapprove	83.6	81.1	85.6		81.2	83.2	84.1	87.3		87.7	85.7	88.7	78.1	46.4
Item 8640 N(Wtd)	*2617*	*1147*	*1414*		*591*	*804*	*861*	*361*		*1107*	*433*	*265*	*498*	*56*
A53J: Trying a barbiturate (downer, goofball, red, yellow, etc.) once or twice														
1. Don't disapprove	22.3	25.6	19.6		25.8	24.4	17.7	22.9		6.2	17.5	22.3	54.7	78.6
2. Disapprove	23.5	23.0	23.7		27.6	24.1	21.3	20.4		20.8	27.0	28.7	22.8	12.5
3. Strongly disapprove	54.2	51.3	56.6		46.6	51.5	61.0	56.9		73.0	55.5	49.1	22.6	8.9
Item 8650 N(Wtd)	*2622*	*1150*	*1416*		*597*	*804*	*859*	*362*		*1109*	*434*	*265*	*501*	*56*
A53K: Taking barbiturates regularly														
1. Don't disapprove	6.8	9.5	4.6		6.6	7.6	7.0	5.0		2.7	4.8	1.9	14.7	46.4
2. Disapprove	23.1	23.3	23.0		28.6	25.0	18.5	20.6		13.5	21.1	25.5	40.6	33.9
3. Strongly disapprove	70.2	67.1	72.4		64.8	67.5	74.6	74.4		83.8	74.1	72.7	44.8	21.4
Item 8660 N(Wtd)	*2617*	*1150*	*1411*		*594*	*805*	*858*	*360*		*1102*	*436*	*267*	*498*	*56*

CAUTION: Items were rearranged after 1975; changes in context may produce spurious "trends" (see page 12).

QUESTIONNAIRE FORM 3 1975	TOTAL	SEX			REGION					ILLICIT DRUG USE: LIFETIME				
		M	F		NE	NC	S	W		None	Marijuana Only	Few Pills	More Pills	Any Heroin
Weighted No. of Cases:	3049	1356	1559		681	961	975	432		1125	438	268	507	57
% of Weighted Total:	100.0	44.5	51.1		22.3	31.5	32.0	14.2		36.9	14.4	8.8	16.6	1.9
A53L: Trying an amphetamine (upper, pep pill, bennie, speed) once or twice														
1. Don't disapprove	25.2	29.1	22.1		28.8	28.1	19.2	27.4		6.4	19.0	26.6	64.7	82.1
2. Disapprove	22.6	21.4	23.7		26.1	22.5	21.1	20.8		21.0	26.1	29.6	17.8	10.7
3. Strongly disapprove	52.2	49.4	54.2		45.2	49.4	59.7	52.1		72.7	54.8	43.8	17.4	7.1
Item 8670 N(Wtd)	2625	1153	1416		598	805	861	361		1108	436	267	501	56
A53M: Taking amphetamines regularly														
1. Don't disapprove	7.9	10.3	6.1		9.4	8.6	6.5	7.5		2.7	5.3	2.2	21.0	37.5
2. Disapprove	23.1	23.4	22.9		26.8	26.1	18.9	20.2		13.4	20.4	27.3	38.9	41.1
3. Strongly disapprove	69.0	66.3	71.0		64.0	65.3	74.5	72.4		83.9	74.1	70.8	39.9	21.4
Item 8680 N(Wtd)	2617	1151	1412		597	802	856	362		1109	436	267	499	56
A53N: Trying cocaine once or twice														
1. Don't disapprove	18.7	25.1	13.5		22.6	18.7	15.0	21.1		4.4	14.3	16.2	48.5	83.9
2. Disapprove	19.6	18.3	20.8		23.1	18.7	18.7	17.7		16.4	22.3	23.3	21.0	12.5
3. Strongly disapprove	61.7	56.7	65.7		54.2	62.4	66.4	61.2		79.2	63.4	60.5	30.5	5.4
Item 8690 N(Wtd)	2612	1145	1412		594	801	856	361		1104	435	266	501	56
A53O: Taking cocaine regularly														
1. Don't disapprove	6.7	10.1	3.8		7.8	6.5	6.5	5.8		3.0	4.4	2.3	15.2	33.9
2. Disapprove	19.2	20.8	17.6		23.6	20.4	15.8	17.2		10.9	17.7	19.0	32.7	53.6
3. Strongly disapprove	74.1	69.1	78.6		68.8	73.2	77.6	76.9		86.2	77.9	78.7	52.1	12.5
Item 8700 N(Wtd)	2588	1138	1397		590	798	840	360		1098	434	263	499	56
A53P: Trying one or two drinks of an alcoholic beverage (beer, wine, liquor)														
1. Don't disapprove	78.4	81.8	75.5		86.2	80.1	73.7	72.4		64.3	90.8	81.6	93.0	98.2
2. Disapprove	12.5	11.0	14.2		9.4	12.0	14.6	13.8		20.4	6.0	12.0	4.0	1.8
3. Strongly disapprove	9.1	7.2	10.3		4.4	7.8	11.7	13.5		15.2	3.2	6.4	3.0	-
Item 8710 N(Wtd)	2607	1145	1408		595	799	852	362		1105	435	267	501	56
A53Q: Taking one or two drinks nearly every day														
1. Don't disapprove	32.4	41.6	24.8		37.5	34.9	29.3	25.8		19.3	39.1	31.3	48.7	58.9
2. Disapprove	40.5	38.3	42.4		41.7	40.5	38.9	42.7		42.1	42.8	39.6	37.1	33.9
3. Strongly disapprove	27.1	20.1	32.8		21.0	24.6	31.9	31.6		38.5	18.2	29.1	14.2	7.1
Item 8720 N(Wtd)	2600	1142	1408		595	800	844	361		1101	435	265	499	56
A53R: Taking four or five drinks nearly every day														
1. Don't disapprove	11.4	17.2	6.5		13.3	13.8	9.6	7.5		5.9	12.6	8.2	17.9	35.7
2. Disapprove	29.4	32.9	26.2		32.3	30.8	27.0	26.5		24.3	32.0	23.2	40.4	41.1
3. Strongly disapprove	59.3	49.9	67.1		54.4	55.4	63.4	65.7		69.9	55.4	68.5	41.6	25.0
Item 8730 N(Wtd)	2602	1145	1406		594	798	848	362		1105	435	267	498	56
A53S: Having five or more drinks once or twice each weekend														
1. Don't disapprove	39.7	49.3	31.7		45.8	44.6	33.5	33.8		22.4	49.1	41.4	62.7	78.6
2. Disapprove	25.2	24.0	26.5		28.4	23.9	24.1	25.5		27.1	27.2	22.9	21.0	16.1
3. Strongly disapprove	35.1	26.7	41.8		26.0	31.5	42.4	41.0		50.5	23.5	35.7	16.4	7.1
Item 8740 N(Wtd)	2603	1144	1408		596	796	849	361		1108	434	266	501	56

CAUTION: Items were rearranged after 1975; changes in context may produce spurious "trends" (see page 12).

QUESTIONNAIRE FORM 3 1975	TOTAL	SEX			REGION					ILLICIT DRUG USE: LIFETIME				
		M	F		NE	NC	S	W		None	Mari- juana Only	Few Pills	More Pills	Any Her- oin
Weighted No. of Cases:	3049	1356	1559		681	961	975	432		1125	438	268	507	57
% of Weighted Total:	100.0	44.5	51.1		22.3	31.5	32.0	14.2		36.9	14.4	8.8	16.6	1.9

A55: How often have you been around people who were taking each of the following to get high or for "kicks"?

A55A: Marijuana (pot, grass) or hashish

	TOTAL	M	F		NE	NC	S	W		None	Mar.	Few	More	Any
1. Never ‡	16.7	12.9	19.8		11.5	17.1	21.8	12.7		32.0	1.2	6.9	3.4	-
2. Once or twice	22.5	20.7	24.4		19.7	23.1	24.3	21.0		35.4	13.9	17.6	6.4	-
3. Occasionally	26.7	28.0	25.6		30.0	25.2	24.1	30.3		23.7	37.4	36.4	19.6	25.0
4. Often	34.1	38.4	30.2		38.8	34.5	29.7	36.0		9.0	47.6	39.1	70.7	75.0
Item 8750 N(Wtd)	2528	1107	1377		583	765	827	353		1101	433	261	499	56

A55B: LSD

	TOTAL	M	F		NE	NC	S	W		None	Mar.	Few	More	Any
1. Never ‡	65.0	62.8	66.7		59.2	63.2	70.9	64.2		84.3	65.0	56.7	29.6	14.3
2. Once or twice	18.9	18.9	18.9		23.3	18.6	16.7	18.1		11.2	24.8	30.7	26.8	12.5
3. Occasionally	11.8	13.0	10.9		13.4	13.8	8.2	13.8		4.0	8.7	10.3	32.4	30.4
4. Often	4.2	5.4	3.4		4.0	4.5	4.3	4.3		.5	1.4	1.9	11.3	41.1
Item 8760 N(Wtd)	2503	1096	1363		574	760	820	349		1092	423	261	497	56

A55C: Other psychedelics (mescaline, peyote, THC, etc.) ‡

	TOTAL	M	F		NE	NC	S	W		None	Mar.	Few	More	Any
1. Never ‡	60.3	55.2	64.8		53.5	58.2	67.3	59.9		85.1	55.2	47.9	21.9	10.7
2. Once or twice	17.4	19.2	15.9		20.6	15.6	15.4	20.6		9.8	27.3	30.9	18.1	14.3
3. Occasionally	15.2	17.6	13.0		17.3	19.3	11.0	13.2		4.4	13.6	17.4	38.4	32.1
4. Often	7.1	8.0	6.2		8.7	6.8	6.3	6.6		.7	3.9	3.9	21.7	44.6
Item 8770 N(Wtd)	2508	1096	1368		578	761	819	349		1097	433	259	497	56

A55E: Barbiturates (downers, goofballs, reds, yellows, etc.)

	TOTAL	M	F		NE	NC	S	W		None	Mar.	Few	More	Any
1. Never ‡	52.8	50.4	54.7		48.6	51.6	57.0	52.0		75.3	48.1	40.2	18.0	3.6
2. Once or twice	23.4	24.8	22.2		27.5	20.8	22.1	25.4		16.5	33.5	39.1	22.0	23.2
3. Occasionally	15.9	17.3	14.7		16.2	17.8	13.8	16.0		6.8	14.7	16.5	35.9	30.4
4. Often	7.9	7.4	8.3		7.7	9.7	7.1	6.3		1.4	4.0	3.8	24.0	44.6
Item 8790 N(Wtd)	2501	1092	1366		574	759	818	350		1095	430	261	499	56

A55F: Tranquilizers (Librium, Valium, Miltown)

	TOTAL	M	F		NE	NC	S	W		None	Mar.	Few	More	Any
1. Never ‡	55.2	56.7	54.3		57.0	53.4	55.9	54.3		70.7	58.6	46.5	26.1	12.7
2. Once or twice	22.6	22.3	23.2		23.0	23.1	20.6	25.7		18.2	24.9	28.3	27.3	18.2
3. Occasionally	14.2	13.9	14.2		13.4	14.8	15.0	12.6		8.4	11.4	18.2	26.5	27.3
4. Often	8.0	7.2	8.4		6.6	8.7	8.6	7.4		2.7	5.1	6.6	20.0	41.8
Item 8800 N(Wtd)	2493	1089	1360		575	757	811	350		1091	430	258	499	55

A55G: Cocaine ("coke")

	TOTAL	M	F		NE	NC	S	W		None	Mar.	Few	More	Any
1. Never ‡	67.7	64.0	70.9		64.6	68.4	71.8	61.7		86.5	69.1	67.0	31.8	3.6
2. Once or twice	18.7	19.4	18.0		21.4	18.8	16.5	19.1		9.5	22.9	21.5	34.6	21.4
3. Occasionally	9.2	12.7	6.4		10.6	9.5	6.3	13.4		3.1	6.0	7.7	23.7	35.7
4. Often	4.4	3.9	4.5		3.5	3.4	5.3	5.7		1.0	2.1	3.8	9.9	39.3
Item 8810 N(Wtd)	2499	1090	1366		576	756	816	350		1094	433	261	497	56

A55H: Heroin (smack, horse)

	TOTAL	M	F		NE	NC	S	W		None	Mar.	Few	More	Any
1. Never ‡	83.1	82.5	83.8		82.1	83.7	82.5	84.9		91.3	86.1	87.3	66.7	14.3
2. Once or twice	11.9	12.0	11.6		12.8	11.8	12.1	10.0		6.2	9.7	9.3	26.9	30.4
3. Occasionally	3.2	3.5	2.9		2.9	3.2	3.5	3.4		1.9	3.0	1.9	4.2	28.6
4. Often	1.8	1.9	1.7		2.3	1.3	2.0	1.7		.6	1.2	1.9	2.2	26.8
Item 8820 N(Wtd)	2485	1083	1358		577	747	810	350		1088	431	259	495	56

‡ = Wording changed in subsequent years.

CAUTION: Items were rearranged after 1975; changes in context may produce spurious "trends" (see page 12).

	TOTAL	SEX			REGION					ILLICIT DRUG USE: LIFETIME				
QUESTIONNAIRE FORM 3 **1975**		M	F		NE	NC	S	W		None	Mari- juana Only	Few Pills	More Pills	Any Her- oin
Weighted No. of Cases:	*3049*	*1356*	*1559*		*681*	*961*	*975*	*432*		*1125*	*438*	*268*	*507*	*57*
% of Weighted Total:	*100.0*	*44.5*	*51.1*		*22.3*	*31.5*	*32.0*	*14.2*		*36.9*	*14.4*	*8.8*	*16.6*	*1.9*
A55I: Other narcotics (methadone, opium, codeine, paregoric, etc.)														
1. Never ‡	71.0	68.4	73.5		68.5	70.9	74.2	67.2		87.3	73.8	73.4	36.3	10.7
2. Once or twice	17.6	19.2	16.0		21.4	16.2	15.2	20.4		8.9	18.9	20.5	33.9	32.1
3. Occasionally	8.1	8.9	7.4		7.3	9.7	6.7	9.5		3.2	5.4	5.4	21.6	23.2
4. Often	3.3	3.4	3.1		2.6	3.2	3.9	2.9		.6	1.6	1.2	8.3	33.9
Item 8830 N(Wtd)	*2486*	*1082*	*1360*		*575*	*752*	*811*	*348*		*1091*	*428*	*259*	*496*	*56*
A55K: Alcoholic beverages (beer, wine, liquor)														
1. Never ‡	3.6	3.3	3.8		2.1	3.3	4.6	4.6		6.0	1.2	1.5	1.6	-
2. Once or twice	7.9	6.1	9.3		7.5	6.9	7.9	10.6		13.8	2.3	5.0	1.4	-
3. Occasionally	26.8	25.4	27.9		27.3	24.5	29.3	24.9		38.6	20.1	21.5	10.8	16.1
4. Often	61.8	65.1	59.0		63.1	65.3	58.1	60.3		41.8	76.4	71.6	86.0	83.9
Item 8840 N(Wtd)	*2508*	*1094*	*1371*		*583*	*758*	*818*	*350*		*1104*	*432*	*261*	*499*	*56*

‡ = Wording changed in subsequent years.
CAUTION: Items were rearranged after 1975; changes in context may produce spurious "trends" (see page 12).

QUESTIONNAIRE FORM 4 1975	TOTAL	SEX			REGION					ILLICIT DRUG USE: LIFETIME				
		M	F		NE	NC	S	W		None	Mari- juana Only	Few Pills	More Pills	Any Her- oin
Weighted No. of Cases:	3041	1398	1520		668	975	968	430		1030	456	267	465	40
% of Weighted Total:	100.0	46.0	50.0		22.0	32.1	31.8	14.1		33.9	15.0	8.8	15.3	1.3

A01: Looking ahead to the next five years, do you think that things in this country will get better or worse?

	TOTAL	M	F		NE	NC	S	W		None	Mari- juana Only	Few Pills	More Pills	Any Her- oin
1. Get much better	4.0	5.0	2.9		3.8	3.5	5.3	2.4		2.9	6.2	3.0	4.1	5.0
2. Get somewhat better	33.9	39.1	29.5		35.8	33.6	36.0	26.9		33.9	38.0	33.7	34.2	20.0
3. Stay about the same	17.6	16.8	18.1		17.3	17.5	17.9	17.5		16.8	15.6	18.7	17.4	20.0
4. Get somewhat worse	35.0	30.0	39.9		35.0	35.8	31.8	40.3		36.1	33.8	35.2	36.8	35.0
5. Get much worse	9.5	9.1	9.6		8.3	9.5	8.9	13.0		10.3	6.6	9.7	7.3	20.0
Item 9940 N(Wtd)	2981	1394	1517		654	959	944	424		1027	455	267	465	40

A02: Looking ahead to the next five years, do you think that things in the rest of the world will get better or worse?

	TOTAL	M	F		NE	NC	S	W		None	Mari- juana Only	Few Pills	More Pills	Any Her- oin
1. Get much better	2.3	2.2	2.4		2.5	2.0	3.0	1.2		1.6	3.3	1.5	1.9	-
2. Get somewhat better	20.4	21.8	18.9		24.3	18.7	20.9	17.0		18.6	24.0	19.1	18.7	20.0
3. Stay about the same	21.9	22.2	21.6		22.3	24.2	19.2	22.4		20.7	22.4	25.1	22.4	10.0
4. Get somewhat worse	42.1	40.3	43.7		40.4	42.8	43.4	40.3		44.4	42.2	38.2	45.4	32.5
5. Get much worse	13.3	13.5	13.5		10.8	12.3	13.5	19.3		14.6	8.1	16.5	11.6	37.5
Item 9950 N(Wtd)	2973	1393	1511		651	956	941	424		1025	455	267	465	40

A03: How do you think your own life will go in the next five years-- do you think it will get better or worse?

	TOTAL	M	F		NE	NC	S	W		None	Mari- juana Only	Few Pills	More Pills	Any Her- oin
1. Get much better	37.2	35.2	38.9		37.1	35.3	39.0	38.0		33.9	40.8	35.6	40.4	37.5
2. Get somewhat better	45.5	46.9	44.6		46.6	48.5	41.7	45.3		48.5	43.2	47.2	44.3	40.0
3. Stay about the same	13.5	13.7	13.2		12.0	13.2	14.9	13.7		14.1	11.6	13.9	11.2	15.0
4. Get somewhat worse	2.8	2.9	2.6		3.4	2.2	3.0	3.1		2.6	2.9	2.2	3.2	5.0
5. Get much worse	1.0	1.3	.7		.9	.9	1.5	-		.9	1.5	1.1	.9	2.5
Item 9960 N(Wtd)	2970	1391	1511		650	956	940	424		1026	456	267	465	40

A06: Some people think a lot about the social problems of the nation and the world, and about how they might be solved. Others spend little time thinking about these issues. How much do you think about such things?

	TOTAL	M	F		NE	NC	S	W		None	Mari- juana Only	Few Pills	More Pills	Any Her- oin
1. Never	1.6	2.1	1.1		1.4	1.5	1.7	1.9		1.3	1.1	.8	2.0	7.9
2. Seldom	11.3	11.7	10.8		13.2	11.8	9.2	12.2		10.7	11.9	13.0	10.3	13.2
3. Sometimes	47.9	48.6	47.2		47.4	48.6	45.8	51.8		47.3	48.6	47.7	47.6	47.4
4. Quite often	30.3	28.5	32.2		29.3	29.6	33.6	26.3		31.7	29.3	30.9	32.3	18.4
5. A great deal	8.9	9.1	8.7		8.7	8.5	9.7	8.1		8.9	9.0	7.6	7.9	13.2
Item 6880 N(Wtd)	2930	1358	1505		642	943	926	419		1015	444	262	458	38

The next questions are about work.

A08: Different people may look for different things in their work. Below is a list of some of these things. Please read each one, then indicate how important this thing is for you.

A08A: A job where you can see the results of what you do

	TOTAL	M	F		NE	NC	S	W		None	Mari- juana Only	Few Pills	More Pills	Any Her- oin
1. Not important	1.3	1.7	.7		1.7	1.4	1.2	.7		1.0	1.1	2.3	1.5	5.0
2. A little important	7.8	7.2	8.4		8.0	7.9	7.5	8.3		7.9	6.8	5.6	7.1	10.0
3. Pretty important	37.5	37.4	37.5		34.6	40.3	34.4	42.3		36.8	37.0	40.2	41.9	40.0
4. Very important	53.4	53.7	53.3		55.7	50.4	56.9	48.7		54.4	55.1	51.9	49.2	45.0
Item 10090 N(Wtd)	2972	1389	1515		653	955	941	423		1028	454	266	463	40

CAUTION: Items were rearranged after 1975; changes in context may produce spurious "trends" (see page 12).

QUESTIONNAIRE FORM 4 1975	TOTAL	SEX			REGION					ILLICIT DRUG USE: LIFETIME				
		M	F		NE	NC	S	W		None	Mari-juana Only	Few Pills	More Pills	Any Her-oin
Weighted No. of Cases:	3041	1398	1520		668	975	968	430		1030	456	267	465	40
% of Weighted Total:	100.0	46.0	50.0		22.0	32.1	31.8	14.1		33.9	15.0	8.8	15.3	1.3

A08B: A job that has high status and prestige

	TOTAL	M	F		NE	NC	S	W		None	Mari-juana Only	Few Pills	More Pills	Any Her-oin
1. Not important	12.2	10.8	13.6		14.4	11.1	9.2	18.3		13.7	10.6	12.4	13.8	15.0
2. A little important	30.3	26.7	33.6		28.3	34.5	27.0	31.6		30.5	31.0	34.1	30.8	17.5
3. Pretty important	35.2	36.6	34.0		37.8	34.7	36.2	30.6		36.4	35.8	33.0	34.9	35.0
4. Very important	22.2	25.8	18.8		19.5	19.8	27.7	19.7		19.4	22.6	21.0	20.3	30.0
Item 10100 N(Wtd)	2940	1385	1490		646	945	928	421		1016	452	267	458	40

A08C: A job which is interesting to do

	TOTAL	M	F		NE	NC	S	W		None	Mari-juana Only	Few Pills	More Pills	Any Her-oin
1. Not important	.3	.5	.2		.2	.5	.2	.2		.2	-	.4	.9	2.5
2. A little important	1.1	1.8	.4		1.1	1.2	1.1	1.4		.6	.4	1.1	1.1	-
3. Pretty important	10.4	11.8	8.7		11.5	11.8	8.1	10.2		8.2	9.7	12.0	10.5	12.5
4. Very important	88.2	85.9	90.7		87.1	86.6	90.5	88.4		90.9	89.8	86.5	87.8	85.0
Item 10110 N(Wtd)	2961	1386	1509		651	952	935	423		1026	453	267	459	40

A08D: A job where the chances for advancement and promotion are good

	TOTAL	M	F		NE	NC	S	W		None	Mari-juana Only	Few Pills	More Pills	Any Her-oin
1. Not important	2.6	2.7	2.4		3.1	2.0	1.5	5.2		2.4	2.9	1.1	2.8	5.0
2. A little important	10.6	8.3	12.7		13.3	9.6	7.5	15.2		11.3	11.3	12.0	10.6	7.5
3. Pretty important	30.2	27.4	32.7		30.1	33.8	26.5	30.3		32.0	26.3	31.8	32.8	15.0
4. Very important	56.7	61.6	52.3		53.4	54.6	64.4	49.3		54.2	59.6	55.1	53.8	72.5
Item 10120 N(Wtd)	2970	1388	1515		652	954	942	422		1028	453	267	463	40

A08E: A job that gives you an opportunity to be directly helpful to others

	TOTAL	M	F		NE	NC	S	W		None	Mari-juana Only	Few Pills	More Pills	Any Her-oin
1. Not important	2.2	3.5	.8		2.9	2.3	1.5	1.9		1.8	2.9	1.1	2.6	7.5
2. A little important	11.5	17.1	6.1		13.5	12.6	10.3	8.7		11.4	11.7	9.0	13.6	5.0
3. Pretty important	33.5	38.1	29.1		30.6	32.5	34.4	38.1		29.9	34.1	34.1	34.2	52.5
4. Very important	52.9	41.4	64.0		53.0	52.6	54.0	51.3		56.9	51.3	55.8	49.6	35.0
Item 10130 N(Wtd)	2974	1389	1517		653	953	945	423		1029	454	267	462	40

A08F: A job which provides you with a chance to earn a good deal of money

	TOTAL	M	F		NE	NC	S	W		None	Mari-juana Only	Few Pills	More Pills	Any Her-oin
1. Not important	3.4	3.5	3.4		4.1	3.3	2.8	3.8		4.0	2.9	3.4	3.7	7.5
2. A little important	12.9	9.2	16.4		13.3	12.3	9.2	21.7		16.2	12.1	16.1	10.2	-
3. Pretty important	35.5	32.2	38.5		35.6	38.4	33.8	33.1		37.1	39.4	36.7	34.8	17.5
4. Very important	48.2	55.1	41.7		46.9	46.1	54.3	41.4		42.7	45.8	44.2	51.1	75.0
Item 10140 N(Wtd)	2970	1388	1514		652	951	943	423		1029	454	267	462	40

A08G: A job where you have the chance to be creative

	TOTAL	M	F		NE	NC	S	W		None	Mari-juana Only	Few Pills	More Pills	Any Her-oin
1. Not important	5.9	6.0	5.8		7.5	5.5	5.9	4.7		6.9	5.5	5.6	5.8	5.0
2. A little important	24.8	25.7	23.8		25.0	26.2	23.9	23.4		25.4	23.4	26.2	19.4	30.0
3. Pretty important	34.7	36.1	33.2		32.3	35.1	36.0	34.8		36.0	34.7	34.8	31.7	22.5
4. Very important	34.6	32.3	37.2		35.2	33.2	34.4	37.4		31.7	36.4	33.3	43.0	42.5
Item 10150 N(Wtd)	2969	1389	1512		653	954	939	423		1026	453	267	463	40

A08H: A job where the skills you learn will not go out of date

	TOTAL	M	F		NE	NC	S	W		None	Mari-juana Only	Few Pills	More Pills	Any Her-oin
1. Not important	3.8	4.1	3.5		4.9	3.9	3.2	3.6		3.7	3.5	5.3	3.2	7.5
2. A little important	10.2	8.8	11.6		12.0	8.9	10.1	10.5		10.6	9.0	9.0	9.1	5.0
3. Pretty important	30.9	30.2	31.2		33.3	35.0	24.6	31.8		31.9	29.7	36.1	30.3	32.5
4. Very important	55.1	56.9	53.7		50.1	52.1	62.1	54.4		53.7	57.7	49.6	57.4	57.5
Item 10160 N(Wtd)	2965	1387	1511		651	952	940	421		1027	454	266	462	40

CAUTION: Items were rearranged after 1975; changes in context may produce spurious "trends" (see page 12).

QUESTIONNAIRE FORM 4 1975	TOTAL	SEX			REGION					ILLICIT DRUG USE: LIFETIME				
		M	F		NE	NC	S	W		None	Mari- juana Only	Few Pills	More Pills	Any Her- oin
Weighted No. of Cases:	3041	1398	1520		668	975	968	430		1030	456	267	465	40
% of Weighted Total:	100.0	46.0	50.0		22.0	32.1	31.8	14.1		33.9	15.0	8.8	15.3	1.3
A08I: A job that gives you a chance to make friends														
1. Not important	1.5	1.9	1.1		1.8	1.6	1.4	.9		1.4	1.5	1.1	1.7	2.5
2. A little important	8.1	10.2	6.2		10.3	8.3	6.6	7.8		8.5	5.9	6.4	7.6	7.5
3. Pretty important	33.3	38.5	28.5		33.4	33.2	33.1	34.4		30.2	37.2	34.0	31.5	35.0
4. Very important	57.0	49.4	64.2		54.4	57.2	58.8	56.9		59.9	55.1	58.9	59.1	55.0
Item 10170 N(Wtd)	2966	1388	1510		652	953	939	422		1025	454	265	460	40
A08J: A job which uses your skills and abilities--lets you do the things you can do best														
1. Not important	.6	.7	.5		.9	.4	.5	.5		.7	.2	.4	.4	2.5
2. A little important	3.6	3.7	3.4		4.4	3.2	3.7	3.3		2.8	2.9	3.0	3.0	10.0
3. Pretty important	26.1	29.5	22.9		27.7	25.6	24.9	27.0		24.5	31.5	29.2	23.8	22.5
4. Very important	69.7	65.9	73.2		66.9	70.9	70.8	69.0		72.1	65.4	67.0	72.7	67.5
Item 10180 N(Wtd)	2970	1391	1512		653	952	943	423		1028	454	267	462	40
A08K: A job that is worthwhile to society														
1. Not important	3.4	4.0	2.9		4.9	4.1	1.9	2.9		3.2	2.0	2.6	4.4	15.0
2. A little important	13.3	15.5	11.5		13.5	15.0	11.9	12.4		11.7	16.1	12.5	14.4	15.0
3. Pretty important	38.6	41.8	35.4		38.7	38.7	36.4	42.5		38.1	36.8	36.6	42.6	37.5
4. Very important	44.7	38.7	50.3		42.7	42.3	49.7	42.3		46.9	44.9	48.3	38.4	35.0
Item 10190 N(Wtd)	2953	1377	1508		651	948	933	421		1021	454	265	458	40
A08L: A job where you have more than two weeks vacation														
1. Not important	22.5	17.3	27.2		27.1	22.4	19.5	22.7		24.5	25.1	24.1	18.6	17.5
2. A little important	33.9	29.7	38.1		32.4	35.2	34.3	32.5		35.6	27.3	34.6	35.3	22.5
3. Pretty important	24.3	26.6	22.1		23.2	23.5	26.8	22.0		24.8	26.0	22.6	24.2	22.5
4. Very important	19.3	26.5	12.7		17.5	18.9	19.4	22.7		14.9	21.8	18.4	22.1	37.5
Item 10200 N(Wtd)	2969	1389	1512		652	952	942	422		1027	454	266	462	40
A08M: A job where you get a chance to participate in decision making														
1. Not important	7.5	5.9	8.9		8.6	8.7	6.0	6.1		8.0	7.1	4.5	9.5	7.5
2. A little important	24.6	21.2	27.7		25.7	25.6	22.6	25.1		27.6	23.0	21.7	23.9	25.0
3. Pretty important	42.1	43.5	40.8		42.3	41.1	43.1	41.8		39.9	43.3	46.4	39.3	32.5
4. Very important	25.8	29.3	22.6		23.4	24.5	28.3	26.7		24.5	26.9	27.3	27.5	35.0
Item 10210 N(Wtd)	2971	1390	1513		653	954	941	423		1028	453	267	461	40
A08O: A job which allows you to establish roots in a community and not have to move from place to place														
1. Not important	12.9	13.2	12.3		13.8	12.6	11.9	14.0		9.9	13.9	12.8	16.8	30.0
2. A little important	17.6	18.6	16.6		18.9	17.4	16.2	19.7		14.4	19.2	19.2	22.0	30.0
3. Pretty important	32.9	31.3	34.2		37.5	34.4	28.7	32.2		35.1	35.3	33.8	28.7	15.0
4. Very important	36.6	36.8	37.0		29.8	35.7	43.4	34.4		40.7	31.6	34.2	32.4	25.0
Item 10230 N(Wtd)	2964	1386	1510		651	950	941	422		1025	453	266	463	40
A08P: A job which leaves you mostly free of supervision by others														
1. Not important	10.0	8.5	11.2		11.7	9.0	9.1	11.4		11.0	9.1	6.7	7.6	22.5
2. A little important	26.0	22.4	29.1		23.5	26.1	28.1	24.5		27.9	24.3	21.0	24.5	12.5
3. Pretty important	40.2	39.7	40.7		40.2	42.9	37.6	39.8		41.8	41.8	44.6	37.3	40.0
4. Very important	23.9	29.4	19.0		24.6	21.9	25.2	24.0		19.3	24.8	27.3	30.8	25.0
Item 10240 N(Wtd)	2947	1382	1497		650	946	931	420		1019	452	267	458	40

CAUTION: Items were rearranged after 1975; changes in context may produce spurious "trends" (see page 12).

QUESTIONNAIRE FORM 4 1975	TOTAL	SEX			REGION					ILLICIT DRUG USE: LIFETIME				
		M	F		NE	NC	S	W		None	Mari-juana Only	Few Pills	More Pills	Any Her-oin
Weighted No. of Cases:	3041	1398	1520		668	975	968	430		1030	456	267	465	40
% of Weighted Total:	100.0	46.0	50.0		22.0	32.1	31.8	14.1		33.9	15.0	8.8	15.3	1.3
A08Q: A job that offers a reasonably predictable, secure future														
1. Not important	2.0	1.9	2.1		2.8	2.0	1.2	2.9		1.2	2.0	2.3	2.4	12.8
2. A little important	6.2	5.7	6.5		7.1	5.8	5.9	6.3		5.9	5.5	6.5	6.5	10.3
3. Pretty important	31.2	30.5	31.9		30.5	34.0	26.5	36.8		30.4	35.6	33.5	31.0	28.2
4. Very important	60.5	61.8	59.4		59.6	58.2	66.3	54.1		62.5	56.9	57.4	60.2	51.3
Item 10250 N(Wtd)	2945	1376	1501		646	947	936	416		1022	452	263	462	39
A08R: A job where you can learn new things, learn new skills														
1. Not important	1.7	3.0	.6		2.8	1.8	1.4	1.0		1.9	1.3	.7	1.3	2.5
2. A little important	12.5	13.9	11.4		14.3	13.9	10.8	10.5		12.8	14.8	12.7	13.7	22.5
3. Pretty important	40.0	40.3	39.6		40.5	40.7	39.4	38.7		41.9	38.6	42.3	40.7	25.0
4. Very important	45.8	42.8	48.5		42.3	43.7	48.4	50.1		43.5	45.5	44.2	44.6	50.0
Item 10260 N(Wtd)	2958	1384	1506		652	950	935	421		1024	453	267	460	40
A08S: A job where you do not have to pretend to be a type of person that you are not														
1. Not important	5.0	6.7	3.3		4.5	4.8	6.2	3.5		4.7	4.6	3.4	4.1	5.0
2. A little important	5.5	8.5	2.8		5.1	6.4	4.5	6.6		5.5	5.3	4.5	3.7	17.5
3. Pretty important	16.8	20.1	13.5		18.1	18.5	14.1	16.3		15.0	21.0	15.5	15.2	15.0
4. Very important	72.7	64.8	80.3		72.4	70.2	75.2	73.5		74.8	68.8	76.6	77.0	65.0
Item 10270 N(Wtd)	2959	1380	1511		651	950	935	423		1026	452	265	461	40
A08T: A job that most people look up to and respect														
1. Not important	8.6	10.0	7.0		10.2	6.3	8.1	11.9		9.2	8.0	7.6	8.7	17.9
2. A little important	19.6	19.5	19.3		23.7	20.8	16.3	17.6		17.9	19.6	20.8	23.4	23.1
3. Pretty important	36.5	36.0	36.9		35.0	38.8	34.6	37.9		37.1	38.9	34.5	34.1	30.8
4. Very important	35.4	34.4	36.9		31.1	34.1	40.9	32.9		35.8	33.3	37.1	33.6	30.8
Item 10280 N(Wtd)	2950	1376	1507		646	947	937	420		1027	450	264	461	39
A08U: A job that permits contact with a lot of people														
1. Not important	8.8	10.9	6.8		7.2	8.6	10.6	8.0		9.6	8.2	9.4	6.5	7.5
2. A little important	20.7	26.6	15.2		20.7	22.6	20.7	16.3		20.7	20.3	17.2	22.3	20.0
3. Pretty important	34.0	34.9	32.8		34.4	34.0	31.5	39.0		33.3	34.0	36.0	30.1	47.5
4. Very important	36.4	27.5	45.2		37.6	34.8	37.2	36.6		36.5	37.3	37.8	41.1	22.5
Item 10290 N(Wtd)	2963	1383	1511		651	950	939	423		1025	453	267	462	40

CAUTION: Items were rearranged after 1975; changes in context may produce spurious "trends" (see page 12).

QUESTIONNAIRE FORM 4 1975	TOTAL	SEX			REGION					ILLICIT DRUG USE: LIFETIME				
		M	F		NE	NC	S	W		None	Mari- juana Only	Few Pills	More Pills	Any Her- oin
Weighted No. of Cases:	3041	1398	1520		668	975	968	430		1030	456	267	465	40
% of Weighted Total:	100.0	46.0	50.0		22.0	32.1	31.8	14.1		33.9	15.0	8.8	15.3	1.3

A09: What kind of work do you think you will be doing when you are 30 years old? Mark the one that comes closest to what you expect to be doing.

	TOTAL	M	F		NE	NC	S	W		None	Mari- juana Only	Few Pills	More Pills	Any Her- oin
01. Laborer (car washer, sanitary worker, farm laborer)	.4	.9	-		1.0	.5	-	.2		.2	.7	-	.9	-
02. Service worker (cook, waiter, barber, janitor, gas station attendant, practical nurse, beautician)	2.0	.7	3.1		2.6	2.3	1.3	1.7		1.6	1.6	1.9	3.1	
03. Operative or semi-skilled worker (garage worker, taxicab, bus or truck driver, assembly line worker, welder)	2.1	4.0	.3		1.8	2.5	2.1	1.5		1.8	1.9	.4	2.7	
04. Sales clerk in a retail store (shoe salesperson, department store clerk, drug store clerk)	1.8	.5	2.9		1.6	3.3	.4	1.5		1.7	2.8	1.2	.9	-
05. Clerical or office worker (bank teller, bookkeeper, secretary, typist, postal clerk or carrier, ticket agent)	11.5	1.8	20.3		9.1	11.8	13.1	11.2		12.7	10.9	12.3	10.3	17.1
06. Protective service (police officer, fireman, detective)	2.5	4.0	1.3		2.6	1.9	3.1	2.7		2.7	2.8	2.3	3.1	-
07. Military service	2.8	5.2	.6		2.1	1.5	4.7	2.5		3.2	2.3	.4	2.2	5.7
08. Craftsman or skilled worker (carpenter, electrician, brick layer, mechanic, machinist, tool and die maker, telephone installer)	9.2	19.0	.3		8.1	11.0	8.5	8.5		6.3	10.4	7.3	9.6	5.7
09. Farm owner, farm manager	2.9	5.2	.8		1.9	2.9	3.9	1.7		3.4	2.1	3.8	2.5	2.9
10. Owner of small business (restaurant owner, shop owner)	3.0	4.1	1.9		4.5	2.1	2.4	4.2		2.7	3.7	2.7	3.8	2.9
11. Sales representative (insurance agent, real estate broker, bond salesman)	.7	1.1	.5		.6	.5	1.1	.7		.2	.5	1.2	1.8	-
12. Manager or administrator (office manager, sales manager, school administrator, government official)	3.3	4.0	2.5		3.4	2.7	3.5	4.2		2.4	4.2	1.9	4.5	2.9
13. Professional without doctoral degree (registered nurse, librarian, engineer, architect, social worker, technician, accountant, actor, artist, musician)	27.5	22.5	32.4		31.3	26.3	26.6	26.4		31.6	24.3	34.2	25.4	17.1
14. Professional with doctoral degree or equivalent (lawyer, physician, dentist, scientist, college professor)	10.7	13.2	8.3		12.8	9.7	8.7	14.4		11.7	15.7	8.5	7.4	11.4
15. Homemaker or housewife only ‡	4.7	.1	8.9		2.9	5.9	4.1	6.0		5.5	3.2	6.9	3.8	8.6
16. don't know ‡	15.0	13.9	15.9		14.2	15.1	16.3	12.9		12.5	13.0	15.0	17.9	31.4
Item 10320 N(Wtd)	2857	1329	1462		626	926	903	402		1009	432	260	448	35

A09A: If you were to get enough money to live as comfortably as you'd like for the rest of your life, would you want to work?

	TOTAL	M	F		NE	NC	S	W		None	Mari- juana Only	Few Pills	More Pills	Any Her- oin
1. I would want to work	80.8	80.3	81.2		80.0	83.9	78.4	80.3		81.6	83.2	82.7	74.2	75.0
2. I would not want to work	19.2	19.7	18.7		20.0	16.1	21.5	19.7		18.4	16.8	17.3	25.8	25.0
Item 8100 N(Wtd)	2943	1376	1500		645	949	932	416		1021	446	266	461	40

A11: How much do you agree or disagree with each statement below?

A11A: One sees so few good or happy marriages that one questions it as a way of life

	TOTAL	M	F		NE	NC	S	W		None	Mari- juana Only	Few Pills	More Pills	Any Her- oin
1. Disagree	30.2	28.3	32.7		31.3	28.7	30.6	31.3		36.6	30.8	29.8	22.4	23.1
2. Mostly disagree	23.1	23.2	23.2		21.4	25.6	21.0	25.1		25.4	26.1	23.8	21.7	23.1
3. Neither	20.4	24.4	16.3		19.8	20.0	19.7	23.6		17.2	19.0	19.6	26.3	30.8
4. Mostly agree	17.6	16.3	18.6		18.8	17.8	17.4	15.4		14.8	16.5	14.7	20.6	17.9
5. Agree	8.7	7.8	9.2		8.5	8.0	11.3	4.3		6.0	7.8	11.7	9.0	2.6
Item 10470 N(Wtd)	2921	1365	1489		645	942	919	415		1018	448	265	456	39

‡ = Wording changed in subsequent years.

CAUTION: Items were rearranged after 1975; changes in context may produce spurious "trends" (see page 12).

	TOTAL	SEX			REGION					ILLICIT DRUG USE: LIFETIME				
QUESTIONNAIRE FORM 4 **1975**		M	F		NE	NC	S	W		None	Mari- juana Only	Few Pills	More Pills	Any Her- oin
Weighted No. of Cases:	3041	1398	1520		668	975	968	430		1030	456	267	465	40
% of Weighted Total:	100.0	46.0	50.0		22.0	32.1	31.8	14.1		33.9	15.0	8.8	15.3	1.3

A11B: It is usually a good idea for a couple to live together before getting married in order to find out whether they really get along

	TOTAL	M	F		NE	NC	S	W		None	Mari- juana Only	Few Pills	More Pills	Any Her- oin
1. Disagree	32.6	25.1	39.8		24.2	28.6	40.9	35.6		46.6	22.7	31.5	15.8	22.5
2. Mostly disagree	15.4	13.4	17.0		11.9	18.2	15.3	14.2		17.7	16.3	15.0	11.9	10.0
3. Neither	17.6	20.0	15.2		20.1	17.7	16.3	16.0		15.8	23.1	15.4	16.7	10.0
4. Mostly agree	17.2	20.1	14.6		21.1	19.3	13.2	15.1		10.7	19.2	22.5	26.8	25.0
5. Agree	17.3	21.4	13.4		22.5	16.2	14.1	18.9		9.2	18.9	15.7	28.8	32.5
Item 10480 N(Wtd)	2964	1382	1515		653	951	936	424		1029	454	267	462	40

A11C: Having a close intimate relationship with only one partner is too restrictive for the average person

	TOTAL	M	F		NE	NC	S	W		None	Mari- juana Only	Few Pills	More Pills	Any Her- oin
1. Disagree	36.2	28.8	43.4		36.6	34.5	35.7	41.0		43.2	32.8	40.8	29.7	27.5
2. Mostly disagree	23.9	25.1	22.7		25.4	25.3	21.9	22.7		24.1	27.3	21.3	23.9	22.5
3. Neither	15.5	18.7	12.4		14.9	15.6	15.4	15.9		12.3	15.9	12.7	20.4	22.5
4. Mostly agree	14.6	16.8	12.6		14.5	15.0	15.4	12.1		12.0	14.5	14.2	16.7	25.0
5. Agree	9.8	10.6	8.8		8.5	9.7	11.7	8.1		8.3	9.5	11.2	9.3	2.5
Item 10490 N(Wtd)	2949	1377	1504		650	946	931	422		1022	454	267	461	40

A11E: Having a job takes away from a woman's relationship with her husband

	TOTAL	M	F		NE	NC	S	W		None	Mari- juana Only	Few Pills	More Pills	Any Her- oin
1. Disagree	41.1	26.8	53.7		44.8	37.8	43.2	38.6		40.6	39.6	42.3	40.9	35.0
2. Mostly disagree	24.7	26.4	23.6		27.0	26.9	20.5	25.7		24.9	28.3	24.3	27.9	25.0
3. Neither	19.2	25.3	13.6		15.4	20.4	20.4	20.2		20.0	20.4	19.1	16.9	20.0
4. Mostly agree	9.8	13.6	6.4		8.6	9.7	9.4	12.4		10.2	6.2	9.4	8.4	15.0
5. Agree	5.2	7.9	2.7		4.2	5.4	6.5	3.3		4.3	5.5	4.9	5.8	5.0
Item 10500 N(Wtd)	2951	1376	1507		649	948	933	420		1023	452	267	462	40

A11G: Having a job gives a wife more of a chance to develop herself as a person

	TOTAL	M	F		NE	NC	S	W		None	Mari- juana Only	Few Pills	More Pills	Any Her- oin
1. Disagree	5.6	7.5	3.6		7.4	3.9	5.9	6.2		5.3	3.3	5.2	5.0	17.5
2. Mostly disagree	5.3	7.0	3.8		5.2	5.7	4.6	6.2		5.8	6.2	2.6	3.5	2.5
3. Neither	17.3	21.9	13.1		14.8	17.1	16.6	23.7		19.6	17.4	16.1	17.4	20.0
4. Mostly agree	32.6	37.5	28.1		31.3	33.8	32.2	32.7		29.9	35.5	36.3	33.8	35.0
5. Agree	39.2	26.1	51.4		41.4	39.5	40.8	31.3		39.5	37.5	40.4	40.5	25.0
Item 10510 N(Wtd)	2952	1374	1511		649	951	930	422		1023	453	267	459	40

A11H: Being a father and raising children is one of the most fulfilling experiences a man can have

	TOTAL	M	F		NE	NC	S	W		None	Mari- juana Only	Few Pills	More Pills	Any Her- oin
1. Disagree	5.0	4.4	5.4		5.5	4.6	4.6	5.7		5.1	3.8	3.4	4.8	2.5
2. Mostly disagree	6.0	6.3	5.8		5.9	6.6	5.9	5.7		5.5	6.6	4.9	6.1	15.0
3. Neither	23.4	23.5	23.0		21.7	26.9	19.2	27.5		23.3	23.3	23.2	26.8	17.5
4. Mostly agree	30.1	31.4	29.5		31.9	31.5	28.4	28.0		31.6	32.4	28.5	30.3	32.5
5. Agree	35.5	34.4	36.4		35.0	30.4	41.9	33.0		34.4	33.9	39.9	32.0	27.5
Item 10520 N(Wtd)	2913	1372	1475		642	936	918	418		1013	442	263	459	40

A11I: Most mothers should spend more time with their children than they do now

	TOTAL	M	F		NE	NC	S	W		None	Mari- juana Only	Few Pills	More Pills	Any Her- oin
1. Disagree	4.2	3.7	4.3		5.0	3.9	3.8	4.8		4.3	3.8	4.9	3.7	10.0
2. Mostly disagree	7.5	6.6	8.3		9.6	9.2	5.4	5.0		6.5	8.0	9.4	12.5	12.5
3. Neither	24.9	31.0	19.3		29.1	25.2	20.4	27.4		22.7	28.5	27.4	28.7	22.5
4. Mostly agree	29.9	30.8	29.0		28.0	31.7	28.5	31.7		29.3	33.4	28.9	25.8	20.0
5. Agree	33.5	27.8	39.2		28.2	30.0	41.9	31.0		37.2	26.1	29.3	29.1	37.5
Item 10530 N(Wtd)	2941	1369	1506		646	944	931	419		1024	452	266	457	40

CAUTION: Items were rearranged after 1975; changes in context may produce spurious "trends" (see page 12).

QUESTIONNAIRE FORM 4 1975	TOTAL	SEX			REGION					ILLICIT DRUG USE: LIFETIME				
		M	F		NE	NC	S	W		None	Mari- juana Only	Few Pills	More Pills	Any Her- oin
Weighted No. of Cases:	3041	1398	1520		668	975	968	430		1030	456	267	465	40
% of Weighted Total:	100.0	46.0	50.0		22.0	32.1	31.8	14.1		33.9	15.0	8.8	15.3	1.3

A11K: If a wife works, her husband should take a greater part in housework and child-care

	TOTAL	M	F		NE	NC	S	W		None	Mari-juana Only	Few Pills	More Pills	Any Heroin
1. Disagree	6.3	7.3	5.2		6.8	5.1	7.0	7.0		5.8	3.1	7.1	4.8	15.0
2. Mostly disagree	8.5	7.9	8.9		8.7	9.2	7.7	8.2		7.2	10.9	6.4	6.5	12.5
3. Neither	15.7	17.4	14.2		17.1	16.1	14.6	15.1		15.5	15.8	18.4	15.4	15.0
4. Mostly agree	38.5	40.4	36.9		38.8	39.6	35.6	41.6		38.0	42.8	36.7	42.6	42.5
5. Agree	31.0	27.0	34.7		28.5	29.9	35.2	27.9		33.5	27.2	31.8	30.7	17.5
Item 10540 N(Wtd)	2939	1365	1509		645	946	933	416		1025	449	267	462	40

A14: Some people think that there ought to be changes in the amount of influence and power that certain organizations have in our society. Do you think the following organizations should have more influence, less influence, or about the same amount of influence as they have now?

A14A: Large corporations?

	TOTAL	M	F		NE	NC	S	W		None	Mari-juana Only	Few Pills	More Pills	Any Heroin
1. Much less	13.2	14.9	11.8		18.2	12.2	9.4	16.0		12.8	11.9	15.5	17.0	17.5
2. Less	37.1	39.7	35.0		37.1	38.7	33.4	41.9		41.4	40.6	37.4	35.9	15.0
3. Same as now	25.6	24.5	26.5		21.5	27.6	27.7	23.1		25.3	24.5	28.7	28.3	25.0
4. More	8.4	7.1	9.5		7.8	8.1	10.6	5.5		8.1	7.3	6.8	7.6	17.5
5. Much more	3.2	3.6	2.7		3.1	3.0	3.8	2.6		1.9	3.3	1.9	2.4	15.0
8. No opinion	12.4	10.2	14.5		12.3	10.5	15.1	10.7		10.4	12.1	9.4	8.5	10.0
Item 10570 N(Wtd)	2929	1374	1492		642	939	927	420		1017	453	265	459	40

A14B: Major labor unions?

	TOTAL	M	F		NE	NC	S	W		None	Mari-juana Only	Few Pills	More Pills	Any Heroin
1. Much less	8.8	11.0	6.7		8.5	11.2	6.2	9.8		10.3	7.8	11.3	8.8	5.0
2. Less	24.1	26.5	22.4		24.2	22.5	23.7	28.9		25.6	26.0	24.5	23.5	17.5
3. Same as now	28.7	29.3	28.0		29.5	30.9	25.7	28.9		28.1	31.6	32.1	28.1	35.0
4. More	17.9	15.9	19.7		15.9	18.3	19.8	15.8		18.1	15.8	14.7	20.2	17.5
5. Much more	7.9	8.2	7.6		8.9	6.6	9.3	6.2		6.6	8.2	8.3	8.6	15.0
8. No opinion	12.6	9.0	15.5		13.0	10.5	15.4	10.3		11.4	10.9	9.4	11.0	10.0
Item 10580 N(Wtd)	2916	1368	1485		637	936	925	418		1013	450	265	455	40

A14C: Churches and religious organizations?

	TOTAL	M	F		NE	NC	S	W		None	Mari-juana Only	Few Pills	More Pills	Any Heroin
1. Much less	4.2	5.6	3.1		5.0	4.4	2.3	7.1		3.0	6.0	1.9	5.9	15.0
2. Less	7.6	8.6	6.8		11.2	6.5	5.6	8.8		6.5	8.4	9.5	9.6	7.5
3. Same as now	31.8	34.6	29.3		39.5	34.1	24.4	31.4		27.5	39.2	32.6	36.2	35.0
4. More	25.5	24.5	26.3		23.4	27.4	25.5	24.5		28.6	25.0	20.8	25.3	17.5
5. Much more	23.8	20.0	27.5		13.7	20.3	36.0	19.5		29.8	15.3	27.7	16.6	22.5
8. No opinion	7.1	6.8	6.9		7.2	7.4	6.3	8.3		4.6	6.0	7.6	6.5	2.5
Item 10590 N(Wtd)	2925	1365	1496		641	936	928	420		1014	452	264	459	40

A14D: The national news media (TV, magazines, news services)?

	TOTAL	M	F		NE	NC	S	W		None	Mari-juana Only	Few Pills	More Pills	Any Heroin
1. Much less	6.9	7.8	6.1		4.8	6.6	8.2	7.9		7.8	5.6	7.6	5.5	7.7
2. Less	18.6	18.8	18.7		18.0	21.2	16.1	19.5		20.3	16.9	23.5	19.1	23.1
3. Same as now	41.4	41.0	41.7		43.6	42.1	36.8	46.7		43.0	46.0	40.2	41.0	25.6
4. More	18.0	18.0	17.8		19.4	17.0	19.9	13.8		16.0	16.4	20.5	19.3	17.9
5. Much more	8.8	10.0	7.8		7.3	7.9	11.4	7.9		6.7	9.8	4.9	10.7	12.8
8. No opinion	6.3	4.5	7.8		7.0	5.3	7.7	4.3		6.3	5.3	3.4	4.4	10.3
Item 10600 N(Wtd)	2917	1366	1489		640	933	924	420		1017	450	264	456	39

A14E: The Presidency and the administration?

	TOTAL	M	F		NE	NC	S	W		None	Mari-juana Only	Few Pills	More Pills	Any Heroin
1. Much less	6.3	6.1	6.7		6.7	5.0	6.2	8.9		5.6	6.7	3.8	10.0	10.3
2. Less	19.3	19.1	19.4		21.3	19.6	17.3	20.3		17.9	21.1	20.4	22.7	15.4
3. Same as now	33.9	34.7	33.3		32.3	35.1	33.5	34.2		37.7	34.1	40.4	27.9	38.5
4. More	17.6	19.0	16.4		15.8	19.6	18.3	14.6		19.3	18.0	15.1	14.6	17.9
5. Much more	10.5	11.2	9.5		9.8	10.1	12.3	8.6		8.0	9.5	9.8	11.1	7.7
8. No opinion	12.3	9.9	14.7		14.1	10.7	12.3	13.2		11.5	10.4	9.8	13.3	10.3
Item 10610 N(Wtd)	2917	1366	1488		640	935	924	418		1016	451	265	458	39

CAUTION: Items were rearranged after 1975; changes in context may produce spurious "trends" (see page 12).

QUESTIONNAIRE FORM 4 1975	TOTAL	SEX			REGION				ILLICIT DRUG USE: LIFETIME				
		M	F		NE	NC	S	W	None	Mari- juana Only	Few Pills	More Pills	Any Her- oin
Weighted No. of Cases:	3041	1398	1520		668	975	968	430	1030	456	267	465	40
% of Weighted Total:	100.0	46.0	50.0		22.0	32.1	31.8	14.1	33.9	15.0	8.8	15.3	1.3

A14F: The Congress--that is, the U.S. Senate and House of Representatives?

1. Much less	4.1	4.5	3.9		4.9	4.1	4.0	3.8	3.6	4.4	2.3	5.9	7.7
2. Less	14.2	15.4	13.3		11.9	13.1	15.9	16.7	14.1	15.3	14.7	16.8	10.3
3. Same as now	35.3	35.7	34.9		34.0	35.7	35.5	36.2	39.7	34.1	36.2	29.0	38.5
4. More	21.9	22.4	21.6		23.3	22.9	21.3	18.8	21.3	22.3	25.3	20.3	25.6
5. Much more	11.0	12.0	10.0		12.1	11.3	9.9	11.2	9.1	11.3	10.6	12.2	7.7
8. No opinion	13.4	9.9	16.3		14.1	12.8	13.5	13.6	12.4	12.6	10.9	15.7	10.3
Item 10620 N(Wtd)	2921	1370	1489		639	936	927	420	1016	452	265	458	39

A14G: The U.S. Supreme Court?

1. Much less	2.9	3.7	2.4		2.8	3.4	2.7	2.4	2.0	2.7	2.3	6.4	10.3
2. Less	8.5	8.5	8.4		7.7	8.2	9.0	9.3	9.3	8.9	7.5	9.6	-
3. Same as now	40.3	40.5	40.3		40.9	39.2	38.6	45.6	41.9	40.2	44.5	37.5	41.0
4. More	24.0	25.1	23.0		23.3	25.8	24.7	19.3	23.7	25.6	25.7	20.4	33.3
5. Much more	10.6	12.6	8.6		10.3	9.6	11.7	11.2	10.0	10.7	8.3	12.1	10.3
8. No opinion	13.6	9.7	17.3		15.0	13.7	13.4	12.2	13.3	12.0	11.7	14.0	5.1
Item 10630 N(Wtd)	2909	1365	1481		634	930	926	419	1013	450	265	456	39

A14H: All the courts and the justice system in general?

1. Much less	2.8	3.5	2.1		3.3	2.8	2.5	2.4	1.9	2.9	1.9	4.4	7.5
2. Less	8.2	7.8	8.6		8.3	8.0	8.2	8.8	7.1	7.5	9.8	13.6	15.0
3. Same as now	39.6	40.5	39.0		36.9	41.2	37.4	44.5	40.2	41.2	39.0	39.7	32.5
4. More	26.1	26.8	25.2		26.7	27.5	25.4	23.3	27.6	27.2	28.0	19.7	30.0
5. Much more	10.9	12.2	9.5		10.7	8.8	13.5	9.8	10.1	11.1	10.6	11.0	7.5
8. No opinion	12.5	9.2	15.5		14.1	11.7	12.9	11.2	13.1	10.4	10.2	11.8	7.5
Item 10640 N(Wtd)	2910	1367	1480		637	928	925	420	1013	452	264	456	40

A14I: The police and other law enforcement agencies?

1. Much less	3.1	4.3	1.9		3.3	3.2	2.7	3.1	1.1	2.4	2.7	6.3	15.4
2. Less	8.3	8.7	8.0		10.6	8.7	6.2	8.8	3.8	9.3	8.0	15.7	20.5
3. Same as now	27.6	29.5	25.8		26.5	25.0	27.4	35.3	25.0	29.4	28.4	32.7	28.2
4. More	30.9	28.3	33.5		30.3	35.3	28.6	27.3	37.2	33.8	33.0	20.0	7.7
5. Much more	23.6	23.6	23.4		22.2	21.9	28.5	18.7	27.5	19.0	23.9	18.3	17.9
8. No opinion	6.5	5.6	7.4		7.0	5.8	6.8	6.6	5.4	5.8	3.8	7.0	10.3
Item 10650 N(Wtd)	2918	1366	1490		641	931	924	422	1017	452	264	459	39

A14J: The U.S. military?

1. Much less	5.5	7.5	3.7		7.4	4.6	4.5	6.7	3.6	7.5	4.5	8.3	10.0
2. Less	9.4	10.3	8.4		9.9	9.5	7.3	13.4	9.0	8.6	9.8	10.9	15.0
3. Same as now	41.4	38.9	43.5		38.2	45.0	39.5	42.5	43.1	39.8	48.1	40.3	35.0
4. More	19.3	20.2	18.6		21.4	18.0	20.3	16.7	21.3	20.1	14.8	18.6	17.5
5. Much more	13.2	16.1	10.7		9.7	12.9	17.2	10.3	11.3	13.3	14.0	13.6	7.5
8. No opinion	11.2	7.2	14.9		13.3	10.0	11.3	10.7	11.7	10.6	8.7	8.3	15.0
Item 10660 N(Wtd)	2911	1369	1480		639	929	924	419	1012	452	264	457	40

A22: These questions are about pollution and the environment. Please mark the circle that shows how much you agree or disagree with each statement below.

A22A: In general, pollution has increased in the U.S. in the last ten years

1. Disagree	1.3	2.2	.3		2.2	.8	1.2	1.0	1.4	1.3	.4	.7	2.6
2. Mostly disagree	3.9	6.1	1.8		2.9	4.6	3.8	3.9	3.1	4.9	3.0	4.4	-
3. Neither	6.8	6.7	6.9		7.1	7.8	5.4	7.1	6.3	7.5	4.9	4.6	5.3
4. Mostly agree	32.0	31.3	33.0		31.7	34.2	30.3	31.2	31.9	30.2	32.7	32.0	34.2
5. Agree	56.1	53.7	58.1		55.9	52.7	59.2	57.0	57.2	56.1	59.0	58.3	57.9
Item 9970 N(Wtd)	2863	1334	1474		631	916	910	407	1016	451	266	456	38

CAUTION: Items were rearranged after 1975; changes in context may produce spurious "trends" (see page 12).

QUESTIONNAIRE FORM 4 1975	TOTAL	SEX M	SEX F		REGION NE	NC	S	W		ILLICIT DRUG USE: LIFETIME None	Marijuana Only	Few Pills	More Pills	Any Heroin
Weighted No. of Cases:	3041	1398	1520		668	975	968	430		1030	456	267	465	40
% of Weighted Total:	100.0	46.0	50.0		22.0	32.1	31.8	14.1		33.9	15.0	8.8	15.3	1.3

A22B: The dangers of pollution are not really as great as government, the media, and environmental groups would like us to believe

	TOTAL	M	F		NE	NC	S	W		None	Marij	Few	More	Her
1. Disagree	33.1	32.9	33.2		32.6	29.6	34.5	38.7		32.0	36.4	35.5	36.1	44.4
2. Mostly disagree	29.4	29.6	29.4		30.5	31.5	27.1	27.9		31.3	30.0	28.3	30.6	19.4
3. Neither	14.7	12.9	16.4		14.9	14.7	15.0	14.5		14.3	12.2	15.1	12.8	13.9
4. Mostly agree	15.4	15.9	14.8		12.9	18.2	15.2	13.5		16.5	14.0	11.7	14.1	19.4
5. Agree	7.4	8.9	6.1		9.3	6.1	8.4	5.5		5.9	7.3	9.4	6.4	-
Item 9980 N(Wtd)	2851	1329	1468		626	914	909	401		1015	450	265	454	36

A22C: America needs growth to survive, and that is going to require some increase in pollution

1. Disagree	26.8	26.2	27.2		27.9	24.3	26.7	31.0		26.6	26.8	37.9	26.2	31.6
2. Mostly disagree	26.2	26.0	26.3		24.3	29.1	25.2	24.3		27.7	26.6	21.8	27.0	15.8
3. Neither	19.9	18.6	20.9		18.2	21.2	18.6	22.3		19.4	19.4	11.9	20.9	15.8
4. Mostly agree	18.3	20.6	16.5		18.8	18.4	18.9	15.5		18.6	19.9	18.4	18.9	28.9
5. Agree	8.9	8.6	9.1		10.6	6.9	10.6	7.0		7.7	7.4	10.0	7.0	7.9
Item 9990 N(Wtd)	2836	1327	1458		621	911	905	400		1006	448	261	455	38

A22D: People will have to change their buying habits and way of life to correct our environmental problems

1. Disagree	4.4	5.3	3.5		4.8	3.2	5.7	3.3		4.0	2.7	5.7	3.3	2.6
2. Mostly disagree	9.1	10.0	8.4		7.3	7.2	12.4	8.8		7.9	8.2	7.6	9.7	13.2
3. Neither	18.1	17.9	18.5		17.4	19.6	18.9	13.8		17.4	17.8	11.8	19.4	31.6
4. Mostly agree	39.1	39.0	39.2		37.5	42.7	34.6	43.3		40.7	38.1	46.9	37.1	26.3
5. Agree	29.3	27.8	30.4		32.7	27.2	28.3	30.8		30.2	33.2	27.5	30.5	26.3
Item 10000 N(Wtd)	2843	1326	1464		626	908	908	400		1011	449	262	453	38

A22E: Government should take action to solve our environmental problems even if it means that some of the products we now use would have to be changed or banned

1. Disagree	3.4	3.6	3.1		3.8	2.0	4.0	4.5		3.5	2.5	1.9	3.3	2.6
2. Mostly disagree	6.3	7.3	5.4		4.3	6.0	7.8	6.5		6.3	5.6	3.8	6.5	18.4
3. Neither	16.9	15.9	17.6		16.3	19.1	16.1	14.5		16.5	16.2	17.2	17.1	18.4
4. Mostly agree	37.9	38.8	37.2		34.1	39.1	37.4	42.0		38.0	37.1	44.8	35.6	39.5
5. Agree	35.6	34.3	36.8		41.6	33.7	34.7	32.8		35.7	41.1	32.6	37.6	21.1
Item 10010 N(Wtd)	2828	1320	1455		625	907	896	400		1007	448	261	449	38

A22F: Government should place higher taxes on products which cause pollution in their manufacture or disposal, so that companies will be encouraged to find better ways to produce them

1. Disagree	13.6	13.5	13.4		13.0	9.8	18.2	12.6		13.5	12.9	10.3	13.5	16.7
2. Mostly disagree	11.6	10.6	12.5		11.4	12.4	11.3	10.6		12.5	11.6	8.0	12.1	5.6
3. Neither	18.0	17.3	18.7		17.9	20.4	16.1	17.3		16.7	17.6	19.5	18.0	22.2
4. Mostly agree	28.3	29.7	27.0		26.6	30.4	25.5	32.2		28.3	28.0	32.8	27.0	30.6
5. Agree	28.5	28.8	28.4		31.1	26.9	28.9	27.4		28.8	30.0	29.8	29.7	22.2
Item 10020 N(Wtd)	2820	1315	1451		621	900	901	398		1009	450	262	445	36

A22G: I wish that government would ban throwaway bottles and beverage cans

1. Disagree	7.8	7.8	7.9		7.6	4.7	10.7	8.8		8.5	5.1	3.4	9.1	5.3
2. Mostly disagree	9.5	9.0	9.7		7.3	9.8	11.1	8.3		8.9	10.1	10.3	10.0	15.8
3. Neither	25.3	23.2	27.3		24.2	28.1	24.4	23.0		24.8	27.7	23.3	24.4	31.6
4. Mostly agree	23.5	22.6	24.4		25.0	25.1	19.1	28.0		25.8	21.7	27.1	20.4	18.4
5. Agree	33.9	37.3	30.6		36.0	32.4	34.7	32.0		31.9	35.6	35.9	35.9	26.3
Item 10030 N(Wtd)	2812	1308	1449		620	897	895	400		1008	447	262	451	38

CAUTION: Items were rearranged after 1975; changes in context may produce spurious "trends" (see page 12).

QUESTIONNAIRE FORM 4 1975	TOTAL	SEX			REGION					ILLICIT DRUG USE: LIFETIME				
		M	F		NE	NC	S	W		None	Mari- juana Only	Few Pills	More Pills	Any Her- oin
Weighted No. of Cases:	3041	1398	1520		668	975	968	430		1030	456	267	465	40
% of Weighted Total:	100.0	46.0	50.0		22.0	32.1	31.8	14.1		33.9	15.0	8.8	15.3	1.3

A22H: T.V. commercials stimulate people to buy a lot of things they don't really need

	TOTAL	M	F		NE	NC	S	W		None	Mari- juana Only	Few Pills	More Pills	Any Her- oin
1. Disagree	2.7	4.2	1.4		2.9	1.3	4.2	2.2		3.2	2.9	.4	1.8	7.9
2. Mostly disagree	4.6	5.4	3.7		4.0	4.7	5.5	3.5		4.1	6.7	2.3	2.9	15.8
3. Neither	8.8	10.4	7.4		7.0	10.3	8.7	8.5		7.2	9.3	9.1	7.9	5.3
4. Mostly agree	30.9	32.8	29.3		31.2	31.3	29.8	32.1		32.0	29.6	35.7	30.5	36.8
5. Agree	53.0	47.1	58.2		55.0	52.4	51.8	54.0		53.4	51.8	52.1	56.7	34.2
Item 10040 N(Wtd)	2840	1318	1469		625	907	906	402		1013	450	263	453	38

A22I: T.V. commercials do a lot of good by showing new products that we might not know about otherwise

	TOTAL	M	F		NE	NC	S	W		None	Mari- juana Only	Few Pills	More Pills	Any Her- oin
1. Disagree	9.5	9.3	9.6		12.8	8.4	6.1	14.8		9.0	9.6	7.6	13.2	13.2
2. Mostly disagree	15.4	14.0	16.6		17.9	16.3	12.1	16.5		15.6	6.7	17.1	16.5	21.1
3. Neither	22.7	21.7	23.8		23.4	25.0	18.1	26.6		23.1	25.4	24.0	22.5	18.4
4. Mostly agree	32.4	33.7	31.6		29.8	33.4	35.1	27.8		33.9	28.5	33.1	31.7	28.9
5. Agree	20.0	21.3	18.3		15.9	16.8	28.7	14.0		18.6	20.3	18.3	16.1	15.8
Item 10050 N(Wtd)	2831	1316	1461		624	907	901	399		1013	449	263	454	38

A22L: My family and I often buy things we don't really need; we could get along with much less

	TOTAL	M	F		NE	NC	S	W		None	Mari- juana Only	Few Pills	More Pills	Any Her- oin
1. Disagree	7.9	7.8	7.7		8.2	6.7	9.9	5.7		7.5	7.4	4.6	6.7	-
2. Mostly disagree	13.0	13.2	12.9		13.7	11.6	13.7	14.0		12.8	14.5	10.7	12.0	28.9
3. Neither	17.6	22.3	13.5		16.4	19.6	17.3	15.7		17.0	15.6	15.7	18.4	18.4
4. Mostly agree	34.8	33.4	36.4		34.9	37.4	31.1	36.9		37.0	30.6	39.8	35.7	23.7
5. Agree	26.6	23.2	29.6		26.7	24.8	28.0	27.7		25.7	32.1	28.7	27.1	26.3
Item 10060 N(Wtd)	2820	1313	1457		622	900	897	401		1009	448	261	451	38

A22M: By the year 2000, engineers and scientists will probably have invented devices that will solve our pollution problems

	TOTAL	M	F		NE	NC	S	W		None	Mari- juana Only	Few Pills	More Pills	Any Her- oin
1. Disagree	9.4	9.9	8.9		10.8	8.3	8.7	11.3		10.3	8.9	5.8	12.4	5.4
2. Mostly disagree	17.0	17.0	17.2		18.5	16.2	16.1	18.5		18.7	17.1	18.2	15.7	24.3
3. Neither	29.4	26.6	32.0		25.3	31.0	29.4	32.5		28.5	27.6	33.3	28.7	24.3
4. Mostly agree	30.1	31.8	28.4		30.9	32.1	29.9	24.8		30.4	30.5	29.1	30.2	35.1
5. Agree	14.1	14.7	13.5		14.5	12.4	15.9	13.3		12.0	15.6	13.6	13.0	16.2
Item 10070 N(Wtd)	2814	1308	1455		612	901	901	400		1005	449	258	453	37

A23: In your own actions--the things you buy and the things you do-- how much of an effort do you make to conserve energy and protect the environment?

	TOTAL	M	F		NE	NC	S	W		None	Mari- juana Only	Few Pills	More Pills	Any Her- oin
1. None	5.2	5.2	5.1		6.3	5.8	4.0	4.2		4.5	6.0	3.0	5.3	5.3
2. A little	26.8	28.3	25.8		28.5	28.4	26.6	21.6		26.9	29.2	27.8	27.6	28.9
3. Some	56.1	53.5	58.1		51.4	56.2	57.8	59.2		56.8	52.5	60.1	56.1	42.1
4. Quite a bit	11.9	13.0	11.1		13.8	9.6	11.7	14.7		11.7	12.5	8.7	10.7	26.3
Item 10080 N(Wtd)	2829	1311	1463		622	906	900	402		1012	448	263	456	38

A27: How closely do your ideas agree with your parents' ideas about (...)

Our ideas are...

A27A: What you should do with your life.

	TOTAL	M	F		NE	NC	S	W		None	Mari- juana Only	Few Pills	More Pills	Any Her- oin
1. Very similar	22.3	21.3	23.4		22.3	20.1	23.4	24.6		28.8	22.0	16.3	15.6	13.5
2. Mostly similar	45.3	46.6	44.0		46.0	45.0	44.6	46.3		45.7	45.7	47.9	41.4	40.5
3. Mostly different	17.4	16.9	17.6		16.5	20.1	16.1	15.6		13.8	15.8	18.3	26.5	21.6
4. Very different	11.4	10.9	11.8		11.9	11.0	12.6	8.7		8.4	12.7	14.8	12.7	21.6
8. Don't know	3.7	4.2	3.2		3.3	3.8	3.3	4.9		3.4	3.8	2.7	3.7	2.7
Item 11230 N(Wtd)	2732	1252	1430		611	875	855	391		1014	449	257	456	37

CAUTION: Items were rearranged after 1975; changes in context may produce spurious "trends" (see page 12).

QUESTIONNAIRE FORM 4 1975	TOTAL	SEX			REGION					ILLICIT DRUG USE: LIFETIME				
		M	F		NE	NC	S	W		None	Mari- juana Only	Few Pills	More Pills	Any Her- oin
Weighted No. of Cases:	3041	1398	1520		668	975	968	430		1030	456	267	465	40
% of Weighted Total:	100.0	46.0	50.0		22.0	32.1	31.8	14.1		33.9	15.0	8.8	15.3	1.3

A27B: What you do in your leisure time

1. Very similar	9.6	9.1	10.3		9.1	8.0	11.7	9.5		13.5	8.1	8.6	5.7	10.8
2. Mostly similar	33.7	32.0	35.0		33.6	36.3	30.2	35.6		39.1	34.8	31.5	25.4	16.2
3. Mostly different	31.3	32.2	30.5		31.1	31.3	30.8	32.3		27.6	34.1	34.2	36.9	29.7
4. Very different	21.8	22.4	21.2		22.5	21.4	23.3	17.9		16.7	20.0	21.8	30.0	37.8
8. Don't know	3.6	4.3	3.0		3.6	3.0	3.8	4.4		3.2	3.1	3.5	2.0	5.4
Item 11240 N(Wtd)	2711	1243	1418		605	873	844	390		1009	446	257	453	37

A27C: How you dress--what clothes you wear

1. Very similar	18.4	16.1	20.6		17.8	16.4	20.0	20.0		23.0	17.1	16.3	15.8	10.8
2. Mostly similar	44.7	44.0	45.2		45.1	44.8	43.1	47.4		45.7	47.4	47.1	40.2	27.0
3. Mostly different	20.3	20.4	19.9		19.2	21.3	20.5	19.2		18.9	20.0	17.9	22.0	37.8
4. Very different	14.2	15.7	12.9		15.5	15.4	14.0	10.3		10.4	12.5	16.7	19.6	24.3
8. Don't know	2.4	3.8	1.3		2.5	2.1	2.5	2.8		2.0	2.9	1.6	2.4	2.7
Item 11250 N(Wtd)	2725	1250	1426		608	877	850	390		1015	449	257	455	37

A27D: How you spend your money

1. Very similar	11.0	9.0	12.9		9.5	9.7	12.6	12.6		13.9	9.4	10.0	8.3	13.5
2. Mostly similar	37.1	31.6	41.7		34.9	38.4	35.6	41.0		43.7	36.3	38.2	26.5	5.4
3. Mostly different	28.3	31.1	25.9		31.6	29.6	25.8	25.4		24.6	32.1	28.2	33.8	27.0
4. Very different	20.5	24.0	17.4		21.0	18.5	23.3	17.9		15.5	19.2	20.8	28.9	45.9
8. Don't know	3.2	4.3	2.0		3.0	3.6	2.7	3.1		2.4	3.1	2.3	2.4	8.1
Item 11260 N(Wtd)	2727	1250	1428		610	877	850	390		1014	449	259	456	37

A27E: What things are O.K. to do when you are on a date

1. Very similar	12.3	8.9	15.4		9.1	10.0	15.9	14.4		17.6	10.3	10.9	7.7	8.3
2. Mostly similar	28.9	27.1	30.2		26.2	29.2	29.3	31.4		34.3	25.7	27.1	20.9	13.9
3. Mostly different	22.1	24.8	20.1		22.2	25.5	20.0	19.3		18.8	26.0	26.0	25.3	16.7
4. Very different	21.8	21.2	22.4		26.3	19.8	22.0	19.3		14.1	23.3	27.1	33.5	52.8
8. Don't know	14.9	18.1	11.9		16.2	15.5	13.0	15.7		15.3	15.0	8.5	12.6	8.3
Item 11270 N(Wtd)	2710	1244	1417		604	870	847	389		1007	447	258	454	36

A27F: Whether it is O.K. to drink

1. Very similar	25.4	20.2	30.1		19.4	20.8	30.5	33.6		37.4	15.8	21.3	14.1	13.9
2. Mostly similar	29.6	30.4	29.0		33.6	31.6	28.4	21.5		30.3	36.4	24.8	25.2	19.4
3. Mostly different	18.9	20.8	17.2		20.1	21.1	16.0	18.5		15.2	20.1	22.1	22.5	27.8
4. Very different	21.2	23.6	19.0		23.4	21.8	18.3	22.8		11.9	23.4	28.7	35.1	38.9
8. Don't know	4.9	5.0	4.6		3.6	4.6	6.8	3.3		5.1	4.0	2.7	3.1	2.8
Item 11280 N(Wtd)	2713	1241	1423		608	867	849	390		1010	448	258	453	36

A27G: Whether it is O.K. to use marijuana

1. Very similar	42.0	39.2	45.1		35.7	40.8	46.4	45.4		67.4	25.5	35.7	15.2	16.7
2. Mostly similar	14.8	14.3	15.4		16.4	13.6	14.8	15.2		15.3	15.7	14.3	10.6	11.1
3. Mostly different	9.0	8.7	9.2		10.6	10.0	6.7	9.5		3.7	14.1	10.9	13.7	16.7
4. Very different	27.4	29.9	24.6		32.2	28.3	23.9	25.0		7.5	38.5	34.9	55.4	50.0
8. Don't know	6.8	7.8	5.7		5.1	7.3	8.2	4.9		5.9	6.3	4.3	4.9	5.6
Item 11290 N(Wtd)	2704	1237	1420		603	873	840	388		1010	447	258	453	36

A27H: Whether it is O.K. to use other drugs

1. Very similar	53.2	49.4	57.2		44.9	52.9	58.2	56.2		73.1	49.0	51.9	23.5	13.9
2. Mostly similar	14.5	13.7	15.1		19.3	13.8	11.9	14.6		13.3	17.4	16.7	12.6	13.9
3. Mostly different	4.6	4.8	4.2		5.1	4.7	3.7	5.6		2.3	4.0	4.3	10.4	13.9
4. Very different	20.7	23.6	18.1		24.9	21.6	17.7	19.0		5.7	22.7	21.7	49.2	55.6
8. Don't know	6.9	8.6	5.4		5.8	7.1	8.5	4.9		5.6	6.9	5.4	4.2	5.6
Item 11300 N(Wtd)	2706	1239	1417		602	870	843	390		1010	449	258	451	36

CAUTION: Items were rearranged after 1975; changes in context may produce spurious "trends" (see page 12).

QUESTIONNAIRE FORM 4 1975	TOTAL	SEX			REGION					ILLICIT DRUG USE: LIFETIME				
		M	F		NE	NC	S	W		None	Mari- juana Only	Few Pills	More Pills	Any Her- oin
Weighted No. of Cases:	3041	1398	1520		668	975	968	430		1030	456	267	465	40
% of Weighted Total:	100.0	46.0	50.0		22.0	32.1	31.8	14.1		33.9	15.0	8.8	15.3	1.3

A27I: What values are important in life

	TOTAL	M	F		NE	NC	S	W		None	Mar	Few	More	Any
1. Very similar	26.9	23.7	29.7		23.5	24.8	29.5	31.1		35.3	24.2	25.1	16.6	5.3
2. Mostly similar	46.4	48.6	44.4		48.7	47.6	44.9	43.0		45.8	48.1	50.6	48.0	42.1
3. Mostly different	14.4	14.3	14.7		15.0	15.8	12.1	15.3		10.1	13.6	14.7	21.9	31.6
4. Very different	7.6	7.7	7.5		7.7	7.4	8.6	5.7		4.9	9.6	7.7	8.8	15.8
8. Don't know	4.8	5.7	3.8		5.2	4.4	4.8	4.9		3.9	4.5	1.9	4.9	5.3
Item 11310 N(Wtd)	2701	1235	1419		600	867	848	386		1011	447	259	452	38

A27J: The value of education

	TOTAL	M	F		NE	NC	S	W		None	Mar	Few	More	Any
1. Very similar	39.4	37.0	41.3		36.6	35.6	44.1	42.0		48.4	35.6	37.1	28.4	21.1
2. Mostly similar	42.7	43.8	42.0		42.8	45.7	39.8	42.0		39.9	46.5	45.6	43.7	39.5
3. Mostly different	9.1	9.3	9.1		10.5	11.6	6.4	7.5		5.6	8.9	10.0	16.9	13.2
4. Very different	7.0	7.5	6.6		8.0	5.0	8.5	7.0		4.6	7.8	5.0	9.3	21.1
8. Don't know	1.8	2.5	1.1		2.2	2.2	1.2	1.6		1.4	1.1	2.3	2.0	5.3
Item 11320 N(Wtd)	2697	1231	1418		601	864	846	386		1010	447	259	451	38

A27K: What are appropriate roles for women

	TOTAL	M	F		NE	NC	S	W		None	Mar	Few	More	Any
1. Very similar	19.3	14.2	23.7		16.1	18.1	21.6	21.6		23.6	19.8	20.5	12.4	10.5
2. Mostly similar	42.1	41.9	42.2		39.5	44.0	42.4	40.8		42.7	40.8	47.9	41.8	28.9
3. Mostly different	15.6	17.2	14.2		17.8	15.1	13.9	17.1		13.5	13.5	15.4	21.6	26.3
4. Very different	7.6	6.5	8.4		9.7	7.2	7.0	6.5		6.2	8.6	7.3	8.2	18.4
8. Don't know	15.5	20.2	11.5		16.9	15.7	15.1	13.8		14.1	17.3	8.1	16.2	13.2
Item 11330 N(Wtd)	2684	1222	1414		597	862	841	385		1006	444	259	450	38

A27L: Conservation and pollution issues

	TOTAL	M	F		NE	NC	S	W		None	Mar	Few	More	Any
1. Very similar	16.1	14.7	17.6		16.8	14.1	17.1	17.5		19.1	16.7	14.5	14.7	21.1
2. Mostly similar	42.3	45.4	39.5		42.9	41.0	41.2	46.2		44.3	41.5	46.1	40.3	28.9
3. Mostly different	10.2	12.4	8.2		10.3	13.4	6.8	10.4		9.1	10.8	14.5	10.0	13.2
4. Very different	5.5	6.4	4.8		5.2	4.7	6.1	6.8		4.1	6.8	3.1	6.0	10.5
8. Don't know	25.9	21.2	30.0		24.9	26.9	28.8	18.8		23.3	23.9	22.3	29.2	26.3
Item 11340 N(Wtd)	2673	1219	1407		595	859	837	383		1004	443	256	449	38

A27M: Racial issues

	TOTAL	M	F		NE	NC	S	W		None	Mar	Few	More	Any
1. Very similar	18.5	17.6	19.1		16.9	13.6	23.1	22.1		19.9	17.9	17.3	16.6	13.2
2. Mostly similar	37.1	41.5	33.3		35.1	37.9	36.7	39.2		39.9	37.4	35.0	30.6	26.3
3. Mostly different	18.5	16.7	20.2		21.0	19.9	16.5	15.8		17.9	19.1	22.4	21.5	23.7
4. Very different	10.8	10.4	11.4		12.2	11.5	8.9	11.2		8.4	11.9	10.2	14.2	13.2
8. Don't know	15.1	13.9	16.1		14.7	17.1	14.7	11.7		13.9	13.2	15.4	17.1	21.1
Item 11350 N(Wtd)	2685	1223	1414		599	860	841	385		1008	446	254	451	38

A27N: Religion

	TOTAL	M	F		NE	NC	S	W		None	Mar	Few	More	Any
1. Very similar	30.5	25.5	35.1		22.2	28.4	37.7	32.6		39.3	26.5	28.4	19.5	36.8
2. Mostly similar	34.0	36.9	31.5		35.7	34.4	33.5	31.5		32.8	33.9	38.5	32.3	15.8
3. Mostly different	14.8	15.6	14.1		16.7	15.6	12.4	15.5		13.9	15.9	12.5	19.0	18.4
4. Very different	12.0	12.8	11.3		17.0	11.1	9.5	11.9		7.2	15.5	11.7	17.7	21.1
8. Don't know	8.6	9.2	8.0		8.3	10.6	6.9	8.5		6.6	8.1	8.9	11.5	7.9
Item 11360 N(Wtd)	2688	1222	1417		599	858	844	387		1011	446	257	452	38

A27O: Politics

	TOTAL	M	F		NE	NC	S	W		None	Mar	Few	More	Any
1. Very similar	13.5	14.1	13.0		13.0	12.0	16.2	11.4		15.6	13.3	14.0	9.1	13.2
2. Mostly similar	35.4	38.2	32.5		31.6	35.5	36.7	38.1		38.1	35.5	31.9	31.7	23.7
3. Mostly different	13.0	14.3	12.2		15.7	13.9	10.5	13.0		12.2	13.0	19.5	14.6	18.4
4. Very different	8.4	9.9	7.1		10.0	7.5	8.0	9.1		6.3	10.6	7.4	11.8	15.8
8. Don't know	29.7	23.5	35.2		29.6	31.2	28.8	28.8		27.9	27.6	27.2	33.0	28.9
Item 11370 N(Wtd)	2684	1222	1413		598	859	841	386		1008	445	257	451	38

CAUTION: Items were rearranged after 1975; changes in context may produce spurious "trends" (see page 12).

QUESTIONNAIRE FORM 4 1975	TOTAL	SEX			REGION					ILLICIT DRUG USE: LIFETIME				
		M	F		NE	NC	S	W		None	Mari-juana Only	Few Pills	More Pills	Any Her-oin
Weighted No. of Cases:	3041	1398	1520		668	975	968	430		1030	456	267	465	40
% of Weighted Total:	100.0	46.0	50.0		22.0	32.1	31.8	14.1		33.9	15.0	8.8	15.3	1.3

A28: People have different opinions about world problems. How much do you agree or disagree with each of the following statements?

A28A: I feel that I can do very little to change the way the world is today

	TOTAL	M	F		NE	NC	S	W		None	Mari-juana Only	Few Pills	More Pills	Any Her-oin
1. Disagree	9.6	9.2	10.0		9.3	8.7	10.6	9.8		10.0	10.1	8.9	8.9	10.5
2. Mostly disagree	24.3	22.1	26.2		22.4	23.9	24.5	28.0		26.4	23.4	32.7	21.5	13.2
3. Neither	24.8	25.0	24.6		21.9	25.8	23.9	29.0		23.2	25.6	21.8	26.8	26.3
4. Mostly agree	27.7	28.3	27.0		30.4	31.2	24.9	21.9		28.3	26.1	23.3	28.2	34.2
5. Agree	13.6	15.3	12.1		16.0	10.5	16.0	11.6		12.1	14.6	13.2	14.5	13.2
Item 10920 N(Wtd)	2660	1214	1403		589	855	836	379		1012	445	257	447	38

A28B: It does little good to clean up air and water pollution because this society will not last long enough for it to matter

	TOTAL	M	F		NE	NC	S	W		None	Mari-juana Only	Few Pills	More Pills	Any Her-oin
1. Disagree	41.5	38.8	43.4		43.5	40.0	39.9	45.4		42.2	44.8	42.0	38.2	34.2
2. Mostly disagree	30.8	31.1	30.8		32.1	30.6	30.3	30.3		33.0	31.5	33.9	29.9	28.9
3. Neither	17.2	18.0	16.6		13.2	20.6	16.2	17.7		15.5	16.2	12.5	21.2	23.7
4. Mostly agree	6.4	7.1	5.7		6.6	6.4	7.0	4.7		5.0	4.7	8.2	7.1	13.2
5. Agree	4.2	5.0	3.5		4.8	2.3	6.8	1.6		4.3	2.7	3.5	3.6	-
Item 10930 N(Wtd)	2654	1210	1400		589	853	833	379		1010	444	257	448	38

A28C: When things get tough enough, we'll put our minds to it and find a technological solution

	TOTAL	M	F		NE	NC	S	W		None	Mari-juana Only	Few Pills	More Pills	Any Her-oin
1. Disagree	8.2	6.8	9.3		9.6	6.9	7.6	10.1		7.7	7.0	9.4	9.8	7.9
2. Mostly disagree	15.5	15.1	15.9		14.4	15.5	14.6	18.9		15.9	16.2	11.8	17.2	23.7
3. Neither	22.7	20.6	24.4		22.9	24.6	20.9	22.1		21.0	24.1	22.8	24.0	23.7
4. Mostly agree	36.6	39.7	34.1		35.9	39.3	36.4	32.2		36.5	37.4	41.7	35.6	23.7
5. Agree	17.1	17.8	16.4		17.3	13.9	20.6	16.8		18.9	15.3	14.2	13.2	18.4
Item 10940 N(Wtd)	2631	1200	1387		585	843	827	376		1009	444	254	441	38

A28D: When I think about all the terrible things that have been happening, it is hard for me to hold out much hope for the world

	TOTAL	M	F		NE	NC	S	W		None	Mari-juana Only	Few Pills	More Pills	Any Her-oin
1. Disagree	15.5	15.2	15.9		14.7	12.5	17.9	18.3		18.1	15.3	16.5	11.2	7.9
2. Mostly disagree	29.2	29.2	29.0		31.8	28.6	29.3	26.5		30.3	31.7	33.1	26.0	31.6
3. Neither	23.2	26.0	20.8		24.1	28.1	17.7	23.1		21.8	25.5	18.1	23.3	23.7
4. Mostly agree	23.3	22.5	24.3		21.4	22.9	24.5	24.7		21.6	19.6	22.4	30.9	28.9
5. Agree	8.8	7.2	10.0		8.0	8.0	10.7	7.2		8.2	8.0	10.2	8.9	7.9
Item 10950 N(Wtd)	2627	1201	1382		585	840	825	377		1007	439	254	447	38

A28E: I often wonder if there is any real purpose to my life in light of the world situation

	TOTAL	M	F		NE	NC	S	W		None	Mari-juana Only	Few Pills	More Pills	Any Her-oin
1. Disagree	22.2	22.3	22.1		22.2	17.9	24.5	26.6		28.2	22.2	24.8	14.6	7.9
2. Mostly disagree	23.1	23.2	22.9		23.3	23.7	21.8	24.2		25.3	21.3	23.6	20.4	23.7
3. Neither	24.8	25.8	23.9		23.1	26.6	24.7	23.9		22.2	28.6	19.3	27.2	21.1
4. Mostly agree	21.7	20.4	22.8		21.2	23.9	20.4	20.5		17.4	17.9	25.2	26.7	36.8
5. Agree	8.2	8.2	8.3		10.2	7.9	8.8	5.1		6.8	10.0	7.1	10.8	10.5
Item 10960 N(Wtd)	2616	1195	1380		580	838	822	376		1003	441	254	445	38

A28F: My guess is that this country will be caught up in a major world upheaval in the next 10 years

	TOTAL	M	F		NE	NC	S	W		None	Mari-juana Only	Few Pills	More Pills	Any Her-oin
1. Disagree	11.1	13.0	9.2		10.7	11.3	11.9	9.4		10.5	15.3	9.9	8.6	2.6
2. Mostly disagree	16.1	18.1	14.1		15.1	17.3	15.2	16.6		17.0	16.4	15.4	18.6	7.9
3. Neither	36.8	33.9	39.6		36.2	37.9	35.9	37.3		36.7	36.9	38.3	33.0	39.5
4. Mostly agree	22.8	21.7	23.9		24.4	21.8	23.1	21.4		22.8	19.1	25.3	24.0	28.9
5. Agree	13.3	13.3	13.2		13.5	11.6	13.8	15.5		13.0	12.3	11.1	15.6	23.7
Item 10970 N(Wtd)	2597	1187	1367		577	833	814	373		1002	439	253	442	38

CAUTION: Items were rearranged after 1975; changes in context may produce spurious "trends" (see page 12).

QUESTIONNAIRE FORM 4 1975	TOTAL	SEX			REGION					ILLICIT DRUG USE: LIFETIME				
		M	F		NE	NC	S	W		None	Mari- juana Only	Few Pills	More Pills	Any Her- oin
Weighted No. of Cases:	3041	1398	1520		668	975	968	430		1030	456	267	465	40
% of Weighted Total:	100.0	46.0	50.0		22.0	32.1	31.8	14.1		33.9	15.0	8.8	15.3	1.3
A28G: Nuclear or biological annihilation will probably be the fate of all mankind, within my lifetime														
1. Disagree	21.5	25.7	17.6		20.1	21.0	22.0	23.4		23.5	23.3	18.5	18.0	7.9
2. Mostly disagree	21.1	21.2	21.0		25.2	20.7	19.1	20.2		24.5	22.9	17.3	20.8	15.8
3. Neither	35.8	29.9	41.3		34.3	35.0	36.4	38.2		33.1	33.7	42.1	36.3	42.1
4. Mostly agree	14.2	15.3	13.2		12.8	16.2	15.4	9.7		12.6	12.7	13.8	16.7	21.1
5. Agree	7.5	7.8	7.0		7.7	7.2	7.2	8.3		6.4	7.4	8.3	8.2	10.5
Item 10980 N(Wtd)	2576	1189	1345		571	823	810	372		991	433	254	438	38
A28H: The human race has come through tough times before, and will do so again														
1. Disagree	3.9	4.9	3.0		3.6	2.9	4.8	4.6		4.4	4.3	3.5	2.5	2.6
2. Mostly disagree	7.0	7.2	6.8		6.5	8.0	6.0	7.2		6.8	6.6	7.4	8.3	10.5
3. Neither	22.2	21.3	22.9		20.0	23.1	22.0	23.6		21.0	22.6	20.7	25.5	26.3
4. Mostly agree	38.6	38.2	39.3		39.9	42.1	34.5	37.8		39.2	37.8	41.0	38.0	42.1
5. Agree	28.4	28.4	28.0		30.0	23.8	32.7	26.5		28.7	28.5	27.7	26.0	18.4
Item 10990 N(Wtd)	2613	1190	1381		584	839	817	373		1001	442	256	447	38
A29: Some people think about what's going on in government very often, and others are not that interested. How much of an interest do you take in government and current events?														
1. No interest at all	9.2	12.3	6.7		8.4	7.7	11.5	8.5		9.9	8.0	11.3	8.5	-
2. Very little interest	22.7	25.1	20.6		19.8	22.1	24.8	23.8		24.5	22.7	23.0	20.9	23.5
3. Some interest	47.1	45.4	48.3		46.9	49.3	44.5	48.2		44.7	48.9	46.9	47.6	52.9
4. A lot of interest	17.1	13.3	20.2		18.6	17.6	15.9	15.9		17.2	16.7	16.4	17.1	14.7
5. A very great interest	4.0	3.8	4.1		6.4	3.3	3.2	3.6		3.6	3.7	2.3	6.1	5.9
Item 6330 N(Wtd)	2591	1173	1379		580	829	818	365		1007	436	256	445	34
A32: In particular, there has been a great deal of public debate about whether marijuana use should be legal. Which of the following policies would you favor?														
1. Using marijuana shoud be entirely legal	27.3	29.9	25.0		33.7	25.2	24.0	29.2		9.0	37.3	27.5	55.2	72.5
2. It shoud be a minor violation --like a parking ticket-- but not a crime	25.3	24.8	25.6		28.4	26.2	22.3	24.9		20.3	32.7	30.2	28.8	12.5
3. It should be a crime	30.5	28.8	32.3		22.3	29.8	36.6	31.7		51.0	12.9	27.9	9.2	10.0
4. Don't know	16.8	16.6	17.0		15.6	18.7	16.9	14.2		19.8	17.1	14.1	6.8	7.5
Item 10880 N(Wtd)	2541	1155	1351		578	813	797	353		1017	450	262	455	40
A33: If it were legal for people to use marijuana, should it also be legal to sell marijuana?														
1. No	27.8	27.3	28.5		25.3	27.8	28.4	30.2		40.5	16.4	22.8	12.9	17.5
2. Yes, but only to adults	37.1	40.3	33.8		39.6	36.3	38.4	32.1		26.3	43.7	44.1	48.6	35.0
3. Yes, to anyone	16.2	16.1	16.2		15.7	17.7	15.3	15.6		11.6	16.9	16.7	26.4	37.5
4. Don't know	18.9	16.2	21.4		19.4	18.2	18.0	22.3		21.6	23.1	16.3	12.0	10.0
Item 10890 N(Wtd)	2544	1152	1357		578	813	795	358		1021	451	263	459	40
A34: If marijuana were legal to use and legally available, which of the following would you be most likely to do?														
1. Not use it, even if it were legal and available	53.2	48.6	57.8		45.4	50.1	59.1	59.7		83.4	31.6	48.7	18.3	12.5
2. Try it	8.2	8.8	7.9		7.7	10.4	8.3	3.9		8.8	11.1	9.9	4.1	2.5
3. Use it about as often as I do now	22.7	24.4	20.5		30.1	22.1	16.9	24.8		.7	37.1	26.2	52.1	42.5
4. Use it more often than I do now	6.0	6.8	5.5		6.1	7.7	5.2	4.2		.2	6.4	5.3	16.8	37.5
5. Use it less than I do now	1.3	2.0	.7		1.6	.7	1.5	1.4		.2	1.3	1.1	3.7	-
6. Don't know	8.5	9.4	7.6		9.2	8.8	8.8	5.6		6.7	12.7	9.1	4.8	5.0
Item 10900 N(Wtd)	2529	1144	1349		575	806	793	355		1020	450	263	459	40

CAUTION: Items were rearranged after 1975; changes in context may produce spurious "trends" (see page 12).

QUESTIONNAIRE FORM 4 1975	TOTAL	SEX			REGION					ILLICIT DRUG USE: LIFETIME				
		M	F		NE	NC	S	W		None	Mari- juana Only	Few Pills	More Pills	Any Her- oin
Weighted No. of Cases:	*3041*	*1398*	*1520*		*668*	*975*	*968*	*430*		*1030*	*456*	*267*	*465*	*40*
% of Weighted Total:	*100.0*	*46.0*	*50.0*		*22.0*	*32.1*	*31.8*	*14.1*		*33.9*	*15.0*	*8.8*	*15.3*	*1.3*

A35: How do you think your parents feel (or would feel) about you doing each of the following things?

A35A: Smoking one or more packs of cigarettes per day

1. Not disapprove	11.5	11.7	11.1		13.4	11.3	11.3	8.9		5.1	14.2	14.5	20.8	15.0
2. Disapprove	37.1	41.0	33.7		42.2	35.4	39.1	28.1		31.7	35.7	37.4	46.0	50.0
3. Strongly disapprove	51.5	47.3	55.2		44.3	53.3	49.6	63.0		63.2	50.1	48.5	33.3	32.5
Item 11380 N(Wtd)	*2495*	*1133*	*1332*		*569*	*796*	*780*	*349*		*1018*	*451*	*262*	*457*	*40*

A35B: Trying marijuana (pot,grass) once or twice.

1. Not disapprove	9.2	9.6	8.6		11.9	8.7	6.9	10.9		1.8	11.3	11.5	20.5	25.0
2. Disapprove	22.4	23.7	21.1		24.0	24.2	19.2	22.9		14.5	25.1	27.9	31.7	35.0
3. Strongly disapprove	68.4	66.7	70.4		64.0	67.0	73.9	66.5		83.7	63.6	60.7	47.8	40.0
Item 11390 N(Wtd)	*2489*	*1131*	*1329*		*570*	*792*	*778*	*349*		*1014*	*451*	*262*	*458*	*40*

A35C: Smoking marijuana occasionally

1. Not disapprove	4.3	4.7	4.0		6.3	3.8	3.1	5.5		.6	4.2	3.8	11.2	20.0
2. Disapprove	16.9	17.7	15.9		18.1	19.8	13.5	15.8		7.8	17.8	22.5	31.1	27.5
3. Strongly disapprove	78.8	77.6	80.1		75.6	76.4	83.5	79.0		91.6	78.0	74.0	57.8	50.0
Item 11400 N(Wtd)	*2484*	*1131*	*1324*		*569*	*792*	*775*	*348*		*1015*	*449*	*262*	*457*	*40*

A35D: Smoking marijuana regularly

1. Not disapprove	1.9	2.1	1.5		2.8	1.4	1.4	2.6		.6	1.3	1.9	4.4	7.5
2. Disapprove	12.1	12.9	11.2		13.7	14.4	9.5	9.7		4.7	11.9	13.0	25.3	32.5
3. Strongly disapprove	86.1	84.9	87.2		83.3	84.3	89.2	87.7		94.7	86.7	85.1	70.0	57.5
Item 11410 N(Wtd)	*2480*	*1127*	*1325*		*568*	*792*	*772*	*349*		*1014*	*452*	*262*	*454*	*40*

A35E: Trying LSD once or twice

1. Not disapprove	1.0	1.4	.6		2.1	.5	.6	.6		.3	.9	1.1	2.2	10.0
2. Disapprove	7.2	7.2	7.0		7.6	8.8	6.0	5.7		4.9	4.2	8.0	12.5	25.0
3. Strongly disapprove	91.8	91.4	92.4		90.2	90.7	93.4	93.7		94.9	94.9	91.2	85.1	62.5
Item 11420 N(Wtd)	*2482*	*1127*	*1326*		*569*	*793*	*772*	*348*		*1014*	*452*	*262*	*457*	*40*

A35F: Trying an amphetamine (upper, pep pill, bennie, speed) once or twice

1. Not disapprove	2.0	2.1	1.8		3.3	1.9	1.3	1.4		.4	1.6	1.5	5.7	7.5
2. Disapprove	10.0	8.9	10.9		11.1	11.0	8.0	10.4		6.5	5.8	13.0	19.7	32.5
3. Strongly disapprove	88.0	88.9	87.2		85.6	87.0	90.5	88.2		93.1	92.9	85.5	74.8	57.5
Item 11430 N(Wtd)	*2478*	*1125*	*1324*		*569*	*791*	*771*	*347*		*1014*	*450*	*262*	*456*	*40*

A35G: Taking one or two drinks nearly every day

1. Not disapprove	10.5	13.7	7.6		10.2	9.8	10.9	11.5		6.8	11.3	11.8	15.8	20.0
2. Disapprove	23.8	25.5	22.4		28.6	24.8	22.3	17.0		18.8	25.5	23.3	31.0	30.0
3. Strongly disapprove	65.8	60.9	70.0		61.3	65.5	66.8	71.2		74.4	63.2	64.5	53.2	50.0
Item 11440 N(Wtd)	*2476*	*1127*	*1320*		*569*	*789*	*771*	*347*		*1014*	*451*	*262*	*455*	*40*

A35H: Taking four or five drinks nearly every day

1. Not disapprove	2.8	3.7	1.8		1.8	3.2	3.4	2.6		1.6	2.0	2.7	4.6	10.0
2. Disapprove	15.6	17.9	13.6		17.3	16.3	13.6	15.6		10.2	18.1	12.6	24.4	32.5
3. Strongly disapprove	81.6	78.3	84.5		80.9	80.5	83.0	81.8		88.3	79.9	84.7	70.9	57.5
Item 11450 N(Wtd)	*2473*	*1124*	*1320*		*566*	*790*	*771*	*347*		*1013*	*452*	*262*	*454*	*40*

CAUTION: Items were rearranged after 1975; changes in context may produce spurious "trends" (see page 12).

QUESTIONNAIRE FORM 4 1975	TOTAL	SEX			REGION					ILLICIT DRUG USE: LIFETIME				
		M	F		NE	NC	S	W		None	Mari- juana Only	Few Pills	More Pills	Any Her- oin
Weighted No. of Cases:	*3041*	*1398*	*1520*		*668*	*975*	*968*	*430*		*1030*	*456*	*267*	*465*	*40*
% of Weighted Total:	*100.0*	*46.0*	*50.0*		*22.0*	*32.1*	*31.8*	*14.1*		*33.9*	*15.0*	*8.8*	*15.3*	*1.3*
A35I: Having five or more drinks once or twice each weekend														
1. Not disapprove	14.7	18.7	11.1		18.8	16.3	11.5	11.2		6.3	19.3	12.6	25.6	30.0
2. Disapprove	23.0	25.0	21.3		25.5	24.9	19.9	21.6		16.6	27.9	26.7	30.4	25.0
3. Strongly disapprove	62.3	56.4	67.6		55.6	58.7	68.5	67.4		77.2	52.8	60.7	44.3	45.0
Item 11460 N(Wtd)	*2476*	*1126*	*1321*		*568*	*790*	*772*	*347*		*1014*	*451*	*262*	*454*	*40*

CAUTION: Items were rearranged after 1975; changes in context may produce spurious "trends" (see page 12).

QUESTIONNAIRE FORM 5 1975	TOTAL	SEX			REGION					ILLICIT DRUG USE: LIFETIME				
		M	F		NE	NC	S	W		None	Mari-juana Only	Few Pills	More Pills	Any Her-oin
Weighted No. of Cases:	3046	1413	1545		668	970	980	428		1136	516	309	523	73
% of Weighted Total:	100.0	46.4	50.7		21.9	31.8	32.2	14.1		37.3	16.9	10.1	17.2	2.4

A04: Of all the problems facing the nation today, how often do you worry about each of the following?

A04A: Chance of nuclear war

	TOTAL	M	F		NE	NC	S	W		None	Mj	Few	More	Her
1. Never	22.9	19.9	25.4		27.1	24.6	18.3	22.5		23.0	23.3	19.9	25.3	30.1
2. Seldom	36.9	40.1	34.1		37.3	34.2	38.0	40.3		39.2	37.3	37.8	34.9	31.5
3. Sometimes	32.6	32.8	32.7		29.1	35.6	33.2	30.1		31.5	34.8	35.5	30.3	24.7
4. Often	7.6	7.2	7.8		6.5	5.5	10.5	7.1		6.5	4.9	6.5	9.4	13.7
Item 11660 N(Wtd)	3002	1407	1538		660	955	965	422		1131	515	307	521	73

A04B: Population growth

	TOTAL	M	F		NE	NC	S	W		None	Mj	Few	More	Her
1. Never	12.8	13.8	11.8		15.6	13.0	10.6	13.0		13.7	11.7	12.7	13.7	15.1
2. Seldom	29.3	32.3	26.6		30.3	33.0	26.7	25.5		30.1	30.2	27.7	26.4	32.9
3. Sometimes	38.4	35.9	40.8		36.4	37.8	39.6	40.0		38.7	37.9	39.1	39.9	39.7
4. Often	19.5	17.9	20.8		17.6	16.0	23.1	21.7		17.5	20.0	20.5	20.0	12.3
Item 11670 N(Wtd)	3000	1408	1536		659	954	964	423		1132	514	307	519	73

A04C: Crime and violence

	TOTAL	M	F		NE	NC	S	W		None	Mj	Few	More	Her
1. Never	1.8	3.0	.8		2.4	2.1	1.7	.9		1.8	1.0	.7	1.7	7.0
2. Seldom	11.1	16.7	6.0		12.1	12.1	10.2	9.2		9.1	13.2	10.4	14.4	12.7
3. Sometimes	33.6	37.4	30.2		35.9	34.1	28.6	40.5		34.9	35.0	37.1	33.2	23.9
4. Often	53.5	43.0	63.1		49.5	51.8	59.6	49.5		54.2	50.7	51.8	50.7	54.9
Item 11680 N(Wtd)	2999	1404	1538		660	954	963	422		1130	515	307	521	71

A04D: Pollution

	TOTAL	M	F		NE	NC	S	W		None	Mj	Few	More	Her
1. Never	4.0	3.9	4.2		4.8	3.1	4.8	3.3		3.9	2.7	3.6	4.6	2.7
2. Seldom	17.8	18.3	17.3		15.9	20.4	17.8	14.7		16.4	17.9	18.2	17.0	28.8
3. Sometimes	41.1	39.9	42.1		38.1	42.2	43.4	37.7		42.2	43.5	41.4	38.5	31.5
4. Often	37.1	37.8	36.4		41.1	34.1	34.0	44.3		37.4	35.7	36.8	40.0	35.6
Item 11690 N(Wtd)	3002	1407	1540		661	955	965	422		1133	515	307	522	73

A04E: Energy shortages

	TOTAL	M	F		NE	NC	S	W		None	Mj	Few	More	Her
1. Never	3.3	3.1	3.6		3.8	3.8	2.3	4.0		3.7	2.3	1.6	3.5	5.5
2. Seldom	17.1	15.3	18.2		19.3	17.9	14.9	17.0		16.7	16.1	18.7	16.7	17.8
3. Sometimes	43.7	42.8	44.9		43.4	42.8	43.6	46.6		45.1	44.9	37.4	44.6	41.1
4. Often	35.9	38.8	33.3		33.5	35.6	39.2	32.6		34.4	36.6	42.3	35.4	34.2
Item 11700 N(Wtd)	2993	1406	1535		659	951	960	423		1130	514	305	520	73

A04F: Race relations

	TOTAL	M	F		NE	NC	S	W		None	Mj	Few	More	Her
1. Never	15.6	16.8	14.3		20.5	17.4	10.4	15.9		14.4	15.2	16.3	17.8	19.2
2. Seldom	35.0	38.8	31.3		33.4	36.5	34.8	34.8		37.4	34.0	32.9	34.9	32.9
3. Sometimes	30.1	28.9	31.6		30.2	28.6	32.0	29.1		30.2	30.9	35.8	29.2	24.7
4. Often	19.3	15.4	22.9		16.0	17.5	22.9	20.1		18.1	19.8	15.0	18.0	23.3
Item 11710 N(Wtd)	2995	1405	1534		655	954	964	422		1130	514	307	518	73

A04G: Hunger and poverty

	TOTAL	M	F		NE	NC	S	W		None	Mj	Few	More	Her
1. Never	6.3	9.5	3.1		8.2	6.8	5.0	5.5		5.4	7.2	5.2	6.2	12.5
2. Seldom	28.7	39.1	19.3		29.5	31.2	27.0	26.1		27.4	32.1	30.6	29.0	27.8
3. Sometimes	37.9	34.0	41.4		35.9	37.8	37.2	43.4		40.5	36.2	41.0	37.7	33.3
4. Often	27.0	17.5	36.1		26.6	24.2	30.7	25.1		26.7	24.5	22.8	27.1	26.4
Item 11720 N(Wtd)	2999	1404	1541		658	955	963	422		1132	514	307	520	72

CAUTION: Items were rearranged after 1975; changes in context may produce spurious "trends" (see page 12).

QUESTIONNAIRE FORM 5 1975	TOTAL	SEX			REGION					ILLICIT DRUG USE: LIFETIME				
		M	F		NE	NC	S	W		None	Mari- juana Only	Few Pills	More Pills	Any Her- oin
Weighted No. of Cases:	*3046*	*1413*	*1545*		*668*	*970*	*980*	*428*		*1136*	*516*	*309*	*523*	*73*
% of Weighted Total:	*100.0*	*46.4*	*50.7*		*21.9*	*31.8*	*32.2*	*14.1*		*37.3*	*16.9*	*10.1*	*17.2*	*2.4*

A04H: Using open land for housing or industry

1. Never	27.7	25.3	29.6		29.2	27.8	30.1	19.5		28.6	24.1	30.4	27.4	37.0
2. Seldom	30.2	30.9	29.7		27.4	31.0	31.9	28.8		32.4	32.2	33.3	25.5	17.8
3. Sometimes	22.8	23.3	22.2		21.1	23.6	22.8	23.6		21.8	24.7	19.0	24.4	20.5
4. Often	19.4	20.4	18.5		22.5	17.7	15.2	28.3		17.3	19.2	17.6	22.8	24.7
Item 11730　N(Wtd)	*2996*	*1404*	*1539*		*658*	*956*	*962*	*420*		*1131*	*515*	*306*	*521*	*73*

A04I: Urban decay

1. Never	35.3	35.9	35.0		33.3	34.6	40.0	29.2		34.8	34.6	36.1	35.3	41.1
2. Seldom	37.0	38.2	35.8		33.5	40.3	34.7	40.2		38.3	39.6	34.8	36.6	28.8
3. Sometimes	21.3	20.0	22.4		24.5	18.6	20.8	23.6		20.8	20.7	23.0	22.2	16.4
4. Often	6.4	6.0	6.8		8.7	6.6	4.4	7.0		6.1	5.5	6.2	6.0	12.3
Item 11740　N(Wtd)	*2967*	*1391*	*1525*		*657*	*946*	*948*	*415*		*1122*	*512*	*305*	*519*	*73*

A04J: Economic problems

1. Never	4.8	4.6	4.9		5.5	5.2	4.1	5.0		3.5	3.9	4.9	5.2	11.1
2. Seldom	20.5	20.3	20.9		19.7	21.5	19.9	21.2		20.0	20.4	20.9	20.0	20.8
3. Sometimes	43.0	43.4	42.1		42.4	42.3	44.9	40.8		42.1	46.9	40.2	43.4	38.9
4. Often	31.6	31.7	32.1		32.4	30.9	31.2	32.8		34.2	28.8	34.0	31.3	27.8
Item 11750　N(Wtd)	*3001*	*1407*	*1538*		*660*	*955*	*962*	*424*		*1133*	*514*	*306*	*521*	*72*

A04K: Drug abuse

1. Never	10.7	15.9	5.9		13.5	11.4	7.5	12.1		8.7	8.9	7.8	15.7	24.7
2. Seldom	25.8	29.4	22.3		27.5	25.4	22.6	31.2		23.3	31.1	27.4	28.5	17.8
3. Sometimes	32.9	32.2	33.9		30.5	33.3	33.9	32.9		35.8	34.4	32.9	25.9	17.8
4. Often	30.7	22.6	37.9		28.4	29.8	36.1	23.6		32.4	25.8	31.9	29.7	39.7
Item 11760　N(Wtd)	*3003*	*1407*	*1540*		*659*	*957*	*965*	*423*		*1131*	*515*	*307*	*522*	*73*

A06: Some people think a lot about the social problems of the nation and the world, and about how they might be solved. Others spend little time thinking about these issues. How much do you think about such things?

1. Never	2.4	3.1	1.6		3.7	2.2	1.6	2.6		1.8	2.4	3.2	2.3	2.8
2. Seldom	16.3	18.0	14.6		20.5	15.0	14.7	16.4		15.6	18.2	16.2	16.2	18.3
3. Sometimes	48.5	48.8	48.2		46.9	51.3	48.5	44.8		47.6	49.0	51.6	48.5	42.3
4. Quite often	26.7	23.5	29.8		24.1	26.3	27.2	30.0		29.5	24.1	25.3	26.7	29.6
5. A great deal	6.1	6.7	5.8		4.9	5.3	7.9	6.0		5.5	6.1	3.9	6.0	8.5
Item 6880　N(Wtd)	*2963*	*1381*	*1528*		*655*	*940*	*948*	*420*		*1123*	*510*	*308*	*517*	*71*

A09: Apart from the particular kind of work you want to do, how would you rate each of the following settings as a place to work?

A09A: Working in a large corporation

1. Not at all acceptable	11.3	10.9	11.6		12.3	10.6	10.8	12.4		12.4	9.2	12.3	13.3	15.9
2. Somewhat acceptable	28.1	26.9	28.9		29.9	28.3	25.2	31.3		30.4	28.8	28.2	27.9	15.9
3. Acceptable	46.8	48.5	45.7		44.9	46.8	49.4	43.7		44.1	51.3	46.9	44.7	50.7
4. Desirable	13.9	13.7	13.8		12.9	14.2	14.7	12.6		13.1	10.5	12.6	14.3	17.4
Item 11800　N(Wtd)	*2977*	*1397*	*1532*		*652*	*944*	*962*	*419*		*1126*	*513*	*309*	*517*	*69*

A09B: Working in a small business

1. Not at all acceptable	4.9	4.7	5.1		5.1	3.3	5.7	6.5		5.2	4.5	3.6	3.7	1.4
2. Somewhat acceptable	20.6	21.3	19.8		21.8	19.6	21.6	18.9		18.3	24.0	21.0	20.5	23.2
3. Acceptable	52.1	54.0	50.4		50.5	54.3	50.0	53.8		53.3	51.5	51.1	50.3	60.9
4. Desirable	22.4	20.0	24.7		22.6	22.7	22.7	20.6		23.2	20.1	23.9	25.3	15.9
Item 11810　N(Wtd)	*2974*	*1396*	*1531*		*651*	*944*	*962*	*418*		*1125*	*513*	*309*	*517*	*69*

CAUTION: Items were rearranged after 1975; changes in context may produce spurious "trends" (see page 12).

QUESTIONNAIRE FORM 5 1975	TOTAL	SEX			REGION					ILLICIT DRUG USE: LIFETIME				
		M	F		NE	NC	S	W		None	Mari- juana Only	Few Pills	More Pills	Any Her- oin
Weighted No. of Cases:	3046	1413	1545		668	970	980	428		1136	516	309	523	73
% of Weighted Total:	100.0	46.4	50.7		21.9	31.8	32.2	14.1		37.3	16.9	10.1	17.2	2.4
A09C: Working in a government agency														
1. Not at all acceptable	15.2	15.0	15.2		15.5	18.8	13.5	10.6		14.4	14.1	16.0	16.2	21.7
2. Somewhat acceptable	25.5	26.7	24.5		23.6	27.7	24.6	26.0		24.1	27.5	31.6	27.0	26.1
3. Acceptable	40.3	41.7	39.0		38.9	38.9	40.8	44.6		42.6	40.8	38.4	35.5	31.9
4. Desirable	18.9	16.5	21.3		22.2	14.6	21.2	18.6		18.8	17.8	14.0	21.2	21.7
Item 11820 N(Wtd)	2967	1396	1524		653	941	959	415		1122	512	307	518	69
A09D: Working in the military service														
1. Not at all acceptable	39.2	36.7	41.7		41.5	39.8	36.7	40.2		38.4	39.8	41.2	44.6	47.8
2. Somewhat acceptable	29.4	30.4	28.0		25.6	32.4	27.9	32.1		29.2	27.7	30.8	27.6	24.6
3. Acceptable	20.9	22.0	20.4		22.5	19.4	21.6	20.3		21.7	21.8	19.8	17.4	17.4
4. Desirable	10.5	10.9	9.9		10.4	8.5	14.0	7.2		10.7	10.5	8.4	10.4	10.1
Item 11830 N(Wtd)	2974	1395	1533		653	942	960	418		1125	513	308	518	69
A09E: Working in a school or university														
1. Not at all acceptable	19.2	23.5	15.4		18.4	21.7	19.1	15.3		17.3	16.6	22.7	20.3	23.2
2. Somewhat acceptable	28.4	32.9	23.8		27.9	28.6	28.7	28.2		27.1	35.0	27.6	27.0	23.2
3. Acceptable	35.5	31.5	39.3		35.4	34.5	34.8	39.7		37.6	32.4	34.4	34.7	36.2
4. Desirable	16.8	12.1	21.5		18.4	15.1	17.4	16.7		18.1	15.8	15.3	18.0	18.8
Item 11840 N(Wtd)	2977	1394	1535		653	944	963	418		1127	512	308	518	69
A09F: Working in a police department or police agency														
1. Not at all acceptable	26.6	28.2	25.2		30.9	26.2	25.8	22.2		23.8	22.9	28.8	34.6	47.8
2. Somewhat acceptable	25.4	26.7	24.2		23.4	28.2	24.8	23.4		24.2	29.8	25.9	25.1	20.3
3. Acceptable	31.3	30.2	32.0		29.4	31.5	31.1	34.4		33.9	29.8	30.1	26.7	17.4
4. Desirable	16.7	15.0	18.6		16.2	14.0	18.3	19.6		18.1	17.6	15.5	13.5	15.9
Item 11850 N(Wtd)	2974	1396	1530		653	942	962	418		1125	510	309	517	69
A09G: Working in a social service organization														
1. Not at all acceptable	16.0	24.3	8.5		19.7	17.4	13.2	13.2		16.1	16.1	15.4	15.1	14.9
2. Somewhat acceptable	29.7	38.8	21.0		26.8	30.4	32.2	26.9		30.0	31.6	31.1	26.6	26.9
3. Acceptable	32.6	29.1	35.8		30.5	32.8	33.4	34.1		32.6	31.8	28.9	32.8	34.3
4. Desirable	21.7	7.8	34.7		23.1	19.4	21.2	25.7		21.2	20.6	24.9	25.6	23.9
Item 11860 N(Wtd)	2957	1388	1521		650	937	954	416		1121	510	305	516	67
A09H: Working with a small group of partners														
1. Not at all acceptable	10.0	8.7	11.3		10.9	7.9	11.9	8.6		8.4	9.6	11.0	11.4	5.8
2. Somewhat acceptable	23.8	21.6	25.8		21.7	24.4	25.1	22.5		23.8	24.7	18.5	22.2	15.9
3. Acceptable	45.6	48.1	42.6		45.6	46.5	44.9	45.0		48.1	46.0	45.5	42.5	52.2
4. Desirable	20.7	21.6	20.2		21.7	21.2	18.0	23.9		19.6	19.8	25.0	24.1	27.5
Item 11870 N(Wtd)	2970	1396	1527		653	939	960	418		1125	511	308	518	69
A09I: Working on your own (self-employed)														
1. Not at all acceptable	13.5	6.9	19.3		13.8	13.1	12.8	15.6		12.9	14.5	17.5	13.2	7.2
2. Somewhat acceptable	18.7	13.4	23.7		19.9	17.4	19.6	17.9		21.6	14.7	18.8	18.6	10.1
3. Acceptable	31.2	32.7	29.9		30.4	31.7	32.4	28.7		31.8	30.6	27.8	30.9	26.1
4. Desirable	36.6	47.1	27.1		35.9	37.9	35.3	37.6		33.8	40.1	35.9	37.5	58.0
Item 11880 N(Wtd)	2973	1395	1530		652	942	961	418		1126	509	309	517	69
A11: If you were to get enough money to live as comfortably as you'd like for the rest of your life, would you want to work?														
1. I would want to work	84.5	84.6	84.5		83.8	86.1	84.1	83.4		86.9	83.9	86.6	81.0	74.3
2. I would not want to work	15.4	15.4	15.4		16.2	13.9	16.0	16.6		13.1	15.9	13.8	19.0	25.7
Item 8100 N(Wtd)	2957	1386	1525		649	936	956	415		1123	508	305	516	70

CAUTION: Items were rearranged after 1975; changes in context may produce spurious "trends" (see page 12).

QUESTIONNAIRE FORM 5 1975	TOTAL	SEX			REGION					ILLICIT DRUG USE: LIFETIME				
		M	F		NE	NC	S	W		None	Mari- juana Only	Few Pills	More Pills	Any Her- oin
Weighted No. of Cases:	3046	1413	1545		668	970	980	428		1136	516	309	523	73
% of Weighted Total:	100.0	46.4	50.7		21.9	31.8	32.2	14.1		37.3	16.9	10.1	17.2	2.4

A12A: Most people will have fuller and happier lives if they get married than if they do not ‡

1. Disagree	12.8	10.8	14.7		15.4	13.0	11.6	10.5		11.5	11.1	8.4	14.3	22.9
2. Mostly disagree	12.1	9.7	14.2		13.6	11.0	12.2	12.4		11.2	9.9	14.6	14.5	15.7
3. Neither	28.7	30.4	26.9		32.0	29.4	25.6	29.4		26.4	30.4	30.7	30.1	27.1
4. Mostly agree	32.0	34.1	30.1		27.4	31.5	35.8	31.7		33.9	34.3	31.1	27.6	25.7
5. Agree	14.4	15.0	13.9		11.6	15.1	15.0	15.8		16.9	13.8	15.2	13.5	10.0
Item 12150 N(Wtd)	2979	1397	1536		654	943	962	419		1129	513	309	518	70

A12B: Parents should encourage just as much independence in their daughters as in their sons

1. Disagree	3.5	5.1	2.2		2.9	3.3	4.6	2.9		4.0	2.7	2.6	2.3	7.1
2. Mostly disagree	8.0	13.1	3.3		9.6	8.7	6.4	7.9		7.3	10.8	8.1	6.9	8.6
3. Neither	9.6	14.6	4.8		8.4	10.0	9.1	11.7		10.4	12.9	5.8	7.3	10.0
4. Mostly agree	30.3	35.7	25.3		26.9	30.2	33.3	28.9		32.0	26.2	34.0	27.2	15.7
5. Agree	48.6	31.4	64.3		52.2	48.0	46.6	48.6		46.5	47.6	49.5	56.4	58.6
Item 12160 N(Wtd)	2978	1396	1536		655	944	962	418		1129	511	309	518	70

A12D: Being a mother and raising children is one of the most fulfilling experiences a woman can have

1. Disagree	5.0	3.5	5.9		6.0	5.4	4.3	3.9		4.4	4.8	3.0	6.2	11.9
2. Mostly disagree	6.9	5.7	8.0		5.8	6.8	8.0	6.1		6.0	7.9	6.7	7.8	4.5
3. Neither	23.5	30.6	17.3		21.7	26.8	19.0	29.3		23.0	24.8	22.5	26.0	26.9
4. Mostly agree	31.4	30.6	32.0		34.1	30.3	31.5	29.1		31.8	30.2	34.6	31.8	23.9
5. Agree	33.3	29.6	36.8		32.5	30.7	37.1	31.3		34.8	32.7	32.9	28.2	34.3
Item 12170 N(Wtd)	2888	1319	1528		637	911	932	409		1098	504	298	503	67

A12G: Most fathers should spend more time with their children than they do now.

1. Disagree	1.1	1.3	1.0		1.7	.8	1.0	1.2		1.2	.4	.7	2.5	1.4
2. Mostly disagree	2.2	3.0	1.6		2.2	2.0	2.6	1.9		1.9	2.8	1.0	1.4	5.7
3. Neither	10.8	12.6	8.8		12.7	12.6	7.2	11.8		9.1	10.8	11.1	13.6	11.4
4. Mostly agree	32.8	36.6	29.4		32.1	35.0	29.7	35.5		33.7	34.2	28.1	31.8	24.3
5. Agree	53.1	46.6	59.1		51.3	49.6	59.4	49.6		54.0	51.9	58.8	50.8	57.1
Item 12180 N(Wtd)	2964	1386	1532		647	943	957	417		1129	509	306	516	70

A12H: The husband should make all the important decisions in the family

1. Disagree	31.7	19.8	42.9		34.5	32.1	30.1	30.6		31.9	32.4	31.8	35.7	42.0
2. Mostly disagree	19.9	20.7	19.2		22.2	20.6	16.4	22.7		20.6	19.5	23.1	18.7	21.7
3. Neither	21.2	27.1	15.7		21.1	22.6	18.3	24.2		19.6	23.2	16.9	25.1	21.7
4. Mostly agree	16.1	19.1	13.0		11.5	14.2	22.5	13.2		16.2	15.0	14.9	13.3	4.3
5. Agree	11.1	13.4	9.2		10.6	10.6	12.7	9.3		11.6	9.9	13.3	7.1	10.1
Item 12190 N(Wtd)	2964	1389	1529		653	939	954	418		1124	513	308	518	69

A15: Thinking about the country as a whole, would you say relations between white people and black people have been getting better, getting worse, or staying pretty much the same?

1. Better	23.0	22.2	23.6		18.6	19.9	26.7	28.2		22.0	21.5	26.7	27.4	22.9
2. A little better	44.4	44.7	44.0		47.2	44.8	40.8	48.0		44.0	47.1	42.2	42.5	45.7
3. Same	20.4	20.1	20.9		22.4	21.5	20.7	14.2		21.8	19.7	16.8	20.7	12.9
4. A little worse	7.8	8.1	7.6		7.8	9.6	7.3	5.3		7.6	7.7	9.6	6.8	7.1
5. Worse	4.3	4.9	3.8		4.0	4.3	4.5	4.3		4.6	3.9	4.6	2.7	11.4
Item 11950 N(Wtd)	2948	1371	1531		644	934	956	415		1125	507	303	518	70

‡ = Wording changed in subsequent years.

CAUTION: Items were rearranged after 1975; changes in context may produce spurious "trends" (see page 12).

QUESTIONNAIRE FORM 5 1975	TOTAL	SEX M	F		REGION NE	NC	S	W		ILLICIT DRUG USE: LIFETIME None	Mari- juana Only	Few Pills	More Pills	Any Her- oin
Weighted No. of Cases:	*3046*	*1413*	*1545*		*668*	*970*	*980*	*428*		*1136*	*516*	*309*	*523*	*73*
% of Weighted Total:	*100.0*	*46.4*	*50.7*		*21.9*	*31.8*	*32.2*	*14.1*		*37.3*	*16.9*	*10.1*	*17.2*	*2.4*
A19A: We ought to worry about our own country and let the rest of the world take care of itself														
1. Disagree	12.6	11.8	13.5		10.9	11.8	16.1	9.1		11.8	12.9	10.5	12.8	14.1
2. Mostly disagree	22.4	20.2	24.5		18.5	24.1	22.9	23.3		25.6	18.2	25.5	21.9	22.5
3. Neither	15.7	14.9	16.4		16.5	15.3	14.3	19.0		16.2	18.4	15.7	13.6	14.1
4. Mostly agree	32.5	33.7	31.7		34.5	32.0	31.4	33.4		32.9	31.6	31.4	35.7	23.9
5. Agree	16.8	19.4	13.9		19.8	16.8	15.3	15.1		13.5	18.8	17.0	16.1	25.4
Item 12070 N(Wtd)	*2941*	*1378*	*1521*		*650*	*924*	*950*	*416*		*1125*	*512*	*306*	*516*	*71*
A19C: It would be better if we all felt more like citizens of the world than of any particular country														
1. Disagree	7.1	8.0	6.2		7.2	5.4	8.3	8.0		7.8	6.5	5.2	6.2	8.6
2. Mostly disagree	11.9	14.9	9.2		11.7	12.1	11.8	11.7		11.0	12.0	13.7	13.8	10.0
3. Neither	23.4	23.8	22.6		27.9	20.5	22.8	24.3		21.2	29.5	24.5	24.3	14.3
4. Mostly agree	27.0	25.5	28.5		25.1	30.7	24.0	28.4		28.4	25.6	26.8	24.7	28.6
5. Agree	30.7	27.8	33.5		28.3	31.3	33.0	27.7		31.8	26.4	29.4	31.1	38.6
Item 12080 N(Wtd)	*2916*	*1367*	*1508*		*642*	*924*	*938*	*412*		*1120*	*508*	*306*	*514*	*70*
A19E: I find it hard to be sympathetic toward starving people in foreign lands, when there is so much trouble in our own country														
1. Disagree	20.2	10.9	28.9		18.4	17.8	23.7	20.2		20.6	16.8	23.2	22.2	28.2
2. Mostly disagree	23.2	22.0	24.5		21.9	23.5	22.4	26.5		24.8	20.2	22.5	25.3	14.1
3. Neither	18.4	21.1	15.9		18.9	20.8	15.1	20.0		20.6	17.8	15.0	16.7	14.1
4. Mostly agree	22.3	27.1	18.0		22.3	23.6	21.9	20.2		19.8	28.2	23.2	22.8	21.1
5. Agree	15.9	19.0	12.8		18.5	14.1	16.9	13.0		14.2	17.0	15.7	13.0	22.5
Item 12090 N(Wtd)	*2931*	*1372*	*1517*		*647*	*922*	*947*	*415*		*1124*	*511*	*306*	*514*	*71*
A19F: Maybe some minority groups do get unfair treatment, but that's no business of mine														
1. Disagree	34.1	22.7	44.9		32.5	32.9	33.1	41.6		36.8	31.1	32.7	35.5	36.6
2. Mostly disagree	32.7	36.2	29.6		33.2	33.3	30.9	34.6		32.6	33.7	36.6	34.5	16.9
3. Neither	20.9	25.4	16.4		22.5	22.2	20.3	16.2		19.5	22.8	17.3	21.7	28.2
4. Mostly agree	7.7	9.8	5.7		6.5	7.7	9.5	5.8		6.3	7.5	9.2	5.6	9.9
5. Agree	4.6	5.9	3.3		5.4	3.8	6.3	1.7		4.7	4.9	4.2	2.7	7.0
Item 12100 N(Wtd)	*2919*	*1371*	*1507*		*644*	*922*	*940*	*413*		*1121*	*508*	*306*	*516*	*71*
A19G: I get very upset when I see other people treated unfairly														
1. Disagree	3.6	4.0	3.2		2.9	3.6	3.9	3.9		3.9	2.5	2.3	5.1	1.4
2. Mostly disagree	4.8	6.6	3.2		5.3	4.3	5.2	4.3		3.4	5.5	5.6	5.5	11.3
3. Neither	11.9	15.9	8.1		14.9	11.5	10.5	10.9		10.8	12.3	14.1	11.3	12.7
4. Mostly agree	34.6	40.8	29.1		35.1	37.4	32.9	31.6		34.6	39.1	33.3	33.6	25.4
5. Agree	45.1	32.8	56.4		41.8	43.0	47.5	49.0		47.5	40.6	45.1	44.5	49.3
Item 12110 N(Wtd)	*2925*	*1374*	*1510*		*646*	*922*	*943*	*414*		*1123*	*512*	*306*	*512*	*71*
A19I: I would agree to a good plan to make a better life for the poor, even if it cost me money														
1. Disagree	5.9	7.2	4.7		7.6	7.2	3.8	4.8		5.4	6.7	6.9	5.7	8.6
2. Mostly disagree	11.2	14.0	8.6		12.1	10.7	11.8	9.4		9.6	14.9	12.1	10.7	8.6
3. Neither	29.4	30.5	28.3		31.3	30.5	27.4	29.0		30.7	30.2	30.8	30.0	18.6
4. Mostly agree	34.1	32.5	35.8		34.2	33.3	33.5	37.0		33.8	27.5	34.1	39.0	32.9
5. Agree	19.4	15.9	22.6		14.9	18.4	23.5	19.8		20.3	21.0	16.1	14.4	30.0
Item 12120 N(Wtd)	*2911*	*1368*	*1503*		*643*	*918*	*936*	*414*		*1120*	*510*	*305*	*513*	*70*

CAUTION: Items were rearranged after 1975; changes in context may produce spurious ''trends'' (see page 12).

QUESTIONNAIRE FORM 5 1975	TOTAL	SEX			REGION					ILLICIT DRUG USE: LIFETIME				
		M	F		NE	NC	S	W		None	Mari- juana Only	Few Pills	More Pills	Any Her- oin
Weighted No. of Cases:	3046	1413	1545		668	970	980	428		1136	516	309	523	73
% of Weighted Total:	100.0	46.4	50.7		21.9	31.8	32.2	14.1		37.3	16.9	10.1	17.2	2.4

A19K: It's not really my problem if others are in trouble and need help

1. Disagree	34.1	24.8	43.1		31.7	32.2	35.1	39.9		35.5	33.0	38.0	35.1	32.4
2. Mostly disagree	38.4	41.9	35.1		40.4	39.5	35.4	39.6		39.9	37.1	36.4	41.5	23.9
3. Neither	16.8	18.9	14.8		18.4	18.4	15.0	14.7		17.3	18.6	13.8	14.2	14.1
4. Mostly agree	7.3	9.5	5.3		5.6	6.6	10.1	4.6		5.0	7.8	8.9	7.2	18.3
5. Agree	3.4	4.9	1.7		3.9	3.2	4.3	1.4		2.2	3.3	3.0	1.9	11.3
Item 12130 N(Wtd)	2909	1360	1509		643	916	936	414		1119	512	305	513	71

A20: If you have at least an average income in the future, how likely is it that you will contribute money to the following organizations? If you have already contributed, mark the last circle only. Are you likely to contribute to...

A20A: The United Fund or other community charities?

1. Definitely not	3.0	4.7	1.5		3.1	3.4	2.0	3.9		2.6	2.7	3.0	3.5	7.1
2. Probably not	10.8	12.3	9.2		9.9	11.9	9.3	13.2		9.4	12.4	10.9	11.0	21.4
3. Don't know	34.6	34.8	34.4		34.6	36.1	31.5	38.1		32.9	31.6	37.1	37.8	31.4
4. Probably will	34.3	34.0	34.9		35.5	31.5	36.7	33.0		36.6	34.9	34.8	31.9	24.3
5. Definitely will	5.0	3.6	6.4		4.4	4.5	6.7	3.4		6.2	5.9	3.0	2.5	4.3
6. Already have	12.3	10.7	13.7		12.4	12.6	13.8	8.3		12.3	12.5	11.6	13.3	11.4
Item 12200 N(Wtd)	2880	1351	1487		636	911	923	409		1108	510	302	511	70

A20B: International relief organizations (CARE, UNICEF, etc.)?

1. Definitely not	3.7	5.8	1.9		2.7	4.6	2.9	5.1		3.2	3.9	2.3	3.7	8.6
2. Probably not	10.2	13.6	7.3		11.7	10.6	8.6	10.8		9.5	13.7	9.9	9.6	17.1
3. Don't know	25.6	29.2	21.9		23.6	24.4	26.5	29.4		24.1	25.2	26.3	26.2	30.0
4. Probably will	39.3	37.1	41.5		37.2	38.2	42.2	38.7		41.1	37.0	38.5	39.8	17.1
5. Definitely will	7.7	5.3	10.2		6.9	8.1	9.3	4.9		8.2	7.4	5.3	7.6	14.3
6. Already have	13.4	9.2	17.2		18.1	14.2	10.4	11.3		14.0	12.7	17.8	13.1	11.4
Item 12210 N(Wtd)	2881	1350	1490		640	906	926	408		1110	511	304	512	70

A20C: Minority group organizations (NAACP, SCLS, etc.)?

1. Definitely not	10.3	14.2	7.0		8.6	10.0	12.7	8.3		11.6	9.6	8.3	10.0	10.0
2. Probably not	23.3	24.4	22.3		24.6	23.7	21.3	24.5		22.2	26.0	25.1	24.2	25.7
3. Don't know	42.2	39.4	44.5		41.7	43.3	40.7	44.4		42.9	37.2	49.2	45.7	40.0
4. Probably will	18.0	17.1	19.0		18.2	17.5	17.8	18.9		17.9	19.4	13.5	16.4	14.3
5. Definitely will	4.6	3.3	5.9		5.0	4.0	5.5	3.2		4.3	5.7	2.6	2.7	8.6
6. Already have	1.6	1.6	1.3		1.7	1.4	1.8	1.0		1.1	2.3	1.0	.8	1.4
Item 12220 N(Wtd)	2874	1347	1487		638	906	923	408		1110	511	303	512	70

A20D: Church or religious organizations?

1. Definitely not	5.6	7.7	3.8		6.9	5.7	2.8	9.5		3.2	7.1	5.0	10.0	17.1
2. Probably not	7.8	8.2	7.6		10.8	7.6	5.4	9.0		5.6	7.7	11.5	18.6	
3. Don't know	13.7	14.2	12.9		13.0	15.4	11.0	16.6		9.2	15.7	14.8	18.0	15.7
4. Probably will	23.2	23.4	22.9		24.5	24.5	21.8	21.5		24.4	23.4	24.5	19.0	18.6
5. Definitely will	15.4	14.9	15.6		12.2	14.0	21.1	10.5		17.7	13.2	12.8	11.4	14.3
6. Already have	34.4	31.5	37.4		32.4	32.7	37.9	32.9		40.0	32.9	35.9	29.9	15.7
Item 12230 N(Wtd)	2879	1348	1491		638	907	924	410		1116	508	298	511	70

A20E: Political parties or organizations?

1. Definitely not	19.3	20.1	18.8		23.1	20.9	14.4	21.5		18.1	19.6	24.4	20.8	28.6
2. Probably not	27.4	25.7	29.2		29.0	27.4	26.2	28.0		24.3	28.7	30.4	27.8	32.9
3. Don't know	30.9	29.5	31.6		29.9	28.3	34.7	30.2		31.9	29.1	23.4	32.4	24.3
4. Probably will	16.2	17.7	15.0		12.2	16.6	20.1	12.9		19.1	14.3	16.8	13.3	7.1
5. Definitely will	2.8	3.1	2.3		3.0	3.3	2.1	2.7		2.9	3.7	2.3	2.0	4.3
6. Already have	3.3	3.9	3.0		3.0	3.5	2.6	5.1		3.7	4.3	2.6	3.3	2.9
Item 12240 N(Wtd)	2867	1344	1482		632	905	919	410		1107	509	303	510	70

CAUTION: Items were rearranged after 1975; changes in context may produce spurious "trends" (see page 12).

QUESTIONNAIRE FORM 5 1975	TOTAL	SEX			REGION					ILLICIT DRUG USE: LIFETIME				
		M	F		NE	NC	S	W		None	Mari-juana Only	Few Pills	More Pills	Any Her-oin
Weighted No. of Cases:	3046	1413	1545		668	970	980	428		1136	516	309	523	73
% of Weighted Total:	100.0	46.4	50.7		21.9	31.8	32.2	14.1		37.3	16.9	10.1	17.2	2.4

A20F: Citizen lobbies (Common Cause, Public Citizen, etc.)?

1. Definitely not	7.7	9.4	6.3		7.8	7.9	7.1	8.6		7.3	8.8	5.3	8.6	14.3
2. Probably not	21.4	20.0	22.8		22.5	21.9	20.6	20.3		21.9	20.5	23.5	21.0	20.0
3. Don't know	47.7	45.7	49.2		45.7	47.8	48.8	48.0		49.7	44.8	48.7	46.3	32.9
4. Probably will	18.1	18.9	17.4		17.6	17.1	19.1	19.1		16.0	21.1	19.2	19.2	17.1
5. Definitely will	3.9	4.4	3.4		5.1	4.5	3.3	2.2		3.5	4.3	3.3	3.1	10.0
6. Already have	1.2	1.6	.8		1.3	.8	1.4	1.5		1.6	.4	.3	1.6	4.3
Item 12250 N(Wtd)	2871	1345	1487		632	910	921	408		1109	511	302	510	70

A20G: Charities to help fight diseases (Cancer, Heart Disease, etc.)?

1. Definitely not	1.4	2.2	.8		1.6	1.8	.9	2.0		1.2	2.3	.7	1.0	2.9
2. Probably not	1.8	2.8	1.0		2.5	2.5	.5	2.2		.9	3.3	2.6	1.0	7.1
3. Don't know	8.2	11.1	5.2		9.1	7.3	7.4	10.8		7.1	7.8	5.3	9.6	12.9
4. Probably will	33.3	40.7	26.7		33.4	34.1	29.0	41.3		33.2	33.7	30.4	30.7	38.6
5. Definitely will	30.5	25.3	35.4		27.7	31.4	34.3	24.7		33.3	30.3	28.4	29.7	17.1
6. Already have	24.7	18.0	30.9		25.7	22.9	28.1	19.1		24.3	22.5	33.0	27.9	20.0
Item 12260 N(Wtd)	2877	1345	1493		638	905	925	409		1111	511	303	512	70

A20H: Organizations concerned with population problems (Planned Parenthood, ZPG, etc.)?

1. Definitely not	5.9	7.6	4.4		5.2	6.9	4.3	8.1		6.1	5.5	5.0	4.3	18.6
2. Probably not	14.1	16.0	12.6		16.8	13.3	12.2	15.9		16.9	16.2	12.9	10.7	10.0
3. Don't know	38.8	42.8	34.9		41.4	38.5	39.4	33.7		39.5	36.2	37.3	37.0	30.0
4. Probably will	28.0	24.8	30.8		24.7	27.3	30.4	29.3		25.4	29.7	27.1	31.4	24.3
5. Definitely will	11.6	7.3	15.6		10.7	11.8	12.5	10.8		10.8	11.4	15.2	13.5	14.3
6. Already have	1.7	1.4	1.8		1.3	2.3	1.2	2.0		1.2	1.0	2.3	3.1	1.4
Item 12270 N(Wtd)	2880	1350	1489		636	912	923	409		1113	511	303	513	70

A20I: Organizations concerned with environmental problems (Sierra Club, Friends of Earth, etc.)?

1. Definitely not	4.8	5.6	4.2		5.7	5.4	3.8	4.4		4.4	4.5	3.3	5.1	12.9
2. Probably not	11.9	11.7	12.2		11.5	11.0	13.4	11.0		11.0	15.0	10.6	11.9	8.6
3. Don't know	37.6	35.7	39.0		33.3	41.3	39.8	31.3		40.3	32.5	37.4	33.7	31.4
4. Probably will	28.6	28.6	28.7		29.7	26.5	27.4	34.2		30.0	28.2	29.1	29.8	22.9
5. Definitely will	13.4	13.8	13.0		16.0	12.6	12.3	13.4		11.0	16.4	14.6	14.6	20.0
6. Already have	3.8	4.7	2.9		3.9	3.2	3.3	5.6		3.2	3.4	5.0	5.1	4.3
Item 12280 N(Wtd)	2873	1345	1488		636	908	921	409		1114	507	302	513	70

Now we have a different kind of question.

A21: These questions are about whether you think women are discriminated against in each of the following areas. How many women are discriminated against... ‡

A21A: In getting a college education?

1. None ‡	34.6	39.0	30.6		35.4	33.6	36.5	31.6		33.4	34.1	40.2	35.8	43.5
2. A few ‡	27.2	26.3	28.1		30.0	28.9	24.6	25.1		26.5	30.2	27.5	27.2	21.7
3. Some	18.9	15.3	22.0		16.5	19.2	19.1	21.2		20.6	17.1	20.3	18.9	10.1
4. Many ‡	4.4	3.1	5.5		3.8	4.3	4.5	5.1		4.7	4.3	2.6	4.5	7.2
5. Most ‡	1.2	1.0	1.4		.6	.9	2.1	.7		1.3	.6	1.0	.6	1.4
8. Don't know	13.8	15.3	12.5		13.7	13.3	13.2	16.3		13.5	13.7	8.8	13.0	15.9
Item 12290 N(Wtd)	2888	1348	1500		636	915	926	411		1115	510	306	514	69

‡ = Wording changed in subsequent years.

CAUTION: Items were rearranged after 1975; changes in context may produce spurious "trends" (see page 12).

QUESTIONNAIRE FORM 5 1975	TOTAL	SEX			REGION					ILLICIT DRUG USE: LIFETIME				
		M	F		NE	NC	S	W		None	Mari-juana Only	Few Pills	More Pills	Any Her-oin
Weighted No. of Cases:	3046	1413	1545		668	970	980	428		1136	516	309	523	73
% of Weighted Total:	100.0	46.4	50.7		21.9	31.8	32.2	14.1		37.3	16.9	10.1	17.2	2.4
A21B: In gaining positions of leadership over men and women?														
1. None ‡	4.8	6.6	3.3		4.1	4.1	5.9	5.1		5.0	4.1	6.9	3.9	8.7
2. A few ‡	16.4	20.4	12.4		17.0	14.4	17.7	16.6		14.9	21.6	15.7	15.0	20.3
3. Some	25.8	27.0	24.4		24.2	28.3	22.7	30.0		26.1	23.8	24.3	27.6	27.5
4. Many ‡	30.6	27.1	34.2		32.9	30.4	30.2	28.0		30.3	31.4	32.8	31.7	21.7
5. Most ‡	13.6	9.0	17.8		14.5	13.0	14.1	12.2		15.6	12.6	14.4	12.6	4.3
8. Don't know	8.9	9.9	7.9		7.4	9.8	9.2	8.3		8.1	6.7	5.9	9.5	15.9
Item 12300 N(Wtd)	2880	1343	1497		636	908	926	410		1113	509	305	515	69
A21C: In obtaining executive positions in business?														
1. None ‡	5.9	6.5	5.3		5.4	4.4	7.5	6.2		5.5	6.9	5.9	6.2	11.6
2. A few ‡	14.7	15.0	14.2		12.8	15.0	16.1	14.1		14.0	14.2	14.4	15.1	17.4
3. Some	24.1	25.6	22.5		24.5	25.3	22.1	25.7		24.7	23.7	23.0	22.3	30.4
4. Many ‡	29.8	28.9	31.0		32.4	31.5	27.9	25.9		30.1	29.8	32.1	32.0	20.3
5. Most ‡	16.0	12.9	18.9		15.2	15.2	17.0	16.8		17.0	14.6	20.0	16.5	8.7
8. Don't know	9.5	11.2	7.9		9.8	8.7	9.3	11.4		8.8	10.8	4.9	7.8	11.6
Item 12310 N(Wtd)	2880	1344	1499		633	913	928	405		1116	507	305	516	69
A21D: In obtaining top jobs in the professions?														
1. None ‡	7.6	8.4	6.9		6.0	7.0	9.6	6.6		6.8	8.6	6.6	7.8	14.5
2. A few ‡	16.6	16.7	16.6		18.3	14.7	17.9	15.4		17.0	18.6	13.1	16.0	18.8
3. Some	25.7	27.6	23.8		26.7	25.1	25.1	26.7		25.9	23.7	25.9	28.3	27.5
4. Many ‡	27.3	25.4	28.9		27.3	29.7	26.0	24.8		28.3	29.5	31.1	23.3	21.7
5. Most ‡	14.2	11.4	17.0		13.7	14.7	13.6	15.0		14.4	11.5	16.1	16.1	4.3
8. Don't know	8.6	10.6	6.9		7.7	8.6	7.9	11.3		7.5	8.0	6.9	9.3	13.0
Item 12320 N(Wtd)	2880	1345	1497		633	911	927	408		1116	511	305	515	69
A21E: In getting skilled labor jobs?														
1. None ‡	8.1	9.5	6.9		6.0	8.6	9.3	7.6		7.7	7.8	5.9	8.7	11.6
2. A few ‡	17.7	17.8	17.3		18.2	17.4	18.3	16.3		17.3	17.0	21.0	17.1	24.6
3. Some	26.9	28.3	25.8		28.3	24.8	27.8	27.8		27.6	26.2	27.2	25.6	26.1
4. Many ‡	24.3	23.1	25.5		23.4	26.5	22.5	24.9		24.6	26.6	25.6	25.8	10.1
5. Most ‡	11.8	10.4	13.2		13.8	10.7	11.8	11.1		12.8	11.0	10.2	11.7	10.1
8. Don't know	11.2	11.0	11.3		10.4	12.1	10.4	12.3		10.0	11.2	9.8	10.9	18.8
Item 12330 N(Wtd)	2872	1341	1493		632	910	924	406		1111	511	305	515	69
A21F: In getting elected to political office?														
1. None ‡	4.8	7.1	2.9		3.9	5.4	5.2	4.2		4.7	4.3	5.6	4.3	10.1
2. A few ‡	14.0	18.2	9.8		13.7	11.9	15.0	17.0		13.0	17.1	14.7	11.1	18.8
3. Some	21.1	24.2	18.1		22.4	17.8	23.6	20.9		20.2	21.8	22.2	20.0	20.3
4. Many ‡	26.6	22.4	30.6		27.4	28.5	25.3	24.3		27.8	27.5	25.2	28.4	15.9
5. Most ‡	24.4	18.7	29.6		25.0	27.8	21.4	22.6		25.6	21.4	24.2	28.4	23.2
8. Don't know	9.1	9.5	8.9		7.6	8.8	9.6	11.1		8.7	8.0	8.2	8.0	11.6
Item 12340 N(Wtd)	2879	1343	1498		635	910	928	407		1117	510	306	514	69
A21G: In getting equal pay for equal work?														
1. None ‡	9.8	13.7	6.4		8.8	10.2	11.3	7.1		8.7	11.9	7.8	9.2	18.8
2. A few ‡	18.6	21.4	15.9		18.9	17.7	18.8	19.8		17.5	18.8	23.9	15.8	29.0
3. Some	22.4	23.7	21.0		23.7	21.9	20.3	26.2		21.9	21.1	25.2	24.2	20.3
4. Many ‡	24.2	19.3	28.8		26.6	26.4	21.3	22.5		25.3	24.9	22.5	28.5	8.7
5. Most ‡	18.0	13.4	22.3		14.6	16.3	22.3	17.4		20.1	14.9	16.0	16.4	13.0
8. Don't know	6.9	8.5	5.6		7.5	7.6	6.0	6.8		6.5	8.2	4.6	6.0	8.7
Item 12350 N(Wtd)	2882	1342	1501		636	910	927	409		1119	511	306	513	69

‡ = Wording changed in subsequent years.

CAUTION: Items were rearranged after 1975; changes in context may produce spurious "trends" (see page 12).

QUESTIONNAIRE FORM 5 1975	TOTAL	SEX			REGION					ILLICIT DRUG USE: LIFETIME				
		M	F		NE	NC	S	W		None	Mari-juana Only	Few Pills	More Pills	Any Her-oin
Weighted No. of Cases:	3046	1413	1545		668	970	980	428		1136	516	309	523	73
% of Weighted Total:	100.0	46.4	50.7		21.9	31.8	32.2	14.1		37.3	16.9	10.1	17.2	2.4
A22: Do you have a driver's license?														
1. Yes	88.7	93.3	84.3		83.8	92.4	88.6	88.0		86.9	89.6	91.6	91.7	92.8
2. No, but I soon will-- GO TO Q.A27	8.7	5.8	11.7		13.6	5.9	7.4	10.3		9.9	8.2	8.1	6.9	4.3
3. No--GO TO Q.A27	2.6	.9	4.0		2.4	1.7	4.0	1.8		3.2	2.2	.3	1.6	1.4
Item 11960 N(Wtd)	2818	1332	1448		625	891	903	400		1098	500	297	508	69
A23: Do you own a car?														
1. Yes	45.4	57.1	33.3		39.1	43.7	52.8	42.0		40.2	47.4	44.5	48.0	59.4
2. No, but I expect to own one in another year or two	34.2	29.1	39.2		36.6	33.3	31.1	39.7		33.2	35.1	31.4	36.8	37.5
3. No	20.4	13.8	27.5		24.2	23.1	16.1	18.3		26.7	17.4	24.1	15.0	3.1
Item 11970 N(Wtd) ★	2505	1244	1224		524	824	801	355		956	447	274	467	64
A24: Are you able to use a car belonging to your parents when ‡ you want to?														
1. Yes, whenever I wish	31.2	31.0	31.0		27.3	29.8	35.1	31.3		33.0	30.8	21.4	31.7	42.2
2. Yes, most of the time	47.4	46.6	48.5		46.1	49.4	46.0	47.6		50.4	47.8	52.0	41.3	26.6
3. Sometimes	13.1	14.5	11.9		16.5	13.2	12.0	10.3		10.6	13.0	17.3	14.2	25.0
4. Rarely	5.4	4.8	5.8		6.1	4.4	5.2	7.1		4.4	4.8	5.9	7.9	3.1
5. Never	3.0	3.1	2.8		4.1	3.1	1.8	3.7		1.6	3.4	3.0	5.0	3.1
Item 11980 N(Wtd) ★	2456	1224	1198		510	812	783	351		939	439	271	458	64
A35: How do you feel about each of the following?														
A35A: How much do you enjoy shopping for things like clothes, records, sporting goods, and books?														
1. Not at all	2.3	4.0	.9		4.1	2.5	1.0	2.2		2.2	3.5	2.0	1.4	9.9
2. Not very much	12.7	19.6	6.3		11.4	14.8	10.1	15.5		12.3	12.5	12.4	12.4	14.1
3. Pretty much	38.4	48.1	29.7		36.9	41.1	35.2	41.8		38.8	37.0	39.2	38.6	45.1
4. Very much	46.7	28.3	63.2		47.4	41.6	53.7	40.3		46.7	47.0	46.4	47.7	31.0
Item 12020 N(Wtd)	2842	1323	1487		639	891	907	407		1126	513	306	518	71
A35B: How much do you care about having the latest fashion in your clothes, records, leisure activities, and so on?														
1. Not at all	4.4	6.2	2.8		5.0	4.4	3.4	5.4		4.3	3.9	5.2	4.2	9.9
2. Not very much	27.0	31.2	23.3		29.0	26.7	22.8	33.6		30.3	24.3	26.1	26.3	15.5
3. Pretty much	39.8	40.2	39.6		36.7	44.4	37.3	39.8		41.6	40.9	38.2	37.1	52.1
4. Very much	28.9	22.5	34.3		29.0	24.6	36.4	21.0		23.8	31.1	30.1	32.4	23.9
Item 12030 N(Wtd)	2835	1317	1486		637	886	907	405		1124	511	306	518	71
A35C: How much do you care about whether your family has most of the things your friends and neighbors have?														
1. Not at all	25.3	20.8	29.3		28.6	27.7	19.0	28.8		24.6	21.7	24.8	29.3	36.6
2. Not very much	49.8	51.3	48.1		50.9	49.1	49.2	50.9		51.6	51.3	49.0	48.6	35.2
3. Pretty much	19.1	21.9	16.6		15.7	17.9	24.0	16.1		18.5	21.3	20.9	17.2	14.1
4. Very much	5.9	5.9	5.9		4.9	5.4	7.9	4.2		5.3	5.7	5.6	4.8	15.5
Item 12040 N(Wtd)	2826	1310	1484		637	882	904	403		1120	511	306	518	71
A36: When you are older, do you expect to own more possessions than your parents do now, or about the same, or less?														

★=excludes respondents for whom question was inappropriate.   ‡=Wording changed in subsequent years.

CAUTION: Items were rearranged after 1975; changes in context may produce spurious "trends" (see page 12).

QUESTIONNAIRE FORM 5 1975	TOTAL	SEX			REGION					ILLICIT DRUG USE: LIFETIME				
		M	F		NE	NC	S	W		None	Mari- juana Only	Few Pills	More Pills	Any Her- oin
Weighted No. of Cases:	3046	1413	1545		668	970	980	428		1136	516	309	523	73
% of Weighted Total:	100.0	46.4	50.7		21.9	31.8	32.2	14.1		37.3	16.9	10.1	17.2	2.4

I expect to own...

	TOTAL	M	F		NE	NC	S	W		None	Mari- juana Only	Few Pills	More Pills	Any Her- oin
1. Much less than my parents	2.5	2.5	2.4		1.9	2.5	2.0	4.0		2.4	2.0	1.3	3.3	5.6
2. Somewhat less than my parents	11.3	10.3	12.4		9.4	14.0	7.9	15.8		11.5	9.0	11.5	14.6	11.3
3. About as much as my parents	42.5	36.7	47.5		42.7	39.8	44.0	44.4		46.2	40.7	42.8	37.8	32.4
4. Somewhat more than my parents	35.0	39.3	31.2		35.3	36.5	36.8	27.6		33.0	37.4	37.5	34.3	28.2
5. Much more than my parents	8.8	11.2	6.7		10.5	7.2	9.2	8.3		7.0	11.0	6.6	10.1	22.5
Item 12050 N(Wtd)	2808	1305	1473		637	880	894	399		1119	511	304	513	71

A37: Compared with your parents, what is the smallest amount that you could be content or satisfied to own?

The least I could be content to own is...

	TOTAL	M	F		NE	NC	S	W		None	Mari- juana Only	Few Pills	More Pills	Any Her- oin
1. Much less than my parents	12.6	11.6	13.5		9.7	12.8	11.0	20.0		10.9	13.9	11.6	16.3	23.9
2. Somewhat less than my parents	35.1	32.6	37.4		33.4	38.8	31.7	37.0		37.6	33.9	38.7	32.9	23.9
3. About as much as my parents	38.8	40.2	37.4		42.4	36.9	41.7	31.1		39.0	39.3	39.4	35.7	28.2
4. Somewhat more than my parents	10.7	12.7	9.0		11.4	9.7	11.8	9.4		9.6	10.5	8.6	12.5	16.9
5. Much more than my parents	2.8	2.9	2.7		2.9	1.8	3.9	2.5		2.9	2.4	2.0	2.5	7.0
Item 12060 N(Wtd)	2767	1288	1448		616	873	883	395		1104	504	302	510	71

Do you agree or disagree with each statement below?

A39A: I take a positive attitude toward myself

	TOTAL	M	F		NE	NC	S	W		None	Mari- juana Only	Few Pills	More Pills	Any Her- oin
1. Disagree	2.8	1.9	3.8		4.9	2.1	2.0	2.8		2.4	1.6	4.3	4.1	4.2
2. Mostly disagree	6.8	5.8	7.8		8.3	7.4	5.4	6.1		6.3	5.5	4.9	8.4	15.5
3. Neither	15.2	15.3	14.8		15.7	13.6	16.5	15.1		15.5	15.5	15.7	15.1	14.1
4. Mostly agree	44.6	43.8	45.3		41.5	49.2	40.6	48.6		42.4	46.7	52.5	46.8	36.6
5. Agree	30.6	33.4	28.3		29.6	27.7	35.5	27.4		33.4	30.6	23.0	25.6	29.6
Item 12550 N(Wtd)	2779	1289	1462		629	874	885	391		1119	510	305	511	71

A39B: Good luck is more important than hard work for success

	TOTAL	M	F		NE	NC	S	W		None	Mari- juana Only	Few Pills	More Pills	Any Her- oin
1. Disagree	37.8	33.6	41.5		37.8	35.9	41.2	33.9		37.6	37.6	38.2	40.9	33.8
2. Mostly disagree	36.8	37.1	36.5		37.8	38.3	32.5	41.6		37.5	36.4	40.5	35.4	29.6
3. Neither	15.6	16.9	14.5		13.7	16.6	15.3	17.1		16.8	14.8	12.1	14.7	12.7
4. Mostly agree	6.8	8.8	4.9		7.2	6.0	7.5	6.4		5.0	8.1	6.5	6.3	15.5
5. Agree	3.0	3.5	2.5		3.5	3.0	3.5	1.0		3.1	3.0	2.6	2.5	8.5
Item 12560 N(Wtd)	2773	1283	1461		627	871	884	392		1116	508	306	511	71

A39C: I feel I am a person of worth, on an equal plane with others

	TOTAL	M	F		NE	NC	S	W		None	Mari- juana Only	Few Pills	More Pills	Any Her- oin
1. Disagree	1.7	1.2	2.2		2.6	1.0	1.5	2.3		1.9	1.2	2.0	1.2	5.6
2. Mostly disagree	3.9	3.4	4.4		4.8	3.6	3.8	3.9		3.1	3.5	3.6	5.1	4.2
3. Neither	11.6	10.8	12.1		11.0	14.1	10.1	10.3		10.3	13.1	8.9	13.1	11.3
4. Mostly agree	41.8	42.5	41.1		40.4	44.9	39.2	42.8		43.9	39.8	45.4	39.7	42.3
5. Agree	41.0	42.2	40.3		41.2	36.3	45.6	41.0		40.7	42.5	40.5	40.9	39.4
Item 12570 N(Wtd)	2765	1281	1456		626	870	880	388		1118	510	304	511	71

A39D: I am able to do things as well as most other people

	TOTAL	M	F		NE	NC	S	W		None	Mari- juana Only	Few Pills	More Pills	Any Her- oin
1. Disagree	1.1	.8	1.4		1.3	1.3	1.0	.5		1.4	.6	1.0	1.4	-
2. Mostly disagree	3.1	2.4	3.6		3.3	3.7	2.9	2.1		2.0	2.9	2.6	3.5	11.3
3. Neither	8.0	7.3	8.3		7.0	9.6	5.9	10.8		7.6	7.1	6.9	9.0	9.9
4. Mostly agree	46.6	44.8	48.5		47.5	48.2	46.0	43.1		48.6	44.0	52.3	47.0	36.6
5. Agree	41.1	44.7	38.1		40.8	37.2	44.1	43.3		40.4	45.2	36.9	39.1	42.3
Item 12580 N(Wtd)	2765	1275	1463		627	865	883	390		1116	509	306	509	71

CAUTION: Items were rearranged after 1975; changes in context may produce spurious "trends" (see page 12).

QUESTIONNAIRE FORM 5 1975	TOTAL	SEX			REGION					ILLICIT DRUG USE: LIFETIME				
		M	F		NE	NC	S	W		None	Marijuana Only	Few Pills	More Pills	Any Heroin
Weighted No. of Cases:	3046	1413	1545		668	970	980	428		1136	516	309	523	73
% of Weighted Total:	100.0	46.4	50.7		21.9	31.8	32.2	14.1		37.3	16.9	10.1	17.2	2.4

A39E: Every time I try to get ahead, something or somebody stops me

1. Disagree	17.0	16.2	18.1		19.9	14.9	15.7	20.2		18.7	17.3	20.7	14.5	16.9
2. Mostly disagree	32.9	32.0	33.6		34.2	32.8	31.1	34.8		35.0	35.6	34.9	30.2	14.1
3. Neither	26.6	26.3	26.7		24.8	26.6	26.2	30.4		25.2	26.0	25.7	29.0	18.3
4. Mostly agree	17.0	18.3	15.7		13.0	19.8	20.1	10.0		14.4	13.8	15.1	20.6	32.4
5. Agree	6.5	7.2	6.0		8.1	5.8	6.8	4.9		6.7	7.5	3.9	5.7	16.9
Item 12590 N(Wtd)	2764	1278	1456		629	865	879	391		1116	508	304	510	71

A39F: Planning only makes a person unhappy since plans hardly ever work out anyway

1. Disagree	26.8	23.8	29.7		23.3	24.9	28.8	32.2		30.5	25.9	29.5	22.5	18.3
2. Mostly disagree	33.2	34.0	32.6		32.4	35.5	31.1	34.0		34.6	34.3	31.5	33.6	23.9
3. Neither	16.9	18.2	15.5		18.3	16.1	15.4	19.8		15.2	17.8	15.1	19.0	15.5
4. Mostly agree	16.0	18.1	14.0		17.2	17.2	16.5	10.1		13.6	15.0	17.0	17.8	26.8
5. Agree	7.2	6.0	8.3		8.8	6.3	8.2	3.9		6.2	6.9	6.6	7.1	15.5
Item 12600 N(Wtd)	2753	1272	1453		627	859	878	388		1112	505	305	506	71

A39G: People who accept their condition in life are happier than those who try to change things

1. Disagree	15.3	15.2	15.5		17.3	12.8	16.0	15.9		15.0	17.4	15.5	14.2	12.7
2. Mostly disagree	25.9	25.8	25.8		26.8	26.0	23.9	28.8		26.7	24.3	27.6	27.8	22.5
3. Neither	22.4	24.3	20.7		21.6	24.7	19.7	24.7		23.2	19.1	20.4	22.0	22.5
4. Mostly agree	21.7	22.8	20.7		20.8	21.7	24.1	17.5		20.6	23.3	21.4	22.6	25.4
5. Agree	14.7	11.8	17.4		13.6	14.7	16.2	13.1		14.4	16.0	15.5	13.4	18.3
Item 12610 N(Wtd)	2747	1267	1452		624	857	877	389		1115	507	304	508	71

A39H: On the whole, I'm satisfied with myself

1. Disagree	2.9	3.2	2.7		4.2	2.6	2.9	1.8		2.1	2.4	4.3	4.3	5.7
2. Mostly disagree	7.5	7.6	7.4		8.2	8.0	5.9	8.8		5.9	6.9	7.2	10.7	10.0
3. Neither	11.8	11.9	11.1		12.5	13.8	9.0	12.7		10.5	10.1	13.1	13.6	17.1
4. Mostly agree	43.1	44.0	42.6		42.5	42.7	44.5	41.7		44.7	43.2	43.0	43.7	34.3
5. Agree	34.7	33.2	36.3		32.7	32.9	37.7	35.0		36.8	37.7	32.5	27.9	34.3
Item 12620 N(Wtd)	2746	1268	1450		623	860	877	386		1113	507	305	506	70

A39I: People like me don't have much of a chance to be successful in life

1. Disagree	51.9	49.4	54.4		51.6	46.6	55.0	57.3		52.5	56.5	57.4	48.1	45.1
2. Mostly disagree	29.0	31.2	27.2		30.3	34.1	25.1	24.7		27.8	29.8	28.5	31.4	32.4
3. Neither	12.5	12.4	12.3		11.5	13.0	12.0	14.1		12.7	8.9	9.2	15.2	9.9
4. Mostly agree	4.5	4.9	4.1		4.3	4.2	5.6	2.8		4.1	4.2	3.6	4.3	11.3
5. Agree	2.0	2.2	1.9		2.1	2.1	2.4	.8		2.9	.8	1.0	1.0	2.8
Item 12630 N(Wtd)	2745	1266	1451		624	856	877	389		1117	503	305	507	71

A40: Some people think about what's going on in government very often, and others are not that interested. How much of an interest do you take in government and current events?

1. No interest at all	4.5	5.2	3.7		5.5	5.3	4.3	1.8		3.5	3.5	5.6	5.1	15.5
2. Very little interest	18.9	15.6	21.7		22.3	18.5	17.5	17.8		14.9	16.3	23.7	24.7	25.4
3. Some interest	47.0	42.7	50.8		46.8	49.1	44.7	47.9		50.4	49.2	46.1	40.2	39.4
4. A lot of interest	20.9	24.4	17.7		18.0	19.9	22.2	24.2		21.5	22.6	17.4	22.5	16.9
5. A very great interest	8.8	12.0	6.1		7.4	7.1	11.5	8.2		9.7	8.3	6.9	7.3	4.2
Item 6330 N(Wtd)	2743	1261	1454		618	856	882	388		1123	508	304	507	71

CAUTION: Items were rearranged after 1975; changes in context may produce spurious "trends" (see page 12).

	TOTAL	SEX			REGION					ILLICIT DRUG USE: LIFETIME				
QUESTIONNAIRE FORM 5 1975		M	F		NE	NC	S	W		None	Mari- juana Only	Few Pills	More Pills	Any Her- oin
Weighted No. of Cases:	3046	1413	1545		668	970	980	428		1136	516	309	523	73
% of Weighted Total:	100.0	46.4	50.7		21.9	31.8	32.2	14.1		37.3	16.9	10.1	17.2	2.4

A41: The next questions ask for your opinions on the effects of using certain drugs and other substances. First, how much do you think people risk harming themselves (physically or in other ways), if they...

A41A: Smoke one or more packs of cigarettes per day

	TOTAL	M	F		NE	NC	S	W		None	Mari- juana Only	Few Pills	More Pills	Any Her- oin
1. No risk	3.2	3.5	2.7		3.5	3.7	2.9	2.5		1.9	2.9	3.3	1.8	17.4
2. Slight risk	9.3	10.4	8.3		11.2	9.6	9.2	5.6		5.4	9.9	15.4	11.5	14.5
3. Moderate risk	34.5	35.2	33.6		33.7	36.7	34.9	30.0		30.0	36.0	37.0	42.7	34.8
4. Great risk	51.3	48.7	54.2		48.8	49.0	51.2	60.8		60.1	49.6	43.3	43.7	34.8
5. Can't say drug unfamiliar	1.7	2.2	1.3		2.7	1.2	1.8	1.0		2.7	1.4	1.0	.4	-
Item 12360 N(Wtd)	2755	1273	1451		623	862	877	393		1127	514	305	513	69

A41B: Try marijuana (pot,grass) once or twice

	TOTAL	M	F		NE	NC	S	W		None	Mari- juana Only	Few Pills	More Pills	Any Her- oin
1. No risk	39.6	42.7	36.4		51.0	39.1	29.6	45.1		15.5	56.6	47.5	68.1	75.4
2. Slight risk	26.2	24.8	27.6		25.4	25.4	28.2	24.9		28.5	27.7	30.2	20.0	8.7
3. Moderate risk	14.2	13.7	14.9		11.2	16.8	14.9	12.3		21.5	9.2	11.5	6.0	5.8
4. Great risk	15.1	13.4	16.7		8.5	14.1	21.0	14.6		26.0	4.9	8.5	4.5	10.1
5. Can't say drug unfamiliar	4.8	5.3	4.4		3.9	4.7	6.4	3.3		8.5	1.4	2.3	1.4	-
Item 12370 N(Wtd)	2751	1273	1447		623	859	878	390		1125	512	305	514	69

A41C: Smoke marijuana occasionally

	TOTAL	M	F		NE	NC	S	W		None	Mari- juana Only	Few Pills	More Pills	Any Her- oin
1. No risk	23.2	25.9	20.2		29.9	24.5	16.2	25.4		4.7	26.8	29.8	49.0	73.9
2. Slight risk	26.1	27.0	25.6		30.8	23.8	22.7	31.6		16.9	42.4	29.5	30.5	4.3
3. Moderate risk	27.4	24.9	29.8		25.0	27.8	30.5	23.8		39.3	22.1	27.5	12.7	11.6
4. Great risk	18.1	16.7	19.5		10.4	18.6	24.1	16.1		30.4	7.4	9.2	5.9	11.6
5. Can't say drug unfamiliar	5.2	5.6	4.8		3.9	5.5	6.7	3.4		8.7	1.6	3.3	2.0	-
Item 12380 N(Wtd)	2739	1265	1444		623	857	872	386		1124	512	305	512	69

A41D: Smoke marijuana regularly

	TOTAL	M	F		NE	NC	S	W		None	Mari- juana Only	Few Pills	More Pills	Any Her- oin
1. No risk	10.5	13.8	7.4		12.4	11.1	8.1	11.4		2.2	9.0	13.3	22.3	53.6
2. Slight risk	16.4	17.3	15.2		20.6	16.1	12.6	19.1		4.5	23.8	18.9	31.6	20.3
3. Moderate risk	25.1	26.0	24.3		28.5	25.6	21.2	26.9		19.4	36.5	29.6	26.0	8.7
4. Great risk	43.3	37.6	48.7		34.8	41.5	52.5	40.1		66.1	28.7	34.9	18.4	17.4
5. Can't say drug unfamiliar	4.7	5.4	4.2		3.7	5.7	5.5	2.6		7.8	2.0	3.3	2.0	-
Item 12390 N(Wtd)	2738	1267	1443		621	857	873	387		1123	512	301	512	69

A41E: Try LSD once or twice

	TOTAL	M	F		NE	NC	S	W		None	Mari- juana Only	Few Pills	More Pills	Any Her- oin
1. No risk	5.9	6.5	5.2		6.9	6.1	5.0	5.7		2.5	4.1	6.6	10.1	33.3
2. Slight risk	14.2	14.4	13.8		15.5	16.2	11.1	14.9		7.6	11.9	11.4	28.8	33.3
3. Moderate risk	22.1	20.8	23.1		25.6	24.2	16.2	24.9		18.3	25.0	29.5	25.0	17.4
4. Great risk	49.4	48.1	50.8		44.0	45.7	57.4	48.3		61.3	49.9	43.3	31.2	15.9
5. Can't say drug unfamiliar	8.4	10.1	7.1		7.9	7.8	10.3	6.4		10.4	9.0	6.2	5.1	1.4
Item 12400 N(Wtd)	2737	1267	1442		620	854	874	389		1124	511	305	513	69

A41F: Take LSD regularly

	TOTAL	M	F		NE	NC	S	W		None	Mari- juana Only	Few Pills	More Pills	Any Her- oin
1. No risk	2.6	2.8	2.2		2.4	2.9	2.5	2.1		1.6	2.3	2.3	1.6	17.4
2. Slight risk	1.5	1.8	1.1		1.8	1.9	1.1	1.0		.4	.2	1.0	4.1	11.6
3. Moderate risk	6.3	7.0	5.3		7.1	7.3	5.0	5.4		2.6	5.1	7.2	13.3	15.9
4. Great risk	81.4	77.6	85.1		81.2	79.6	81.5	85.3		85.3	84.0	83.6	75.2	53.6
5. Can't say drug unfamiliar	8.3	10.7	6.2		7.4	8.3	9.7	6.4		10.1	8.4	5.9	5.5	2.9
Item 12410 N(Wtd)	2739	1267	1444		621	854	876	388		1126	512	305	513	69

CAUTION: Items were rearranged after 1975; changes in context may produce spurious "trends" (see page 12).

QUESTIONNAIRE FORM 5 1975	TOTAL	SEX			REGION					ILLICIT DRUG USE: LIFETIME				
		M	F		NE	NC	S	W		None	Marijuana Only	Few Pills	More Pills	Any Heroin
Weighted No. of Cases:	3046	1413	1545		668	970	980	428		1136	516	309	523	73
% of Weighted Total:	100.0	46.4	50.7		21.9	31.8	32.2	14.1		37.3	16.9	10.1	17.2	2.4
A41G: Try heroin (smack,horse) once or twice														
1. No risk	3.9	4.7	3.1		4.0	4.2	3.7	3.4		1.9	3.1	4.6	4.1	33.3
2. Slight risk	7.1	7.0	7.3		8.1	6.3	6.3	9.0		4.4	4.3	9.5	13.1	17.4
3. Moderate risk	20.1	18.4	21.2		22.5	23.3	15.0	20.4		18.3	20.5	21.4	23.1	21.7
4. Great risk	60.1	58.9	61.3		57.9	57.2	64.0	61.0		65.0	63.7	57.2	53.8	27.5
5. Can't say drug unfamiliar	8.9	10.9	7.1		7.4	8.9	11.1	6.2		10.4	8.4	7.6	6.3	-
Item 12420 N(Wtd)	2731	1264	1440		618	851	875	387		1124	512	304	511	69
A41H: Take heroin occasionally														
1. No risk	2.7	3.0	2.3		2.4	3.4	2.4	2.1		2.0	2.3	2.3	1.6	19.1
2. Slight risk	1.2	1.3	1.2		1.1	1.1	1.8	.5		.8	.4	1.0	2.3	8.8
3. Moderate risk	11.9	10.4	13.0		13.7	13.2	9.2	12.1		10.0	9.4	16.2	15.0	22.1
4. Great risk	75.6	74.4	76.8		75.3	73.2	76.3	79.6		77.3	80.2	72.9	74.3	51.5
5. Can't say drug unfamiliar	8.6	10.9	6.6		7.3	9.1	10.3	5.7		10.1	7.4	7.6	6.6	-
Item 12430 N(Wtd)	2733	1264	1441		620	853	871	388		1127	511	303	513	68
A41I: Take heroin regularly														
1. No risk	2.5	2.9	2.0		2.3	2.9	2.4	1.8		1.8	2.4	2.3	1.2	14.5
2. Slight risk	.3	.5	.1		.3	.4	.3	-		-	-	-	.6	2.9
3. Moderate risk	1.5	1.6	1.4		1.5	2.1	1.3	.8		1.6	.8	.7	1.8	5.8
4. Great risk	87.2	84.4	89.8		88.5	85.8	85.5	92.2		86.7	89.4	90.2	89.2	76.8
5. Can't say drug unfamiliar	8.5	10.8	6.5		7.6	8.8	10.4	4.9		9.9	7.7	6.9	7.3	1.4
Item 12440 N(Wtd)	2728	1261	1439		616	851	873	387		1126	509	305	509	69
A41J: Try barbiturates (downers, goofballs,reds,yellows,etc.) once or twice														
1. No risk	9.1	9.6	8.6		11.8	9.9	6.7	8.6		2.9	5.5	10.8	20.0	46.4
2. Slight risk	18.1	18.0	18.0		17.9	20.3	15.7	18.7		9.7	15.8	26.9	34.2	24.6
3. Moderate risk	28.3	25.2	31.2		31.0	29.0	23.8	32.5		28.2	30.9	32.5	26.3	20.3
4. Great risk	34.8	36.6	33.3		29.2	31.5	42.5	33.8		45.9	39.5	23.3	15.1	8.7
5. Can't say drug unfamiliar	9.7	10.6	8.9		10.0	9.2	11.3	6.8		13.3	8.6	6.9	4.3	1.4
Item 12450 N(Wtd)	2723	1259	1437		619	851	868	385		1125	512	305	509	69
A41K: Take barbiturates regularly														
1. No risk	2.9	3.1	2.6		2.7	3.5	3.0	1.8		1.7	2.3	2.6	3.1	17.4
2. Slight risk	3.3	4.0	2.9		3.4	4.6	2.4	2.6		1.2	1.0	3.3	8.8	17.4
3. Moderate risk	15.4	15.6	15.0		16.5	17.3	12.4	16.3		7.7	12.7	21.4	30.9	26.1
4. Great risk	69.1	66.5	71.7		67.9	65.6	71.4	73.6		77.6	75.6	65.8	52.3	39.1
5. Can't say drug unfamiliar	9.2	10.7	7.8		9.5	9.1	10.7	5.4		11.9	8.2	7.2	4.7	-
Item 12460 N(Wtd)	2724	1258	1438		619	850	868	387		1124	512	304	511	69
A41L: Try amphetamines (uppers,pep pills,bennies,speed) once or twice														
1. No risk	10.4	10.5	10.2		12.4	11.5	7.2	11.7		2.9	5.5	11.5	26.2	44.9
2. Slight risk	17.2	17.6	16.7		17.9	17.7	15.1	19.9		9.4	14.9	25.6	32.8	18.8
3. Moderate risk	27.9	25.2	30.4		29.8	28.9	24.4	30.8		28.4	30.9	32.1	23.8	23.2
4. Great risk	35.4	36.6	34.4		31.1	33.3	41.6	32.6		46.8	39.7	24.6	13.7	13.0
5. Can't say drug unfamiliar	9.0	10.0	8.2		8.7	8.6	11.6	4.9		12.5	8.8	6.6	3.5	-
Item 12470 N(Wtd)	2727	1260	1439		620	849	872	386		1127	511	305	512	69
A41M: Take amphetamines regularly														
1. No risk	3.0	3.4	2.6		3.1	3.7	2.5	2.6		1.5	2.9	3.0	3.7	13.0
2. Slight risk	4.1	4.2	3.8		4.5	5.6	2.3	3.9		1.0	.8	2.6	13.1	24.6
3. Moderate risk	14.3	15.1	13.4		14.4	14.6	12.7	17.1		7.4	12.4	22.1	28.4	17.4
4. Great risk	69.0	66.5	71.6		68.3	67.5	69.7	71.8		77.5	74.9	64.4	50.3	44.9
5. Can't say drug unfamiliar	9.6	10.9	8.6		9.5	8.8	12.7	4.7		12.6	9.2	7.9	4.7	-
Item 12480 N(Wtd)	2716	1253	1435		618	845	867	386		1121	509	303	511	69

CAUTION: Items were rearranged after 1975; changes in context may produce spurious "trends" (see page 12).

QUESTIONNAIRE FORM 5 1975	TOTAL	SEX			REGION					ILLICIT DRUG USE: LIFETIME				
		M	F		NE	NC	S	W		None	Mari- juana Only	Few Pills	More Pills	Any Her- oin
Weighted No. of Cases:	3046	1413	1545		668	970	980	428		1136	516	309	523	73
% of Weighted Total:	100.0	46.4	50.7		21.9	31.8	32.2	14.1		37.3	16.9	10.1	17.2	2.4

A41N: Try cocaine once or twice

1. No risk	8.9	10.4	7.4		10.6	9.0	7.1	10.2		2.4	4.7	8.6	21.5	52.2
2. Slight risk	13.6	14.1	13.1		15.6	13.5	10.7	16.9		6.5	12.4	18.5	27.8	14.9
3. Moderate risk	23.9	22.5	25.1		25.3	26.9	20.1	23.7		22.4	26.9	26.4	23.7	20.9
4. Great risk	42.6	42.2	43.4		37.5	39.5	50.8	39.3		55.2	45.6	35.0	20.9	11.9
5. Can't say drug unfamiliar	10.9	10.8	11.2		11.0	11.1	11.3	9.9		13.4	10.6	11.6	6.1	-
Item 12490 N(Wtd)	2714	1254	1432		616	844	870	384		1123	509	303	511	67

A41O: Take cocaine regularly

1. No risk	3.4	4.0	2.6		3.1	3.5	3.1	3.6		1.5	2.4	3.9	4.3	23.2
2. Slight risk	2.8	3.7	2.1		3.3	3.8	1.3	3.4		.9	1.4	2.6	6.1	21.7
3. Moderate risk	10.3	11.0	9.3		13.9	9.3	8.2	11.2		3.8	8.7	13.5	24.2	11.6
4. Great risk	73.1	70.7	75.6		69.1	72.6	76.0	74.2		80.8	78.5	68.8	58.9	42.0
5. Can't say drug unfamiliar	10.5	10.6	10.4		10.6	10.8	11.4	7.8		12.9	9.3	11.2	6.5	-
Item 12500 N(Wtd)	2703	1249	1426		611	846	862	384		1117	506	304	508	69

A41P: Try one or two drinks of an alcoholic beverage (beer, wine, liquor)

1. No risk	48.3	51.8	45.3		55.4	49.4	41.8	49.4		31.5	57.2	54.6	70.3	69.6
2. Slight risk	32.1	30.3	33.5		32.1	31.3	33.3	30.9		38.3	32.0	33.9	20.7	14.5
3. Moderate risk	12.7	10.3	14.7		8.6	14.0	14.5	11.9		19.1	8.2	8.9	6.3	4.3
4. Great risk	5.3	5.8	5.0		2.8	3.7	8.1	7.3		8.4	2.3	2.3	1.6	11.6
5. Can't say drug unfamiliar	1.6	1.8	1.5		1.1	1.6	2.3	.5		2.6	.2	.3	1.0	-
Item 12510 N(Wtd)	2718	1253	1438		617	849	867	385		1125	512	304	511	69

A41Q: Take one or two drinks nearly every day

1. No risk	11.1	14.8	7.6		14.6	12.6	7.8	9.7		5.4	12.7	11.8	17.3	35.3
2. Slight risk	26.3	28.8	24.1		26.7	25.4	28.6	22.5		21.2	30.5	28.2	31.1	22.1
3. Moderate risk	39.2	36.1	42.1		42.6	40.0	34.3	43.3		41.5	39.1	43.9	36.0	27.9
4. Great risk	21.5	18.0	24.8		14.5	20.2	26.6	24.0		28.9	17.0	15.1	14.4	16.2
5. Can't say drug unfamiliar	1.8	2.2	1.5		1.6	1.8	2.6	.5		3.0	.6	1.0	1.2	-
Item 12520 N(Wtd)	2716	1255	1434		615	847	871	383		1125	511	305	508	68

A41R: Take four or five drinks nearly every day

1. No risk	4.5	6.1	2.9		5.0	5.3	3.9	3.1		2.7	3.7	4.3	4.7	24.6
2. Slight risk	7.8	10.3	5.4		9.4	8.7	6.5	6.3		5.0	9.2	7.6	12.5	13.0
3. Moderate risk	22.7	26.4	19.1		24.4	21.8	24.3	18.2		17.9	25.6	26.4	27.1	18.8
4. Great risk	63.5	55.3	71.2		59.9	62.4	63.3	71.6		71.6	60.9	61.4	55.1	43.5
5. Can't say drug unfamiliar	1.6	1.9	1.3		1.3	1.9	2.0	.8		2.8	.6	.3	.8	1.4
Item 12530 N(Wtd)	2715	1256	1433		616	848	867	384		1126	511	303	510	69

A41S: Have five or more drinks once or twice each weekend

1. No risk	10.9	14.9	7.2		13.8	12.5	8.1	8.6		4.8	11.4	10.2	18.9	33.3
2. Slight risk	19.1	22.3	16.2		24.5	18.6	17.6	14.8		12.8	26.8	19.3	25.0	23.2
3. Moderate risk	30.5	30.2	30.6		32.3	29.6	28.9	33.2		26.7	31.5	37.0	35.2	20.3
4. Great risk	37.8	30.6	44.5		27.9	37.4	42.9	42.6		53.1	29.2	32.5	20.3	18.8
5. Can't say drug unfamiliar	1.8	2.0	1.5		1.5	1.9	2.5	.5		2.5	1.2	1.0	.6	4.3
Item 12540 N(Wtd)	2715	1253	1435		616	845	869	385		1125	511	305	512	69

CAUTION: Items were rearranged after 1975; changes in context may produce spurious "trends" (see page 12).

Cross-Time Index of Questionnaire Items, 1975-1978

Introduction to the Indexing Conventions

This cross-time index of question locations is organized in numerical sequence according to item reference number, which is the unique numerical identifier assigned to each question in the study.

The Content Index may be used in two major ways:

1. **Locating a Question Across Years.** Having located a question of interest in the Descriptive Results section, the reader may determine in what other years that same question has appeared simply by looking it up here under its unique item reference number. The Index will show all years in which that item has appeared and also show its location each year (by questionnaire form, section, and item number). All items will retain their unique reference numbers in future years as well, and thus may be located in exactly the same way in subsequent volumes in this series.

EXAMPLE: A reader interested in a particular item about enjoying the fast pace of today's life would find that it has been assigned item Reference Number 1210. The index entry for item 1210 shows that this item has appeared in Section A of questionnaire Form 1 in all annual surveys in the series. Its question number was 4B in 1975 and 2B thereafter. By looking up the same item reference number in the index of any other volume of interest, the reader can ascertain the page location in that volume for the descriptive results on the same question.

2. **Locating Questions by Subject Area.** Given an interest in some particular subject area, one can quickly scan the Index to locate all questions dealing with that area. Table 3 shows the 19 general subject areas into which all items are classified, along with the alphabetical code assigned each

area. (Category A, Drugs, is further subdivided into numerically identified subcategories.)

EXAMPLE: A reader interested in items dealing with religion should first locate the relevant code in Table 3: Code G, "Religion." The second step is to scan all pages of the item index looking for entries in Column G under the heading Subject Area, noting for every item showing a G, its item reference number and page location in this volume. The reader may or may not find the abbreviated description of the item (given in the third column of the index and further described below) helpful in deciding whether to look up a particular item in the Descriptive Results section. Some of these descriptions are rather clear as to their meaning, but others are less so.

Definitions of the Column Headings

The definitions of column headings, and the conventions used for the entries in each column, are given below under the numbers indicated in the following key.

① **Item Reference Number.** A unique identification number is assigned to each question for the duration of this research and reporting series. It appears below that question in the Descriptive Results section, as well as in this index and the indices of all other volumes in the series.

② **Page Location.** The second column of the Question Index gives the page number of the present volume on which a verbatim statement of the question may be found along with this year's descriptive results.

③ **Item Description (Abbreviated).** This is a brief mnemonic description — up to 16 characters in length — which attempts to characterize the content of the question. Originally developed for question identification on OSIRIS computer files, it may in many cases allow one to determine the relevance of the question to one's own interest and thus reduce the number of irrelevant questions which must be looked up in the Descriptive Results section.

④ **Questionnaire Location by Year.** An entry is provided for every year in which an item appeared in one of the study's questionnaire forms. The six (or fewer) characters comprising the entry indicate the form in which the question appeared, the section of that form, and the question number. Take as an example the questionnaire location 1A004A. This location code indicates that the question appeared in Form 1, Section A, and was labeled as Question 4a.

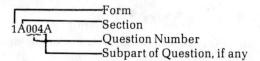

Occasionally an entry will be enclosed in parentheses. This indicates that there was a change (usually minor) in the wording of the question and/or the answer alternatives in subsequent years.

A form number (ranging from 1 to 5) is usually shown in the first character location. However, two substitute characters will replace the form number at times:

+ A plus sign indicates that the item appeared in all five forms that year and that it appeared in the same location on all forms.

* An asterisk indicates that the item appeared in four forms (Forms 2 through 5) and in the same location on all forms.

⑤ **Subject Area.** Table 3 shows the subject content areas which have been distinguished here and gives the alphabetical code assigned to each of them. Every question item in the index has been classified into one or more of the subject areas, and the alphabetical codes for those subject areas are printed in the appropriate column(s) next to each item under the general heading "Subject Area." A separate column has been assigned to each subject area code to facilitate rapid scanning. (Note that area A, dealing with drugs, has been given numerically identified subcategories because there were so many questions dealing with this general subject area.)

Figure 2

Guide to Cross-Time Index

① ITEM REFERENCE NUMBER	② PAGE LOCATION (IN THIS VOLUME)	③ ITEM DESCRIPTION (ABBREVIATED)	④ QUESTIONNAIRE LOCATION BY YEAR (FORM, SECTION, AND QUESTION NUMBER) 1975	1976	1977	1978	⑤ SUBJECT AREA A	B	C	D	E	F	G	H	I	J	K	L	M	N	O	P	Q	R	S
10		R'S BIRTH YEAR		+C001	+C001	+C001																		R	
20		R'S BIRTH MONTH		+C002	+C002	+C002																		R	
30		R'S SEX		+C003	+C003	+C003																		R	
40		R'S RACE		+C004	+C004	+C004																		R	
50		R SPD >TIM R-URB		+C005	+C005	+C005																		R	
60		R NOT MARRIED		+C006	+C006	+C006					D													R	
80		R'S HSHLD ALONE		+C007A	+C007A	+C007A														M				R	
90		R'S HSHLD FATHER		+C007B	+C007B	+C007B														M				R	
100		R'S HSHLD MOTHER		+C007C	+C007C	+C007C														M				R	
110		R'S HSHLD BR/SR		+C007D	+C007D	+C007D														M				R	
120		R'S HSHLD GRPRNT		+C007E	+C007E	+C007E														M				R	
130		R'S HSHLD SPOUSE		+C007F	+C007F	+C007F														M				R	
140		R'S HSHLD CHLDRN		+C007G	+C007G	+C007G														M				R	
150		R'S HSHLD RELTVS		+C007H	+C007H	+C007H														M				R	
160		R'S HSHLD NONRLT		+C007I	+C007I	+C007I														M				R	
310		FATHR EDUC LEVEL		+C008	+C008	+C008			B															R	
320		MOTHR EDUC LEVEL		+C009	+C009	+C009			B															R	
330		MOTH PD JB R YNG		+C010	+C010	+C010				C														R	
340		R'S POLTL PRFNC		+C011	+C011	+C011									H									R	
350		R'POL BLF RADCL		+C012	+C012	+C012									H									R	
360		R'S RELGS PRFNC		+C013A	+C013A	+C013A								G										R	
370		R'ATTND REL SVC		+C013B	+C013B	+C013B								G										R	
380		RLGN IMP R'S LF		+C013C	+C013C	+C013C								G										R	
390		WHEN R XPCT GRAD		+C014	+C014	+C014			B															R	
400		R'S HS PROGRAM		+C015	+C015	+C015			B															R	
410		RT SF SCH AB>AVG		+C016	+C016	+C016																		R	
420		RT SF INTELL>AVG		+C017	+C017	+C017																		R	
430		#DA/4W SC MS ILL		+C018A	+C018A	+C018A			B																
440		#DA/4W SC MS CUT		+C018B	+C018B	+C018B			B																
450		#DA/4W SC MS OTH		+C018C	+C018C																				
460		#DA/4W SKP CLASS		+C019																				
470		R HS GRADE/D=1		+C0..																			R	
480		R WL DO VOC/TEC																					R	
490		R WL DO ARMD FC																						
500		R WL DO 2YR CLG																						
510		R WL DO 4YR CLG																						
520		R WL DO GRD/...																						
530		R WNT...																						

Table 3

Subject Area Key
(Referenced by letter in the Question Index)

A. **Drugs.** Drug use and related attitudes and beliefs, drug availability and exposure, surrounding conditions and social meaning of drug use. Views of significant others regarding drugs.

A01   Use of Drugs
        A01A — . . . in lifetime
        A01B — . . . in the last 12 months
        A01C — . . . in the last 30 days
        A01D — Quantity used
        A01E — How high? (How often?)
        A01F — How long high?
        A01G — Incidence of first use
        A01H — Use with other drugs
        A01I — Try to stop?
        A01J — . . . on doctor's orders?
        A01K — Bad trip?
        A01L — Kinds of drugs

A02   Exposure to Drug Use
        A02A — Friends' use of drugs
        A02B — Exposure to users

A03   Availability of Drugs

A04   Expected Future Use

A05   Conditions of Use
        A05A — Alone
        A05B — With others
        A05C — Settings
        A05D — Mode of drug administration

A06   Reasons for Use, Abstention, and Stopping

A07   Problems with Drugs

A08   Sources of Help regarding Drugs

A09   Parental Awareness of Use

A10   Drug Education

A11   Own Attitudes regarding Drugs and Drug Users
        A11A — For adults
        A11C — For own children
        A11D — Perception of drug users

A12   Others' Attitudes regarding Drugs and Drug Users
        A12A — Parents
        A12B — Friends
        A12C — Students in school
        A12D — Perception of Drug Users

Table 3 (continued)

A13   Legal Issues regarding Drugs
        A13A — Preferred legality for adults
        A13C — Own response to legalization
        A13D — Knowledge of marijuana laws

A14   Risk of Drug Harm
        A14A — To self
        A14B — To others

B. **Education.** Educational lifestyle, values, experiences, and environments. Media usage.

C. **Work and Leisure.** Vocational values, meaning of work and leisure, work and leisure activities, preferences regarding occupational characteristics and type of work setting.

D. **Sex Roles and Family.** Values, attitudes, and expectations about marriage, family structure, sex roles, and sex discrimination.

E. **Family Plans and Population Concerns.** Values, attitudes, and expectations about personal family plans. Views on sexual mores and concerns about overpopulation.

F. **Conservation, Materialism, Equity, Etc.** Values, attitudes, and expectations related to conservation, pollution, materialism, equity, and the sharing of resources. Preferences regarding type of dwelling and urbanicity.

G. **Religion.** Religious affiliation, practices, and views.

H. **Politics.** Political affiliation, activities, and views.

I. **Social Change.** Values, attitudes, and expectations about social change.

J. **Social Problems.** Concern with various social problems facing the nation and the world.

K. **Major Social Institutions.** Confidence in and commitment to various major social institutions (business, unions, branches of government, press, organized religion, military, etc.).

L. **Military.** Views about the armed services and the use of military force. Personal plans for military service.

M. **Interpersonal Relationships.** Qualitative and quantitative characteristics of cross-age and peer relationships. Interpersonal conflict.

N. **Race Relations.** Attitudes toward and experiences with other racial groups.

O. **Concern for Others.** Radius of concern for others, voluntary and charitable activities.

P. **Happiness.** Happiness and life satisfaction, overall and in specific life domains.

Q. **Other Personality Variables.** Attitudes about self (including self-esteem), locus of control, loneliness, optimism, trust in others, somatic symptoms, importance placed on various life goals, counter-culture orientation.

R. **Background and School.** Demographic and family background characteristics, curriculum and grades in high school, victimization in school.

S. **Deviant Behavior and Victimization.** Delinquent behaviors, driving violations and accidents, violations and accidents under the influence of drugs, victimization experiences.

ITEM REFERENCE NUMBER	PAGE LOCATION (IN THIS VOLUME)	ITEM DESCRIPTION (ABBREVIATED)	QUESTIONNAIRE LOCATION BY YEAR (FORM, SECTION, AND QUESTION NUMBER)				SUBJECT AREA																		
			1975	1976	1977	1978	A	B	C	D	E	F	G	H	I	J	K	L	M	N	O	P	Q	R	S
10		R'S BIRTH YEAR		+C001	+C001	+C001																		R	
20		R'S BIRTH MONTH		+C002	+C002	+C002																		R	
30		R'S SEX		+C003	+C003	+C003																		R	
40		R'S RACE		+C004	+C004	+C004																		R	
50		R SPD >TIM R-URB		+C005	+C005	+C005																		R	
60		R NOT MARRIED		+C006	+C006	+C006				D														R	
80		R'S HSHLD ALONE		+C007A	+C007A	+C007A														M				R	
90		R'S HSHLD FATHER		+C007B	+C007B	+C007B														M				R	
100		R'S HSHLD MOTHER		+C007C	+C007C	+C007C														M				R	
110		R'S HSHLD BR/SR		+C007D	+C007D	+C007D														M				R	
120		R'S HSHLD GRPRNT		+C007E	+C007E	+C007E														M				R	
130		R'S HSHLD SPOUSE		+C007F	+C007F	+C007F														M				R	
140		R'S HSHLD CHLDRN		+C007G	+C007G	+C007G														M				R	
150		R'S HSHLD RELTVS		+C007H	+C007H	+C007H														M				R	
160		R'S HSHLD NONRLT		+C007I	+C007I	+C007I														M				R	
310		FATHR EDUC LEVEL		+C008	+C008	+C008		B																R	
320		MOTHR EDUC LEVEL		+C009	+C009	+C009		B																R	
330		MOTH PD JB R YNG		+C010	+C010	+C010			C															R	
340		R'S POLTL PRFNC		+C011	+C011	+C011								H										R	
350		R'POL BLF RADCL		+C012	+C012	+C012								H										R	
360		R'S RELGS PRFNC		+C013A	+C013A	+C013A							G											R	
370		R'ATTND REL SVC		+C013B	+C013B	+C013B							G											R	
380		RLGN IMP R'S LF		+C013C	+C013C	+C013C							G											R	
390		WHEN R XPCT GRAD		+C014	+C014	+C014		B																R	
400		R'S HS PROGRAM		+C015	+C015	+C015		B																R	
410		RT SF SCH AB>AVG		+C016	+C016	+C016																		R	
420		RT SF INTELL>AVG		+C0,17	+C017	+C017																		R	
430		#DA/4W SC MS ILL		+C018A	+C018A	+C018A		B																	
440		#DA/4W SC MS CUT		+C018B	+C018B	+C018B		B																	
450		#DA/4W SC MS OTH		+C018C	+C018C	+C018C		B																	
460		#DA/4W SKP CLASS		+C019	+C019	+C019		B																	
470		R HS GRADE/D=1		+C020	+C020	+C020																		R	
480		R WL DO VOC/TEC		+C021A	+C021A	+C021A		B	C																R	
490		R WL DO ARMD FC		+C021B	+C021B	+C021B		B											L						R	
500		R WL DO 2YR CLG		+C021C	+C021C	+C021C		B																	R	
510		R WL DO 4YR CLG		+C021D	+C021D	+C021D		B																	R	
520		R WL DO GRD/PRF		+C021E	+C021E	+C021E		B																	R	
530		R WNTDO VOC/TEC		+C022A	+C022A	+C022A		B	C																R	
540		R WNTDO ARMD FC		+C022B	+C022B	+C022B		B											L						R	
550		R WNTDO 2YR CLG		+C022C	+C022C	+C022C		B																	R	
560		R WNTDO 4YR CLG		+C022D	+C022D	+C022D		B																	R	
570		R WNTDO GRD/PRF		+C022E	+C022E	+C022E		B																	R	
580		R WNTDO NONE		+C022F	+C022F	+C022F		B																	R	
590		HRS/W WRK SCHYR		+C023	+C023	+C023			C																	
600		R$/AVG WEEK JOB		+C024A	+C024A	+C024A																			R	
610		R$/AVG WEEK OTH		+C024B	+C024B	+C024B																			R	
620		#X/AV WK GO OUT		+C025	+C025	+C025			C											M					
630		#X DATE 3+/WK		+C026	+C026	+C026			C											M					
640		DRIVE>200 MI/WK		+C027	+C027	+C027						F													
650		#X/12MO R TCKTD		+C028	+C028	+C028	A07A																		S
660		#TCKTS AFT DRNK		+C029A	+C029A	+C029A	A07A																		S
670		#TCKTS AFT MARJ		+C029B	+C029B	+C029B	A07A																		S
680		#TCKTS AFT OTDG		+C029C	+C029C	+C029C	A07A																		S
690		#ACCIDNTS/12 MO		+C030	+C030	+C030	A07A																		S
700		#ACDTS AFT DRNK		+C031A	+C031A	+C031A	A07A																		S
710		#ACDTS AFT MARJ		+C031B	+C031B	+C031B	A07A																		S
720		#ACDTS AFT OTDG		+C031C	+C031C	+C031C	A07A																		S
730		R'S BRANCH SERV		+C032	+C032	+C032													L					R	
740		R XPCTS B OFFCR		+C033	+C033	+C033													L					R	
750		R XPCTS MLTR CR		+C034	+C034	+C034													L					R	
760	28	EVR SMK CIG,REGL	1A018	+B001	+B001	(+B001)	A01A																		
	16		*B01				A01A																		
780	29	#CIGS SMKD/30DAY	1A020	1B003	1B003	1B003	A01C																		
	16		*B02	*B02	*B02	*B02	A01C																		
790		EVER DRINK		*B03	*B03	*B03	A01A																		
	16		*B03				A01A																		

ITEM REFERENCE NUMBER	PAGE LOCATION (IN THIS VOLUME)	ITEM DESCRIPTION (ABBREVIATED)	QUESTIONNAIRE LOCATION BY YEAR (FORM, SECTION, AND QUESTION NUMBER)				SUBJECT AREA A B C D E F G H I J K L M N O P Q R S
			1975	1976	1977	1978	
810	30	#X DRNK/LIFETIME	1A028A	1B007A	1B007A	1B007A	A01A
	16		*B04A	*B04A	*B04A	*B04A	A01A
820	30	#X DRNK/LAST12MO	1A028B	1B007B	1B007B	1B007B	A01B
	16		*B04B	*B04B	*B04B	*B04B	A01B
830	30	#X DRNK/LAST30DA	1A028C	1B007C	1B007C	1B007C	A01C
	16		*B04C	*B04C	*B04C	*B04C	A01C
840	17	#X DRK ENF FL HI	*B05	*B05	*B05	*B05	A01E
850	31	5+DRK ROW/LST 2W	1A035	1B012	1B012	1B012	A01D
	17		*B06	*B06	*B06	*B06	A01D
860	33	#XMJ+HS/LIFETIME	1A044A				A01A
	17		*B07A	*B07A	*B07A	*B07A	A01A
870	33	#XMJ+HS/LAST12MO	1A044B				A01B
	17		*B07B	*B07B	*B07B	*B07B	A01B
880	33	#XMJ+HS/LAST30DA	1A044C				A01C
	18		*B07C	*B07C	*B07C	*B07C	A01C
890	34	#X LSD/LIFETIME	1A057A	1B029A	1B029A	1B029A	A01A
	18		*B08A	*B08A	*B08A	*B08A	A01A
900	35	#X LSD/LAST 12MO	1A057B	1B029B	1B029B	1B029B	A01B
	18		*B08B	*B08B	*B08B	*B08B	A01B
910	35	#X LSD/LAST 30DA	1A057C	1B029C	1B029C	1B029C	A01C
	18		*B08C	*B08C	*B08C	*B08C	A01C
920	36	#X PSYD/LIFETIME	1A071A	1B038A	1B038A	1B038A	A01A
	18		*B09A	*B09A	*B09A	*B09A	A01A
930	36	#X PSYD/LAST12MO	1A071B	1B038B	1B038B	1B038B	A01B
	19		*B09B	*B09B	*B09B	*B09B	A01B
940	37	#X PSYD/LAST30DA	1A071C	1B038C	1B038C	1B038C	A01C
	19		*B09C	*B09C	*B09C	*B09C	A01C
950	46	#X COKE/LIFETIME	1A144A	1B076A	1B076A	1B076A	A01A
	19		*B10A	*B10A	*B10A	*B10A	A01A
960	46	#X COKE/LAST12MO	1A144B	1B076B	1B076B	1B076B	A01B
	19		*B10B	*B10B	*B10B	*B10B	A01B
970	47	#X COKE/LAST30DA	1A144C	1B076C	1B076C	1B076C	A01C
	19		*B10C	*B10C	*B10C	*B10C	A01C
980	38	#X AMPH/LIFETIME	1A087A	1B043A	1B043A	1B043A	A01A
	20		*B11A	*B11A	*B11A	*B11A	A01A
990	38	#X AMPH/LAST12MO	1A087B	1B043B	1B043B	1B043B	A01B
	20		*B11B	*B11B	*B11B	*B11B	A01B
1000	38	#X AMPH/LAST30DA	1A087C	1B043C	1B043C	1B043C	A01C
	20		*B11C	*B11C	*B11C	*B11C	A01C
1010	40	#X QUAD/LIFETIME	1A102A	1B053A	1B053A	1B053A	A01A
	20		*B12A	*B12A	*B12A	*B12A	A01A
1020	40	#X QUAD/LAST12MO	1A102B	1B053B	1B053B	1B053B	A01B
	20		*B12B	*B12B	*B12B	*B12B	A01B
1030	41	#X QUAD/LAST30DA	1A102C	1B053C	1B053C	1B053C	A01C
	20		*B12C	*B12C	*B12C	*B12C	A01C
1040	42	#X BRBT/LIFETIME	1A116A	1B057A	1B057A	1B057A	A01A
	21		*B13A	*B13A	*B13A	*B13A	A01A
1050	42	#X BRBT/LAST12MO	1A116B	1B057B	1B057B	1B057B	A01B
	21		*B13B	*B13B	*B13B	*B13B	A01B
1060	42	#X BRBT/LAST30DA	1A116C	1B057C	1B057C	1B057C	A01C
	21		*B13C	*B13C	*B13C	*B13C	A01C
1070	44	#X TRQL/LIFETIME	1A131A	1B067A	1B067A	1B067A	A01A
	21		*B14A	*B14A	*B14A	*B14A	A01A
1080	45	#X TRQL/LAST12MO	1A131B	1B067B	1B067B	1B067B	A01B
	21		*B14B	*B14B	*B14B	*B14B	A01B
1090	45	#X TRQL/LAST30DA	1A131C	1B067C	1B067C	1B067C	A01C
	22		*B14C	*B14C	*B14C	*B14C	A01C
1100	48	#X "H"/LIFETIME	1A158A	1B085A	1B085A	1B085A	A01A
	22		*B15A	*B15A	*B15A	*B15A	A01A
1110	48	#X "H"/LAST 12MO	1A158B	1B085B	1B085B	1B085B	A01B
	22		*B15B	*B15B	*B15B	*B15B	A01B
1120	48	#X "H"/LAST 30DA	1A158C	1B085C	1B085C	1B085C	A01C
	22		*B15C	*B15C	*B15C	*B15C	A01C
1130	50	#X NARC/LIFETIME	1A173A	1B095A	1B095A	1B095A	A01A
	22		*B16A	*B16A	*B16A	*B16A	A01A
1140	50	#X NARC/LAST12MO	1A173B	1B095B	1B095B	1B095B	A01B

ITEM REFERENCE NUMBER	PAGE LOCATION (IN THIS VOLUME)	ITEM DESCRIPTION (ABBREVIATED)	QUESTIONNAIRE LOCATION BY YEAR (FORM, SECTION, AND QUESTION NUMBER) 1975	1976	1977	1978	SUBJECT AREA A	B C D E F G H I J K L M N O P Q R S
	23		*B16B	*B16B	*B16B	*B16B	A01B	
1150	51	#X NARC/LAST30DA	1A173C	1B095C	1B095C	1B095C	A01C	
	23		*B16C	*B16C	*B16C	*B16C	A01C	
1160		#X INHL/LIFETIME		*B17A	*B17A	*B17A	A01A	
1170		#X INHL/LAST12MO		*B17B	*B17B	*B17B	A01B	
1180		#X INHL/LAST30DA		*B17C	*B17C	*B17C	A01C	
1190		VRY HPY THS DAYS		+A001	+A001	+A001		P Q R
1200	24	US NEEDS PLANNG	1A004A	1A002A	1A002A	1A002A		I
1210	24	ENJOY FAST PACE	1A004B	1A002B	1A002B	1A002B		I Q
1220	24	THG CHG 2 QUICK	1A004D	1A002C	1A002C	1A002C		I Q
1230	24	X AHEAD TOUGHER	1A004G	1A002D	1A002D	1A002D		I Q
1240	24	TM SPT ADLT MST	1A006	1A003	1A003	1A003		M
1250	25	LK MR TM ADLT	1A007	1A004	1A004	1A004		M
1260	25	LK MR TM YG CHD	1A008	1A005	1A005	1A005		M
1270	25	SAT PRESENT JOB	1A009A	1A006A	1A006A	1A006A		C P
1280	25	SAT NEIGHBORHOD	1A009B	1A006B	1A006B	1A006B		P
1290	25	SAT PRSNL SAFTY	1A009C	1A006C	1A006C	1A006C		P
1300	26	SAT OWN PROP SF	1A009D	1A006D	1A006D	1A006D		P
1310	26	SAT EDUC EXPRNCS	1A009E	1A006E	1A006E	1A006E		B P
1320	26	SAT OWN FRIENDS	1A009F	1A006F	1A006F	1A006F		M P
1330	26	SAT GT ALNG PRNT	1A009G	1A006G	1A006G	1A006G		M P
1340	26	SAT YOURSELF	1A009H	1A006H	1A006H	1A006H		P Q
1350	26	SAT STD OF LVG	1A009I	1A006I	1A006I	1A006I		F P
1360	27	SAT TIME FR THGS	1A009J	1A006J	1A006J	1A006J		P
1370	27	SAT SPD LEISR	1A009K	1A006K	1A006K	1A006K		C P
1380	27	SAT LIFE AS WHLE	1A009L	1A006L	1A006L	1A006L		P
1390		SAT GOVT OPRTNG		1A006M	1A006M	1A006M		H K
1400		SAT AMT OF FUN		1A006N	1A006N	1A006N		P Q R
1410		IMP B SUCCSS WK		1A007A	1A007A	1A007A		C Q
1420		IMP GD MRRG&FAM		1A007B	1A007B	1A007B		D Q
1430		IMP LOTS OF $		1A007C	1A007C	1A007C		F Q
1440		IMP TM RCRN&HBY		1A007D	1A007D	1A007D		C Q
1450		IMP STRG FRDSHP		1A007E	1A007E	1A007E		M Q
1460		IMP STEADY WORK		1A007F	1A007F	1A007F		C Q
1470		IMP CNTRBTN SOC		1A007G	1A007G	1A007G		O Q
1480		IMP LDR COMUNTY		1A007H	1A007H	1A007H		M Q
1490		IMP CHLD BTR OPP		1A007I	1A007I	1A007I		Q
1500		IMP LIV CLS PRNT		1A007J	1A007J	1A007J		M Q
1510		IMP GT AWY AREA		1A007K	1A007K	1A007K		Q
1520		IMP CRRCT INEQL		1A007L	1A007L	1A007L		O Q
1530		IMP NEW XPRNCE		1A007M	1A007M	1A007M		Q
1540		IMP FND PRPS LF		1A007N	1A007N	1A007N		Q
1550	27	PPL CAN B TRSTD	1A010	1A008	1A008	1A008		Q
1560	27	PPL TRY B HLPFL	1A011	1A009	1A009	1A009		Q
1570	27	PPL TRY BE FAIR	1A012	1A010	1A010	1A010		Q
1580		-OBY LW=-GD CTZN		1A011A	1A011A	1A011A		H
1590		GD CTZN ALG GOVT		1A011B	1A011B	1A011B		H
1600	28	GD CTZN CHG GOVT	1A013B	1A011C	1A011C	1A011C		H
1610		VOTE->MAJ IMPCT		1A011D	1A011D	1A011D		H I
1620		CTZN GRP HV EFCT		1A011E	1A011E	1A011E		H I
1630	28	OUR SYST ST BS	1A013C	1A011F	1A011F	1A011F		H
1640	28	US NEEDS GROWTH	1A013E	1A011G	1A011G	1A011G		F
1650	24	LV THNGS TO GOD	1A004C	1A011H	1A011H	1A011H		I
1660	28	GO SCH ENJY XPR	1A013I	1A011I	1A011I	1A011I		B
1670	28	DO WL SC IMP/JB	1A013H	1A011J	1A011J	1A011J		B C
1680	29	SMK CIG DLY/12G	1A019	1B002	1B002	(1B002)	A01G	
1690	29	*TRY STP SMK&FL	1A021	1B004	1B004	1B004	A01I	
1700	29	*WNT STP SMK NW	1A022	1B005	1B005	1B005	A01I	
1710	29	NO SMK IN 5 YR	1A023	1B006	1B006	1B006	A04A	
1720		#X/YR ALC ALONE		1B008A	1B008A	1B008A	A05A	
1730		#X/YR ALC-2 PPL		1B008B	1B008B	1B008B	A05B	
1740		#X/YR ALC@PARTY		1B008C	1B008C	1B008C	A05C	
1750		#X/YR ALC-DT/SP		1B008D	1B008D	1B008D	A05B	
1760		#X/YR ALC-ADLTS		1B008E	1B008E	1B008E	A05B	
1770		#X/YR ALC-DATIM		1B008F	1B008F	1B008F	A05C	
1780		#X/YR ALC@HOME		1B008G	1B008G	1B008G	A05C	

ITEM REFERENCE NUMBER	PAGE LOCATION (IN THIS VOLUME)	ITEM DESCRIPTION (ABBREVIATED)	QUESTIONNAIRE LOCATION BY YEAR (FORM, SECTION, AND QUESTION NUMBER)				SUBJECT AREA	
			1975	1976	1977	1978	A	B C D E F G H I J K L M N O P Q R S
1790		#X/YR ALC@SCHL		1B008H	1B008H	1B008H	A05C	
1810		#X/YR ALCIN CAR		1B008I	1B008I	1B008I	A05C	
1820		ALC EXPERIMENT		1B009A	1B009A	1B009A	A06A	
1830	31	ALC RELAX	1A032A	1B009B	1B009B	1B009B	A06A	
1840	31	ALC GET HIGH	1A032B	1B009C	1B009C	1B009C	A06A	
1850	31	ALC SEEK INSGHT	1A032C	1B009D	1B009D	1B009D	A06A	
1860	31	ALC GD TM FRNDS	1A032D	1B009E	1B009E	1B009E	A06A	
1870	31	ALC FIT IN GRP	1A032E	1B009F	1B009F	1B009F	A06A	
1880	31	ALC GET AWY PRB	1A032F	1B009G	1B009G	1B009G	A06A	
1890	31	ALC BOREDOM	1A032G	1B009H	1B009H	1B009H	A06A	
1900	31	ALC ANGR&FRSTRN	1A032H	1B009I	1B009I	1B009I	A06A	
1910	31	ALC GT THRU DAY	1A032J	1B009J	1B009J	1B009J	A06A	
1920	31	ALC INCRS EF DR	1A032K	1B009K	1B009K	1B009K	A06A	
1930	31	ALC DECRS EF DR	1A032L	1B009L	1B009L	1B009L	A06A	
1940		ALC GET SLEEP		1B009M	1B009M	1B009M	A06A	
1950	31	ALC TASTES GOOD	1A032N	1B009N	1B009N	1B009N	A06A	
1960	31	ALC I AM HOOKED	1A032M	1B009O	1B009O	1B009O	A06A	
1970	31	#X DRK ENF FL 4	1A033	1B010	1B010	1B010	A01E	
1980	31	DRK AL,HI24+HR	1A034	1B011	1B011	1B011	A01F	
1990	32	#X/2W,3-4 DR RW	1A036	1B013	1B013	1B013	A01D	
2000	32	#X/2WK,2 DRK RW	1A037	1B014	1B014	1B014	A01D	
2010	32	#X/2WK,JST 1DRK	1A038	1B015	1B015	1B015	A01D	
2020	32	*TRY STP ALC&FL	1A039	1B016	1B016	1B016	A01D	
2030	32	NO ALC IN 5 YR	1A040	1B017	1B017	1B017	A04A	
2040		#X HASH/LIFETIM		1B018A	1B018A	1B018A	A01A	
2050		#X HASH/LAST12M		1B018B	1B018B	1B018B	A01B	
2060		#X HASH/LAST30D		1B018C	1B018C	1B018C	A01C	
2070		#X MARJ/LIFETIME		1B019A	1B019A	1B019A	A01A	
2080		#X MARJ/LAST12MO		1B019B	1B019B	1B019B	A01B	
2090		#X MARJ/LAST30DA		1B019C	1B019C	1B019C	A01C	
2100		#X/YR MJ ALONE		1B020A	1B020A	1B020A	A05A	
2110		#X/YR MJ-2 PPL		1B020B	1B020B	1B020B	A05B	
2120		#X/YR MJ@PARTY		1B020C	1B020C	1B020C	A05C	
2130		#X/YR MJ-DT/SP		1B020D	1B020D	1B020D	A05B	
2140		#X/YR MJ-ADLTS		1B020E	1B020E	1B020E	A05B	
2150		#X/YR MJ-DATIME		1B020F	1B020F	1B020F	A05C	
2160		#X/YR MJ@HOME		1B020G	1B020G	1B020G	A05C	
2170		#X/YR MJ@SCHL		1B020H	1B020H	1B020H	A05C	
2190		#X/YR MJIN CAR		1B020I	1B020I	1B020I	A05C	
2200		#X OVL MJ+ ALC		1B021	1B021	1B021	A06A	
2210	33	MJ EXPERIMENT	1A049A	1B022A	1B022A	1B022A	A06A	
2220	33	MJ RELAX	1A049B	1B022B	1B022B	1B022B	A06A	
2230	33	MJ GET HIGH	1A049C	1B022C	1B022C	1B022C	A06A	
2240	33	MJ SEEK INSIGHT	1A049D	1B022D	1B022D	1B022D	A06A	
2250	33	MJ GD TM FRNDS	1A049E	1B022E	1B022E	1B022E	A06A	
2260	33	MJ FIT IN GRP	1A049F	1B022F	1B022F	1B022F	A06A	
2270	33	MJ GET AWY PRB	1A049G	1B022G	1B022G	1B022G	A06A	
2280	33	MJ BOREDOM	1A049H	1B022H	1B022H	1B022H	A06A	
2290	33	MJ ANGR&FRUSTRN	1A049I	1B022I	1B022I	1B022I	A06A	
2300	33	MJ GET THRU DAY	1A049K	1B022J	1B022J	1B022J	A06A	
2310	33	MJ INCRS EF DRG	1A049L	1B022K	1B022K	1B022K	A06A	
2320	33	MJ DECRS EF DRG	1A049M	1B022L	1B022L	1B022L	A06A	
2330		MJ I AM HOOKED		1B022M	1B022M	1B022M	A06A	
2340	34	MJ/HSH,VRY HIGH	1A050	1B023	1B023	1B023	A01E	
2350	34	MJ/HSH,HI 24+HR	1A051	1B024	1B024	1B024	A01F	
2360		JOINT/DA LST MO		1B025	1B025	1B025	A01D	
2370		OZS.MJ LST MO/6		1B026	1B026	1B026	A01D	
2380	34	*TRY STP MJ &FL	1A052	1B027	1B027	1B027	A01I	
2390	34	NO MJ/HSH IN5YR	1A053	1B028	1B028	1B028	A04A	
2400		#X/YR LSD ALONE		1B030A	1B030A	1B030A	A05A	
2410		#X/YR LSD-2 PPL		1B030B	1B030B	1B030B	A05B	
2420		#X/YR LSD@PARTY		1B030C	1B030C	1B030C	A05C	
2430		#X/YR LSD-DT/SP		1B030D	1B030D	1B030D	A05B	
2440		#X/YR LSD-ADLTS		1B030E	1B030E	1B030E	A05B	
2450		#X/YR LSD-DATIM		1B030F	1B030F	1B030F	A05C	
2460		#X/YR LSD@HOME		1B030G	1B030G	1B030G	A05C	

ITEM REFERENCE NUMBER	PAGE LOCATION (IN THIS VOLUME)	ITEM DESCRIPTION (ABBREVIATED)	QUESTIONNAIRE LOCATION BY YEAR (FORM, SECTION, AND QUESTION NUMBER)				SUBJECT AREA	
			1975	1976	1977	1978	A	B C D E F G H I J K L M N O P Q R S
2470		#X/YR LSD@SCHL		1B030H	1B030H	1B030H	A05C	
2490		#X/YR LSDIN CAR		1B030I	1B030I	1B030I	A05C	
2500		#X OVL LSD+ ALC		1B031A	1B031A	1B031A	A01H	
2510		#X OVL LSD+ MJ		1B031B	1B031B	1B031B	A01H	
2520	35	LSD EXPERIMENT	1A062A	1B032A	1B032A	1B032A	A06A	
2530	35	LSD RELAX	1A062B	1B032B	1B032B	1B032B	A06A	
2540	35	LSD GET HIGH	1A062C	1B032C	1B032C	1B032C	A06A	
2550	35	LSD SEEK INSGHT	1A062D	1B032D	1B032D	1B032D	A06A	
2560	35	LSD GD TM FRNDS	1A062E	1B032E	1B032E	1B032E	A06A	
2570	35	LSD FIT IN GRP	1A062F	1B032F	1B032F	1B032F	A06A	
2580	35	LSD GT AWY PRB	1A062G	1B032G	1B032G	1B032G	A06A	
2590	35	LSD BOREDOM	1A062H	1B032H	1B032H	1B032H	A06A	
2600	35	LSD ANGR&FRSTRN	1A062I	1B032I	1B032I	1B032I	A06A	
2610	35	LSD GT THRU DAY	1A062K	1B032J	1B032J	1B032J	A06A	
2620	35	LSD INCRS EF DR	1A062L	1B032K	1B032K	1B032K	A06A	
2630	35	LSD DCRS EF DRG	1A062M	1B032L	1B032L	1B032L	A06A	
2640		LSD I AM HOOKED		1B032M	1B032M	1B032M	A06A	
2650	35	LSD,GET VERY HI	1A063	1B033	1B033	1B033	A01E	
2660	35	LSD,HIGH 24+ HR	1A064	1B034	1B034	1B034	A01F	
2670	36	1+ BAD TRIP LSD	1A065	1B035	1B035	1B035	A01K	
2680	36	*TRY STP LSD&FL	1A066	1B036	1B036	1B036	A01I	
2690	36	NO LSD IN 5 YRS	1A067	1B037	1B037	1B037	A04A	
2700	37	PSYD,GT VERY HI	1A077	1B039	1B039	1B039	A01E	
2710	37	PSYD,HI 24+ HRS	1A078	1B040	1B040	1B040	A01F	
2720	37	TKN YR,MESCALIN	1A079A	1B041A	1B041A	1B041A	A01L	
2730	37	TKN YR,PEYOTE	1A079B	1B041B	1B041B	1B041B	A01L	
2740	37	TKN YR,PSILOCYB	1A079C	1B041C	1B041C	1B041C	A01L	
2750		TKN YR,PCP		1B041D	1B041D	1B041D	A01L	
2760	37	TKN YR,CNCT THC	1A079D	1B041E	1B041E	1B041E	A01L	
2770	37	TKN YR,OTH PSYD	1A079E	1B041F	1B041F	1B041F	A01L	
2780	37	TKN YR,DK NAME	1A079F	1B041G	1B041G	1B041G	A01L	
2790	37	DR TOLD TK AMPH	1A085	1B042	1B042	1B042	A01J	
2800		#X/YR AMPH ALNE		1B044A	1B044A	1B044A	A05A	
2810		#X/YR AMPH-2PPL		1B044B	1B044B	1B044B	A05B	
2820		#X/YR AMPH@PRTY		1B044C	1B044C	1B044C	A05C	
2830		#X/YR AMPH-DT/S		1B044D	1B044D	1B044D	A05B	
2840		#X/YR AMPH-ADLT		1B044E	1B044E	1B044E	A05B	
2850		#X/YR AMPH-DATM		1B044F	1B044F	1B044F	A05C	
2860		#X/YR AMPH@HOME		1B044G	1B044G	1B044G	A05C	
2880		#X/YR AMPH@SCHL		1B044H	1B044H	1B044H	A05C	
2890		#X/YR AMPH@CAR		1B044I	1B044I	1B044I	A05C	
2900		#X OVL AMPH+ALC		1B045A	1B045A	1B045A	A01H	
2910		#X OVL AMPH+MJ		1B045B	1B045B	1B045B	A01H	
2920		#X OVL AMPH+LSD		1B045C	1B045C	1B045C	A01H	
2930		#X OVL AMPH+PSY		1B045D	1B045D	1B045D	A01H	
2940	39	AMPH EXPERIMENT	1A092A	1B046A	1B046A	1B046A	A06A	
2950	39	AMPH RELAX	1A092B	1B046B	1B046B	1B046B	A06A	
2960	39	AMPH GET HIGH	1A092C	1B046C	1B046C	1B046C	A06A	
2970	39	AMPH SK INSIGHT	1A092D	1B046D	1B046D	1B046D	A06A	
2980	39	AMPH GD TM FRND	1A092E	1B046E	1B046E	1B046E	A06A	
2990	39	AMPH FIT IN GRP	1A092F	1B046F	1B046F	1B046F	A06A	
3000	39	AMPH GT AWY PRB	1A092G	1B046G	1B046G	1B046G	A06A	
3010	39	AMPH BOREDOM	1A092H	1B046H	1B046H	1B046H	A06A	
3020	39	AMPH ANGR&FRSTN	1A092I	1B046I	1B046I	1B046I	A06A	
3030	39	AMPH GT THRU DA	1A092K	1B046J	1B046J	1B046J	A06A	
3040	39	AMPH INCR EF DR	1A092L	1B046K	1B046K	1B046K	A06A	
3050	39	AMPH DCRS EF DR	1A092M	1B046L	1B046L	1B046L	A06A	
3060	39	AMPH STAY AWAKE	1A092N	1B046M	1B046M	1B046M	A06A	
3070	39	AMPH GET>ENERGY	1A092O	1B046N	1B046N	1B046N	A06A	
3080	39	AMPH LOSE WGHT	1A092P	1B046O	1B046O	1B046O	A06A	
3090	39	AMPH I AM HOOKD	1A092Q	1B046P	1B046P	1B046P	A06A	
3100	39	AMPH,GT VERY HI	1A093	1B047	1B047	1B047	A01E	
3110	39	AMPH,HI 24+ HRS	1A094	1B048	1B048	1B048	A01F	
3120	39	TKN YR,BENZDRIN	1A095A	1B049A	1B049A	1B049A	A01L	
3130	39	TKN YR,DEXEDRIN	1A095B	1B049B	1B049B	1B049B	A01L	
3140	39	TKN YR,METHDRIN	1A095C	1B049C	1B049C	1B049C	A01L	

ITEM REFERENCE NUMBER	PAGE LOCATION (IN THIS VOLUME)	ITEM DESCRIPTION (ABBREVIATED)	QUESTIONNAIRE LOCATION BY YEAR (FORM, SECTION, AND QUESTION NUMBER)				SUBJECT AREA	
			1975	1976	1977	1978	A	B C D E F G H I J K L M N O P Q R S
3150	39	TKN YR,RITALIN	1A095D	1B049D	1B049D	1B049D	A01L	
3160	39	TKN YR,PRELUDIN	1A095E	1B049E	1B049E	1B049E	A01L	
3170	39	TKN YR,DEXAMYL	1A095F	1B049F	1B049F	1B049F	A01L	
3180	39	TKN YR,METHAMPH	1A095G	1B049G	1B049G	1B049G	A01L	
3190	39	TKN YR,OTH AMPH	1A095H	1B049H	1B049H	1B049H	A01L	
3200	39	TKN YR,DNT KN N	1A095I	1B049I	1B049I	1B049I	A01L	
3210		MTHD AMPH-MOUTH		1B050A	1B050A	1B050A	A05D	
3220		MTHD AMPH-INJCT		1B050B	1B050B	1B050B	A05D	
3230		MTHD AMPH-OTHER		1B050C	1B050C	1B050C	A05D	
3240	40	*TRY STP AMP&FL	1A096	1B051	1B051	1B051	A01I	
3250	40	NO AMPH IN 5YR	1A097	1B052	1B052	1B052	A04A	
3260	41	QUAD GT VERY HI	1A108	1B054	1B054	1B054	A01E	
3270	41	QUAD,HI 24+ HRS	1A109	1B055	1B055	1B055	A01F	
3280	41	DR TOLD TK BARB	1A114	1B056	1B056	1B056	A01J	
3290		#X/YR BRBT ALNE		1B058A	1B058A	1B058A	A05A	
3300		#X/YR BRBT-2PPL		1B058B	1B058B	1B058B	A05B	
3310		#X/YR BRBT@PRTY		1B058C	1B058C	1B058C	A05C	
3320		#X/YR BRBT-DT/S		1B058D	1B058D	1B058D	A05B	
3330		#X/YR BRBT-ADLT		1B058E	1B058E	1B058E	A05B	
3340		#X/YR BRBT-DATM		1B058F	1B058F	1B058F	A05C	
3350		#X/YR BRBT@HOME		1B058G	1B058G	1B058G	A05C	
3360		#X/YR BRBT@SCHL		1B058H	1B058H	1B058H	A05C	
3380		#X/YR BRBT@CAR		1B058I	1B058I	1B058I	A05C	
3390		#X OVL BARB+ALC		1B059A	1B059A	1B059A	A01H	
3400		#X OVL BARB+MJ		1B059B	1B059B	1B059B	A01H	
3410		#X OVL BARB+LSD		1B059C	1B059C	1B059C	A01H	
3420		#X OVL BARB+PSY		1B059D	1B059D	1B059D	A01H	
3430		#X OVL BARB+AMP		1B059E	1B059E	1B059E	A01H	
3440		#X OVL BARB+QUA		1B059F	1B059F	1B059F	A01H	
3450	43	BARB EXPERIMENT	1A121A	1B060A	1B060A	1B060A	A06A	
3460	43	BARB RELAX	1A121B	1B060B	1B060B	1B060B	A06A	
3470	43	BARB GET HIGH	1A121C	1B060C	1B060C	1B060C	A06A	
3480	43	BARB SK INSIGHT	1A121D	1B060D	1B060D	1B060D	A06A	
3490	43	BARB GD TM FRND	1A121E	1B060E	1B060E	1B060E	A06A	
3500	43	BARB FIT IN GRP	1A121F	1B060F	1B060F	1B060F	A06A	
3510	43	BARB GT AWY PRB	1A121G	1B060G	1B060G	1B060G	A06A	
3520	43	BARB BOREDOM	1A121H	1B060H	1B060H	1B060H	A06A	
3530	43	BARB ANGR&FRSTN	1A121I	1B060I	1B060I	1B060I	A06A	
3540	43	BARB GT THRU DA	1A121K	1B060J	1B060J	1B060J	A06A	
3550	43	BARB INCR EF DR	1A121L	1B060K	1B060K	1B060K	A06A	
3560	43	BARB DCRS EF DR	1A121M	1B060L	1B060L	1B060L	A06A	
3570	43	BARB GET SLEEP	1A121N	1B060M	1B060M	1B060M	A06A	
3575		BARB RLV PHYS PN				1B060N	A06A	
3580	43	BARB I AM HOOKD	1A121O	1B060N	1B060N	1B060O	A06A	
3590	43	BARB,GT VERY HI	1A122	1B061	1B061	1B061	A01E	
3600	43	BARB,HI 24+ HRS	1A123	1B062	1B062	1B062	A01F	
3610	43	TKN YR,PHNOBARB	1A124A	1B063A	1B063A	1B063A	A01L	
3620	43	TKN YR,SECONAL	1A124B	1B063B	1B063B	1B063B	A01L	
3630	43	TKN YR,TUINAL	1A124C	1B063C	1B063C	1B063C	A01L	
3640	43	TKN YR,NEMBUTAL	1A124D	1B063D	1B063D	1B063D	A01L	
3650	43	TKN YR,LUMINAL	1A124E	1B063E	1B063E	1B063E	A01L	
3660	43	TKN YR,DESBUTAL	1A124F	1B063F	1B063F	1B063F	A01L	
3670	43	TKN YR,AMYTAL	1A124G	1B063G	1B063G	1B063G	A01L	
3680	43	TKN YR,ADRNOCAL	1A124H	1B063H	1B063H	1B063H	A01L	
3690	43	TKN YR,OTH BRBT	1A124I	1B063I	1B063I	1B063I	A01L	
3700	43	TKN YR,DNT KNOW	1A124J	1B063J	1B063J	1B063J	A01L	
3710	44	TRY STP BARB&FL	1A125	1B064	1B064	1B064	A01I	
3720	44	NO BARB IN 5YR	1A126	1B065	1B065	1B065	A04A	
3730	44	DR TOLD TK TRNQ	1A129	1B066	1B066	1B066	A01J	
3740		#X/YR TRQL ALNE		1B068A	1B068A	1B068A	A05A	
3750		#X/YR TRQL-2PPL		1B068B	1B068B	1B068B	A05B	
3760		#X/YR TRQL@PRTY		1B068C	1B068C	1B068C	A05C	
3770		#X/YR TRQL-DT/S		1B068D	1B068D	1B068D	A05B	
3780		#X/YR TRQL-ADLT		1B068E	1B068E	1B068E	A05B	
3790		#X/YR TRQL-DATM		1B068F	1B068F	1B068F	A05C	
3800		#X/YR TRQL@HOME		1B068G	1B068G	1B068G	A05C	

ITEM REFERENCE NUMBER	PAGE LOCATION (IN THIS VOLUME)	ITEM DESCRIPTION (ABBREVIATED)	QUESTIONNAIRE LOCATION BY YEAR (FORM, SECTION, AND QUESTION NUMBER)				SUBJECT AREA	
			1975	1976	1977	1978	A	B C D E F G H I J K L M N O P Q R S
3810		#X/YR TRQL@SCHL		1B068H	1B068H	1B068H	A05C	
3830		#X/YR TRQL@CAR		1B068I	1B068I	1B068I	A05C	
3840		#X OVL TRQL+ALC		1B069A	1B069A	1B069A	A01H	
3850		#X OVL TRQL+MJ		1B069B	1B069B	1B069B	A01H	
3860		#X OVL TRQL+LSD		1B069C	1B069C	1B069C	A01H	
3870		#X OVL TRQL+PSY		1B069D	1B069D	1B069D	A01H	
3880		#X OVL TRQL+AMP		1B069E	1B069E	1B069E	A01H	
3890		#X OVL TRQL+QUA		1B069F	1B069F	1B069F	A01H	
3900		#X OVL TRQL+BRB		1B069G	1B069G	1B069G	A01H	
3910	45	TRNQ EXPERIMENT	1A136A	1B070A	1B070A	1B070A	A06A	
3920	45	TRNQ RELAX	1A136B	1B070B	1B070B	1B070B	A06A	
3930	45	TRNQ GET HIGH	1A136C	1B070C	1B070C	1B070C	A06A	
3940	45	TRNQ SK INSIGHT	1A136D	1B070D	1B070D	1B070D	A06A	
3950	45	TRNQ GD TM FRND	1A136E	1B070E	1B070E	1B070E	A06A	
3960	45	TRNQ FIT IN GRP	1A136F	1B070F	1B070F	1B070F	A06A	
3970	45	TRNQ GT AWY PRB	1A136G	1B070G	1B070G	1B070G	A06A	
3980	45	TRNQ BOREDOM	1A136H	1B070H	1B070H	1B070H	A06A	
3990	45	TRNQ ANGR&FRSTN	1A136I	1B070I	1B070I	1B070I	A06A	
4000	45	TRNQ GT THRU DA	1A136K	1B070J	1B070J	1B070J	A06A	
4010	45	TRNQ INCR EF DR	1A136L	1B070K	1B070K	1B070K	A06A	
4020	45	TRNQ DCRS EF DR	1A136M	1B070L	1B070L	1B070L	A06A	
4030	45	TRNQ GET SLEEP	1A136N	1B070M	1B070M	1B070M	A06A	
4035		TRNQ RLV PHYS PN				1B070N	A06A	
4040	45	TRNQ I AM HOOKD	1A136O	1B070N	1B070N	1B070O	A06A	
4050	45	TRNQ,GT VERY HI	1A137	1B071	1B071	1B071	A01E	
4060	46	TRNQ,HI 24+ HRS	1A138	1B072	1B072	1B072	A01F	
4070		TKN YR,LIBRIUM		1B073A	1B073A	1B073A	A01L	
4080		TKN YR,VALIUM		1B073B	1B073B	1B073B	A01L	
4090		TKN YR,MILTOWN		1B073C	1B073C	1B073C	A01L	
4100		TKN YR,EQUANIL		1B073D	1B073D	1B073D	A01L	
4110		TKN YR,MEPRBMTE		1B073E	1B073E	1B073E	A01L	
4120		TKN YR,SERAX		1B073F	1B073F	1B073F	A01L	
4130		TKN YR,ATARAX		1B073G	1B073G	1B073G	A01L	
4140		TKN YR,TRANXENE		1B073H	1B073H	1B073H	A01L	
4150		TKN YR,VISTARIL		1B073I	1B073I	1B073I	A01L	
4160		TKN YR,DNT KNW		1B073J	1B073J	1B073J	A01L	
4170	46	*TRY STP TRQ&FL	1A139	1B074	1B074	1B074	A01I	
4180	46	NO TRNQ IN 5YR	1A140	1B075	1B075	1B075	A04A	
4190		#X/YR COKE ALNE		1B077A	1B077A	1B077A	A05A	
4200		#X/YR COKE-2PPL		1B077B	1B077B	1B077B	A05B	
4210		#X/YR COKE@PRTY		1B077C	1B077C	1B077C	A05C	
4220		#X/YR COKE-DT/S		1B077D	1B077D	1B077D	A05B	
4230		#X/YR COKE-ADLT		1B077E	1B077E	1B077E	A05B	
4240		#X/YR COKE-DATM		1B077F	1B077F	1B077F	A05C	
4250		#X/YR COKE@HOME		1B077G	1B077G	1B077G	A05C	
4260		#X/YR COKE@SCHL		1B077H	1B077H	1B077H	A05C	
4280		#X/YR COKE@CAR		1B077I	1B077I	1B077I	A05C	
4290		#X OVL COKE+ALC		1B078A	1B078A	1B078A	A01H	
4300		#X OVL COKE+MJ		1B078B	1B078B	1B078B	A01H	
4310		#X OVL COKE+LSD		1B078C	1B078C	1B078C	A01H	
4320		#X OVL COKE+PSY		1B078D	1B078D	1B078D	A01H	
4330		#X OVL COKE+AMP		1B078E	1B078E	1B078E	A01H	
4340		#X OVL COKE+QUA		1B078F	1B078F	1B078F	A01H	
4350		#X OVL COKE+BRB		1B078G	1B078G	1B078G	A01H	
4360		#X OVL COKE+TRN		1B078H	1B078H	1B078H	A01H	
4370	47	COKE EXPERIMENT	1A149A	1B079A	1B079A	1B079A	A06A	
4380	47	COKE RELAX	1A149B	1B079B	1B079B	1B079B	A06A	
4390	47	COKE GET HIGH	1A149C	1B079C	1B079C	1B079C	A06A	
4400	47	COKE SK INSIGHT	1A149D	1B079D	1B079D	1B079D	A06A	
4410	47	COKE GD TM FRND	1A149E	1B079E	1B079E	1B079E	A06A	
4420	47	COKE FIT IN GRP	1A149F	1B079F	1B079F	1B079F	A06A	
4430	47	COKE GT AWY PRB	1A149G	1B079G	1B079G	1B079G	A06A	
4440	47	COKE BOREDOM	1A149H	1B079H	1B079H	1B079H	A06A	
4450	47	COKE ANGR&FRSTN	1A149I	1B079I	1B079I	1B079I	A06A	
4460	47	COKE GT THRU DA	1A149K	1B079J	1B079J	1B079J	A06A	
4470	47	COKE INCR EF DR	1A149L	1B079K	1B079K	1B079K	A06A	

ITEM REFERENCE NUMBER	PAGE LOCATION (IN THIS VOLUME)	ITEM DESCRIPTION (ABBREVIATED)	QUESTIONNAIRE LOCATION BY YEAR (FORM, SECTION, AND QUESTION NUMBER)				SUBJECT AREA	
			1975	1976	1977	1978	A	B C D E F G H I J K L M N O P Q R S
4480	47	COKE DCRS EF DR	1A149M	1B079L	1B079L	1B079L	A06A	
4490		COKE STAY AWAKE		1B079M	1B079M	1B079M	A06A	
4500	47	COKE GET>ENERGY	1A149N	1B079N	1B079N	1B079N	A06A	
4510	47	COKE I AM HOOKD	1A149O	1B079O	1B079O	1B079O	A06A	
4520	47	COK,GET VERY HI	1A150	1B080	1B080	1B080	A01E	
4530	47	COK,HIGH 24+ HR	1A151	1B081	1B081	1B081	A01F	
4540	47	*TRY STP COK&FL	1A152	1B082	1B082	1B082	A01I	
4550	48	MTHD COKE SNORT	1A153A	1B083A	1B083A	1B083A	A05D	
4560	48	MTHD COKE-SMOKE	1A153B	1B083B	1B083B	1B083B	A05D	
4570	48	MTHD COKE-INJCT	1A153C	1B083C	1B083C	1B083C	A05D	
4580	48	MTHD COKE-MOUTH	1A153D	1B083D	1B083D	1B083D	A05D	
4590	48	MTHD COKE-OTHER	1A153E	1B083E	1B083E	1B083E	A05D	
4600	48	NO COKE IN 5YR	1A154	1B084	1B084	1B084	A04A	
4610		#X/YR HER ALONE		1B086A	1B086A	1B086A	A05A	
4620		#X/YR HER-2 PPL		1B086B	1B086B	1B086B	A05B	
4630		#X/YR HER@PARTY		1B086C	1B086C	1B086C	A05C	
4640		#X/YR HER-DA/SP		1B086D	1B086D	1B086D	A05B	
4650		#X/YR HER-ADULT		1B086E	1B086E	1B086E	A05B	
4660		#X/YR HER-DATIM		1B086F	1B086F	1B086F	A05C	
4670		#X/YR HER@HOME		1B086G	1B086G	1B086G	A05C	
4680		#X/YR HER@SCHL		1B086H	1B086H	1B086H	A05C	
4700		#X/YR HER@CAR		1B086I	1B086I	1B086I	A05C	
4710		#X OVL HER +ALC		1B087A	1B087A	1B087A	A01H	
4720		#X OVL HER +MJ		1B087B	1B087B	1B087B	A01H	
4730		#X OVL HER +LSD		1B087C	1B087C	1B087C	A01H	
4740		#X OVL HER +PSY		1B087D	1B087D	1B087D	A01H	
4750		#X OVL HER +AMP		1B087E	1B087E	1B087E	A01H	
4760		#X OVL HER +QUA		1B087F	1B087F	1B087F	A01H	
4770		#X OVL HER +BRB		1B087G	1B087G	1B087G	A01H	
4780		#X OVL HER +TRN		1B087H	1B087H	1B087H	A01H	
4790		#X OVL HER +COK		1B087I	1B087I	1B087I	A01H	
4800	49	HERIN EXPERMENT	1A163A	1B088A	1B088A	1B088A	A06A	
4810	49	HERIN RELAX	1A163B	1B088B	1B088B	1B088B	A06A	
4820	49	HERIN GET HIGH	1A163C	1B088C	1B088C	1B088C	A06A	
4830	49	HERIN SK INSIGT	1A163D	1B088D	1B088D	1B088D	A06A	
4840	49	HERIN GD TM FRN	1A163E	1B088E	1B088E	1B088E	A06A	
4850	49	HERIN FT IN GRP	1A163F	1B088F	1B088F	1B088F	A06A	
4860	49	HERIN GT AWY PB	1A163G	1B088G	1B088G	1B088G	A06A	
4870	49	HERIN BOREDOM	1A163H	1B088H	1B088H	1B088H	A06A	
4880	49	HERIN ANGR&FRST	1A163I	1B088I	1B088I	1B088I	A06A	
4890	49	HERIN GT THR DA	1A163K	1B088J	1B088J	1B088J	A06A	
4900	49	HERIN INC EF DG	1A163L	1B088K	1B088K	1B088K	A06A	
4910	49	HERIN DEC EF DG	1A163M	1B088L	1B088L	1B088L	A06A	
4920	49	HERIN I AM HOOK	1A163N	1B088M	1B088M	1B088M	A06A	
4930	49	HER,GT VERY HI	1A164	1B089	1B089	1B089	A01E	
4940	49	HER,HI 24+ HRS	1A165	1B090	1B090	1B090	A01F	
4950	49	TRY STP HER& FL	1A166	1B091	1B091	1B091	A01I	
4960	49	METHD HRN SNORT	1A167A	1B092A	1B092A	1B092A	A05D	
4970	49	METHD HRN-SMOKE	1A167B	1B092B	1B092B	1B092B	A05D	
4980	49	METHD HRN-INJCT	1A167C	1B092C	1B092C	1B092C	A05D	
4990	49	METHD HRN-MOUTH	1A167D	1B092D	1B092D	1B092D	A05D	
5000	49	METHD HRN-OTHER	1A167E	1B092E	1B092E	1B092E	A05D	
5010	50	NO HER IN 5 YR	1A168	1B093	1B093	1B093	A04A	
5020	50	DR TOLD TK NARC	1A171	1B094	1B094	1B094	A01J	
5030		#X/YR NARC ALNE		1B096A	1B096A	1B096A	A05A	
5040		#X/YR NARC-2PPL		1B096B	1B096B	1B096B	A05B	
5050		#X/YR NARC@PRTY		1B096C	1B096C	1B096C	A05C	
5060		#X/YR NARC-DT/S		1B096D	1B096D	1B096D	A05B	
5070		#X/YR NARC-ADLT		1B096E	1B096E	1B096E	A05B	
5080		#X/YR NARC-DATM		1B096F	1B096F	1B096F	A05C	
5090		#X/YR NARC@HOME		1B096G	1B096G	1B096G	A05C	
5100		#X/YR NARC@SCHL		1B096H	1B096H	1B096H	A05C	
5120		#X/YR NARC @CAR		1B096I	1B096I	1B096I	A05C	
5130		#X OVL NARC+ALC		1B097A	1B097A	1B097A	A01H	
5140		#X OVL NARC+MJ		1B097B	1B097B	1B097B	A01H	
5150		#X OVL NARC+LSD		1B097C	1B097C	1B097C	A01H	

ITEM REFERENCE NUMBER	PAGE LOCATION (IN THIS VOLUME)	ITEM DESCRIPTION (ABBREVIATED)	QUESTIONNAIRE LOCATION BY YEAR (FORM, SECTION, AND QUESTION NUMBER)				SUBJECT AREA	
			1975	1976	1977	1978	A	B C D E F G H I J K L M N O P Q R S
5160		#X OVL NARC+PSY		1B097D	1B097D	1B097D	A01H	
5170		#X OVL NARC+AMP		1B097E	1B097E	1B097E	A01H	
5180		#X OVL NARC+QUA		1B097F	1B097F	1B097F	A01H	
5190		#X OVL NARC+BRB		1B097G	1B097G	1B097G	A01H	
5200		#X OVL NARC+TRN		1B097H	1B097H	1B097H	A01H	
5210		#X OVL NARC+COK		1B097I	1B097I	1B097I	A01H	
5220		#X OVL NARC+HER		1B097J	1B097J	1B097J	A01H	
5230	51	NARC EXPERIMENT	1A178A	1B098A	1B098A	1B098A	A06A	
5240	51	NARC RELAX	1A178B	1B098B	1B098B	1B098B	A06A	
5250	51	NARC GET HIGH	1A178C	1B098C	1B098C	1B098C	A06A	
5260	51	NARC SK INSIGTS	1A178D	1B098D	1B098D	1B098D	A06A	
5270	51	NARC GD TM FRND	1A178E	1B098E	1B098E	1B098E	A06A	
5280	51	NARC FIT IN GRP	1A178F	1B098F	1B098F	1B098F	A06A	
5290	51	NARC GT AWY PBM	1A178G	1B098G	1B098G	1B098G	A06A	
5300	51	NARC BOREDOM	1A178H	1B098H	1B098H	1B098H	A06A	
5310	51	NARC ANGR&FRSTN	1A178I	1B098I	1B098I	1B098I	A06A	
5320	51	NARC GT THRU DA	1A178K	1B098J	1B098J	1B098J	A06A	
5330	51	NARC INC EF DG	1A178L	1B098K	1B098K	1B098K	A06A	
5340	51	NARC DEC EF DG	1A178M	1B098L	1B098L	1B098L	A06A	
5350		NARC GET SLEEP		1B098M	1B098M	1B098M	A06A	
5360	51	NARC SBST HERIN	1A178O	1B098N	1B098N	1B098N	A06A	
5363		NARC RLV PHYS PN				1B098O	A06A	
5366		NARC RLV COUGHNG				1B098P	A06A	
5370	51	NARC I AM HOOKD	1A178N	1B098O	1B098O	1B098Q	A06A	
5380	51	NARC,GT VERY HI	1A179	1B099	1B099	1B099	A01E	
5390	51	NARC,HI 24+ HRS	1A180	1B100	1B100	1B100	A01F	
5400	52	NARC TKN MTHDNE	1A181A	1B101A	1B101A	1B101A	A01L	
5410	52	NARC TKN OPIUM	1A181B	1B101B	1B101B	1B101B	A01L	
5420	52	NARC TKN MRPHNE	1A181C	1B101C	1B101C	1B101C	A01L	
5430	52	NARC TKN CODEIN	1A181D	1B101D	1B101D	1B101D	A01L	
5440	52	NARC TKN DEMROL	1A181E	1B101E	1B101E	1B101E	A01L	
5450	52	NARC TKN PARGRC	1A181F	1B101F	1B101F	1B101F	A01L	
5460	52	NARC TKN TALWIN	1A181G	1B101G	1B101G	1B101G	A01L	
5470	52	NARC TKN LDANUM	1A181H	1B101H	1B101H	1B101H	A01L	
5480	52	NARC TKN OTHER	1A181I	1B101I	1B101I	1B101I	A01L	
5490	52	NARC TKN DNT KN	1A181J	1B101J	1B101J	1B101J	A01L	
5500	52	TRY STP NARC&FL	1A182	1B102	1B102	1B102	A01I	
5510	52	METH NARC SNORT	1A183A	1B103A	1B103A	1B103A	A05D	
5520	52	METH NARC SMOKE	1A183B	1B103B	1B103B	1B103B	A05D	
5530	52	METH NARC INJCT	1A183C	1B103C	1B103C	1B103C	A05D	
5540	52	METH NARC MOUTH	1A183D	1B103D	1B103D	1B103D	A05D	
5550	52	METH NARC OTHER	1A183E	1B103E	1B103E	1B103E	A05D	
5560	52	NO NARC IN 5YR	1A184	1B104	1B104	1B104	A04A	
5570	29	GR 1ST SMOK DLY	1A019	1B105A	1B105A	1B105A	A01G	
					3E12A	3E12A	A01G	
5580	30	GR 1ST TRY ALC	1A027	1B105B	1B105B	1B105B	A01G	
					3E12B	3E12B	A01G	
5590	32	GR 1ST TRY MJ	1A043	1B105C	1B105C	1B105C	A01G	
					3E12C	3E12C	A01G	
5600	34	GR 1ST TRY LSD	1A056	1B105D	1B105D	1B105D	A01G	
					3E12D	3E12D	A01G	
5610	36	GR 1ST TRY PSY	1A070	1B105E	1B105E	1B105E	A01G	
					3E12E	3E12E	A01G	
5620	38	GR 1ST TRY AMP	1A086	1B105F	1B105F	1B105F	A01G	
					3E12F	3E12F	A01G	
5630	40	GR 1ST TRY QUA	1A101	1B105G	1B105G	1B105G	A01G	
					3E12G	3E12G	A01G	
5640	42	GR 1ST TRY BRB	1A115	1B105H	1B105H	1B105H	A01G	
					3E12H	3E12H	A01G	
5650	44	GR 1ST TRY TRN	1A130	1B105I	1B105I	1B105I	A01G	
					3E12I	3E12I	A01G	
5660	46	GR 1ST TRY COK	1A143	1B105J	1B105J	1B105J	A01G	
					3E12J	3E12J	A01G	
5670	48	GR 1ST TRY HER	1A157	1B105K	1B105K	1B105K	A01G	
					3E12K	3E12K	A01G	
5680	50	GR 1ST TRY NRC	1A172	1B105L	1B105L	1B105L	A01G	

ITEM REFERENCE NUMBER	PAGE LOCATION (IN THIS VOLUME)	ITEM DESCRIPTION (ABBREVIATED)	QUESTIONNAIRE LOCATION BY YEAR (FORM, SECTION, AND QUESTION NUMBER)				SUBJECT AREA																		
			1975	1976	1977	1978	A	B	C	D	E	F	G	H	I	J	K	L	M	N	O	P	Q	R	S
		GR 1ST TRY INHAL			3E12L	3E12L	A01G																		
5685						3E12M	A01G																		
5690	63	US GO WAR FR OTH	2A38B	2A18B	2A18B	2A18B								H				L							
5700		*SC WRK NVR MNG		1D002	1D002	1D002		B																	
5710		*MST COUR V DUL		1D003	1D003	1D003		B																	
5720		*LRN SCH NT IMPT		1D004	1D004	1D004		B																	
5730		LOT CMPTN GRADE		1D005	1D005	1D005		B																	
5740		STDTS DSLK CHTG		1D006	1D006	1D006		B																	
5750		ST -LK PROV TCH		1D007	1D007	1D007		B																	
5760		FRD NCG/TCH -LK		1D008	1D008	1D008		B																	
5770		R IN WK-STDY PG		1D009	1D009	1D009		B	C																
5780		#X/YR COUNS IND		1D010	1D010	1D010		B											M						
5790		#X/YR COUNS GRP		1D011	1D011	1D011		B											M						
5800		R LK C COUNS MR		1D012	1D012	1D012		B											M						
5810		CSLNG VRY HLPFL		(1D013)	1D013	1D013		B											M						
5820		DALY WATCH TV		2A02A	2A02A	2A02A		B	C																
5830		DALY GO TO MOVIE		2A02B	2A02B	2A02B		B	C																
5840		DALY ART,MSC,PLA		2A02C	2A02C	2A02C		B	C																
5850		DALY RIDE FORFUN			2A02D	2A02D			C																
5860		DALY CMNTY AFFRS		2A02E	2A02E	2A02E			C													O			
5870		DALY PLA MSC,SNG		2A02F	2A02F	2A02F			C																
5880		DALY CREAT WRTNG		2A02G	2A02G	2A02G			C																
5890		DALY ACTV SPORTS		2A02H	2A02H	2A02H			C																
5900		DALY ART/CRAFTS		2A02I	2A02I	2A02I			C																
5910		DALY WRK HSE,CAR		2A02J	2A02J	2A02J			C																
5920		DALY VIST W/FRDS		2A02K	2A02K	2A02K			C											M					
5930		DALY GO SHOPPING		2A02L	2A02L	2A02L			C			F													
5940		DALY ALONE LEISR		(2A02M)	2A02M	2A02M			C																
5950		DALY READ BK,MAG		2A02N	2A02N	2A02N		B	C																
5960		DALY GO TO BARS		2A02O	2A02O	2A02O			C																
5970		DALY GO TO PARTY		2A02P	2A02P	2A02P			C																
5980		DALY GO CHURCH		2A02Q					C				G												
5990	60	US 2 MUCH PROFIT	2A23J	2A03A	2A03A	2A03A						F									O			
6000	61	2MUCH CNCRN MTRL	2A23K	2A03B	2A03B	2A03B						F												
6010	61	ENCOURG PPL BUY>	2A23L	2A03C	2A03C	2A03C						F												
6020	61	-WRNG ADVERTISNG	2A23M	2A03D	2A03D	2A03D						F												
6030	61	MOR SHORTGS FUTR	2A23N	2A03E	2A03E	2A03E						F												
6040	59	APRV PETITIONS	2A21A	2A04A	2A04A	2A04A								H	I									
6050	59	APRV BOYCOTT	2A21B	2A04B	2A04B	2A04B								H	I									
6060	59	APRV LWFL DMSTN	2A21C	2A04C	2A04C	2A04C								H	I									
6070	59	APRV OCCUPY BLDG	2A21D	2A04D	2A04D	2A04D								H	I									
6080	59	APRV WLDCAT STRK	2A21E	2A04E	2A04E	2A04E								H	I									
6090	59	APRV BLK TRAFFIC	2A21F	2A04F	2A04F	2A04F								H	I									
6100	59	APRV DAMAG THING	2A21G	2A04G	2A04G	2A04G								H	I									
6110	60	APRV PSNL VIOLNC	2A21H	2A04H	2A04H	2A04H								H	I									
6120	53	DFNTLY PRFR MATE	2A10	2A05	2A05	2A05				D														
6130	53	THINK WILL MARRY	2A11	2A06	2A06	2A06				D														
6140	53	LIKLY STAY MARRD	2A12A	2A07A	2A07A	2A07A				D														
6150	53	LIKLY HAVE KIDS	2A12B	2A07B	2A07B	2A07B				D	E													
6160	54	-CHL,HB WK1.,W=0	2A15A	2A08A	2A08A	2A08A			C	D														
6170	54	-CHL,HB WK1.,W.5	2A15B	2A08B	2A08B	2A08B			C	D														
6180	54	-CHL,HB&WF WK 1.	2A15C	2A08C	2A08C	2A08C			C	D														
6190	54	-CHL,HB&WF WK .5	2A15D	2A08D	2A08D	2A08D			C	D														
6200	54	-CHL,W WK 1.,H.5	2A15E	2A08E	2A08E	2A08E			C	D														
6210	54	-CHL,W WK 1.,H=0	2A15F	2A08F	2A08F	2A08F			C	D														
6220	55	PSCH,HB WK1.,W=0	2A16A	2A09A	2A09A	2A09A			C	D														
6230	55	PSCH,HB WK1.,W.5	2A16B	2A09B	2A09B	2A09B			C	D														
6240	55	PSCH,HB&WF WK 1.	2A16C	2A09C	2A09C	2A09C			C	D														
6250	55	PSCH,HB&WF WK .5	2A16D	2A09D	2A09D	2A09D			C	D														
6260	55	PSCH,WF WK1.,H.5	2A16E	2A09E	2A09E	2A09E			C	D														
6270	55	PSCH,WF WK1.,H=0	2A16F	2A09F	2A09F	2A09F			C	D														
6280	55	H WK,W -WK,W CCR	2A17A	2A10A	2A10A	2A10A				D														
6290	56	H WK,W -WK,W>CCR	2A17B	2A10B	2A10B	2A10B				D														
6300	56	H WK,W -WK,=CHCR	2A17C	2A10C	2A10C	2A10C				D														
6310	56	H WK,W -WK,H>CCR	2A17D	2A10D	2A10D	2A10D				D														
6320	56	H WK,W -WK,H CCR	2A17E	2A10E	2A10E	2A10E				D														

ITEM REFERENCE NUMBER	PAGE LOCATION (IN THIS VOLUME)	ITEM DESCRIPTION (ABBREVIATED)	1975	1976	1977	1978	A	B	C	D	E	F	G	H	I	J	K	L	M	N	O	P	Q	R	S
6330	61	INTEREST IN GOVT	2A31	2A11	2A11	2A11									H									Q		
	102		4A29	3E01	3E01	3E01									H									Q		
	115		5A40	4A18	4A18	4A18									H									Q		
				5A19	5A19	5A19									H									Q		
6340	61	GOVT PPL -DSHNST	2A32	2A12	2A12	2A12									H			K								
6350	62	GOVT DSNT WASTE$	2A33	2A13	2A13	2A13									H			K								
6360	62	NEVER TRUST GOVT	2A34	2A14	2A14	2A14									H			K								
6370	62	GVT PPL DK DOING	2A35	2A15	2A15	2A15									H			K								
6380	62	GOVT RUN FOR PPL	2A36	2A16	2A16	2A16									H			K								
6390	62	DO OR PLN VOTE	2A37A	2A17A	2A17A	2A17A									H	I										
6400	63	DO OR PLN WRITE	2A37B	2A17B	2A17B	2A17B									H	I										
6410	63	DO OR PLN GIVE $	2A37C	2A17C	2A17C	2A17C									H	I										
6420	63	DO OR PLN WK CPG	2A37D	2A17D	2A17D	2A17D									H	I										
6430	63	DO OR PLN DEMNST	2A37E	2A17E	2A17E	2A17E									H	I										
6440	63	DO OR PLN BOYCOT	2A37F	2A17F	2A17F	2A17F									H	I										
6450	63	US SHD DISARM	2A38A	2A18A	2A18A	2A18A									H				L							
6460	64	US WAR PRTCT ECN	2A38C	2A18C	2A18C	2A18C									H				L							
6470	64	US ONLY WAR DFNS	2A38D	2A18D	2A18D	2A18D									H				L							
6480	64	-US MIL PWR>USSR	2A38E	2A18E	2A18E	2A18E									H				L							
6490	64	US NEED>PWR OTHS	2A38F	2A18F	2A18F	2A18F									H				L							
6500	64	US FRN PLCY NRRW	2A38G	2A18G	2A18G	2A18G									H				L							
6510	64	SRVCMEN SHD OBEY	2A38H	2A18H	2A18H	2A18H													L							
6520	65	FRQ FIGHT PARNTS	2A39A	2A19A	2A19A	2A19A														M						S
6530	65	FRQ HIT SUPRVISR	2A39B	2A19B	2A19B	2A19B														M						S
6540	65	FRQ FGT WRK/SCHL	2A39C	2A19C	2A19C	2A19C		B	C																	S
6550	65	FRQ GANG FIGHT	2A39D	2A19D	2A19D	2A19D																				S
6560	65	FRQ HURT SM1 BAD	2A39E	2A19E	2A19E	2A19E																				S
6570	65	FRQ THREAT WEAPN	2A39F	2A19F	2A19F	2A19F																				S
6580	66	FRQ STEAL <$50	2A39G	2A19G	2A19G	2A19G																				S
6590	66	FRQ STEAL >$50	2A39H	2A19H	2A19H	2A19H																				S
6600	66	FRQ SHOPLIFT	2A39I	2A19I	2A19I	2A19I																				S
6610	66	FRQ CAR THEFT	2A39J	2A19J	2A19J	2A19J																				S
6620	66	FRQ STEAL CAR PT	2A39K	2A19K	2A19K	2A19K																				S
6630	66	FRQ TRESPAS BLDG	2A39L	2A19L	2A19L	2A19L																				S
6640	67	FRQ ARSON	2A39M	2A19M	2A19M	2A19M																				S
6650	67	FRQ DMG SCH PPTY	2A39N	2A19N	2A19N	2A19N		B																		S
6660	67	FRQ DMG WK PRPTY	2A39O	2A19O	2A19O	2A19O			C																	S
6670	67	FRQ TRUBL POLICE	2A39P	2A19P	2A19P	2A19P																				S
6680		SM1 ROB YRS <$50		2A20A	2A20A	2A20A																			R	S
6690		SM1 ROB YRS >$50		2A20B	2A20B	2A20B																			R	S
6700		SM1 DMG YR PRPTY		2A20C	2A20C	2A20C																			R	S
6710		SM1 INJR U W/WPN		2A20D	2A20D	2A20D																			R	S
6720		SM1 THRTN U W/WP		2A20E	2A20E	2A20E																			R	S
6730		SM1 INJR YU -WPN		2A20F	2A20F	2A20F																			R	S
6740		SM1 THRT U W/INJ		2A20G	2A20G	2A20G																			R	S
6750	67	EASY GT MARIJUAN	2A40A	2A21A	2A21A	2A21A	A03A																			
6760	67	EASY GT LSD	2A40B	2A21B	2A21B	2A21B	A03A																			
6770	68	EASY GT PSYDELIC	2A40C	2A21C	2A21C	2A21C	A03A																			
6780	68	EASY GT AMPHTMNS	2A40D	2A21D	2A21D	2A21D	A03A																			
6790	68	EASY GT BBTUATES	2A40F	2A21E	2A21E	2A21E	A03A																			
6800	68	EASY GT TRANQLIZ	2A40G	2A21F	2A21F	2A21F	A03A																			
6810	68	EASY GT COCAINE	2A40H	2A21G	2A21G	2A21G	A03A																			
6820	68	EASY GT HEROIN	2A40I	2A21H	2A21H	2A21H	A03A																			
6830	68	EASY GT NARCOTIC	2A40J	2A21I	2A21I	2A21I	A03A																			
6840		CMP SATFD W/LIFE		2D01	2D01	2D01																	P	Q	R	
				3D01	3D01	3D01																	P	Q	R	
				4D01	4D01	4D01																	P	Q	R	
				5A21	5A21	5A21																	P	Q	R	
6850	56	HOW GD AS SPOUSE	2A19A	2D02A	2D02A	2D02A				D														Q		
6860	56	HOW GD AS PARENT	2A19B	2D02B	2D02B	2D02B				D														Q		
6870	56	HOW GD AS WORKER	2A19C	2D02C	2D02C	2D02C			C															Q		
6880	*	THK ABT SOC ISSU	*A06	2D03	2D03	2D03											J							Q		
				3A02	3A02	3A02											J							Q		
				4A05	4A05	4A05											J							Q		
				5A02	5A02	5A02											J							Q		
6890	57	DHNSTY LARG CORP	2A20A	2D04A	2D04A	2D04A												K								

*Descriptive results for Forms 2, 3, 4, and 5, respectively, can be found on pages 53, 72, 89, and 106.

ITEM REFERENCE NUMBER	PAGE LOCATION (IN THIS VOLUME)	ITEM DESCRIPTION (ABBREVIATED)	QUESTIONNAIRE LOCATION BY YEAR (FORM, SECTION, AND QUESTION NUMBER)				SUBJECT AREA																		
			1975	1976	1977	1978	A	B	C	D	E	F	G	H	I	J	K	L	M	N	O	P	Q	R	S
6900	57	DHNSTY LBR UNION	2A20B	2D04B	2D04B	2D04B												K								
6910	57	DHNSTY COLL&UNIV	2A20C	2D04C	2D04C	2D04C		B										K								
6920	57	DHNSTY PBLC SCHL	2A20D	2D04D	2D04D	2D04D		B										K								
6930	57	DHNSTY CHURCHES	2A20E	2D04E	2D04E	2D04E							G					K								
6940	57	DHNSTY NEWS MDIA	2A20F	2D04F	2D04F	2D04F		B										K								
6950	58	DHNSTY PRES&ADMN	2A20G	2D04G	2D04G	2D04G								H				K								
6960	58	DHNSTY CONGRESS	2A20H	2D04H	2D04H	2D04H								H				K								
6970	58	DHNSTY SUPRM CRT	2A20I	2D04I	2D04I	2D04I								H				K								
6980	58	DHNSTY JUSTC SYS	2A20J	2D04J	2D04J	2D04J								H				K								
6990	58	DHNSTY POLICE	2A20K	2D04K	2D04K	2D04K												K								
7000	58	DHNSTY MILITARY	2A20L	2D04L	2D04L	2D04L												K	L							
7010	60	2MCH COMPTN SCTY	2A23C	2D05A	2D05A	2D05A																		Q		
7020	60	2MANY YNG SLOPPY	2A23H	2D05B	2D05B	2D05B																		Q		
7030	60	2MUCH HARD ROCK	2A23I	2D05C	2D05C	2D05C																		Q		
7040	60	SHD DO OWN THING	2A23A	2D05D	2D05D	2D05D																		Q		
7050		KICK DO DANGR TH		2D05E	2D05E	2D05E																		Q		
7060		LIKE RISK SOME X		2D05F	2D05F	2D05F																		Q		
7070	69	ALL FRD SMK CIGS	2A41A	2D06A	2D06A	2D06A	A02A																			
7080	69	ALL FRD SMK MARJ	2A41B	2D06B	2D06B	2D06B	A02A																			
7090	69	ALL FRD TAKE LSD	2A41C	2D06C	2D06C	2D06C	A02A																			
7100	69	ALL FRD TK PSYDL	2A41D	2D06D	2D06D	2D06D	A02A																			
7110	69	ALL FRD TK AMPH	2A41E	2D06E	2D06E	2D06E	A02A																			
7120	69	ALL FRD TK QUALD	2A41F	2D06F	2D06F	2D06F	A02A																			
7130	70	ALL FRD TK BARBT	2A41G	2D06G	2D06G	2D06G	A02A																			
7140	70	ALL FRD TK TRNQL	2A41H	2D06H	2D06H	2D06H	A02A																			
7150	70	ALL FRD TK COKE	2A41I	2D06I	2D06I	2D06I	A02A																			
7160	70	ALL FRD TK HERON	2A41J	2D06J	2D06J	2D06J	A02A																			
7170	70	ALL FRD TK NARC	2A41K	2D06K	2D06K	2D06K	A02A																			
7180	70	ALL FRD TK INHL	2A41L	2D06L	2D06L	2D06L	A02A																			
7190	70	ALL FRD DRK ALCL	2A41M	2D06M	2D06M	2D06M	A02A																			
7200	71	ALL FRD GT DRUNK	2A41N	2D06N	2D06N	2D06N	A02A																			
7210		FBD CHLD CIG RGL			2E01A		A11C																			
7220		FBD CHLD MJ OCCS			2E01B		A11C																			
7230		FBD CHLD MJ RGLY			2E01C		A11C																			
7240		FBD CHLD LSD OCC			2E01D		A11C																			
7250		FBD CHLD AMPH OC			2E01E		A11C																			
7260		FBD CHLD BARB OC			2E01F		A11C																			
7270		FBD CHLD COKE OC			2E01G		A11C																			
7280		FBD CHLD HRN OCC			2E01H		A11C																			
7290		FBD CHLD DRNK OC			2E01I		A11C																			
7300		FBD CHLD DRNK RG			2E01J		A11C																			
7310		FBD CHLD DRUNKOC			2E01K		A11C																			
7320		RSK/OT CIG1+PK/D		2E01A			A14B																			
7330		RSK/OT MJ 1-2 X		2E01B			A14B																			
7340		RSK/OT MJ OCSNLY		2E01C			A14B																			
7350		RSK/OT MJ REGLY		2E01D			A14B																			
7360		RSK/OT LSD 1-2 X		2E01E			A14B																			
7370		RSK/OT LSD REGLY		2E01F			A14B																			
7380		RSK/OT 'H' 1-2 X		2E01G			A14B																			
7390		RSK/OT 'H' OCSNL		2E01H			A14B																			
7400		RSK/OT 'H' REGLY		2E01I			A14B																			
7410		RSK/OT BARB 1-2X		2E01J			A14B																			
7420		RSK/OT BARB REGY		2E01K			A14B																			
7430		RSK/OT AMPH 1-2X		2E01L			A14B																			
7440		RSK/OT AMPH REG		2E01M			A14B																			
7450		RSK/OT COKE 1-2X		2E01N			A14B																			
7460		RSK/OT COKE REG		2E01O			A14B																			
7470		RSK/OT 1-2 DRINK		2E01P			A14B																			
7480		RSK/OT 1-2 DR/DA		2E01Q			A14B																			
7490		RSK/OT 4-5 DR/DA		2E01R			A14B																			
7500		RSK/OT 5+DR/WKND		2E01S			A14B																			
7510		PRNT THK U DRINK			2E02	2E01	A09A																			
7520		PRNT THK U SM MJ			2E03	2E02	A09A																			
7530		PRNT THK USE DRG			2E04	2E03	A09A																			
7540		TRN FA/MO DRG HP			2E05A		A08A																			
7550		TRN SR/BR DRG HP			2E05B		A08A																			

ITEM REFERENCE NUMBER	PAGE LOCATION (IN THIS VOLUME)	ITEM DESCRIPTION (ABBREVIATED)	1975	1976	1977	1978	A	B	C	D	E	F	G	H	I	J	K	L	M	N	O	P	Q	R	S
7560		TRN RLTVS DRG HP			2E05C		A08A																			
7570		TRN FRND DRG HP			2E05D		A08A																			
7580		TRN DOCTR DRG HP			2E05E		A08A																			
7590		TRN CLINC DRG HP			2E05F		A08A																			
7600		TRN CNSLR DRG HP			2E05G		A08A																			
7610		TRN TCHR DRG HP			2E05H		A08A																			
7620		TRN MNSTR DRG HP			2E05I		A08A																			
7630		R LIKES SCHOOL		1D001	1D001	1D001		B																Q		
				2E02	2E06	2E06		B																Q		
				3E08	3E07	3E07		B																Q		
				4E10	5E05	5E05		B																Q		
				5E04				B																Q		
7640		HRS/WK SPND HMWK		2E03	2E07	2E07		B																		
7650		PRCL INFL SCL RN		2E04A	2E08A	2E08A		B																		
7660		TCHR INFL SCL RN		2E04B	2E08B	2E08B		B																		
7670		STDS INFL SCL RN		2E04C	2E08C	2E08C		B																		
7680		PRTS INFL SCL RN		2E04D	2E08D	2E08D		B																		
7690		HAD DRUG EDUCATN		2E05	2E09	2E09	A10A																			
7700		NOW OWN HAIR DRY		2E09A								F													R	
7710		NOW OWN WT/S SKI		2E09B								F													R	
7720		NOW OWN CAMERA		2E09C								F													R	
7730		NOW OWN WATCH		2E09D								F													R	
7740		NOW OWN HKG BKPK		2E09E								F													R	
7750		NOW OWN CK RADIO		2E09F								F													R	
7760		NOW OWN EL SHAVR		2E09G								F													R	
7770		NOW OWN TENIS RQ		2E09H								F													R	
7780		NOW OWN TV SET		2E09I								F													R	
7790		NOW OWN BICYCLE		2E09J								F													R	
7800		NOW OWN CAR		2E09K								F													R	
7810		NOW OWN TAPE REC		2E09L								F													R	
7820		NOW OWN ELT CALC		2E09M								F													R	
7830		NOW OWN BT/SNMBL		2E09N								F													R	
7840		DG ED,>DG INTRST		2E06	2E10	2E10	A10A																			
7850		DG ED,SPC COURSE		2E07A	2E11A	2E11A	A10A																			
7860		DG ED,IN REG CRS		2E07B	2E11B	2E11B	A10A																			
7870		DG ED,NT REG CRS		2E07C	2E11C	2E11C	A10A																			
7880		DG ED,SPC DISCUS		2E07D	2E11D	2E11D	A10A																			
7890		DG ED,GRT VALUE		2E08	2E12	2E12	A10A																			
7900		16YR+,TEST->DIPL			2E13A	2E13A		B																		
7910		14YR+,TEST->DIPL			2E13B	2E13B		B																		
7920		ALL STD H.S.TEST			2E13C	2E13C		B																		
7930	73	MEN&WOMN/=$,=WRK	3A17A	3A03A	3A03A	3A03A			C	D																
7940	73	CNSDR WMN/HI JOB	3A17B	3A03B	3A03B	3A03B				D				H												
7950	73	WMN SHD =JOB OPP	3A17C	3A03C	3A03C	3A03C			C	D																
7960	73	WMN SHD =ED OPP	3A17D	3A03D	3A03D	3A03D		B		D																
7970	73	MN=ACHV/WMN=HOME	3A17H	3A03E	3A03E	3A03E				D																
7980	74	CHL SUFF W WK MO	3A17I	3A03F	3A03F	3A03F				D																
7990	74	WK MO AS WRM REL	3A17J	3A03G	3A03G	3A03G			C	D																
8000	80	POLLUT INCREASED	3A31A	3A04A	3A04A	3A04A						F														
8010	80	GOVT DEAL ENV PR	3A31D	3A04B	3A04B	3A04B						F		H												
8020	80	MR$ FR LASTG THG	3A31E	3A04C	3A04C	3A04C						F														
8030	80	USE BYC/MAS TRAN	3A31F	3A04D	3A04D	3A04D						F														
8040	80	EAT DIF->FD STRV	3A31G	3A04E	3A04E	3A04E						F										O				
8050	72	LIK WRK CAN FRGT	3A08D	3A05A	3A05A	3A05A			C																	
8060	72	WRK=ONLY MK LVNG	3A08E	3A05B	3A05B	3A05B			C																	
8070	72	WRK CNTRL PRT LF	3A08G	3A05C	3A05C	3A05C			C																	
8080	72	OVTM 2DO BST JOB	3A08H	3A05D	3A05D	3A05D			C																	
8090	72	SAME JOB MST LIF	3A08I	3A05E	3A05E	3A05E			C																	
8100	73	ENUF$,NT WNT WRK	3A10	3A06	3A06	3A06			C																	
	93		4A09A	4A14	4A14	4A14			C																	
	107		5A11	5A06	5A06	5A06			C																	
8110	74	DES FRND OTH RC	3A19A	3A07A	3A07A	3A07A															N					
8120	74	DES SUPVR DIF RC	3A19B	3A07B	3A07B	3A07B			C												N					
8130	74	DES FAM NX DF RC	3A19C	3A07C	3A07C	3A07C															N					
8140	75	DES CHL FD SM RC	3A19D	3A07D	3A07D	3A07D															N					
8150	75	DES CHL FD OT RC	3A19E	3A07E	3A07E	3A07E															N					

ITEM REFERENCE NUMBER	PAGE LOCATION (IN THIS VOLUME)	ITEM DESCRIPTION (ABBREVIATED)	QUESTIONNAIRE LOCATION BY YEAR (FORM, SECTION, AND QUESTION NUMBER) 1975	1976	1977	1978	SUBJECT AREA A	B	C	D	E	F	G	H	I	J	K	L	M	N	O	P	Q	R	S
8160	75	DES AL WKS SM RC	3A19F	3A08A	3A08A	3A08A			C											N					
8170	75	DES SO WKS DF RC	3A19G	3A08B	3A08B	3A08B			C											N					
8180	75	DES MS WKS DF RC	3A19H	3A08C	3A08C	3A08C			C											N					
8190	75	DES AL NGB SM RC	3A19I	3A09A	3A09A	3A09A														N					
8200	75	DES SO NGB OT RC	3A19J	3A09B	3A09B	3A09B														N					
8210	76	DES MS NGB OT RC	3A19K	3A09C	3A09C	3A09C														N					
8220	76	DES AL CHL SM RC	3A19L	3A10A	3A10A	3A10A		B												N					
8230	76	DES SM CHL OT RC	3A19M	3A10B	3A10B	3A10B		B												N					
8240	76	DES MS CHL OT RC	3A19N	3A10C	3A10C	3A10C		B												N					
8250	77	FRNDS AL OT RC	3A22	3A11	3A11	3A11														N				R	
8260	77	NGBHD AL OT RC	3A23	3A12	3A12	3A12														N				R	
8270	76	ELEMSCH AL OT RC	3A21	3A13	3A13	3A13														N				R	
8280	76	HISCH AL OT RC	3A20	3A14	3A14	3A14														N				R	
8290		WRKRS AL OT RC		3A15	3A15	3A15														N					
8300	77	DO LOT THG OT RC	3A24	3A16	3A16	3A16														N					
8310	77	VRY GD EXP OT RC	3A25	3A17	3A17	3A17														N					
8320	82	MARRD OR ENGAGED	3A41	3A18	3A18	3A18					E													R	
8330	82	WHN WANT GT MARR	3A42	3A19	3A19	3A19					E														
8340	83	THGT LOT HAV CHL	3A43	3A20	3A20	3A20					E														
8350	83	# CHLDN WANT(6+)	3A44	3A21	3A21	3A21					E														
8360	83	IF -POP, MR CHLD	3A45	3A22	3A22	3A22					E														
8370	83	WHN 1ST CHL(5+Y)	3A46	3A23	3A23	3A23					E								M						
8380	77	GD JB LARG CORPS	3A27A	3A24A	3A24A	3A24A											K								
8390	77	GD JB LBR UNIONS	3A27B	3A24B	3A24B	3A24B											K								
8400	78	GD JB COLLG&UNIV	3A27C	3A24C	3A24C	3A24C		B									K								
8410	78	GD JB PBLC SCHOL	3A27D	3A24D	3A24D	3A24D		B									K								
8420	78	GD JB CHURCHES	3A27E	3A24E	3A24E	3A24E							G				K								
8430	78	GD JB NEWS MEDIA	3A27F	3A24F	3A24F	3A24F		B									K								
8440	78	GD JB PRES&ADMIN	3A27G	3A24G	3A24G	3A24G								H			K								
8450	78	GD JB CONGRESS	3A27H	3A24H	3A24H	3A24H								H			K								
8460	79	GD JB SUPRM CRT	3A27I	3A24I	3A24I	3A24I								H			K								
8470	79	GD JB JUSTC SYST	3A27J	3A24J	3A24J	3A24J								H			K								
8480	79	GD JB POLICE	3A27K	3A24K	3A24K	3A24K											K								
8490	79	GD JB MILITARY	3A27L	3A24L	3A24L	3A24L											K	L							
8500	79	MIL TOO MCH INFL	3A28	3A25	3A25	3A25												L							
8510	79	US TOO MCH$ MILT	3A29	3A26	3A26	3A26												L							
8520	83	12MO,#OCC PAINRF	3A48A	3A27A	3A27A	3A27A	A01B																		
8530	84	12MO,#OCC SLP PL	3A48B	3A27B	3A27B	3A27B	A01B																		
8540	84	12MO,#OCC AWK PL	3A48C	3A27C	3A27C	3A27C	A01B																		
8550	84	12MO,#OCC CALM P	3A48D	3A27D	3A27D	3A27D	A01B																		
8560	84	DAP SMK 1PCK CIG	(3A53A)	3A28A	3A28A	3A28A	A11A																		
8570	84	DAP TRY MRJ 1-2T	(3A53B)	3A28B	3A28B	3A28B	A11A																		
8580	85	DAP SMK MRJ OCCS	(3A53C)	3A28C	3A28C	3A28C	A11A																		
8590	85	DAP SMK MRJ REGL	(3A53D)	3A28D	3A28D	3A28D	A11A																		
8600	85	DAP TRY LSD 1-2T	(3A53E)	3A28E	3A28E	3A28E	A11A																		
8610	85	DAP TKG LSD REGL	(3A53F)	3A28F	3A28F	3A28F	A11A																		
8620	85	DAP TRY HRN 1-2T	(3A53G)	3A28G	3A28G	3A28G	A11A																		
8630	85	DAP TKG HRN OCCS	(3A53H)	3A28H	3A28H	3A28H	A11A																		
8640	85	DAP TKG HRN REGL	(3A53I)	3A28I	3A28I	3A28I	A11A																		
8650	85	DAP TRY BRB 1-2T	(3A53J)	3A28J	3A28J	3A28J	A11A																		
8660	85	DAP TKG BRB REGL	(3A53K)	3A28K	3A28K	3A28K	A11A																		
8670	86	DAP TRY AMP 1-2T	(3A53L)	3A28L	3A28L	3A28L	A11A																		
8680	86	DAP TKG AMP REGL	(3A53M)	3A28M	3A28M	3A28M	A11A																		
8690	86	DAP TRY COC 1-2T	(3A53N)	3A28N	3A28N	3A28N	A11A																		
8700	86	DAP TKG COC REGL	(3A53O)	3A28O	3A28O	3A28O	A11A																		
8710	86	DAP TRY DRK ALCL	(3A53P)	3A28P	3A28P	3A28P	A11A																		
8720	86	DAP 1-2 DRK/DAY	(3A53Q)	3A28Q	3A28Q	3A28Q	A11A																		
8730	86	DAP 4-5 DRK/DAY	(3A53R)	3A28R	3A28R	3A28R	A11A																		
8740	86	DAP 5+ DRK WKNDS	(3A53S)	3A28S	3A28S	3A28S	A11A																		
8750	87	OFT W PL TK MARJ	3A55A	5E07A	5E08A	5E08A	A02B																		
8760	87	OFT W PL TK LSD	3A55B	5E07B	5E08B	5E08B	A02B																		
8770	87	OFT W PL TK PSYC	3A55C	5E07C	5E08C	5E08C	A02B																		
8780		OFT W PL TK QUAL		5E07D	5E08D	5E08D	A02B																		
8790	87	OFT W PL TK BARB	3A55E	5E07E	5E08E	5E08E	A02B																		
8800	87	OFT W PL TK TRQL	3A55F	5E07F	5E08F	5E08F	A02B																		
8810	87	OFT W PL TK COKE	3A55G	5E07G	5E08G	5E08G	A02B																		

ITEM REFERENCE NUMBER	PAGE LOCATION (IN THIS VOLUME)	ITEM DESCRIPTION (ABBREVIATED)	QUESTIONNAIRE LOCATION BY YEAR (FORM, SECTION, AND QUESTION NUMBER)				SUBJECT AREA	
			1975	1976	1977	1978	A	B C D E F G H I J K L M N O P Q R S
8820	87	OFT W PL TK HRN	3A55H	5E07H	5E08H	5E08H	A02B	
8830	88	OFT W PL TK NARC	3A55I	5E07I	5E08I	5E08I	A02B	
8835		OFT W PL TK INHL		5E07J	5E08J	5E08J	A02B	
8840	88	OFT W PL TK ALCL	3A55K	5E07K	5E08K	5E08K	A02B	
8850		OFTN SHRTNS BRTH		(3D02A)	3D02A	3D02A		Q
8860		OFTN HEART BEATG		(3D02B)	3D02B	3D02B		Q
8870		OFTN SPLLS DZZNS		(3D02C)	3D02C	3D02C		Q
8880		OFTN HNDS TRMBLE		(3D02D)	3D02D	3D02D		Q
8890		OFTN HNDS SWEATG		(3D02E)	3D02E	3D02E		Q
8900		OFTN CDNT GT GNG		(3D02F)	3D02F	3D02F		Q
8910		12MO REDUCE ALCL		3D03A	3D03A	3D03A	A01I	
8920		12MO REDUCE CIG		3D03B	3D03B	3D03B	A01I	
8930		12MO REDUCE MARJ		3D03C	3D03C	3D03C	A01I	
8940		12MO REDUCE PSYC		3D03D	3D03D	3D03D	A01I	
8950		12MO REDUCE AMPH		3D03E	3D03E	3D03E	A01I	
8960		12MO REDUCE QUAL		3D03F	3D03F	3D03F	A01I	
8970		12MO REDUCE BARB		3D03G	3D03G	3D03G	A01I	
8980		12MO REDUCE COKE		3D03H	3D03H	3D03H	A01I	
8990		12MO REDUCE HRN		3D03I	3D03I	3D03I	A01I	
9000		12MO REDUCE NARC		3D03J	3D03J	3D03J	A01I	
9010		NXT 12MOS USE MJ			3D04	3D04	A01B	
9020		CNCRN PSYCH DAMG		3D04A	3D04A	3D04A	A06A	
9030		CNCRN PHYSCL DMG		3D04B	3D04B	3D04B	A06A	
9040		CNCRN GT ARRESTD		3D04C	3D04C	3D04C	A06A	
9050		CNCRN BECOM ADCT		3D04D	3D04D	3D04D	A06A	
9060		AGST MY BELIEFS		3D04E	3D04E	3D04E	A06A	
9070		CNCRN LEGY&AMBTN		3D04F	3D04F	3D04F	A06A	
9080		CNCRN LOSS CNTRL		3D04G	3D04G	3D04G	A06A	
9090		MJ ->STRNGR DRGS		3D04H	3D04H	3D04H	A06A	
9100		MJ NOT ENJOYABLE		3D04I	3D04I	3D04I	A06A	
9110		PRNTS DISAPPROVE		3D04J	3D04J	3D04J	A06A	
9120		HS/WF DISAPPROVE		3D04K	3D04K	3D04K	A06A	
9130		DONT LIKE USERS		3D04L	3D04L	3D04L	A06A	
9140		FRNDS DNT USE IT		3D04M	3D04M	3D04M	A06A	
9150		PSSBLY BAD TRIP		3D04N	3D04N	3D04N	A06A	
9160		TOO EXPENSIVE			3D04O	3D04O	A06A	
9170		NOT AVAILABLE			3D04P	3D04P	A06A	
9180		NOT WNT GET HIGH			3D04Q	3D04Q	A06A	
9190		AL CS BEHV REGRT		3D05A	3D05A	3D05A	A07A	
9200		AL HURT REL PRNT		3D05A	3D05A	3D05A	A07A	
9210		AL HURT REL SPSE		3D05A	3D05A	3D05A	A07A	
9220		AL HURT REL FRND		3D05A	3D05A	3D05A	A07A	
9230		AL HURT REL TCHR		3D05A	3D05A	3D05A	A07A	
9240		AL INV PL BD INF		3D05A	3D05A	3D05A	A07A	
9250		AL HURT PERF JOB		3D05A	3D05A	3D05A	A07A	
9260		AL CAUS<INTERSTD		3D05A	3D05A	3D05A	A07A	
9270		AL CS<STABL EMTN		3D05A	3D05A	3D05A	A07A	
9280		AL CS HAV<ENERGY		3D05A	3D05A	3D05A	A07A	
9290		AL INTF THNK CLR		3D05A	3D05A	3D05A	A07A	
9300		AL BD PSYCH EFCT		3D05A	3D05A	3D05A	A07A	
9310		AL CS HEALTH BAD		3D05A	3D05A	3D05A	A07A	
9320		AL CS DRIV UNSAF		3D05A	3D05A	3D05A	A07A	
9330		AL GT TRBL W POL		3D05A	3D05A	3D05A	A07A	
9340		AL CS NO PROBLEM			3D05A	3D05A	A07A	
9350		AL NEVER USED DG			3D05A	3D05A	A07A	
9360		MJ CS BEHV REGRT		3D05M	3D05M	3D05M	A07A	
9370		MJ HURT REL PRNT		3D05M	3D05M	3D05M	A07A	
9380		MJ HURT REL SPSE		3D05M	3D05M	3D05M	A07A	
9390		MJ HURT REL FRND		3D05M	3D05M	3D05M	A07A	
9400		MJ HURT REL TCHR		3D05M	3D05M	3D05M	A07A	
9410		MJ INV PL BD INF		3D05M	3D05M	3D05M	A07A	
9420		MJ HURT PERF JOB		3D05M	3D05M	3D05M	A07A	
9430		MJ CAUS<INTERSTD		3D05M	3D05M	3D05M	A07A	
9440		MJ CS<STABL EMTN		3D05M	3D05M	3D05M	A07A	
9450		MJ CS HAV<ENERGY		3D05M	3D05M	3D05M	A07A	
9460		MJ INTF THNK CLR		3D05M	3D05M	3D05M	A07A	

ITEM REFERENCE NUMBER	PAGE LOCATION (IN THIS VOLUME)	ITEM DESCRIPTION (ABBREVIATED)	QUESTIONNAIRE LOCATION BY YEAR (FORM, SECTION, AND QUESTION NUMBER) 1975	1976	1977	1978	SUBJECT AREA A	B C D E F G H I J K L M N O P Q R S
9470		MJ BD PSYCH EFCT		3D05M	3D05M	3D05M	A07A	
9480		MJ CS HEALTH BAD		3D05M	3D05M	3D05M	A07A	
9490		MJ CS DRIV UNSAF		3D05M	3D05M	3D05M	A07A	
9500		MJ GT TRBL W POL		3D05M	3D05M	3D05M	A07A	
9510		MJ CS NO PROBLEM			3D05M	3D05M	A07A	
9520		MJ NEVER USED DG			3D05M	3D05M	A07A	
9530		OT CS BEHV REGRT		3D05O	3D05O	3D05O	A07A	
9540		OT HURT REL PRNT		3D05O	3D05O	3D05O	A07A	
9550		OT HURT REL SPSE		3D05O	3D05O	3D05O	A07A	
9560		OT HURT REL FRND		3D05O	3D05O	3D05O	A07A	
9570		OT HURT REL TCHR		3D05O	3D05O	3D05O	A07A	
9580		OT INV PL BD INF		3D05O	3D05O	3D05O	A07A	
9590		OT HURT PERF JOB		3D05O	3D05O	3D05O	A07A	
9600		OT CAUS<INTERSTD		3D05O	3D05O	3D05O	A07A	
9610		OT CS<STABL EMTN		3D05O	3D05O	3D05O	A07A	
9620		OT CS HAV<ENERGY		3D05O	3D05O	3D05O	A07A	
9630		OT INTF THNK CLR		3D05O	3D05O	3D05O	A07A	
9640		OT BD PSYCH EFCT		3D05O	3D05O	3D05O	A07A	
9650		OT CS HEALTH BAD		3D05O	3D05O	3D05O	A07A	
9660		OT CS DRIV UNSAF		3D05O	3D05O	3D05O	A07A	
9670		OT GT TRBL W POL		3D05O	3D05O	3D05O	A07A	
9680		OT CS NO PROBLEM			3D05O	3D05O	A07A	
9690		OT NEVER USED DG			3D05O	3D05O	A07A	
9700		PRVNT POL TOO >$		3E02A	3E02A	3E02A		F
9710		PRVNT POL CST JB		3E02B	3E02B	3E02B		F
9720		PRVNT POL PPL DK		3E02C	3E02C	3E02C		F
9730		PRVNT POL -ENUF		3E02D	3E02D	3E02D		F
9740		PRVNT POL USELSS		3E02E	3E02E	3E02E		F
9750		FUTR,HAV2 CNSUM<		3E03	3E03	3E03		F
9760	82	GOV HP PRB POPL	3A32N	3E04A	3E04A	3E04A		E H
9770	81	GOV NO POP PLCY	3A32A	3E04B	3E04B	3E04B		E H
9780	81	STR OVPOP,LMT FM	3A32B	3E04C	3E04C	3E04C		E
9790	81	PRV OVPOP,NO CHL	3A32C	3E04D	3E04D	3E04D		E
9800	81	HISCH INS BRTH C	3A32E	3E04E	3E04E	3E04E		B E
9810	81	BRTH CNT IMMORAL	3A32I	3E04F	3E04F	3E04F		E
9820	81	GOV BRTHC NO CST	3A32M	3E04G	3E04G	3E04G		E H
9830	82	US POP SZ LRGER	3A34	3E06	3E05	3E05		E
9840	82	GVNG FOOD O CNTY	3A33	3E05				E O
9850	82	WRLD POP SZ LRGR	3A35	3E07	3E06	3E06		E
9860		HAD SEX ED IN HS		3E09	3E08	3E08		D E
9870		STUDY BC IN HS		3E10	3E09	3E09		D E
9871		SM1 SCL ROB <$50		4E11A	3E10A	3E10A		R S
9872		SM1 SCL ROB >$50		4E11B	3E10B	3E10B		R S
9873		SM1 SCL DMG PRTY		4E11C	3E10C	3E10C		R S
9874		SM1 SCL IN U W/W		4E11D	3E10D	3E10D		R S
9875		SM1 SCL TH U W/W		4E11E	3E10E	3E10E		R S
9876		SM1 SCL IN U -WP		4E11F	3E10F	3E10F		R S
9877		SM1 SCL TH U W/I		4E11G	3E10G	3E10G		R S
9880		DK DO W LEISR TM			3E11A			C
9890		TM QUIK/LEIS HRS			3E11B			C
9900		WASTE LEIS TIME			3E11C			C
9910		ENUF TIME FR THG			3E11D			C
9920		R WL VOTE IN '76		3E11				H
9940	89	FUTR CNTRY WORSE	4A01	4A02	4A02	4A02		I
9950	89	FUTR WORLD WORSE	4A02	4A03	4A03	4A03		I
9960	89	FUTR R LIFE WRSE	4A03	4A04	4A04	4A04		I
9970	96	PLLTN INCR IN US	4A22A	4A06A	4A06A	4A06A		F
9980	97	PLLTN NT SO DANG	4A22B	4A06B	4A06B	4A06B		F
9990	97	PLLTN NEC 4 GRTH	4A22C	4A06C	4A06C	4A06C		F
10000	97	INDVL RESP 4 ENV	4A22D	4A06D	4A06D	4A06D		F
10010	97	GOVT RESP 4 ENV	4A22E	4A06E	4A06E	4A06E		F H
10020	97	GOVT TAX PLLTRS	4A22F	4A06F	4A06F	4A06F		F H
10030	97	GOVT BAN DSPSBLE	4A22G	4A06G	4A06G	4A06G		F H
10040	98	TV COMM CRT NDS	4A22H	4A06H	4A06H	4A06H		B F
10050	98	TV COMMRCLS GOOD	4A22I	4A06I	4A06I	4A06I		B F
10060	98	FAM BUYS THG -ND	4A22L	4A06J	4A06J	4A06J		F

ITEM REFERENCE NUMBER	PAGE LOCATION (IN THIS VOLUME)	ITEM DESCRIPTION (ABBREVIATED)	QUESTIONNAIRE LOCATION BY YEAR (FORM, SECTION, AND QUESTION NUMBER)				SUBJECT AREA																		
			1975	1976	1977	1978	A	B	C	D	E	F	G	H	I	J	K	L	M	N	O	P	Q	R	S
				5A18I	5A18I	5A18I						F													
10070	98	POL SLVD BY 2000	4A22M	4A06K	4A06K	4A06K						F														
10080	98	R EFRT 2 HLP ENV	4A23	4A07	4A07	4A07						F														
10090	89	JOB IMPC SE RSLT	4A08A	4A08A	4A08A	4A08A			C																	
10100	90	JOB IMPC STATUS	4A08B	4A08B	4A08B	4A08B			C																	
10110	90	JOB IMPC INTRSTG	4A08C	4A08C	4A08C	4A08C			C																	
10120	90	JOB IMPC ADVNCMT	4A08D	4A08D	4A08D	4A08D			C																	
10130	90	JOB IMPC HLP OTH	4A08E	4A08E	4A08E	4A08E			C													O				
10140	90	JOB IMPC EARN $	4A08F	4A08F	4A08F	4A08F			C			F														
10150	90	JOB IMPC CREATVY	4A08G	4A08G	4A08G	4A08G			C																	
10160	90	JOB IMPC UTILITY	4A08H	4A08H	4A08H	4A08H			C																	
10170	91	JOB IMPC MK FRND	4A08I	4A08I	4A08I	4A08I			C										M						
10180	91	JOB IMPC USE SKL	4A08J	4A08J	4A08J	4A08J			C																	
10190	91	JOB IMPC WRTHWLE	4A08K	4A08K	4A08K	4A08K			C													O				
10200	91	JOB IMPC VACATN	4A08L	4A08L	4A08L	4A08L			C																	
10210	91	JOB IMPC MK DCSN	4A08M	4A08M	4A08M	4A08M			C																	
10220		JOB IMPC FRE TIM		4A08N	4A08N	4A08N			C																	
10230	91	JOB IMPC NO MVNG	4A08O	4A08O	4A08O	4A08O			C																	
10240	91	JOB IMPC NO SPRV	4A08P	4A08P	4A08P	4A08P			C																	
10250	92	JOB IMPC SECURTY	4A08Q	4A08Q	4A08Q	4A08Q			C																	
10260	92	JOB IMPC LRNING	4A08R	4A08R	4A08R	4A08R		B	C																	
10270	92	JOB IMPC BE SELF	4A08S	4A08S	4A08S	4A08S			C																	
10280	92	JOB IMPC RESPECT	4A08T	4A08T	4A08T	4A08T			C																	
10290	92	JOB IMPC CNTC PL	4A08U	4A08U	4A08U	4A08U			C										M						
10300		JOB IMPC EZ PACE		4A08V	4A08V	4A08V			C																	
10310		JOB IMPC HRD PRB		4A08W	4A08W	4A08W			C																	
10320	93	KIND OF WORK @30	4A09	4A09	4A09	4A09			C																	
10330		R SURE GT THS WK		4A10	4A10	4A10			C																	
10340		R SURE WK GD CHC		4A11	4A11	4A11			C																	
10350		R THNK WK BE SAT		4A12	4A12	4A12			C														P			
10360		JOB OBSTC RELGN		4A13A	4A13A	4A13A			C				G													
10370		JOB OBSTC SEX		4A13B	4A13B	4A13B			C	D																
10380		JOB OBSTC RACE		4A13C	4A13C	4A13C			C											N					
10390		JOB OBSTC BKGRND		4A13D	4A13D	4A13D			C																R	
10400		JOB OBSTC POL VW		4A13E	4A13E	4A13E			C					H											
10410		JOB OBSTC EDUCTN		4A13F	4A13F	4A13F		B	C																	
10420		JOB OBSTC -VOC T		4A13G	4A13G	4A13G			C																	
10430		JOB OBSTC -ABLTY		4A13H	4A13H	4A13H			C																R	
10440		JOB OBSTC - PULL		4A13I	4A13I	4A13I			C																R	
10450		JOB OBSTC -WK HD		4A13J	4A13J	4A13J			C															Q		
10460		JOB OBSTC -CONFM		4A13K	4A13K	4A13K			C															Q		
10470	93	FEW GD MAR, ? IT	4A11A	4A15A	4A15A	4A15A				D																
10480	94	GD LIV TG BF MRG	4A11B	4A15B	4A15B	4A15B				D	E															
10490	94	1 PRTNR=RSTRCTVE	4A11C	4A15C	4A15C	4A15C				D	E															
10500	94	JB INTFR REL HBD	4A11E	4A15D	4A15D	4A15D			C	D																
10510	94	JB DVLP WF PERSN	4A11G	4A15E	4A15E	4A15E			C	D																
10520	94	RS CHLD + FR MAN	4A11H	4A15F	4A15F	4A15F				D																
10530	94	MO SH B W CHL>TM	4A11I	4A15G	4A15G	4A15G				D																
10540	95	WF WK,HBD SHD>HW	4A11K	4A15H	4A15H	4A15H			C	D																
10550		#HRS TV/DAY/5+		4A16	4A16	4A16		B																		
10560		#BKS LAST YR/10+		4A17	4A17	4A17		B																		
10570	95	>INFLC LARG CORP	4A14A	4A19A	4A19A	4A19A												K								
10580	95	>INFLC LBR UNION	4A14B	4A19B	4A19B	4A19B												K								
10590	95	>INFLC CHURCHES	4A14C	4A19C	4A19C	4A19C							G					K								
10600	95	>INFLC NEWS MDIA	4A14D	4A19D	4A19D	4A19D		B										K								
10610	95	>INFLC PRES&ADMN	4A14E	4A19E	4A19E	4A19E								H				K								
10620	96	>INFLC CONGRESS	4A14F	4A19F	4A19F	4A19F								H				K								
10630	96	>INFLC SUPRM CRT	4A14G	4A19G	4A19G	4A19G								H				K								
10640	96	>INFLC JUSTC SYS	4A14H	4A19H	4A19H	4A19H								H				K								
10650	96	>INFLC POLICE	4A14I	4A19I	4A19I	4A19I												K								
10660	96	>INFLC MILITARY	4A14J	4A19J	4A19J	4A19J												K	L							
10760		LAW 4 SMK TOBPUB			4A20K	4A20K	A13A																			
10770		ILGL AD SMK CIG		4A20A			A13A																			
10780		ILGL AD MRJ PRIV		4A20B	4A20A	4A20A	A13A																			
10790		ILGL AD MRJ PUBL		4A20C	4A20B	4A20B	A13A																			
10800		ILGL AD LSD PRIV		4A20D	4A20C	4A20C	A13A																			

ITEM REFERENCE NUMBER	PAGE LOCATION (IN THIS VOLUME)	ITEM DESCRIPTION (ABBREVIATED)	1975	1976	1977	1978	A	B	C	D	E	F	G	H	I	J	K	L	M	N	O	P	Q	R	S
10810		ILGL AD LSD PUBL		4A20E	4A20D	4A20D	A13A																		
10820		ILGL AD AMP PRIV		4A20F	4A20E	4A20E	A13A																		
10830		ILGL AD AMP PUBL		4A20G	4A20F	4A20F	A13A																		
10840		ILGL AD HRN PRIV		4A20H	4A20G	4A20G	A13A																		
10850		ILGL AD HRN PUBL		4A20I	4A20H	4A20H	A13A																		
10860		ILGL AD DRNK PRV		4A20J	4A20I	4A20I	A13A																		
10870		ILGL AD DRNK PBL		4A20K	4A20J	4A20J	A13A																		
10880	102	CRIME 2 USE MARJ	4A32	4A21	4A21	4A21	A13C																		
10890	102	LEGAL 2 SELL MRJ	4A33	4A22	4A22	4A22	A13C																		
10900	102	USE<MJ IF LEGAL	4A34	4A23	4A23	4A23	A13C																		
10910		CMP SATFD W/JOB		4D02	4D02	4D02			C														P			
10920	101	I CNT CHNG WORLD	4A28A	4D03A	4D03A	4D03A									I	J							Q		
10930	101	SOCTY WONT LAST	4A28B	4D03B	4D03B	4D03B						F				J									
10940	101	THG TUF,TCHN SLV	4A28C	4D03C	4D03C	4D03C									I	J							Q		
10950	101	NO HOPE 4 WORLD	4A28D	4D03D	4D03D	4D03D										J							Q		
10960	101	WNDR PURPS 2 LIF	4A28E	4D03E	4D03E	4D03E										J							Q		
10970	101	WRLD UPHVL 10 YR	4A28F	4D03F	4D03F	4D03F										J							Q		
10980	102	ANNIHLTN IN LFTM	4A28G	4D03G	4D03G	4D03G										J							Q		
10990	102	HMN RCE RSILIENT	4A28H	4D03H	4D03H	4D03H										J							Q		
11000		#X BEER/LIFETIME		4D04A	4D04A	4D04A	A01A																		
11010		#X BEER/LAST12MO		4D04B	4D04B	4D04B	A01B																		
11020		#X BEER/LAST30DA		4D04C	4D04C	4D04C	A01C																		
11030		5+BR/LST2WK,10+X		4D05	4D05	4D05	A01D																		
11040		#X WINE/LIFETIME		4D06A	4D06A	4D06A	A01A																		
11050		#X WINE/LAST12MO		4D06B	4D06B	4D06B	A01B																		
11060		#X WINE/LAST30DA		4D06C	4D06C	4D06C	A01C																		
11070		#X 20OZ+ WN/2 WK		4D07	4D07	4D07	A01D																		
11080		#X LIQR/LIFETIME		4D08A	4D08A	4D08A	A01A																		
11090		#X LIQR/LAST12MO		4D08B	4D08B	4D08B	A01B																		
11100		#X LIQR/LAST30DA		4D08C	4D08C	4D08C	A01C																		
11110		#X 5+LIQ/LST 2WK		4D09	4D09	4D09	A01D																		
11120		MLTRY GET AHEAD		4E01A	4E01A	4E01A													L							
11130		MLTRY MORE ED		4E01B	4E01B	4E01B		B											L							
11140		MLTRY ADVNC RESP		4E01C	4E01C	4E01C													L							
11150		MLTRY >FLFLLG JB		4E01D	4E01D	4E01D			C										L							
11160		MLTRY IDEAS HERD		4E01E	4E01E	4E01E													L							
11170		EXTNT MLTRY JSTC		4E02	4E02	4E02													L							
11180		MLTRY DSCRM WOMN		4E03	4E03	4E03					D								L							
11190		MLTRY DSCRM BLKS		4E04	4E04	4E04													L		N					
11200		>FAIR MLTRY CVLN		4E05	4E05	4E05													L							
11210		-MLTRY COUP U.S.		4E06	4E06										H				L							
11220		NT VOL 4 NEC WAR		4E07	4E07	4E06													L							
11230	98	P'IDEA OF DO LIF	4A27A	4E08A	4E08A	4E07A													M						
11240	99	P'IDEA OF LSR TM	4A27B	4E08B	4E08B	4E07B			C										M						
11250	99	P'IDEA OF CLTHES	4A27C	4E08C	4E08C	4E07C													M						
11260	99	P'IDEA OF SPND $	4A27D	4E08D	4E08D	4E07D													M						
11270	99	P'IDEA OF DATE	4A27E	4E08E	4E08E	4E07E													M						
11280	99	P'IDEA OF OK DRK	4A27F	4E08F	4E08F	4E07F													M						
11290	99	P'IDEA OF OK MRJ	4A27G	4E08G	4E08G	4E07G													M						
11300	99	P'IDEA OF OK DRG	4A27H	4E08H	4E08H	4E07H													M						
11310	100	P'IDEA OF VALUES	4A27I	4E08I	4E08I	4E07I													M						
11320	100	P'IDEA OF EDUC	4A27J	4E08J	4E08J	4E07J		B											M						
11330	100	P'IDEA OF SX RLS	4A27K	4E08K	4E08K	4E07K				D									M						
11340	100	P'IDEA OF ECLOGY	4A27L	4E08L	4E08L	4E07L						F							M						
11350	100	P'IDEA OF RCL IS	4A27M	4E08M	4E08M	4E07M													M	N					
11360	100	P'IDEA OF RLGION	4A27N	4E08N	4E08N	4E07N							G						M						
11370	100	P'IDEA OF PLTICS	4A27O	4E08O	4E08O	4E07O								H					M						
11380	103	PRNT DAP CIGS	4A35A	4E09A	4E09A	4E08A	A12A																		
11390	103	PRNT DAP TRY MRJ	4A35B	4E09B	4E09B	4E08B	A12A																		
11400	103	PRNT DAP MJ OCC	4A35C	4E09C	4E09C	4E08C	A12A																		
11410	103	PRNT DAP MJ REG	4A35D	4E09D	4E09D	4E08D	A12A																		
11420	103	PRNT DAP TRY LSD	4A35E	4E09E	4E09E	4E08E	A12A																		
11430	103	PRNT DAP TRY AMP	4A35F	4E09F	4E09F	4E08F	A12A																		
11440	103	PRNT DAP 1-2DR/D	4A35G	4E09G	4E09G	4E08G	A12A																		
11450	103	PRNT DAP 4-5DR/D	4A35H	4E09H	4E09H	4E08H	A12A																		
11460	104	PRNT DAP 5+DR/WE	4A35I	4E09I	4E09I	4E08I	A12A																		

ITEM REFERENCE NUMBER	PAGE LOCATION (IN THIS VOLUME)	ITEM DESCRIPTION (ABBREVIATED)	QUESTIONNAIRE LOCATION BY YEAR (FORM, SECTION, AND QUESTION NUMBER)				SUBJECT AREA																	
			1975	1976	1977	1978	A	B	C	D	E	F	G	H	I	J	K	L	M	N	O	P	Q	R	S
11470		FRD DAP CIGS			4E10A		A12B																		
11480		FRD DAP TRY MARJ			4E10B		A12B																		
11490		FRD DAP MJ OCC			4E10C		A12B																		
11500		FRD DAP MJ REG			4E10D		A12B																		
11510		FRD DAP TRY LSD			4E10E		A12B																		
11520		FRD DAP TRY AMP			4E10F		A12B																		
11530		FRD DAP 1-2DR/DA			4E10G		A12B																		
11540		FRD DAP 4-5DR/DA			4E10H		A12B																		
11550		FRD DAP 5+DR/WKD			4E10I		A12B																		
11560		H&W WK,WF AL HWK			4E11A	4E10A				D															
11570		H&W WK,WF MS HWK			4E11B	4E10B				D															
11580		H&W WK,DO = HWRK			4E11C	4E10C				D															
11590		H&W WK,HB MS HWK			4E11D	4E10D				D															
11600		H&W WK,HB AL HWK			4E11E	4E10E				D															
11610		H&W WK+CH,W CHCR			4E12A	4E11A				D															
11620		H&W WK+CH,W>CHCR			4E12B	4E11B				D															
11630		H&W WK+CH,=CHCAR			4E12C	4E11C				D															
11640		H&W WK+CH,H>CHCR			4E12D	4E11D				D															
11650		H&W WK+CH,H CHCR			4E12E	4E11E				D															
11660	105	WR/NT NUCLER WAR	5A04A	5A03A	5A03A	5A03A											J								
11670	105	WR/NT POP GROWTH	5A04B	5A03B	5A03B	5A03B					E						J								
11680	105	WR/NT CRIME&VLNC	5A04C	5A03C	5A03C	5A03C											J								
11690	105	WR/NT POLLUTION	5A04D	5A03D	5A03D	5A03D						F					J								
11700	105	WR/NT ENRGY SHRT	5A04E	5A03E	5A03E	5A03E						F					J								
11710	105	WR/NT RACE RELTN	5A04F	5A03F	5A03F	5A03F											J				N				
11720	105	WR/NT HNGR&PVRTY	5A04G	5A03G	5A03G	5A03G						F					J								
11730	106	WR/NT USE OPN LD	5A04H	5A03H	5A03H	5A03H						F					J								
11740	106	WR/NT URBN DECAY	5A04I	5A03I	5A03I	5A03I											J								
11750	106	WR/NT ECON PRBLM	5A04J	5A03J	5A03J	5A03J											J								
11760	106	WR/NT DRUG ABUSE	5A04K	5A03K	5A03K	5A03K											J								
11770		XPRC MK R GD SPS		5A04A	5A04A	5A04A				D															
11780		XPRC MK R GD PRT		5A04B	5A04B	5A04B				D															
11790		XPRC MK R GD WKR		5A04C	5A04C	5A04C			C																
11800	106	PLC WRK LG CORPN	5A09A	5A05A	5A05A	5A05A			C																
11810	106	PLC WRK SM BSNSS	5A09B	5A05B	5A05B	5A05B			C																
11820	107	PLC WRK GVT AGCY	5A09C	5A05C	5A05C	5A05C			C					H										
11830	107	PLC WRK MLTY SVC	5A09D	5A05D	5A05D	5A05D			C										L						
11840	107	PLC WRK SCH/UNIV	5A09E	5A05E	5A05E	5A05E		B	C																
11850	107	PLC WRK PLC DEPT	5A09F	5A05F	5A05F	5A05F			C																
11860	107	PLC WRK SOC SVCS	5A09G	5A05G	5A05G	5A05G			C													O			
11870	107	PLC WRK SML GRP	5A09H	5A05H	5A05H	5A05H			C																
11880	107	PLC WRK SLF EMPL	5A09I	5A05I	5A05I	5A05I			C																
11890		RCL CNTCT SCHOOL		5A07A	5A07A	5A07A		B													N				
11900		RCL CNTCT NGHBHD		5A07B	5A07B	5A07B															N				
11910		RCL CNTCT CHURCH		5A07C	5A07C	5A07C								G							N				
11920		RCL CNTCT SPORTS		5A07D	5A07D	5A07D															N				
11930		RCL CNTCT CLUBS		5A07E	5A07E	5A07E															N				
11940		RCL CNTCT JOB		5A07F	5A07F	5A07F			C												N				
11950	108	B/W RLTNS WRSE	5A15	5A08	5A08	5A08															N				
11960	113	DNT HV DRVR LCNS	5A22	5A09	5A09	5A09						F													
11970	113	DONT OWN CAR	5A23	5A10	5A10	5A10						F													
11980	113	NEVR USE OTHS CR	5A24	5A11	5A11	5A11						F													
11990		R CUT DRIVING		5A12	5A12	5A12						F													
12000		R CUT ELECTRICTY		5A13	5A13	5A13						F													
12010		RDCE HEAT R'S HM		5A14	5A14	5A14						F													
12020	113	ENJOY SHOPPING	5A35A	5A15A	5A15A	5A15A						F													
12030	113	CARE LATST FASHN	5A35B	5A15B	5A15B	5A15B						F													
12040	113	CR FAM HV NBR HV	5A35C	5A15C	5A15C	5A15C						F													
12050	113	XPCT 2 OWN>PRNTS	5A36	5A16	5A16	5A16						F													
12060	114	LST CNT OWN>PRNT	5A37	5A17	5A17	5A17						F													
12070	109	WRRY ABT OW CTRY	5A19A	5A18A	5A18A	5A18A																O			
12080	109	BTTR IF CTZ WRLD	5A19C	5A18B	5A18B	5A18B																O			
12090	109	-SYMP TWD STARVG	5A19E	5A18C	5A18C	5A18C						F										O			
12100	109	MNRTY NT MY BSNS	5A19F	5A18D	5A18D	5A18D															N	O			
12110	109	UPST PL TR -FAIR	5A19G	5A18E	5A18E	5A18E																O			
12120	109	HELP POOR W MY $	5A19I	5A18F	5A18F	5A18F																O			

ITEM REFERENCE NUMBER	PAGE LOCATION (IN THIS VOLUME)	ITEM DESCRIPTION (ABBREVIATED)	QUESTIONNAIRE LOCATION BY YEAR (FORM, SECTION, AND QUESTION NUMBER)				SUBJECT AREA																	
			1975	1976	1977	1978	A	B	C	D	E	F	G	H	I	J	K	L	M	N	O	P	Q	R	S
12130	110	-MY PRB OT ND HP	5A19K	5A18G	5A18G	5A18G																O				
12140		RB CHNG ETG HABT		5A18H	5A18H	5A18H						F										O				
12150	108	FULLR LVS IF MRY	5A12A	5A18J	5A18J	5A18J				D																
12160	108	ENCRG=INDP DT/SN	5A12B	5A18K	5A18K	5A18K				D																
12170	108	BNG MOTH V FULFL	5A12D	5A18L	5A18L	5A18L				D																
12180	108	FTHR>TIME W CHLD	5A12G	5A18M	5A18M	5A18M				D																
12190	108	HSB MAK IMP DCSN	5A12H	5A18N	5A18N	5A18N				D																
12200	110	CTB TO UNTD FUND	5A20A	5A20A	5A20A	5A20A																O				
12210	110	CTB TO INTL RELF	5A20B	5A20B	5A20B	5A20B																O				
12220	110	CTB TO MNRTY GRP	5A20C	5A20C	5A20C	5A20C															N	O				
12230	110	CTB TO RELGS ORG	5A20D	5A20D	5A20D	5A20D							G									O				
12240	110	CTB TO PLTCL PTY	5A20E	5A20E	5A20E	5A20E								H								O				
12250	111	CTB TO CTZN LBBY	5A20F	5A20F	5A20F	5A20F								H	I							O				
12260	111	CTB TO VS DISEAS	5A20G	5A20G	5A20G	5A20G																O				
12270	111	CTB TO POP PRBMS	5A20H	5A20H	5A20H	5A20H					E											O				
12280	111	CTB TO ENVIR PBM	5A20I	5A20I	5A20I	5A20I						F										O				
12290	111	DSCM WN COLLG ED	5A21A	5A22A	5A22A	5A22A		B		D																
12300	112	DSCM WN LDRSHP	5A21B	5A22B	5A22B	5A22B				D																
12310	112	DSCM WN EXEC/BSN	5A21C	5A22C	5A22C	5A22C			C	D																
12320	112	DSCM WN TOP/PRFN	5A21D	5A22D	5A22D	5A22D			C	D																
12330	112	DSCM WN SKL LABR	5A21E	5A22E	5A22E	5A22E			C	D																
12340	112	DSCM WN PLTCL OF	5A21F	5A22F	5A22F	5A22F				D				H												
12350	112	DSCM WN =PAY =WK	5A21G	5A22G	5A22G	5A22G			C	D																
12360	116	RSK OF CIG1+PK/D	5A41A	5A23A	5A23A	5A23A	A14A																			
12370	116	RSK OF MJ 1-2 X	5A41B	5A23B	5A23B	5A23B	A14A																			
12380	116	RSK OF MJ OCSNLY	5A41C	5A23C	5A23C	5A23C	A14A																			
12390	116	RSK OF MJ REGLY	5A41D	5A23D	5A23D	5A23D	A14A																			
12400	116	RSK OF LSD 1-2 X	5A41E	5A23E	5A23E	5A23E	A14A																			
12410	116	RSK OF LSD REGLY	5A41F	5A23F	5A23F	5A23F	A14A																			
12420	117	RSK OF 'H' 1-2 X	5A41G	5A23G	5A23G	5A23G	A14A																			
12430	117	RSK OF 'H' OCSNL	5A41H	5A23H	5A23H	5A23H	A14A																			
12440	117	RSK OF 'H' REGLY	5A41I	5A23I	5A23I	5A23I	A14A																			
12450	117	RSK OF BARB 1-2X	5A41J	5A23J	5A23J	5A23J	A14A																			
12460	117	RSK OF BARB REGY	5A41K	5A23K	5A23K	5A23K	A14A																			
12470	117	RSK OF AMPH 1-2X	5A41L	5A23L	5A23L	5A23L	A14A																			
12480	117	RSK OF AMPH REG	5A41M	5A23M	5A23M	5A23M	A14A																			
12490	118	RSK OF COKE 1-2X	5A41N	5A23N	5A23N	5A23N	A14A																			
12500	118	RSK OF COKE REG	5A41O	5A23O	5A23O	5A23O	A14A																			
12510	118	RSK OF 1-2 DRINK	5A41P	5A23P	5A23P	5A23P	A14A																			
12520	118	RSK OF 1-2 DR/DA	5A41Q	5A23Q	5A23Q	5A23Q	A14A																			
12530	118	RSK OF 4-5 DR/DA	5A41R	5A23R	5A23R	5A23R	A14A																			
12540	118	RSK OF 5+DR/WKND	5A41S	5A23S	5A23S	5A23S	A14A																			
12550	114	POS ATT TWD SELF	5A39A	5D01A	5D01A	5D01A																		Q		
12560	114	LUCK>IMP HRD WRK	5A39B	5D01B	5D01B	5D01B																		Q		
12570	114	AM PRSN OF WORTH	5A39C	5D01C	5D01C	5D01C																		Q		
12580	114	DO WELL AS OTHRS	5A39D	5D01D	5D01D	5D01D																		Q		
12590	115	TRY GT AHD,STOPD	5A39E	5D01E	5D01E	5D01E																		Q		
12600	115	PLNNG MKS UNHPPY	5A39F	5D01F	5D01F	5D01F																		Q		
12610	115	ACPT LIFE->HAPPR	5A39G	5D01G	5D01G	5D01G																		Q		
12620	115	SATISFD W MYSELF	5A39H	5D01H	5D01H	5D01H																	P	Q		
12630	115	PPL LK ME -CHANC	5A39I	5D01I	5D01I	5D01I																		Q		
12640		MY PLANS DO WORK			5D01J	5D01J																		Q		
12650		OFTN FEEL LONELY			5D01K	5D01K														M				Q		
12660		-MUCH TO B PROUD			5D01L	5D01L																		Q		
12670		ALWYS SM1 HELP R			5D01M	5D01M														M				Q		
12680		I AM NO GOOD			5D01N	5D01N																		Q		
12690		OFTN FL LEFT OUT			5D01O	5D01O														M				Q		
12700		PPL MASTER FATE			5D01P	5D01P																		Q		
12710		USLY SM1 TALK TO			5D01Q	5D01Q														M				Q		
12720		I DO WRONG THING			5D01R	5D01R																		Q		
12730		OFT WSH MOR FRND			5D01S	5D01S														M				Q		
12740		PLANS->BTR RSLTS			5D01T	5D01T																		Q		
12750		MY LIFE NT USEFL			5D01U	5D01U																		Q		
12760		USLY FRDS BE WTH			5D01V	5D01V														M				Q		
12770		LV TGTH=BD MRLTY		5D05	5D02	5D02				D																
12780		PSN TKG MJ/AMBTS		5D02A			A12D																			

ITEM REFERENCE NUMBER	PAGE LOCATION (IN THIS VOLUME)	ITEM DESCRIPTION (ABBREVIATED)	1975	1976	1977	1978	A	B C D E F G H I J K L M N O P Q R S
12790		PSN TKG MJ/-SOCL		5D02B			A12D	
12800		PSN TKG MJ/CNFMG		5D02C			A12D	
12810		PSN TKG MJ/CRMNL		5D02D			A12D	
12820		PSN TKG MJ/-STBL		5D02E			A12D	
12830		PSN TKG MJ/INTRS		5D02F			A12D	
12840		PSN TKG MJ/RBLS		5D02G			A12D	
12850		PSN TKG MJ/SNSBL		5D02H			A12D	
12860		PSN TKG MJ/SX PR		5D02I			A12D	
12870		PSN TKG MJ/WKWLD		5D02J			A12D	
12880		FAM-MAR=BD MRLTY		5D06	5D03	5D03		D
12890		PSN TKG DG/AMBTS		5D03A			A12D	
12900		PSN TKG DG/-SOCL		5D03B			A12D	
12910		PSN TKG DG/CNFMG		5D03C			A12D	
12920		PSN TKG DG/CRMNL		5D03D			A12D	
12930		PSN TKG DG/-STBL		5D03E			A12D	
12940		PSN TKG DG/INTRS		5D03F			A12D	
12950		PSN TKG DG/RBLS		5D03G			A12D	
12960		PSN TKG DG/SNSBL		5D03H			A12D	
12970		PSN TKG DG/SX PR		5D03I			A12D	
12980		PSN TKG DG/WKWLD		5D03J			A12D	
12990		I HAVE ENOUGH $			5D04A	5D04A		C
13000		I LACK $ FR BILL			5D04B	5D04B		C
13010		I WRY @-FINDG JOB			5D04C	5D04C		C
13020		I CAN FIND JOB			5D04D	5D04D		C
13030		I CAN KEEP MYJOB			5D04E	5D04E		C
13040		I WRY @LOSS MYJOB			5D04F	5D04F		C
13050		R'S STATE LAW/MJ	5D04		5D05	5D05	A13D	
13060		I/MJ USR,>CREATV			5E01A	5E01A	A11D	
13070		I/MJ USR,<SENSBL			5E01B	5E01B	A11D	
13080		I/MJ USR,>INTRST			5E01C	5E01C	A11D	
13090		I/MJ USR,<HRDWKG			5E01D	5E01D	A11D	
13100		I/MJ USR,>INDPND			5E01E	5E01E	A11D	
13110		I/MJ USR,>UNSTBL			5E01F	5E01F	A11D	
13120		I/MJ USR,>CNCRND			5E01G	5E01G	A11D	
13130		I/MJ USR,>WKWLD			5E01H	5E01H	A11D	•
13140		I/MJ USR,>CRMNL			5E01I	5E01I	A11D	
13150		FAM+REL GD/CHILD		5E01A				D M
13160		FAM+REL GD/PARNT		5E01B				D M
13170		FAM+REL GD/GRPNT		5E01C				D M
13180		FAM+REL,R LIK/PT		5E01D				D M
13190		PPL/MJUSR>CREATV			5E02A	5E02A	A12D	
13200		PPL/MJUSR<SENSBL			5E02B	5E02B	A12D	
13210		PPL/MJUSR>INTRST			5E02C	5E02C	A12D	
13220		PPL/MJUSR<HRDWKG			5E02D	5E02D	A12D	
13230		PPL/MJUSR>INDPND			5E02E	5E02E	A12D	
13240		PPL/MJUSR>UNSTBL			5E02F	5E02F	A12D	
13250		PPL/MJUSR>CNCRND			5E02G	5E02G	A12D	
13260		PPL/MJUSR>WKWLD			5E02H	5E02H	A12D	
13270		PPL/MJUSR>CRMNL			5E02I	5E02I	A12D	
13280		FAM+CPL GD/CHILD		5E02A				D
13290		FAM+CPL GD/PARNT		5E02B				D
13300		FAM+CPL GD/GRPNT		5E02C				D
13310		FAM+CPL,LIK/PRNT		5E02D				D
13320		FAM+CPL,LIK/-CHD		5E02E				D
13330		I/DG USR,>CREATV			5E03A	5E03A	A11D	
13340		I/DG USR,<SENSBL			5E03B	5E03B	A11D	
13350		I/DG USR,>INTRST			5E03C	5E03C	A11D	
13360		I/DG USR,<HRDWKG			5E03D	5E03D	A11D	
13370		I/DG USR,>INDPND			5E03E	5E03E	A11D	
13380		I/DG USR,>UNSTBL			5E03F	5E03F	A11D	
13390		I/DG USR,>CNCRND			5E03G	5E03G	A11D	
13400		I/DG USR,>WKWLD			5E03H	5E03H	A11D	
13410		I/DG USR,>CRMNL			5E03I	5E03I	A11D	
13420		CPL+OTH+CHD MAR		5E03A				D
13430		CPL+OTH+CHD DVC		5E03B				D
13440		CPL+OTH+MAR CPL		5E03C				D

ITEM REFERENCE NUMBER	PAGE LOCATION (IN THIS VOLUME)	ITEM DESCRIPTION (ABBREVIATED)	QUESTIONNAIRE LOCATION BY YEAR (FORM, SECTION, AND QUESTION NUMBER)				SUBJECT AREA	
			1975	1976	1977	1978	A	B C D E F G H I J K L M N O P Q R S
13450		CPL+OTH +DIV PRT		5E03D				D
13460		CPL+OTH +UNMARRD		5E03E				D
13470		CPL+OTH,LK,MR PT		5E03F				D
13480		CPL+OTH,LK,DVC P		5E03G				D
13490		PPL/DGUSR>CREATV			5E04A	5E04A	A12D	
13500		PPL/DGUSR<SENSBL			5E04B	5E04B	A12D	
13510		PPL/DGUSR>INTRST			5E04C	5E04C	A12D	
13520		PPL/DGUSR<HRDWKG			5E04D	5E04D	A12D	
13530		PPL/DGUSR>INDPND			5E04E	5E04E	A12D	
13540		PPL/DGUSR>UNSTBL			5E04F	5E04F	A12D	
13550		PPL/DGUSR>CNCRND			5E04G	5E04G	A12D	
13560		PPL/DGUSR>WKWLD			5E04H	5E04H	A12D	
13570		PPL/DGUSR>CRMNL			5E04I	5E04I	A12D	
13580		STS SCH RT FAMLY		5E05A	5E06A	5E06A		B R
13590		STS SCH LDS STU		5E05B	5E06B	5E06B		B M
13600		STS SCH NIC CAR		5E05C	5E06C	5E06C		B F
13610		STS SCH HI GRDE		5E05D	5E06D	5E06D		B
13620		STS SCH GD ATHLT		5E05E	5E06E	5E06E		B
13630		STS SCH INTLCTL		5E05F	5E06F	5E06F		B
13640		STS SCH PLN CLG		5E05G	5E06G	5E06G		B
13650		DRG USE+,MAJ STD		5E06A	5E07A	5E07A	A12C	
13660		DRG USE+,MY FRND		5E06B	5E07B	5E07B	A12B	
13670		DRG USE+,MY FLGS			5E07C	5E07C	A11D	
08780		OFT W PL TK QUAL		5E07D	5E08D	5E08D	A02B	
08835		OFT W PL TK INHL		5E07J	5E08J	5E08J	A02B	
13700		BY SOON HAIR DRY		2E10A				F
13710		BY SOON WT/S SKI		2E10B				F
13720		BY SOON CAMERA		2E10C				F
13730		BY SOON WATCH		2E10D				F
13740		BY SOON HKG BKPK		2E10E				F
13750		BY SOON CK RADIO		2E10F				F
13760		BY SOON EL SHAVR		2E10G				F
13770		BY SOON TENIS RQ		2E10H				F
13780		BY SOON TV SET		2E10I				F
13790		BY SOON BICYCLE		2E10J				F
13800		BY SOON CAR		2E10K				F
13810		BY SOON TAPE REC		2E10L				F
13820		BY SOON ELT CALC		2E10M				F
13830		BY SOON BT/SNMBL		2E10N				F
13835		IMP HAV 1 CAR		3E12A		3E11A		F
13840		IMP HAV 2 CARS		3E12B		3E11B		F
13850		IMP HAV LARG CAR		3E12C		3E11C		F
13860		IMP HAV NW CR OF		3E12D		3E11D		F
13870		IMP HAV NW CLTHS		3E12E		3E11E		F
13880		IMP HAV OWN HSE		3E12F		3E11F		F
13890		IMP HAV BIG YARD		3E12G		3E11G		F
13900		IMP HAV NEAT LWN		3E12H		3E11H		F
13910		IMP HAV APPLINCS		3E12I		3E11I		F
13920		IMP HAV G STEREO		3E12J		3E11J		F
13930		IMP HAV VAC HSE		3E12K		3E11K		F
13940		IMP HAV REC VEH		3E12L		3E11L		F
16320		EFCTV WRIT OFCLS				2E04A		H I
16330		EFCTV WRK PL CPN				2E04B		H I
16340		EFCTV VOTING				2E04C		H I
16350		EFCTV PETITIONS				2E04D		H I
16360		EFCTV BOYCOTT				2E04E		H I
16370		EFCTV LWFL DMSTN				2E04F		H I
16380		EFCTV OCPY BLDGS				2E04G		H I
16390		EFCTV WLDCT STRK				2E04H		H I
16400		EFCTV BLK TRAFIC				2E04I		H I
16410		EFCTV DAMAG THNG				2E04J		H I
16420		EFCTV PSNL VLNC				2E04K		H I
16430		SAT EVB CAR POOL				2E05A		F O
16440		SAT EAT<BEEF>GRN				2E05B		F O
16450		SAT TAX FR ECLGY				2E05C		F
17860		DESRD LVG RURAL				4E09A		F

ITEM REFERENCE NUMBER	PAGE LOCATION (IN THIS VOLUME)	ITEM DESCRIPTION (ABBREVIATED)	QUESTIONNAIRE LOCATION BY YEAR (FORM, SECTION, AND QUESTION NUMBER)				SUBJECT AREA	
			1975	1976	1977	1978	A	B C D E F G H I J K L M N O P Q R S
17870		DESRD LVG SM TWN				4E09B		F
17880		DESRD LVG SM CTY				4E09C		F
17890		DESRD LVG SUBURB				4E09D		F
17900		DESRD LVG LG CTY				4E09E		F
17910		DSRD HSG 1 FAMLY				4E09F		F
17920		DSRD HSG 2 FAMLY				4E09G		F
17930		DSRD HSG CNDMINM				4E09H		F
17940		DSRD HSG APT BLD				4E09I		F
17950		DSRD HSG HI RISE				4E09J		F
20590		12MO NR OTH MARJ		3A29A	3A29A	3A29A	A02B	
20600		12MO NR OTH LSD		3A29B	3A29B	3A29B	A02B	
20610		12MO NR OTH PSYC		3A29C	3A29C	3A29C	A02B	
20620		12MO NR OTH AMPH		3A29D	3A29D	3A29D	A02B	
20630		12MO NR OTH BARB		3A29E	3A29E	3A29E	A02B	
20640		12MO NR OTH TRQL		3A29F	3A29F	3A29F	A02B	
20650		12MO NR OTH COKE		3A29G	3A29G	3A29G	A02B	
20660		12MO NR OTH HRN		3A29H	3A29H	3A29H	A02B	
20670		12MO NR OTH NARC		3A29I	3A29I	3A29I	A02B	
20680		12MO NR OTH ALCL		3A29J	3A29J	3A29J	A02B	

Appendix A
Sampling Error Estimates and Tables

All of the percentages reported in this volume are really *estimates* of the response percentages that would have been obtained if, instead of using a sample survey, we had asked all high schools throughout the United States to participate, and in all schools that agreed to participate we had invited the whole senior class to fill out the questionnaires. The question naturally arises: How accurate are the present percentage estimates based on a limited number of schools and seniors? For any particular percentage resulting from a sample survey we cannot know exactly how much error has resulted from sampling, but we can make reasonably good estimates of "confidence intervals" — ranges within which the "true" population value is very likely to fall. The word "true" in this context is defined quite narrowly; it refers only to the value that would be found if we had set out to survey the total population — all high school seniors in the United States. Thus this concept of "true" population value does *not* take account of biases that might occur due to refusals, distortion of responses, faulty question wording, and other factors. Each of these sources of possible error is discussed in the "Representativeness and Validity" section of the Introduction to this volume. The reader is urged to review this material and take it into account along with the sampling error estimates included in this appendix.

The estimation of confidence intervals in surveys involving complex samples can be a highly complicated combination of statistical science plus informed judgment. It is an area in which there is no single "right answer" or "best approach." We suspect that many of those using this volume will not be especially interested in *how* we have chosen to solve the problems involved in estimating confidence intervals, so long as we provide guidelines

that can be applied in a fairly simple and straightforward manner. This appendix is designed to accomplish that. Appendix B provides a more extensive discussion of how we obtained the confidence intervals shown here, and it also provides guidelines for computing specific confidence intervals for a wider range of possible applications than can be covered in the tables provided in this appendix.

A very rough example of a confidence interval can be stated in these terms: For percentages based on the total sample (all five questionnaire forms), the "true" values are rarely more than 1.5 percent higher or lower than the percentage estimates reported in this volume. How rarely? The chances are much lower than 1 in 20. Indeed, many of the percentages reported for the total sample are accurate to within one percent.

Of course, most of the data reported here are based on items included only in one or another of the five questionnaire forms. Since such percentages are based on only one-fifth of the total sample, they are somewhat less accurate. The loss in accuracy is less than might be imagined, however, for reasons spelled out in Appendix B. For present purposes, it is enough to say that percentages based on 3,000 or more seniors responding to one questionnaire form are rarely (less than 1 in 20) farther than 2.4 percent away from the "true" value.

We have thus far provided two very rough illustrations of confidence intervals — a range of ±1.5 percent for percentages based on the total sample, and a range of ±2.4 percent for percentages based on the number of seniors responding to one questionnaire form. While these two intervals provide some notion of the overall range of accuracy of the sample, they fall short of our needs in a number of respects. We need to be able to assign confidence intervals for subgroups such as males, females, those who plan to complete college, and so forth, all of which involve smaller numbers of cases and thus some reduction in accuracy. We also need to take account of the fact that, other things equal, confidence intervals grow smaller when one moves from the middle of the scale (percentages near 50 percent) to the extremes (e.g., 4 percent or 96 percent). Further, we need to provide guidelines for evaluating the *difference* between two percentages; for example, we may wish to know whether the difference between male and female percentages in response to a particular question is large enough so that it is not likely to be merely the result of sampling error. Another type of difference of considerable interest is that between percentages from two different years; for example, we may wish to know whether an increase in the percentage of daily marijuana users from one year to the next is large enough to be considered a statistically significant change.

Each of the requirements mentioned above is taken into account in the tables of confidence intervals which follow.

Confidence Intervals for Single Percentages

Table A-1 provides confidence intervals for single percentages that are reasonably good approximations for most *variables* and for most *subgroups* (as well as for the total sample). The table entries slightly underestimate the confidence intervals for regional subgroups and for blacks. These underestimates can be corrected reasonably well by multiplying the entries in Table A-1 by a factor of 1.1 for data based on a single form and by a factor of 1.33 for data based on all five forms. A more serious problem is that the table entries substantially underestimate the confidence intervals for certain variables which tend to be somewhat homogeneous within schools, as well as other factors likely to show clustering according to geographical area or socioeconomic level. A discussion of some of these variables is provided at the end of this appendix.

Table A-1 accommodates various numbers of cases (presented as different columns in the table), and various percentages (presented as different rows in the table). The table entries, when added to and subtracted from the observed percentage, establish the 95 percent confidence interval (calculated as 1.96 sampling errors). Thus, for example, to determine the accuracy of a result of 67.4 percent based on a sample of 1,632 cases, one should first look for the closest values in the table (in this case, about 70 percent and a number of cases approximately equal to 1,500); next determine the values to be added to and subtracted from

the observed percentage (in this case the values would be +2.8 percent and -2.9 percent); and then compute the confidence interval around the observed percentage of 67.4 percent (in this case an interval ranging from 64.5 percent to 70.2 percent). This procedure yields an interval such that, for most variables, the chances are 95 in 100 that if all high school seniors in the country had been asked to participate in the survey the resulting percentage would fall within the interval.

Confidence Intervals for Differences between Two Percentages

Table A-2 provides confidence intervals for differences between certain percentages. Specifically, the table can be used for *comparisons* between males and females, between those who do and do not plan to complete four years of college, and between those falling into different categories of the five-level index of drug usage. The above comparisons are appropriate for data from any single year (e.g., male seniors in 1976 compared with female seniors in 1976, or the "marijuana only" seniors in 1977 compared with the "no illicit drugs" seniors in 1977). Table A-2 is also useful in assessing *one-year trends* for any of the above subgroups as well as for the total sample. For example, one may be interested in a confidence interval (or significance level) for the difference between the percentage of female seniors in 1977 who used marijuana and the percentage of female seniors in 1978 who did so. The values in Table A-2 are appropriate for confidence intervals across adjacent years (e.g., 1976 compared with 1977), provided the same subgroup (e.g., females) is being considered both years. The confidence intervals for comparisons across non-adjacent years (e.g., 1976 compared with 1978), are slightly larger.

With appropriate corrections, the entries in Table A-2 can be used for trends covering more than one year and for trends or comparisons involving regional subgroups and blacks. Each of these applications requires some upward adjustment of the table entries; guidelines for such adjustments are provided in the notes accompanying Table A-2.

For information on the derivation of Table A-2 and for guidelines to be used in computing confidence intervals not covered in that table, the reader is referred to Appendix B.

In order to find the appropriate confidence interval in Table A-2, one must first locate that portion of the table which deals with percentage values closest to the two percentages being compared (for example, if one wished to compare a value of 28.1 percent with one of 35.4 percent, the "p = 30 percent or 70 percent" portion of the table would be closest). The next step is to locate the specific table entry which corresponds most closely to the numbers of cases involved in the two percentages being compared (e.g., if those numbers were 1,478 and 1,563 for 28.1 percent and 35.4 percent, the correct table entry would be 3.9 percent). That table entry, when added to and subtracted from the difference between the two percentages, yields the 95 percent confidence interval for the difference. (In the above illustration that would be 7.3 percent ±3.9 percent or an interval from 3.4 percent to 11.2 percent.) The chances are only 1 in 20 that the "true" difference between two percentages lies outside of this interval.

Another use of Table A-2 is to test whether a difference between two percentages is "statistically significant." If the table entry is smaller than the difference between the two percentages (as is true in the above illustration), then the difference is statistically significant at the 95 percent level (sometimes indicated as p<.05).

Some Cautions

The tables provided here are based on averages of large numbers of sampling errors computed across a wide range of the variables which appear in this volume, as well as across all of the subgroups for which data are reported here. We are confident that the values in the tables are reasonably accurate for most purposes, but we must repeat the caution that the tables slightly underestimate confidence intervals for the following groups and comparisons:

    Blacks

    Regions (Northeast, North Central, South, West)

    Comparisons among regions

    Comparisons across non-adjacent years (e.g., 1976 vs. 1978)

A more important problem is that the tables substantially underestimate the confidence intervals for certain variables that, for various reasons, show greater than average homogeneity within schools. After an extensive, but by no means exhaustive, sampling of the kinds of variables which might show such clustering by school, we can provide the following examples of the kinds of variables for which Tables A-1 and A-2 substantially underestimate the confidence intervals.

Variables Related to Educational Background and Aspirations. The questionnaire items dealing with father's education, mother's education, high school curriculum (college preparatory versus all other), and plans for completing four years of college, all show an appreciable amount of clustering by school. Accordingly, for such variables the confidence intervals provided in the tables should be doubled.

Other items dealing with plans for technical/vocational schooling, a two-year college program, or graduate/professional study, also require adjustment. The confidence intervals in the tables should be multiplied by a factor of 1.5 in order to be applicable to these variables.

It seems clear that the common factor underlying these particular variables is the tendency for family socioeconomic level to be somewhat homogeneous within school districts — some schools serve wealthier populations than others. That makes the form of sampling we use somewhat less efficient for measuring those variables (like those listed above) which are closely associated with family socioeconomic level. Therefore, we urge the reader to treat with caution any variables which are likely to be strongly linked to socioeconomic factors. In the absence of more specific computations of sampling errors, a good rule of thumb for dealing with such variables would be to double the confidence intervals provided in Tables A-1 and A-2.

Variables Related to Geographic Location. Another category of variables which are somewhat homogeneous within schools and school districts consists of those things which reflect differences in region and/or urbanicity. An obvious example is a background question asking where the respondent grew up; the response category "on a farm" shows a very high degree of clustering within schools. One would have to more than double the confidence intervals in the tables to deal with such a measure. Similarly high clustering was found for some responses about religious preference; for example, those whose preference is Baptist are located primarily in the South (and probably heavily in rural areas), whereas those whose preference is Jewish are located primarily in the Northeast (especially in larger cities). The confidence intervals in Tables A-1 and A-2 should be multiplied by a factor as large as 3 in order to be applicable to such variables.

Other variables which show some greater than average homogeneity within schools include such ideologically related dimensions as frequency of attending religious services, importance of religion, and political preference. Still other variables showing high homogeneity, probably because of their association with urbanicity, include driving (percentage who usually do not drive at all), working (percentage with no job), and household composition (percentage with father not living in the home). For each of the variables mentioned in this paragraph, the confidence intervals shown in Tables A-1 and A-2 should be multipled by a factor of about 1.5.

Variables Involving Use of Alcohol and Marijuana. Extensive work has been done to compute sampling errors and confidence intervals for the drug use measures included in this volume (see Johnston, Bachman, and O'Malley, 1977, 1979, especially Appendix B). Most drug use variables show sampling errors which lie within the range of those provided in Tables A-1 and A-2. Usage levels for alcohol and marijuana, however, show some

degree of homogeneity within schools, thus requiring that the table levels be adjusted. For items dealing with alcohol use, the table entries should be multiplied by a factor of 1.6; for items dealing with marijuana use, the correction factor is 1.35.

As noted earlier, this appendix has presented guidelines for using the tables of confidence intervals provided herein. Those readers interested in learning more about the rationale underlying such tables, the procedures used to derive the particular tables presented here, and guidelines for further computations of confidence intervals may consult Appendix B of this volume.

Notes to Table A-1

Caution: The entries in this table systematically underestimate confidence intervals for regional subgroups and for blacks. In order to correct these underestimates, the table entries should be multiplied by a factor of 1.10 for data from a single form and by a factor of 1.33 for data based on five forms. Further cautions and corrections are required for some specific variables which relate to educational background and aspirations, geographic location,

and the use of alcohol and marijuana (see discussion in the final sections of Appendix A).

The values in this table, when added to and subtracted from an observed percentage, establish the 95 percent confidence interval around that percentage, incorporating a design effect. Table values were calculated using the following formula (adapted from Hays, 1973, p. 379):

$$\text{lower limit} = p - \frac{2N'p + (1.96)^2 - 1.96\sqrt{4N'p\,(1-p) + (1.96)^2}}{2[N' + (1.96)^2]}$$

$$\text{upper limit} = \frac{2N'p + (1.96)^2 + 1.96\sqrt{4N'p\,(1-p) + (1.96)^2}}{2[N' + (1.96)^2]} - p$$

where p = the percentage, and N' is the "effective N," $N' = N/(1.3 + .00015N)$. (See Appendix B for a discussion of the concept of "effective N.")

Table A-1

Confidence Intervals (95% Level) around Percentage Values

							Number of Cases											
	100	200	300	400	500	700	1000	1500	2000	2500	3000	3500	4000	5000	7000	10000	15000	20000
99% +	0.9	0.8	0.7	0.7	0.6	0.6	0.5	0.5	0.4	0.4	0.4	0.4	0.3	0.3	0.3	0.3	0.3	0.2
−	5.6	3.2	2.4	1.9	1.7	1.3	1.1	0.8	0.7	0.6	0.6	0.6	0.5	0.5	0.4	0.4	0.3	0.3
97% +	2.1	1.8	1.6	1.4	1.3	1.2	1.0	0.9	0.8	0.8	0.7	0.7	0.6	0.6	0.6	0.5	0.5	0.5
−	6.6	4.1	3.2	2.6	2.3	1.9	1.6	1.3	1.1	1.0	0.9	0.9	0.8	0.8	0.7	0.6	0.6	0.5
95% +	3.1	2.5	2.2	2.0	1.8	1.6	1.4	1.2	1.1	1.0	0.9	0.9	0.9	0.8	0.7	0.7	0.6	0.6
−	7.4	4.7	3.7	3.1	2.7	2.3	1.9	1.5	1.4	1.2	1.1	1.1	1.0	0.9	0.8	0.8	0.7	0.7
90% +	4.9	3.8	3.3	2.9	2.7	2.3	2.0	1.7	1.5	1.4	1.3	1.3	1.2	1.1	1.0	0.9	0.9	0.8
−	8.8	5.8	4.6	4.0	3.5	2.9	2.5	2.0	1.8	1.6	1.5	1.4	1.4	1.3	1.1	1.0	0.9	0.9
85% +	6.6	4.8	4.1	3.6	3.3	2.9	2.5	2.1	1.9	1.7	1.6	1.5	1.5	1.4	1.2	1.1	1.0	1.0
−	9.7	6.6	5.3	4.5	4.0	3.4	2.9	2.4	2.1	1.9	1.8	1.7	1.6	1.5	1.3	1.2	1.1	1.1
80% +	7.4	5.6	4.7	4.2	3.8	3.3	2.8	2.4	2.1	2.0	1.8	1.7	1.7	1.5	1.4	1.3	1.2	1.1
−	10.3	7.1	5.7	4.9	4.4	3.7	3.1	2.6	2.3	2.1	2.0	1.8	1.8	1.6	1.5	1.3	1.2	1.2
70% +	9.1	6.8	5.6	5.0	4.5	3.9	3.3	2.8	2.5	2.3	2.1	2.0	1.9	1.8	1.6	1.5	1.4	1.3
−	11.1	7.7	6.3	5.5	4.9	4.2	3.5	2.9	2.6	2.4	2.2	2.1	2.0	1.8	1.7	1.5	1.4	1.3
50% +	11.0	7.9	6.5	5.7	5.1	4.4	3.7	3.1	2.8	2.5	2.4	2.2	2.1	2.0	1.8	1.6	1.5	1.4
−	11.0	7.9	6.5	5.7	5.1	4.4	3.7	3.1	2.8	2.5	2.4	2.2	2.1	2.0	1.8	1.6	1.5	1.4
30% +	11.1	7.7	6.3	5.5	4.9	4.2	3.5	2.9	2.6	2.4	2.2	2.1	2.0	1.8	1.7	1.5	1.4	1.3
−	9.1	6.8	5.6	5.0	4.5	3.9	3.3	2.8	2.5	2.3	2.1	2.0	1.9	1.8	1.6	1.5	1.4	1.3
20% +	10.3	7.1	5.7	4.9	4.4	3.7	3.1	2.6	2.3	2.1	2.0	1.8	1.8	1.6	1.5	1.3	1.2	1.2
−	7.4	5.6	4.7	4.2	3.8	3.3	2.8	2.4	2.1	2.0	1.6	1.7	1.7	1.5	1.4	1.3	1.2	1.1
15% +	9.7	6.6	5.3	4.5	4.0	3.4	2.9	2.4	2.1	1.9	1.8	1.7	1.6	1.5	1.3	1.2	1.1	1.1
−	6.3	4.8	4.1	3.6	3.3	2.9	2.5	2.1	1.9	1.7	1.6	1.5	1.5	1.4	1.2	1.1	1.0	1.0
10% +	8.8	5.8	4.6	4.0	3.5	2.9	2.5	2.0	1.8	1.6	1.5	1.4	1.4	1.3	1.1	1.0	0.9	0.9
−	4.9	3.8	3.3	2.9	2.7	2.3	2.0	1.7	1.5	1.4	1.3	1.3	1.2	1.1	1.0	0.9	0.9	0.8
5% +	7.4	4.7	3.7	3.1	2.7	2.3	1.9	1.5	1.4	1.2	1.1	1.1	1.0	0.9	0.8	0.8	0.7	0.7
−	3.1	2.5	2.2	2.0	1.8	1.6	1.4	1.2	1.1	1.0	0.9	0.9	0.9	0.8	0.7	0.7	0.6	0.6
3% +	6.6	4.1	3.2	2.6	2.3	1.9	1.6	1.3	1.1	1.0	0.9	0.9	0.8	0.8	0.7	0.6	0.6	0.5
−	2.1	1.8	1.6	1.4	1.3	1.2	1.0	0.9	0.8	0.8	0.7	0.7	0.6	0.6	0.6	0.5	0.5	0.5
1% +	5.6	3.2	2.4	1.9	1.7	1.3	1.1	0.8	0.7	0.6	0.6	0.6	0.5	0.5	0.4	0.4	0.3	0.3
−	0.9	0.8	0.7	0.7	0.6	0.6	0.5	0.5	0.4	0.4	0.4	0.4	0.3	0.3	0.3	0.3	0.3	0.2

Notes to Table A-2

The entries in this table (which appear on the next two pages) are appropriate for *comparisons* between (a) males and females, (b) those who do and do not plan four years of college, and (c) those falling into different categories of the five-level index of drug usage. The table entries are also appropriate for *one-year trends* for the total sample and any of the subgroups except region. Most other trends and subgroup comparisons require that the table entries be multiplied by an adjustment factor, given below.

Outline of Steps to Follow (see text of appendix for illustrations)

1. Locate the portion of the table with "p" values closest to the two percentages being compared.

2. Locate the specific entry closest to the weighted Ns for the two percentages.

3. Multiply that entry by any necessary adjustment factor (see below).

4. That table value (or adjusted table value), when added to and subtracted from the difference between the two percentages, yields the 95 percent confidence interval for the difference.

5. Also, if the table value (or adjusted table value) is smaller than the difference between the two percentages, then the difference may be described as "statistically significant at the 95 percent level."

	Adjustment Factor (to be multiplied by table entry)
Adjustment Factors	
For comparisons between blacks and whites	
based on single form data	*
based on five form data	1.25
For comparisons between any two regions	
based on single form data	1.15
based on five form data	1.50
For one-year trends involving any region	
based on single form data	*
based on five form data	1.25
For trends over two or more years involving any region	
based on single form data	*
based on five form data	1.35
For trends over two or more years involving all other groups	
based on single form data	*
based on five form data	1.15

*indicates that no adjustment is necessary for category shown

NOTE: The table entries were calculated using the following formula: $1.96\sqrt{p(1-p)\dfrac{1}{N_1'}+\dfrac{1}{N_2'}}$

where $N_1' = N_1/DEFF$, and $N_2' = N_2/DEFF$, $DEFF = 1.3 + .000075\left[\dfrac{N_1 N_2}{N_1 + N_2}\right]$

Table A-2

Confidence Intervals (95% Confidence Level)
for Differences Between Two Percentages

	N₁=100	200	300	400	500	700	1000	1500	2000	3000	4000	5000	7000	10000	15000	20000
N₂= 100	3.2															
200	2.7	2.2														
300	2.6	2.0	1.8													
400	2.5	1.9	1.7	1.6												
500	2.4	1.9	1.6	1.5	1.4					p = 1% or 99%						
700	2.4	1.8	1.6	1.4	1.3	1.2										
1000	2.3	1.7	1.5	1.3	1.2	1.1	1.0									
1500	2.3	1.7	1.4	1.3	1.2	1.0	0.9	0.8								
2000	2.3	1.7	1.4	1.2	1.1	1.0	0.9	0.8	0.7							
3000	2.3	1.6	1.4	1.2	1.1	1.0	0.8	0.7	0.7	0.6						
4000	2.3	1.6	1.4	1.2	1.1	0.9	0.8	0.7	0.7	0.6	0.6					
5000	2.3	1.6	1.3	1.2	1.1	0.9	0.8	0.7	0.6	0.6	0.5	0.5				
7000	2.3	1.6	1.3	1.2	1.1	0.9	0.8	0.7	0.6	0.5	0.5	0.5	0.4			
10000	2.2	1.6	1.3	1.2	1.0	0.9	0.8	0.7	0.6	0.5	0.5	0.5	0.4	0.4		
15000	2.2	1.6	1.3	1.2	1.0	0.9	0.8	0.6	0.6	0.5	0.5	0.4	0.4	0.4	0.4	
20000	2.2	1.6	1.3	1.1	1.0	0.9	0.8	0.6	0.6	0.5	0.5	0.4	0.4	0.4	0.3	0.3

	N₁=100	200	300	400	500	700	1000	1500	2000	3000	4000	5000	7000	10000	15000	20000
N₂= 100	5.4															
200	4.7	3.8														
300	4.4	3.5	3.1													
400	4.3	3.3	2.9	2.7						p = 3% or 97%						
500	4.2	3.2	2.8	2.6	2.4											
700	4.1	3.1	2.7	2.4	2.3	2.1										
1000	4.0	3.0	2.5	2.3	2.1	1.9	1.8									
1500	4.0	2.9	2.4	2.2	2.0	1.8	1.6	1.5								
2000	3.9	2.9	2.4	2.1	1.9	1.7	1.5	1.4	1.3							
3000	3.9	2.8	2.3	2.1	1.9	1.7	1.5	1.3	1.2	1.1						
4000	3.9	2.8	2.3	2.0	1.9	1.6	1.4	1.2	1.1	1.0	0.9					
5000	3.9	2.8	2.3	2.0	1.8	1.6	1.4	1.2	1.1	1.0	0.9	0.9				
7000	3.9	2.8	2.3	2.0	1.8	1.6	1.4	1.2	1.0	0.9	0.9	0.8	0.8			
10000	3.9	2.8	2.3	2.0	1.8	1.5	1.3	1.1	1.0	0.9	0.8	0.8	0.7	0.7		
15000	3.8	2.7	2.3	2.0	1.8	1.5	1.3	1.1	1.0	0.9	0.8	0.7	0.7	0.6	0.6	
20000	3.8	2.7	2.3	2.0	1.8	1.5	1.3	1.1	1.0	0.9	0.8	0.7	0.7	0.6	0.6	0.6

Table A-2 (continued)

$N_1 =$	100	200	300	400	500	700	1000	1500	2000	3000	4000	5000	7000	10000	15000	20000
$N_2 = 100$	6.9															
200	6.0	4.9														
300	5.6	4.5	4.0													
400	5.5	4.3	3.8	3.5												
500	5.4	4.1	3.6	3.3	3.1											
700	5.2	3.9	3.4	3.1	2.9	2.7										
1000	5.1	3.8	3.2	2.9	2.7	2.5	2.2									
1500	5.1	3.7	3.1	2.8	2.6	2.3	2.1	1.9								
2000	5.0	3.6	3.1	2.7	2.5	2.2	2.0	1.7	1.6							
3000	5.0	3.6	3.0	2.6	2.4	2.1	1.9	1.6	1.5	1.4						
4000	5.0	3.6	3.0	2.6	2.4	2.1	1.8	1.6	1.4	1.3	1.2					
5000	4.9	3.6	2.9	2.6	2.3	2.0	1.8	1.5	1.4	1.2	1.2	1.1				
7000	4.9	3.5	2.9	2.6	2.3	2.0	1.7	1.5	1.3	1.2	1.1	1.0	1.0			
10000	4.9	3.5	2.9	2.5	2.3	2.0	1.7	1.4	1.3	1.1	1.1	1.0	0.9	0.9		
15000	4.9	3.5	2.9	2.5	2.3	2.0	1.7	1.4	1.3	1.1	1.0	1.0	0.9	0.8	0.8	
20000	4.9	3.5	2.9	2.5	2.3	1.9	1.7	1.4	1.3	1.1	1.0	0.9	0.9	0.8	0.7	0.7

p = 5% or 95%

$N_1 =$	100	200	300	400	500	700	1000	1500	2000	3000	4000	5000	7000	10000	15000	20000
$N_2 = 100$	9.5															
200	8.2	6.7														
300	7.8	6.2	5.5													
400	7.5	5.9	5.2	4.8												
500	7.4	5.7	4.9	4.6	4.3											
700	7.2	5.4	4.7	4.3	4.0	3.7										
1000	7.1	5.2	4.5	4.0	3.7	3.4	3.1									
1500	7.0	5.1	4.3	3.8	3.5	3.2	2.8	2.6								
2000	6.9	5.0	4.2	3.7	3.4	3.0	2.7	2.4	2.2							
3000	6.9	4.9	4.1	3.6	3.3	2.9	2.6	2.2	2.1	1.9						
4000	6.8	4.9	4.1	3.6	3.3	2.8	2.5	2.2	2.0	1.8	1.7					
5000	6.8	4.9	4.0	3.6	3.2	2.8	2.4	2.1	1.9	1.7	1.6	1.5				
7000	6.8	4.9	4.0	3.5	3.2	2.8	2.4	2.0	1.8	1.6	1.5	1.4	1.3			
10000	6.8	4.8	4.0	3.5	3.2	2.7	2.3	2.0	1.8	1.6	1.4	1.4	1.3	1.2		
15000	6.8	4.8	4.0	3.5	3.1	2.7	2.3	2.0	1.8	1.5	1.4	1.3	1.2	1.1	1.1	
20000	6.8	4.8	4.0	3.5	3.1	2.7	2.3	1.9	1.7	1.5	1.4	1.3	1.2	1.1	1.0	1.0

p = 10% or 90%

Table A-2 (continued)

$N_1 =$	100	200	300	400	500	700	1000	1500	2000	3000	4000	5000	7000	10000	15000	20000
$N_2 = 100$	11.3															
200	9.8	8.0														
300	9.3	7.3	6.6													
400	9.0	7.0	6.2	5.7												
500	8.8	6.7	5.9	5.4	5.1											
700	8.6	6.5	5.6	5.1	4.8	4.4										
1000	8.4	6.2	5.3	4.8	4.5	4.0	3.7									
1500	8.3	6.1	5.1	4.6	4.2	3.8	3.4	3.0								
2000	8.2	6.0	5.0	4.5	4.1	3.6	3.2	2.9	2.7							
3000	8.2	5.9	4.9	4.3	3.9	3.5	3.0	2.7	2.5	2.2						
4000	8.1	5.8	4.9	4.3	3.9	3.4	2.9	2.6	2.3	2.1	2.0					
5000	8.1	5.8	4.8	4.2	3.8	3.3	2.9	2.5	2.3	2.0	1.9	1.8				
7000	8.1	5.8	4.8	4.2	3.8	3.3	2.8	2.4	2.2	1.9	1.8	1.7	1.6			
10000	8.1	5.8	4.8	4.2	3.8	3.2	2.8	2.4	2.1	1.9	1.7	1.6	1.5	1.4		
15000	8.1	5.7	4.7	4.1	3.7	3.2	2.7	2.3	2.1	1.8	1.7	1.6	1.4	1.3	1.3	
20000	8.0	5.7	4.7	4.1	3.7	3.2	2.7	2.3	2.1	1.8	1.6	1.5	1.4	1.3	1.2	1.2

p = 15% or 85%

$N_1 =$	100	200	300	400	500	700	1000	1500	2000	3000	4000	5000	7000	10000	15000	20000
$N_2 = 100$	12.7															
200	11.0	9.0														
300	10.4	8.2	7.4													
400	10.0	7.8	6.9	6.4												
500	9.8	7.5	6.6	6.1	5.7											
700	9.6	7.2	6.2	5.7	5.3	4.9										
1000	9.4	7.0	6.0	5.4	5.0	4.5	4.1									
1500	9.3	6.8	5.7	5.1	4.7	4.2	3.8	3.4								
2000	9.2	6.7	5.6	5.0	4.6	4.0	3.6	3.2	3.0							
3000	9.1	6.6	5.5	4.9	4.4	3.9	3.4	3.0	2.8	2.5						
4000	9.1	6.5	5.4	4.8	4.3	3.8	3.3	2.9	2.6	2.4	2.2					
5000	9.1	6.5	5.4	4.7	4.3	3.7	3.2	2.8	2.6	2.3	2.1	2.0				
7000	9.1	6.5	5.4	4.7	4.2	3.7	3.2	2.7	2.5	2.2	2.0	1.9	1.8			
10000	9.0	6.5	5.3	4.7	4.2	3.6	3.1	2.7	2.4	2.1	1.9	1.8	1.7	1.6		
15000	9.0	6.4	5.3	4.6	4.2	3.6	3.1	2.6	2.3	2.0	1.9	1.7	1.6	1.5	1.4	
20000	9.0	6.4	5.3	4.6	4.2	3.6	3.1	2.6	2.3	2.0	1.8	1.7	1.6	1.5	1.4	1.3

p = 20% or 80%

Table A-2 (continued)

	$N_1=100$	200	300	400	500	700	1000	1500	2000	3000	4000	5000	7000	10000	15000	20000
$N_2=100$	14.5															
200	12.6	10.3														
300	11.9	9.4	8.4													
400	11.5	8.9	7.9	7.3												
500	11.3	8.6	7.6	7.0	6.6			$p=30\%$ or 70%								
700	11.0	8.3	7.2	6.5	6.1	5.6										
1000	10.8	8.0	6.8	6.2	5.7	5.2	4.7									
1500	10.6	7.8	6.6	5.9	5.4	4.8	4.3	3.9								
2000	10.6	7.7	6.4	5.7	5.2	4.6	4.1	3.7	3.4							
3000	10.5	7.6	6.3	5.6	5.1	4.4	3.9	3.4	3.2	2.9						
4000	10.4	7.5	6.2	5.5	5.0	4.3	3.8	3.3	3.0	2.7	2.5					
5000	10.4	7.5	6.2	5.4	4.9	4.3	3.7	3.2	2.9	2.6	2.4	2.3				
7000	10.4	7.4	6.1	5.4	4.9	4.2	3.6	3.1	2.8	2.5	2.3	2.2	2.1			
10000	10.4	7.4	6.1	5.3	4.8	4.2	3.6	3.0	2.7	2.4	2.2	2.1	1.9	1.8		
15000	10.3	7.4	6.1	5.3	4.8	4.1	3.5	3.0	2.7	2.3	2.1	2.0	1.8	1.7	1.6	
20000	10.3	7.4	6.1	5.3	4.8	4.1	3.5	3.0	2.6	2.3	2.1	2.0	1.8	1.7	1.6	1.5

	$N_1=100$	200	300	400	500	700	1000	1500	2000	3000	4000	5000	7000	10000	15000	20000
$N_2=100$	15.8															
200	13.7	11.2														
300	13.0	10.3	9.2													
400	12.6	9.8	8.6	8.0												
500	12.3	9.4	8.2	7.6	7.2			$p=35\%$ to 65%								
700	12.0	9.0	7.8	7.1	6.7	6.1										
1000	11.8	8.7	7.5	6.7	6.2	5.6	5.1									
1500	11.6	8.5	7.2	6.4	5.9	5.3	4.7	4.3								
2000	11.5	8.4	7.0	6.2	5.7	5.1	4.5	4.0	3.7							
3000	11.4	8.2	6.9	6.1	5.5	4.8	4.3	3.7	3.4	3.1						
4000	11.4	8.2	6.8	6.0	5.4	4.7	4.1	3.6	3.3	3.0	2.8					
5000	11.3	8.1	6.7	5.9	5.4	4.7	4.1	3.5	3.2	2.8	2.7	2.5				
7000	11.3	8.1	6.7	5.9	5.3	4.6	4.0	3.4	3.1	2.7	2.5	2.4	2.2			
10000	11.3	8.1	6.7	5.8	5.3	4.5	3.9	3.3	3.0	2.6	2.4	2.3	2.1	2.0		
15000	11.3	8.0	6.6	5.8	5.2	4.5	3.8	3.3	2.9	2.5	2.3	2.2	2.0	1.9	1.8	
20000	11.3	8.0	6.6	5.8	5.2	4.5	3.8	3.2	2.9	2.5	2.3	2.1	2.0	1.8	1.7	1.6

Appendix B
Procedures Used to Derive Design Effects and Sampling Errors

Appendix A provided a very brief and relatively nontechnical explanation of sampling error estimates, accompanied by two tables of confidence intervals which can be used to ascertain the accuracy of most percentages reported in this volume. The present appendix is intended to provide some background concerning the strategy and rationale involved in computing these confidence intervals. It also offers guidance for those wishing to make sampling computations beyond those contained in Appendix A.

This appendix, like the first, is intended to be readable and usable by the nonstatistician. For that reason, we take the time to outline (albeit briefly) a number of relatively elementary factors involved in estimating confidence intervals.

Factors Influencing the Size of Confidence Intervals

The most straightforward types of samples, from a statistical standpoint at least, are simple random samples. In such samples the confidence limits for a proportion are influenced by the size of the sample or subgroups being considered and also by the size of the proportion. For example, the 95 percent confidence interval for a proportion p based on a simple random sample of N cases is approximated by: $p \pm 1.96 \sqrt{p(1-p)/N}$. In a complex probability sample such as the present one, there are a number of other factors which influence the size of confidence limits. This section lists all of the factors which have been taken into account in calculating confidence intervals for use with the data in this volume, beginning with the most simple factors and then proceeding to the more complex.

Number of Cases (N). Other things equal, the larger a sample (or subgroup within a sample), the smaller or more precise will be the confidence interval for a percentage based on that sample. One of the factors determining the size of the confidence interval is $1/\sqrt{N}$. Thus, for example, if all other things were equal, a sample of 400 would have confidence intervals half as large (or twice as precise) as a sample of 100, because $1/\sqrt{400}$ is half as large as $1/\sqrt{100}$.

Size of Percentage. Other things equal, percentage values around 50 percent have larger confidence intervals than higher or lower percentage values. This is because another of the factors determining the size of the confidence interval is $\sqrt{p(1-p)}$ where p is a proportion ranging from 0 to 1.0 (or, to put it in percentage terms, the factor is $\sqrt{x\%(100-x\%)}$). Thus, for example, a proportion of either .1 or .9 (a percentage of either 10 percent or 90 percent) will have a confidence interval only three-fifths as large as the confidence interval around a proportion of .5 (or 50 percent), because $\sqrt{.1(1-.1)}$ is three-fifths as large as $\sqrt{.5(1-.5)}$.

Design Effects in Complex Samples. Under conditions of simple random sampling, a confidence interval can be determined solely on the basis of the number of cases and the percentage value involved. More complex samples such as the one used in the present study make use of stratification and clustering and often differential weighting of respondent scores, and these all influence sampling error. While stratification tends to heighten the precision of a sample, the effects of clustering and weighting reduce precision (compared with a simple random sample of the same size). Therefore, it is not appropriate to apply the standard,

159

simple random sampling formulas to such complex samples in order to obtain estimates of sampling errors, because they would almost always underestimate the actual sampling errors.

Methods exist for correcting for this underestimation, however. Kish (1965, p. 258) defines a correction term called the design effect (DEFF), where:

$$DEFF = \frac{\text{actual sampling variance}}{\begin{array}{l}\text{expected sampling variance} \\ \text{from a simple random sample} \\ \text{with same number of elements}\end{array}}$$

Thus, if the actual sampling variance in a complex sample is four times as large as the expected sampling variance from a simple random sample with the same number of cases, the DEFF is 4.0. Since confidence intervals are proportionate to the square root of variance, the confidence intervals for such a sample would be twice as large (because the square root of 4 is 2) as the confidence interval for a simple random sample with the same number of cases. A fairly simple and straightforward way of applying the concept of design effect may be to note that an increase in design effect has the same impact on precision as a reduction in the number of cases in a simple random sample. For example, a sample of 16,000 cases with a design effect of 4.0 would have the same degree of precision (the same size confidence intervals around various percentages) as a simple random sample of 4,000.

In principle, every different statistic resulting from a complex sample can have its own design effect, and different statistics in the same sample may have quite different design effects. However, it is not feasible to compute every design effect, nor would it be feasible to report every one. Thus, in practice, design effects are averaged across a number of statistics and these average values are used to estimate the design effects for other statistics based on the same sample. Sometimes a single design effect is applied to all statistics of a given type (e.g., percentages) for a given sample. In the present study, however, a rather extensive exploration of design effects revealed a number of systematic differences. These systematic differences have to do with the particular measures being examined, the subgroups involved, and the question of whether a trend over time is being considered. The most consistent difference involves the number of cases in the group or subgroup for which the design effect is computed.

The Relationship between Subgroup Size and Design Effects. Kish et al. (1976) have observed that design effects tend to be smaller for subgroups than for total samples; moreover, the smaller the

subgroup the smaller the design effect is likely to be. The explanation for this widespread phenomenon is that the average number of cases in each sampling cluster is an important factor in determining the size of the design effect, and as subgroup size decreases so does this average number of cases per cluster. This point is illustrated by several subgroups treated in the present volume — males, females, those planning four years of college, and those not planning four years of college. All (or virtually all) of the schools in the sample have both male and female students, as well as some students who plan four years of college and others who do not. Thus, each of these four subgroups is spread more or less evenly across the full number of clusters (schools). Since each of these subgroups includes roughly half of the total sample, the average number of cases per cluster is about half as large as for the total sample, and this leads to a smaller design effect than is found for the total sample. Other subgroups involving different patterns of drug use are also distributed more or less evenly across all clusters and thus are subject to the same phenomenon of smaller design effects because of the smaller number of cases per cluster.

One very important exception to the pattern of smaller design effects for subgroups involves the four geographic region subgroups presented in this volume. These subgroups do not cut across all clusters; instead, regions have been described as "segregated" subgroups, in contrast to the "cross-class" subgroups discussed above. For such segregated subgroups the average number of cases per cluster is about the same as is found in the total sample, and thus the design effects are not lower than those for the total sample (Kish et al., 1976). Another subgroup which is in some respects similar to regional subgroups is the category of blacks. Black respondents are not found equally across high schools throughout the United States. There are, of course, regional differences in proportions of blacks, and these contribute substantially to this lack of equal distribution. In addition, there are patterns of segregation in housing which continue to be reflected in the unequal distribution of blacks in high schools. The net effect of these several factors is that the black subgroup in our sample is "partially segregated" in a sampling sense as well as in the more usual usage of that word. For that reason, the design effects for blacks are somewhat larger than for other subgroups of approximately similar size.

Because the subgroups consisting of blacks and the four regional groups all have larger design effects than other subgroups of the same size, it is necessary to adjust the confidence intervals for these subgroups as indicated in Appendix A. (At a later point in the present appendix we will say more about these adjustment factors.)

One other kind of "subgroup" must be noted in this discussion of the relationship beteen subgroup size and design effects. One-fifth of the total sample filled out each of the five separate questionnaire forms, and thus the respondents to each of these forms may be viewed as a "cross-class" subgroup of the total sample. The average cluster size for a single form is exactly 20 percent of the average cluster size for the total sample. That means, of course, that the single form samples (which are the basis for the large majority of the data presented in this volume) are distinctly more "efficient" than the sample based on all five forms. Accordingly, single form data have much smaller design effects (as displayed later in this appendix).

Design Effects for Comparisons between Subgroups. We noted above that a number of subgroups treated in this volume can be described as "cross-class" subgroups, meaning that members of the subgroup are distributed more or less evenly across sampling clusters. For these kinds of subgroups, it turns out that *comparisons* are relatively efficient, from a sampling standpoint. The technical explanation for this phenomenon is that there is a higher degree of covariance between such subgroup pairs than would be the case in a comparison of independent subgroups. Now let us offer a fairly nontechnical illustration to indicate why this is so. Suppose that a researcher interested in use of marijuana during the senior year of high school obtained data from five high schools concerning female seniors' marijuana use and data from five other high schools concerning male seniors' marijuana use. Suppose that the percentage values for marijuana use during senior year were as follows:

Female seniors (five schools): 60%, 20%, 65%, 30%, 50%

Male seniors (five other schools): 40%, 80%, 25%, 70%, 60%

Even though there is a difference of ten percentage points between males and females (if the five schools in each case are averaged), there is still so much variability among schools that one would not conclude with very much confidence that females in general are less likely than males to use marijuana during the senior year of high school. Suppose, on the other hand, that the researcher had obtained data from a total of only five schools and had obtained data concerning both male and female seniors in each school as follows:

	Females	Males
School A	60%	70%
School B	20%	25%
School C	65%	80%
School D	30%	40%
School E	50%	60%

The same group of percentages, this time based on five pairings of males and females rather than independent observations, are much more strongly suggestive of systematic differences between the sexes.

A process analogous to that illustrated above is involved when "cross-class" subgroups are compared, and the increased accuracy or sampling efficiency is reflected in relatively small sampling errors and design effects.

Design Effects for Trends. Thus far this discussion of factors influencing design effects and confidence intervals has focused only on groups and subgroups within a single year. But one of the central purposes of the Monitoring the Future project is to monitor trends over time; indeed, the study procedures have been standardized across years insofar as possible in order to provide the opportunity for sensitive measurement of change. One of the factors designed to produce an added degree of consistency from one year to the next is the use of each school for two data collections, which means that for any two successive years half of the sample of schools is the same. This, plus the fact that the other half of the school sample in a given year is from the same primary sampling units as the half sample it replaced, means that there is a good deal of consistency in the sampling and clustering of the sample from one year to the next. As a result, when cross-year comparisons are made (say, between 1976 and 1977), the design effects are appreciably smaller (i.e., the efficiency is greater) than if completely independent samples of schools had been drawn each year. In other words, the 1976 and 1977 samples are not independent; on the contrary, there is a considerable degree of covariance between them. A similar level of covariance occurs between any pair of adjacent-year samples (e.g., 1977 and 1978), because about half of the schools in both samples were the same. This covariance, or partial "matching," reduces the design effect for differences observed between adjacent years, compared to what they would have been with totally independent samples.

It follows from the discussion above that a trend over an interval greater than one year (e.g., a comparison between 1976 and 1978 which involves totally non-overlapping school samples) is likely to have a design effect which is larger than that for a comparison between adjacent-year samples.

Variables with Unusually Large Design Effects. Kish et al. (1976) stress the importance of computing sampling errors for many kinds of variables, and they point out that they have found "very wide ranges in values of sampling errors (standard errors and design effects) between diverse variables within the same survey" (p. 21). Our own experience has been that, among most variables, the variation in sampling errors and design effects seems more random than consistent, and thus we are reasonably comfortable with the use of averaging procedures (described below) in order to derive a set of general purpose tables. There are some important exceptions to the above generalization, however. Variables which are likely to be grouped according to geographical area (region and/or urbanicity), as well as variables that may differ systematically from one school to another, show much higher than usual amounts of homogeneity within sample clusters. It follows necessarily that such variables also have much higher than usual design effects. The variables in the Monitoring the Future study which seem most likely to show such high design effects tend to be grouped into the questionnaire segment dealing with background factors and educational aspirations (Section C of all questionnaire forms). These variables were excluded from the process of computing overall design effects and the confidence intervals provided in Tables A-1 and A-2. Appendix A provides a further discussion of some of these variables and offers some suggestions for adjusting the confidence interval tables to deal with them.

Procedures Used in Deriving Design Effects and Tables of Confidence Intervals

Having taken some pains to review the several factors which can influence design effects and confidence intervals, it is now a fairly simple matter for us to summarize the steps followed to compute the tables of confidence intervals shown in Appendix A. We were heavily influenced in this effort by the work of Kish and his colleagues (Kish, 1965; Kish et al., 1976) in two ways. First, we followed their recommendation that sampling errors be computed and averaged across a goodly number of variables and subgroups. Second, we paid particular attention to their observation that design effects tend to be smaller for subgroups than for total samples (a point discussed earlier in this appendix).

Confidence Intervals for Single Percentages. Our procedure was to compute sampling errors and design effects for most of the variables which are common to all five forms (those in the C sections of all questionnaires, and those in the B sections of Forms 2 through 5), and for every twentieth varia-

ble in the A, D, and E sections of Forms 2 through 5. (Form 1 was omitted because most of this form is comprised of drug-related items, and such items involve high proportions of missing data because respondents are instructed to skip over many questions which are not applicable to them). Design effects were computed for each of the subgroups reported in this volume, as well as for the total sample. Design effects for each subgroup and for the total were averaged across variables for the C section material (all five forms), the B section material (drug use measures, all five forms), and the sampling of variables from the A, D, and E sections (single form data). As noted earlier, the variables which showed unusually high levels of homogeneity within sample clusters were excluded from the C section variables when they were averaged. The 1977 data were used for this analysis. Later replication using 1976 data provided nearly identical values.

The averaging process consisted of taking a mean of the *square roots* of the design effects. Kish and his colleagues (1976) refer to the design effect as DEFF, and to the square root of the design effect as DEFT; thus, $\sqrt{DEFF}$ = DEFT. We will find it useful to use this terminology in what follows. The rationale for computing means of DEFT rather than DEFF is that the former value is directly proportionate to the size of confidence intervals. A further reason for doing so is that the values of DEFT approximate a normal distribution much more closely than the values of DEFF, which are skewed upward. (A comparison of mean DEFTs and median DEFTs showed them to be quite similar, something which certainly is not true of mean and median DEFFs).

Bearing in mind that design effects tend to be smaller for subgroups than for total samples, and bearing in mind also that confidence intervals are directly proportionate to DEFT and to $\sqrt{N}$, we plotted the mean DEFT values for the total sample and for all subgroups, in each case relating DEFT to $\sqrt{N}$. The results are shown in Figure B-1. Note that distinctions are made between "cross-class" and "segregated" subgroups, and between mean DEFTs based on five forms and those based on single forms (the $\sqrt{N}$ values for the latter are, of course, much smaller).*

Setting aside the "segregated" subgroups (regions and blacks) for the moment, it is clear that the rest of the mean DEFTs in Figure B-1 show a very clear and consistent pattern: the higher the value $\sqrt{N}$ the higher the mean DEFT. It turns out that these mean DEFT values are very closely approximated by the function DEFT =

---

*The five form data consisted of C section material, excluding those variables related to region, urbanicity, and/or socioeconomic level.

Figure B-1
Design Effects for Single Percentages

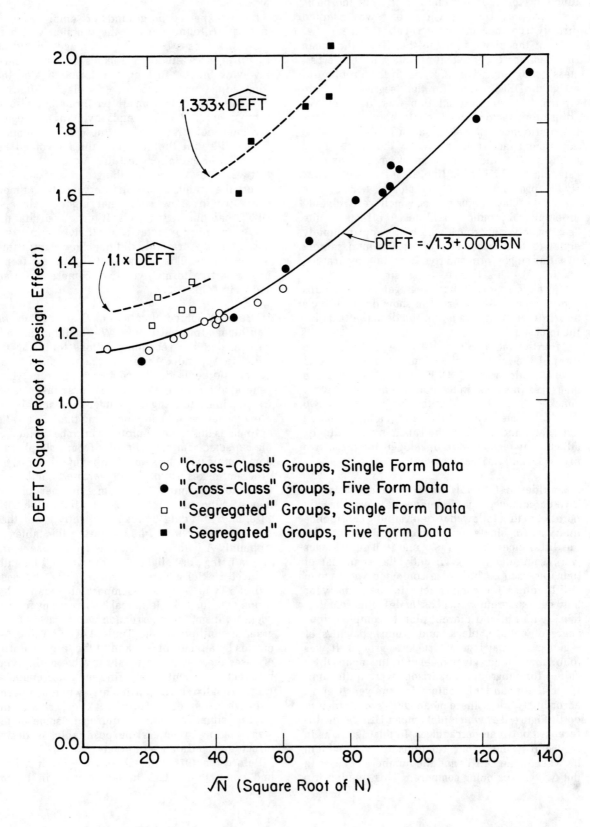

$\sqrt{1.3 + .00015N}$, as shown by the solid line in the figure. (The function can also be stated as DEFF = 1.3 + .00015N.) The particular parameters in that function were derived empirically, but the basic function (i.e., DEFT = $\sqrt{a + bN}$) was adapted directly from the work of Kish et al. (1976).

Given the above function that fitted the mean DEFT values for the total sample and the "cross-class" subgroups, we returned to the problem of assigning DEFT values for the "segregated" subgroups. The simplest solution was to select two adjustment factors which could be multiplied by the confidence interval values in Table A-1. These adjustment factors are shown by the dashed lines in Figure B-1; they correspond to multiplying the "standard" DEFT (solid line) by a factor of 1.1 for single form data and by a factor of 1.33 for five form data. These adjustments, which were selected on empirical grounds, yield design effects for the "segregated" subgroups which are approximately equal to the design effects for the total sample (treating single form and five form data separately, of course). This is reassuring, since Kish et al. (1976) have reported that "segregated" subgroups can in general be expected to show design effects approximately equivalent to the design effects for the total sample.

After the data in Figure B-1 were plotted and the form of the main function (indicated by the solid line) was determined, DEFT values for drug use measures (material in Section B of all forms) were checked. It was found that the DEFTs for only two drug categories, alcohol and marijuana, exceeded the values indicated by the function; accordingly, adjustment factors were developed for these two drugs (1.6 and 1.35, respectively).

Confidence Intervals for Differences between Two Percentages. Our procedure here was directly parallel to that followed in determining confidence intervals for single percentages. DEFT values for the differences between 1977 and 1976 percentages were computed using virtually the same set of items as used earlier. Also computed were mean DEFT values for comparisons in the same year between subgroups such as males and females, those who did and did not plan to complete four years of college, blacks and whites, pairings of regions, and pairings of drug use groups. It was found that, for any given level of N, the mean DEFT values for subgroup comparisons were quite similar to the mean DEFT values for one-year trends; accordingly, all of these mean DEFTs were included in Figure B-2, which plots mean DEFTs for differences between percentages. In this figure, as in Figure B-1, the strong relationship was evident between mean DEFTs and the numbers of cases in the two groups being compared. This relationship

can be verly closely approximated by the function DEFT = $\sqrt{1.3 + .000075N}$ (which can also be stated DEFF = 1.3 + .000075N), where N = $2N_1N_2/N_1 + N_2$.

It was expected on grounds of sampling theory that as we found earlier, the function which fit most differences between percentages would not fit differences involving regions and differences involving blacks. In fact, the data indicated that some adjustment is necessary for black-white comparisons using data from all five forms, and also for comparisons as well as trends involving any region. We have not tried to show those adjustments in Figure B-2, but the several values involved are shown in the guidelines to Table A-2.

It was also expected on the grounds of sampling theory that trends across an interval of two or more years would show somewhat higher values of DEFT than one-year trends. It turned out that this was true only for data from all five forms; data based on one form only did not show significantly higher values. The adjustment factors for trends involving five forms over two or more years are shown in Table A-2.

Use of Weighted Numbers of Cases in Entering Confidence Interval Tables. We should mention in passing that the recommendations for using the tables in Appendix A indicate that *weighted* N values should be used. The computer program which generated our design effect statistics makes use of weights in calculating percentages and actual sampling variances. But in computing the DEFF ratio, defined as the actual sampling variance divided by the expected sampling variance from a simple random sample with the same number of elements, the program makes use of the *unweighted* numbers of cases to determine "the same number of elements." Since the mean weights used in the 1975, 1976, and 1977 data tables are slightly lower than 1.0, this means that when entering the tables in Appendix A with weighted data from those years, one is being very slightly "conservative" (slightly reduced risk of a Type 1 error, slightly increased risk of a Type 2 error). It is important to realize that if one took the trouble to make corrections for this "conservatism," the correction would rarely be as great as multiplying the Table A-1 and Table A-2 entries by a factor of .95; and in the large majority of cases the correction would involve multiplying by a factor of about .98. We find such discrepancies to be trivially small, particularly when compared with what Kish et al. (1976, p. 12) describe as the "heroic simplifications" required in some of the steps leading to general purpose tables of design effects and confidence intervals.

Before the 1978 data tables were produced we had come to realize the advantages in having

Figure B-2
Design Effects for Differences Between Percentages

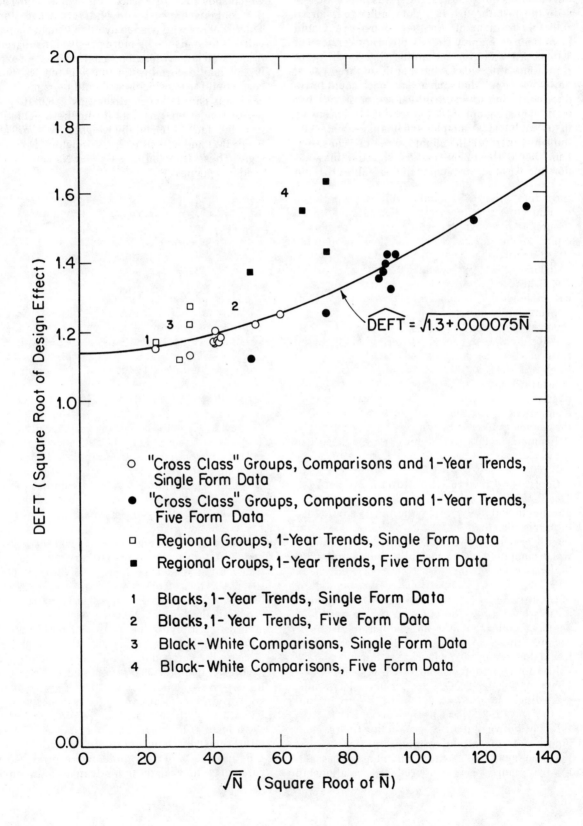

$$\widehat{DEFT} = \sqrt{1.3 + .000075\overline{N}}$$

○   "Cross Class" Groups, Comparisons and 1-Year Trends, Single Form Data

●   "Cross Class" Groups, Comparisons and 1-Year Trends, Five Form Data

□   Regional Groups, 1-Year Trends, Single Form Data

■   Regional Groups, 1-Year Trends, Five Form Data

1   Blacks, 1-Year Trends, Single Form Data

2   Blacks, 1-Year Trends, Five Form Data

3   Black-White Comparisons, Single Form Data

4   Black-White Comparisons, Five Form Data

weighted values which averaged 1.0; accordingly, beginning with the 1978 data, the weighted N values in the tables do approximate the actual numbers of cases quite closely. But it was impractical to redo the 1975 through 1977 data tables to incorporate this refinement. Another alternative would have been to employ slightly different versions of Tables A-1 and A-2, containing slightly different confidence intervals for each of those three years; however, we felt that such an approach could introduce confusion when cross-year comparisons were made. Thus, we opted for the solution which seems to us to be most simple and manageable, even though it involves the slight degree of "conservatism" noted above. For readers who find this solution undesirable, we have included Tables B-1 and B-2, which present weighted and unweighted Ns for the various subgroups for each year. Table B-1 contains Ns for all five forms (except for 1975 which shows Ns for Forms 2 through 5), and Table B-2 contains approximate Ns for a single form. Thus, readers who wish to avoid the slight "conservatism" (and also to be more precise for subgroups in 1978 and later whose average weight is not exactly 1.0) may determine the unweighted Ns. Some correction for missing data should be made in this case; this can be accomplished by calculating the percentage of missing data (using the weighted Ns from the data table and the weighted N from Table B-1 or B-2) and adjusting the unweighted N accordingly. These adjusted unweighted Ns can then be used in Appendix A.

Table B-1

Sample Sizes (Unweighted and Weighted) in Subgroups by Year

| | Number of Cases | | | | | | | |
| | Class of 1975[a] | | Class of 1976 | | Class of 1977 | | Class of 1978 | |
	Unwtd.	Wtd.	Unwtd.	Wtd.	Unwtd.	Wtd.	Unwtd.	Wtd.
Total Sample	12627	12108	16678	15138	18436	15830	18924	18916
Sex:								
Male	5799	5571	7999	7241	8449	7358	8603	8779
Female	6371	6100	7924	7257	9188	7850	9416	9266
Race:								
White	b	b	12933	11796	13818	12240	14663	14847
Black	b	b	1806	1716	2500	1938	2205	2096
Region:								
Northeast	3014	2695	4034	3570	4760	3959	4841	4607
North Central	3951	3832	5098	4687	5697	4758	5576	5411
South	3366	3857	4177	4597	4908	4820	5566	6292
West	2296	1724	3369	2284	3071	2294	2941	2605
College Plans:								
Complete 4 yrs	b	b	7963	6994	8933	7407	9264	8844
None or under 4 yrs	b	b	7179	6877	7764	7048	7857	8413
Illicit Drug Use:								
None	4329	4400	6532	6091	6672	5878	6400	6595
Marijuana Only	2044	1894	3950	3457	4955	4050	5354	5214
Few Pills	1163	1113	1942	1736	2173	1813	2329	2304
More Pills	2157	1989	3427	2987	3857	3266	3906	3885
Any Heroin	231	216	319	268	321	280	289	302

[a] The number of cases shown for 1975 is based on Forms 2 through 5 only, because the data from Form 1 are intentionally-not included in tabulations based on drug and demographic items which appeared in all forms.

[b] Missing data problems were severe for race and college plans in 1975; accordingly, these data have been excluded from all tables in the 1975 report.

Table B-2

Sample Sizes (Unweighted and Weighted) in Subgroups by Year
for Questions on a Single Form

| | Number of Cases | | | | | | | |
| | Class of 1975 | | Class of 1976 | | Class of 1977 | | Class of 1978 | |
	Unwtd.	Wtd.	Unwtd.	Wtd.	Unwtd.	Wtd.	Unwtd.	Wtd.
Total Sample	3157	3027	3336	3028	3687	3166	3785	3783
Sex:								
Male	1450	1393	1600	1488	1690	1472	1721	1756
Female	1371	1525	1585	1451	1838	1570	1883	1853
Race:								
White	a	a	2587	2359	2764	2448	2933	2969
Black	a	a	361	343	500	388	441	419
Region:								
Northeast	754	674	807	714	952	792	968	921
North Central	988	958	1020	937	1139	952	1115	1082
South	842	964	835	919	982	964	1113	1258
West	574	431	674	457	614	459	588	521
College Plans:								
Complete 4 yrs	a	a	1593	1399	1787	1481	1853	1769
None or under 4 yrs	a	a	1436	1375	1553	1410	1571	1683
Illicit Drug Use:								
None	1082	1100	1306	1218	1334	1176	1280	1319
Marijuana Only	511	474	790	691	991	810	1071	1043
Few Pills	291	278	388	347	435	363	466	461
More Pills	539	497	685	597	771	653	781	777
Any Heroin	58	54	64	54	64	56	58	60

[a] Missing data problems were severe for race and college plans in 1975; accordingly, these data have been excluded from all tables in the 1975 report.

Further Applications of these Design Effects and Sampling Errors

One of the reasons for providing the above review of the factors influencing design effects and confidence intervals, and the procedures used in computing our confidence interval tables, is to provide sufficient background and data to permit the interested reader to go beyond the material provided in Appendix A. In this section we consider two specific extensions, the calculation of levels of "statistical significance" higher than 95 percent and the computation of means and their confidence intervals.

Calculating Confidence Intervals for Higher Levels of Statistical Significance. The entries contained in Tables A-1 and A-2 provide the 95 percent confidence level (also referred to as the .05 level of significance). These entries were computed by multiplying the standard error (square root of sample variance) by a factor of 1.96. The 99 percent confidence interval (.01 level of significance) uses a factor of 2.58 standard errors, and the 99.9 percent confidence interval (.001 level of significance) uses a factor of 3.29 standard errors. To convert the entries in Tables A-1 and A-2 to these higher levels, it is necessary only to multiply the entries by the appropriate constant shown below (keeping in mind that any other adjustments required in the tables must also be applied):

Confidence Interval	Significance Level	Multiply entries in Tables A-1 and A-2 by the following:
99%	.01	$2.58/1.96 = 1.32$
99.9%	.001	$3.29/1.96 = 1.68$

Computing Means and Their Confidence Intervals. Many of the questionnaire items included in this volume have ordinal response scales (e.g., agree, agree mostly, neither, disagree mostly, disagree), and it is often the case that a survey analyst will be willing to treat such scales as if they involved equal intervals. In such cases, means and standard deviations are more "efficient" in their use of information than are dichotomies which yield a single percentage or a pair of percentages (e.g., those who respond "agree" or "agree mostly," versus all others). It is a relatively straightforward matter to compute means and standard deviations for the total sample or any of the subgroups treated in this volume. The problem, then, is to be able to specify confidence intervals for the means, or for the differences between pairs of means. In the case of simple random samples, one needs only the means, standard deviations (or variances), and numbers of cases in order to compute confidence intervals. But in complex samples such as the present one, it is also necessary to take account of design effects. If an estimate of design effect is available, one of the simplest procedures to follow is to divide the actual numbers of cases by the design effect (thereby "depreciating" the actual number to its equivalent value in simple random sample terms) and then employ the standard statistical procedures which have been developed for application to simple random samples. Thus, for example, if the design effect (DEFF) for a sample of 18,000 were 4.0, then one could divide the 18,000 by 4.0 and the result, 4,500, could be entered as the value of "N" in statistical tables and formulas designed for use with simple random samples. To take another example, if one were comparing means based on two subgroups, each involving about 9,000 cases, and if DEFF (for both subgroups) was 2.0, then one could compute the significance of the difference between the two means as if the N for each group were 4,500 (i.e., 9,000 divided by 2.0)

In short, the strategy involves dividing the actual number of cases by the appropriate DEFF in order to get a "simple random sampling equivalent N" or, more simply, an "effective N" for use in statistical procedures designed for random samples.

Design Effects for Use in Computing "Effective Ns." In order to employ the strategy outlined above, one must have estimates of design effects which are judged to be appropriate for one's purposes. In the case of means based on the percentages reported in this volume, we are confident (based on personal communications with Kish) that it is appropriate to use the same DEFF values as were used in developing Tables A-1 and A-2. For other, more complex statistics, we cannot make the same assertion, although it is generally the case that design effects for such statistics are not larger than those for means and percentages (Kish and Frankel, 1970; Frankel, 1971).

In Table B-3 we provide guidelines for computing DEFF values for single percentages (or means) and for differences between two percentages (or means). For reasons discussed elsewhere in this appendix, we must provide for different (and somewhat higher) DEFFs for "segregated" subgroups (regional subgroups and sometimes also blacks), and for trends over two or more years (in contrast to one-year trends). And in all instances, of course, the DEFF values are very much influenced by the average size of sampling clusters, which is always dependent on the number of cases

Table B-3
Guidelines for Computing Design Effects (DEFFs) for Percentages
and Means Derived from Monitoring the Future Samples

DEFINITIONS

$$\text{DEFF (design effect)} = \frac{\text{(estimated) sampling variance}}{\substack{\text{expected sampling variance from simple} \\ \text{random sample with same number of elements}}}$$

N = number of respondents on whom a single percentage or mean is based

$\overline{N} = 2N_1 N_2 / (N_1 + N_2)$, for use in comparisons of two percentages or means, based on two groups of sizes N_1 and N_2.

DESIGN EFFECT FORMULAS

1. For single percentages or means involving...
   a. regional subgroups or blacks
      DEFF for single form data .... $(1.3 + .00015N) (1.21)$
      DEFF for five form data .... $(1.3 + .00015N) (1.78)$

   b. all other subgroups or total sample
      DEFF for single form or five form data .... $1.3 + .00015N$

2. For comparisons between...
   a. any two regions
      DEFF for single form data .... $(1.3 + .000075\overline{N}) (1.32)$
      DEFF for five form data .... $(1.3 + .000075\overline{N}) (2.25)$

   b. blacks and whites
      DEFF for single form data .... $1.3 + .000075\overline{N}$
      DEFF for five form data .... $(1.3 + .000075\overline{N}) (1.56)$

   c. genders, college plans groups, or any two "drug use" subgroups
      DEFF for single form or five form data .... $1.3 + .000075\overline{N}$

3. For one-year trends involving...
   a. any region
      DEFF for single form data .... $1.3 + .000075\overline{N}$
      DEFF for five form data .... $(1.3 + .000075\overline{N}) (1.56)$
   b. all other subgroups or total sample
      DEFF for single form or five form data .... $1.3 + .000075\overline{N}$

4. For trends over two or more years involving...
   a. any region
      DEFF for single form data .... $1.3 + .000075\overline{N}$
      DEFF for five form data .... $(1.3 + .000075\overline{N}) (1.82)$
   b. all other subgroups or total sample
      DEFF for single form data .... $1.3 + .000075\overline{N}$
      DEFF for five form data .... $(1.3 + .000075\overline{N}) (1.32)$

(N). Accordingly, all of the design effect formulas in Table B-3 require computations which take account of N. (It should also be noted that the formulas in Table B-3 correspond exactly to the values of design effects and adjustment factors used in Tables A-1 and A-2 in Appendix A.)

A Concluding Note. In their very useful paper dealing with sampling errors for fertility surveys, Kish et al. (1976) commented that some of the methods they used ". . . emerged after several false starts." They went on to say that the volume and diversity of the data they were dealing with ". . . presented new challenges and opportunities." And they added, "Our methods are subject to further developments and modifications, and we invite participation and suggestions" (p. 10). Our own attempts to apply the methods of Kish and his colleagues to the data reported in this volume have been challenged by the diversity of the data, have involved several false starts, and we hope are subject to further developments and modifications. We invite readers to offer their suggestions, and we also encourage readers to inquire about further work that we and/or others may carry out during the coming months and years.

Appendix C
Questionnaire Covers, Instructions, and Sample Page

monitoring the future

a continuing study of the lifestyles and values of youth

This questionnaire is part of a nationwide study of high school seniors, conducted each year by the University of Michigan's Institute for Social Research. The questions ask your opinions about a number of things--the way things are now and the way you think they ought to be in the future. In a sense, many of your answers on this questionnaire will count as "votes" on a wide range of important issues.

If this study is to be helpful, it is important that you answer each question as thoughtfully and frankly as possible. All your answers will be kept strictly confidential, and will never be seen by anyone who knows you.

This study is completely voluntary. If there is any question that you or your parents would find objectionable for any reason, just leave it blank.

In a few months, we would like to mail each of you a summary of the nationwide results from this study. Also, in about a year we would like to mail another questionnaire to some of you, asking about how your plans have worked out and what's happening in your lives.

In order to include you in these mailings, we ask for your name and address on a special form at the end of this questionnaire. This form is to be torn out and handed in separately. Once the address form and the questionnaire have been separated, there is no way they can be matched again, except by using a special computer tape at the University of Michigan. The only purpose for that tape is to match a follow-up questionnaire with this one.

Other seniors have said that these questionnaires are very interesting and that they enjoy filling them out. We hope you will too. Be sure to read the instructions on the other side of this cover page before you begin to answer. Thank you very much for being an important part of this project.

INSTITUTE FOR SOCIAL RESEARCH
THE UNIVERSITY OF MICHIGAN
ANN ARBOR, MICHIGAN

INSTRUCTIONS

1. This is not a test, so there are no right or wrong answers; we would like you to work fairly quickly, so that you can finish.

2. All of the questions should be answered by marking one of the answer spaces. If you don't always find an answer that fits exactly, use the one that comes closest. If any question does not apply to you, or you are not sure of what it means, just leave it blank.

3. Your answers will be read automatically by a machine called an optical mark reader. Please follow these instructions carefully:

    • Use only the black lead pencil you have been given.
    • Make heavy black marks inside the circles.
    • Erase cleanly any answer you wish to change.
    • Make no other markings or comments on the answer pages, since they interfere with the automatic reading. (If you want to add a comment about any question, please use the space provided below.)

These kinds of markings will work: ● ● ●

These kinds of markings will NOT work: ⊙ ● ○

- -

(THIS SPACE FOR WRITTEN COMMENTS)

WHY YOUR NAME AND ADDRESS?

As we told you earlier, we'd like to send you a summary of the nationwide results of the present study, and in about a year we want to mail a shorter questionnaire to some of you. In order to include you in these follow-ups, we would like to have an address where information will be sure to reach you during the coming year.

HOW IS CONFIDENTIALITY PROTECTED?

- The information on this page will be used ONLY for mailing, and will always be kept separate from your answers. A special Grant of Confidentiality from the U.S. government protects all information gathered in this research project.

- The questionnaire and address pages will be collected separately, sealed immediately in separate envelopes, and sent to two different cities for processing.

- Once a questionnaire and address page have been separated, there is no way they can be matched, except by using a special computer tape at the University of Michigan. That tape contains the two DIFFERENT numbers that appear on the back of this address page and on the back of the questionnaire. These numbers will be used ONLY to match a follow-up questionnaire with this one.

> Before filling out this address page, please separate it from the rest of the questionnaire by FOLDING ALONG THE PERFORATED LINE AND TEARING CAREFULLY.

Please **PRINT** your name and the address where you can most likely be reached during the coming year.

Mr.
Miss _____
Ms. FIRST NAME   INITIAL   LAST NAME
Mrs.

STREET _____

CITY _____

STATE _____ ZIP _____

TELEPHONE NO.   (   ) — _____
             AREA

In case we should have trouble getting mail to you, if you move, please **PRINT** the name and address of one other person (with a different address than your own) who will know where to reach you in the future. (Examples of such a person: aunt or uncle, older sister or brother, or close friend.)

Mr.
Miss _____
Ms. FIRST NAME   INITIAL   LAST NAME
Mrs.

STREET _____

CITY _____

STATE _____ ZIP _____

TELEPHONE NO.   (   ) — _____
             AREA

THANK YOU AGAIN FOR YOUR HELP

PART A

*** BEFORE BEGINNING BE SURE YOU HAVE
READ THE INSTRUCTIONS ON THE COVER.**

1. Taking all things together, how would you say things are
these days–would you say you're very happy, pretty
happy, or not too happy these days?

   ○ Very happy
   ○ Pretty happy
   ○ Not too happy

2. Some people think a lot about the social problems of the
nation and the world, and about how they might be solved.
Others spend little time thinking about these issues. How
much do you think about such things?

   ① Never
   ② Seldom
   ③ Sometimes
   ④ Quite often
   ⑤ A great deal

3. Of all the problems facing the nation
today, how often do you worry about
each of the following? (Mark one
circle for each line.)

		Never	Seldom	Sometimes	Often
a.	Chance of nuclear war	①	②	③	④
b.	Population growth	①	②	③	④
c.	Crime and violence	①	②	③	④
d.	Pollution	①	②	③	④
e.	Energy shortages	①	②	③	④
f.	Race relations	①	②	③	④
g.	Hunger and poverty	①	②	③	④
h.	Using open land for housing or industry	①	②	③	④
i.	Urban decay	①	②	③	④
j.	Economic problems	①	②	③	④
k.	Drug abuse	①	②	③	④

4. How well do you think your experiences
and training (at home, school, work, etc.)
have prepared you to be a good. . .

		Poorly	Not So Well	Fairly Well	Well	Very Well
a.	...husband or wife?	①	②	③	④	⑤
b.	...parent?	①	②	③	④	⑤
c.	...worker on a job?	①	②	③	④	⑤

5. Apart from the particular kind of work
you want to do, how would you rate each
of the following settings as a place to
work? (Mark one circle for each line.)

		Not At All Acceptable	Somewhat Acceptable	Acceptable	Desirable
a.	Working in a large corporation	①	②	③	④
b.	Working in a small business	①	②	③	④
c.	Working in a government agency	①	②	③	④
d.	Working in the military service	①	②	③	④
e.	Working in a school or university	①	②	③	④
f.	Working in a police department or police agency	①	②	③	④
g.	Working in a social service organization	①	②	③	④
h.	Working with a small group of partners	①	②	③	④
i.	Working on your own (self-employed)	①	②	③	④

6. If you were to get enough money to live as comfortably as
you'd like for the rest of your life, would you want to
work?

   ① I would want to work
   ② I would not want to work

References

Adelson, J. "What Generation Gap?" *New York Times Magazine.* January 18, 1970, pp. 1-11.

Adelson, J. "Adolescence and the Generation Gap." *Psychology Today,* September 1979, pp. 33-37.

Bachman, J.G.; O'Malley, P.M.; and Johnston, J. Youth in Transition, Volume VI: *Adolescence to Adulthood — A Study of Change and Stability in the Lives of Young Men.* Ann Arbor: Institute for Social Research, 1978.

Bachman, J. G., and Johnston, L. D. *The Monitoring the Future Project Design and Procedures.* Ann Arbor: Institute for Social Research, 1978.

Frankel, M. R. *Inference from Survey Samples:* An Empirical Investigation. Ann Arbor: Institute for Social Research, 1971.

Golladay, M. *The Condition of Education.* National Center for Education Statistics, Washington, D.C.: U.S. Government Printing Office, 1976.

Golladay, M. *The Condition of Education.* National Center for Education Statistics, *Volume 3, Part 1.* Washington, D.C.: U.S. Government Printing Office, 1977.

Hays, William L. *Statistics for the Social Sciences* (2nd ed.). New York: Holt, Rinehart, & Winston, 1973.

Johnston, L. D. *Drugs and American Youth.* Ann Arbor: Institute for Social Research, 1973.

Johnston, L. D.; Bachman, J. G.; and O'Malley, P. M. *Drug Use Among American High School Students 1975-1977* (National Institute on Drug Abuse). Washington, D.C.: U.S. Government Printing Office, 1977.

Johnston, L. D.; Bachman, J. G.; and O'Malley, P. M. *Drugs and the Class of 1978: Behaviors, Attitudes, and Recent National Trends* (National Institute on Drug Abuse). Washington, D.C.: U.S. Government Printing Office, 1979.

Johnston, L. D.; O'Malley, P. M.; and Eveland, L. K. *Some Preliminary Results from Drugs and American Youth II: A Longitudinal Resurvey.* (Interim report to the National Institute on Drug Abuse.) Ann Arbor: Institute for Social Research, 1975.

Kish, L., and Frankel, M. R. "Balanced Repeated Replication for Standard Errors." *Journal of the American Statistical Association, 65 (1970): 1071-1094.*

Kish, L.; Groves R.M.; and Krotki, K.P. *Sampling Errors for Fertility Surveys* (Occasional Papers Series No. 17). Voorburg, Netherlands: International Statistical Institute, 1976.

U. S. Bureau of the Census. *Current Population Reports,* Series P-20, No. 319. School enrollment — social and economic characteristics of students: October 1976. Washington, D.C.: U.S. Government Printing Office, 1978.